# Demanding Development

India's urban slums exhibit dramatic variation in their access to local public goods and services – paved roads, piped water, trash removal, sewers, and streetlights. Why are some vulnerable communities able to demand and secure development from the state while others fail? Drawing on more than two years of fieldwork in the north Indian cities of Bhopal and Jaipur, *Demanding Development* accounts for the uneven success of India's slum residents in securing local public goods and services. Auerbach's theory centers on the political organization of slum settlements and the informal slum leaders who spearhead resident efforts to make claims on the state – in particular, those slum leaders who are party workers. He finds striking variation in the extent to which networks of party workers have spread across slum settlements. *Demanding Development* shows how this variation in the density and partisan distribution of party workers across settlements has powerful consequences for the ability of residents to politically mobilize to improve local conditions.

Adam Michael Auerbach is an assistant professor in the School of International Service at American University, Washington, DC. His doctoral dissertation won the Best Fieldwork Award from the Comparative Democratization Section of the American Political Science Association (APSA), the Best Dissertation Award from the Urban and Local Politics Section of APSA, and APSA's Gabriel A. Almond Award for Best Dissertation in Comparative Politics. His research on politics and development in urban India has appeared in the *American Political Science Review, Contemporary South Asia, Studies in Comparative International Development, World Development,* and *World Politics.*

# Cambridge Studies in Comparative Politics

## General Editors
Kathleen Thelen   *Massachusetts Institute of Technology*
Erik Wibbels   *Duke University*

## Associate Editors
Catherine Boone   *London School of Economics*
Thad Dunning   *University of California, Berkeley*
Anna Grzymala-Busse   *Stanford University*
Torben Iversen   *Harvard University*
Stathis Kalyvas   *Yale University*
Margaret Levi   *Stanford University*
Helen Milner   *Princeton University*
Frances Rosenbluth   *Yale University*
Susan Stokes   *Yale University*
Tariq Thachil   *Vanderbilt University*

## Series Founder
Peter Lange   *Duke University*

## Other Books in the Series
Christopher Adolph, *Bankers, Bureaucrats, and Central Bank Politics: The Myth of Neutrality*
Michael Albertus, *Autocracy and Redistribution: The Politics of Land Reform*
Santiago Anria, *When Movements Become Parties: The Bolivian MAS in Comparative Perspective*
Ben W. Ansell, *From the Ballot to the Blackboard: The Redistributive Political Economy of Education*
Ben W. Ansell and David J. Samuels, *Inequality and Democratization: An Elite-Competition Approach*
Adam Michael Auerbach, *Demanding Development: The Politics of Public Goods Provision in India's Urban Slums*
Ana Arjona, *Rebelocracy: Social Order in the Colombian Civil War*
Leonardo R. Arriola, *Multi-Ethnic Coalitions in Africa: Business Financing of Opposition Election Campaigns*

*Continued after the index*

# Demanding Development

## The Politics of Public Goods Provision in India's Urban Slums

**ADAM MICHAEL AUERBACH**
*American University, Washington, DC*

# CAMBRIDGE
## UNIVERSITY PRESS

University Printing House, Cambridge CB2 8BS, United Kingdom

One Liberty Plaza, 20th Floor, New York, NY 10006, USA

477 Williamstown Road, Port Melbourne, VIC 3207, Australia

314–321, 3rd Floor, Plot 3, Splendor Forum, Jasola District Centre, New Delhi – 110025, India

79 Anson Road, #06–04/06, Singapore 079906

Cambridge University Press is part of the University of Cambridge.

It furthers the University's mission by disseminating knowledge in the pursuit of education, learning, and research at the highest international levels of excellence.

www.cambridge.org
Information on this title: www.cambridge.org/9781108491938
DOI: 10.1017/9781108649377

© Adam Michael Auerbach 2020

This publication is in copyright. Subject to statutory exception and to the provisions of relevant collective licensing agreements, no reproduction of any part may take place without the written permission of Cambridge University Press.

First published 2020

Printed in the United Kingdom by TJ International Ltd. Padstow Cornwall

*A catalogue record for this publication is available from the British Library.*

*Library of Congress Cataloging-in-Publication Data*
NAMES: Auerbach, Adam Michael, 1982– author.
TITLE: Demanding development : the politics of public goods provision in India's urban slums / Adam Michael Auerbach, American University, Washington DC.
DESCRIPTION: Cambridge, United Kingdom ; New York, NY, USA : Cambridge University Press, 2020. | Includes bibliographical references.
IDENTIFIERS: LCCN 2019013486 | ISBN 9781108491938 (hardback : alk. paper) | ISBN 9781108741330 (paperback : alk. paper)
SUBJECTS: LCSH: Marginality, Social – Political aspects – India. | Slums – Political aspects – India. | Slums – Government policy – India. | Urban poor – Political activity – India. | Public goods – Political aspects – India. | Party politics – India. | Municipal government – India.
CLASSIFICATION: LCC HN690.Z9 M2625 2020 | DDC 307.3/3640954–dc23
LC record available at https://lccn.loc.gov/2019013486

ISBN 978-1-108-49193-8 Hardback
ISBN 978-1-108-74133-0 Paperback

Cambridge University Press has no responsibility for the persistence or accuracy of URLs for external or third-party internet websites referred to in this publication and does not guarantee that any content on such websites is, or will remain, accurate or appropriate.

For Prita and Arjun

# Contents

| | |
|---|---|
| *List of Figures* | *page* ix |
| *List of Tables* | xi |
| *Acknowledgments* | xiii |

1  Puzzling Disparities at the Margins of the City   1
    1.1 The Puzzle of Uneven Public Goods Provision
       across Slum Settlements   7
    1.2 Party Workers and Local Development   16
    1.3 Urban Informality and the State   27
    1.4 What Is a Slum?   29
    1.5 Study Settings and Research Design   35
    1.6 Organization of the Book   39

2  Setting the Stage: Governance and Political Parties
    in Urban India   42
    2.1 India at Home in Its Cities and Towns   44
    2.2 The Proliferation of Urban Slums   47
    2.3 Governance in the Post-Decentralization Indian City   49
    2.4 Distributive Politics in India's Slums   56
    2.5 Party Organizations in Bhopal and Jaipur   59
    2.6 Conclusion   63

3  How Party Worker Networks Impact Local Development   65
    3.1 Competition, Connectivity, and Mobilizational
       Capacity   65
    3.2 The Partisan Distribution of Party Workers   80
    3.3 Why Party Worker Networks Vary across Settlements   83
    3.4 Conclusion   90

| | | |
|---|---|---|
| 4 | India's Slum Leaders | 92 |
| | 4.1 Demanding Development in India's Slums | 93 |
| | 4.2 The Pervasiveness of Informal Leadership | 97 |
| | 4.3 The Construction of Informal Leadership | 98 |
| | 4.4 The Problem-Solving Activities of Slum Leaders | 101 |
| | 4.5 The Electoral Activities of Slum Leaders | 105 |
| | 4.6 Motivations to Engage in Slum Leadership | 108 |
| | 4.7 Slum Leaders as Party Workers | 109 |
| | 4.8 Conclusion | 113 |
| 5 | Views from the Ground: Historical Narratives from Eight Squatter Settlements | 114 |
| | 5.1 Jaipur Case Studies | 116 |
| | 5.2 Bhopal Case Studies | 143 |
| | 5.3 Comparative Observations | 164 |
| 6 | Party Workers and Public Goods Provision: Evidence from 111 Settlements | 169 |
| | 6.1 Survey Design and Data | 170 |
| | 6.2 Other Sources of Data | 176 |
| | 6.3 Variables and Their Measurement | 178 |
| | 6.4 Statistical Models and Results | 184 |
| | 6.5 Causality and Historical Sequencing | 200 |
| | 6.6 Conclusion | 205 |
| 7 | Why Party Worker Networks Spread Unevenly Across Settlements | 206 |
| | 7.1 The Correlates of Party Worker Density and Party Representational Balance | 208 |
| | 7.2 Why Are Some Settlements More Populous and Ethnically Diverse than Others? | 213 |
| | 7.3 Conclusion | 220 |
| 8 | Conclusion | 222 |
| | 8.1 Revisiting the Theory and Findings | 223 |
| | 8.2 Implications of the Book's Findings | 228 |

*Appendix A  Measuring Social Capital*  236
*Appendix B  Additional Tables and Figures*  237
*Bibliography*  276
*Index*  293

# Figures

| | | |
|---|---|---|
| 1.1 | An underdeveloped squatter settlement in Jaipur | page 14 |
| 1.2 | A squatter settlement with basic infrastructure in Bhopal | 14 |
| 1.3 | Party flag in a Jaipur squatter settlement | 19 |
| 1.4 | Three levels of party worker density in Kamal Nagar | 20 |
| 1.5 | A squatter settlement in Jaipur | 31 |
| 1.6 | Squatter settlements in southern Bhopal | 34 |
| 2.1 | Sign declaring roadwork funded by MLA and councillor, Bhopal | 43 |
| 2.2 | Political graffiti in a Bhopal slum settlement | 44 |
| 2.3 | Ward councillor overseeing drainage work in a Jaipur slum | 55 |
| 3.1 | Party sign listing local Congress workers, Bhopal | 66 |
| 3.2 | Party sign listing local BJP workers, Bhopal | 67 |
| 3.3 | Local BJP office, Bhopal | 74 |
| 3.4 | Congress party rally, Jaipur | 75 |
| 3.5 | Poster criticizing an MLA, Jaipur, mid-1990s | 77 |
| 3.6 | Congress slum cell protest, Bhopal, mid-1990s | 79 |
| 3.7 | Jawahar Nagar slum protest, Jaipur, early 1980s | 80 |
| 4.1 | Frequency histogram of party worker density | 111 |
| 4.2 | Frequency histogram of party representational balance | 112 |
| 6.1 | Common image of a narrow alleyway in a Bhopal squatter settlement | 172 |
| 6.2 | Ward map of Jaipur with location of sampled settlements | 173 |
| 6.3 | Ward map of Bhopal with location of sampled settlements | 174 |
| 6.4 | The remaining rubble of an evicted slum, Bhopal | 175 |
| 6.5 | A squatter settlement emerging in Jaipur, early 1980s | 201 |
| 6.6 | A squatter settlement emerging in Jaipur, early 1980s | 202 |
| 6.7 | A squatter settlement emerging in Bhopal, early 1980s | 202 |

B.1.A– Marginal effects of party worker density on the outcome
B.1.I  variables, conditional on party representational balance   237
   B.2 Scatterplot of primary development index and party
       worker density                                              242

# Tables

| | | |
|---|---|---|
| 1.1 | Descriptive statistics of slum development indicators in Bhopal and Jaipur | page 13 |
| 4.1 | Slum leader activities: resident level | 105 |
| 4.2 | Slum leader activities: settlement level | 106 |
| 5.1 | Jaipur case studies | 118 |
| 5.2 | Bhopal case studies | 145 |
| 6.1 | Descriptive statistics of settlement-level variables | 179 |
| 6.2 | Paved roads and streetlights | 185 |
| 6.3 | Piped water and sewer connections | 187 |
| 6.4 | Municipal trash removal and government medical camps | 189 |
| 6.5 | Development indices | 191 |
| 7.1 | Correlates of party worker density | 210 |
| 7.2 | Disaggregating INC and BJP party worker densities | 212 |
| 7.3 | Correlates of party representational balance | 214 |
| A.1 | Measuring social capital | 236 |
| B.1 | Dropping party worker density | 243 |
| B.2 | Ethnic diversity reduced models | 245 |
| B.3 | Ethnic diversity components | 246 |
| B.4 | Settlement notification | 247 |
| B.5 | Politically fragmented settlements | 249 |
| B.6 | Swing voters | 251 |
| B.7 | BJP strongholds and years of BJP rule in assembly constituency | 253 |
| B.8 | BJP strongholds and years of BJP rule in municipal ward | 255 |
| B.9 | INC strongholds and years of INC rule in assembly constituency | 257 |

| | | |
|---|---|---|
| B.10 | INC strongholds and years of INC rule in municipal ward | 259 |
| B.11 | Marginal effects of party years in power, conditional on party stronghold | 261 |
| B.12 | Party worker density reduced models | 262 |
| B.13 | Tobit models | 263 |
| B.14 | Fractional logit models | 265 |
| B.15 | Robust regression with Huber weights | 267 |
| B.16 | Using party representational balance (dichotomous measure) | 269 |
| B.17 | Marginal effects of party worker density, conditional on PRB (dichotomous measure) | 271 |
| B.18 | Using Jaipur RAY population data | 272 |
| B.19 | 2015 Ethnic diversity index | 274 |

# Acknowledgments

The foundation of this book, unbeknownst to me at the time, took root in the summer of 2007. I spent that summer in Jaipur taking the American Institute of Indian Studies' Hindi Language Program. Just a few hundred yards behind my host family's house was – and continues to be – a sprawling *kachi basti* (slum settlement), wedged between a drainage basin and the jagged cliffs of the Aravalli Mountains. To reach the nearest path to the mountain, one needs to navigate the winding alleyways of the settlement. The top of the mountain offers sweeping views of the city and, most immediately, the many slum settlements that snake their way northward along the mountain range. During one of my regular walks through the settlement I became acquainted – and on subsequent trips, friends – with the settlement's informal leader, Raju. Though just a few years older than me, Raju's responsibilities dwarfed my own. He had been selected by residents as their *adhyaksh* (president) and was accordingly tasked with petitioning government officials for public services and security from eviction. My interest in understanding how residents of India's urban slums organize and demand development from the state was sparked by my many conversations with Raju. Raju was the first of many slum leaders with whom I spent time for this book, yet I owe him my greatest thanks for introducing me to the complex world of slum leadership.

This book grew out of my doctoral dissertation at the University of Wisconsin–Madison. I am immensely fortunate to have had a group of extraordinary scholars on my dissertation committee, each of whom contributed to this research in substantial and distinct ways: Rikhil Bhavnani, Ivan Ermakoff, Yoshiko Herrera, Melanie Manion, Nadav

Shelef, and Aseema Sinha. Several scholars based in India also shaped this project at its earliest stages in graduate school: Niraja Gopal Jayal, Varsha Joshi, Arup Mitra, and the late Surjit Singh. These scholars – stretching across Madison, Delhi, and Jaipur – have my heartfelt gratitude for their mentorship and many invaluable suggestions on this project. Friends in Madison provided countless insights on this project as well – and offered camaraderie during the grind of dissertation writing. For that, I thank Nick Barnes, Ryan Biava, Leticia Bode, Barry Driscoll, Kyle Hanniman, Aliza Luft, Peter Nasuti, Dave Ohls, Jennifer Petersen, Kerry Ratigan, Emily Sellars, Charlie Taylor, and Kristin Vekasi.

A visiting fellowship at the Kellogg Institute for International Studies, University of Notre Dame, provided a rich intellectual setting for me to embark on the long road of transforming my dissertation into a book. I thank several scholars based at Notre Dame during that 2013–2014 academic year, whose feedback pushed this book forward: Tiffany Barnes, Jaimie Bleck, Sandra Botero, Laura Gomez-Mera, David Nickerson, Alice Wiemers, Sarah Zukerman Daly, and the late Richard Matland. I was also lucky to spend the summer of 2014 at the King's India Institute, King's College London, as a Political Economy of India Fellow, which put me in the company of several leading scholars of Indian politics. In particular, I thank Pranab Bardhan, Anastasia Piliavsky, Lawrence Sáez, and Louise Tillin for their comments on this project during my stay in London.

A number of scholars have provided valuable feedback on small and large portions of this book, during various stages of its writing. I first thank participants of my book workshop, whose detailed comments strengthened this book along numerous fronts: Daniel Esser, Jonathan Fox, Agustina Giraudy, Sarah Khan, Ammar Malik, Irfan Nooruddin, Dave Ohls, Vijayendra Rao, Pavithra Suryanarayan, Emmanuel Teitelbaum, and Milan Vaishnav. For constructive discussions and feedback on assorted parts of my book manuscript and related papers, I also thank Leonardo Arriola, Jennifer Bussell, Ward Berenschot, Lisa Björkman, Kanchan Chandra, Shelby Grossman, Patrick Heller, Christophe Jaffrelot, Francesca Jensenius, Devesh Kapur, Herbert Kitschelt, Anirudh Krishna, Tanu Kumar, Gabrielle Kruks-Wisner, Rabia Malik, Noah Nathan, Philip Oldenburg, Brian Palmer-Rubin, Alison Post, Mark Schneider, Neelanjan Sircar, Dan Slater, Claire Snell-Rood, Tariq Thachil, Ashutosh Varshney, Ajay Verghese, Michael Walton, Erik Wibbels, the late Lloyd and Susan Rudolph, three anonymous reviewers for Cambridge University Press, and participants at seminars held at Arizona State University; Brown University;

the Centre de Sciences Humaines, Delhi; the University of Chicago; the Delhi School of Planning and Architecture; Duke University; Jawaharlal Nehru University; King's College London; the University of Pennsylvania; and Princeton University. Kyle Hanniman, Dave Ohls, Emily Sellars, and Tariq Thachil deserve repeat mentions, and my warmest gratitude, for countless conversations and draft chapters read, as well as their constant encouragement.

The School of International Service at American University has provided an intellectually rich and collegial home for this book's completion. Various parts of this book and related papers have benefitted from the insights of colleagues at American University, foremost among them Keith Darden, Daniel Esser, Jonathan Fox, Agustina Giraudy, Austin Hart, Miles Kahler, Adrienne LeBas, Malini Ranganathan, Rachel Robinson, and Sharon Weiner. I am also lucky to have had the research assistance of Arunjana Das, Kritika Kapoor, Anu Kumar, Julie Radomski, Manaswini Ramkumar, and Anjali Sah, each of whom helped me with various parts of this book, from translations to map-making and several waves of proofreading.

I am fortunate to have worked with Robert Dreesen, my editor at Cambridge University Press, who provided expert guidance on many aspects of the publication process, as well as Robert Judkins, Judieth Sheeja, Sunantha Ramamoorthy, and Jackie Grant, each of whom helped to steer this book through the production process. Many thanks to Kathleen Thelen and Erik Wibbels for their enthusiasm for the book and including it in the Cambridge Studies in Comparative Politics Series.

This book draws on material from my 2016 article "Clients and Communities: The Political Economy of Party Network Organization and Development in India's Urban Slums," *World Politics* 68, no. 1: 111–48. Chapters 5 and 6 draw on material from my 2018 article "Informal Archives: Historical Narratives and the Preservation of Paper in India's Urban Slums," published in *Studies in Comparative International Development* 53, no. 3: 343–64. Chapter 5 also draws on material from my 2017 article "Neighborhood Associations and the Urban Poor: India's Slum Development Committees," published in *World Development* 96: 119–35. I use these previously published materials with permission from Cambridge University Press, Springer Nature, and Elsevier, respectively. I thank the anonymous reviewers who provided incisive comments and suggestions on these articles.

The bulk of the fieldwork on which this book is based was made possible with the support of a Fulbright-Hays Doctoral Dissertation Research Abroad Fellowship, a National Science Foundation Doctoral Dissertation Research Improvement Grant, and a Social Science Research Council International Dissertation Research Fellowship. Early support from the Center for South Asia at the University of Wisconsin–Madison allowed me to gain traction for this project through preliminary fieldwork. A Scott Kloeck-Jenson Fellowship, also from the University of Wisconsin–Madison, gave me the opportunity to hold a summer internship at the National Institute of Urban Affairs in New Delhi, where my interest in urban governance was solidified. Foreign Language and Area Studies Fellowships afforded me the precious gift of several years of Hindi and Urdu coursework.

I was privileged to have worked with outstanding research assistants during my time in Bhopal and Jaipur. I foremost thank Hitesh Pathak for his research assistance and friendship over a year and a half of fieldwork between 2010 and 2012. Much of the data collection for this book would not have been possible without Hitesh's assistance in translating interviews and documents, as well as his role as a team supervisor during the 2012 survey. I also thank the sixteen members of the 2012 survey team, as well as Ved Prakash Sharma and the twelve members of the 2015 survey team, for their hard work and making the daily routine of survey work a pleasure.

I will forever be thankful for and humbled by the warm reception I received from the many people in Bhopal and Jaipur who made this book possible. Over the course of two years, hundreds of residents shared their time, opinions, and stories with me, frequently over cups of *chai* and bowls of *namkeen*. Dozens of slum leaders narrated their political lives and struggles to secure public services, often over a series of interviews that sometimes stretched into the late hours of the night. A group of officials at the Bhopal Municipal Corporation, Jaipur Municipal Corporation, and a constellation of other government departments assisted me in finding what I imagine to them must have been obscure bits of information on past municipal elections, city ward maps, and a wide variety of other materials that provide much of the empirical foundation for this book. An even longer list of elected representatives and political party officers helped me understand the inner workings of party politics in urban India. I hope this book does justice to these many voices.

The Centre for the Study of Law and Governance at Jawaharlal Nehru University, Delhi, and the Institute of Development Studies, Jaipur, provided intellectually stimulating academic homes during my research. I thank Dr. Meera Das and the late Dr. Ishwar Das for graciously hosting me in Bhopal and teaching me a great deal about the history and politics of the city. In Jaipur, I am deeply grateful for a now sixteen-year friendship with the Sharma family. Thanks for bringing me into your family, and for always keeping a box of *mithai* in the refrigerator for me.

My parents, Marcia and Robert Auerbach, have given me far more than a lifetime's worth of love and encouragement. Thanks for always pushing Sarah, Daniel, and me to explore the world and our own potentials. This book would simply not exist without the love, humor, and constant support of my partner, Prita. Who knew that our childhood friendship – stitched together with middle-school dances, pool parties, and neighborhood bike rides in suburban New Jersey – would transform over two decades into this beautiful life together. This book is dedicated to Prita and our little Arjun.

# I

# Puzzling Disparities at the Margins of the City

Ram Nagar has seen little in the way of public services since it was first settled in 1980. The slum's narrow, meandering streets are unpaved and without proper drainage. In the absence of such infrastructure, residents dig shallow channels in front of their homes to remove wastewater, and when it rains, they drop stones and debris in the muddied streets to make crude walkways. Only a handful of water taps have been installed in the settlement. They provide water for just a few hours a day, forcing residents to jostle with one another to fill their plastic buckets. Lacking metered electricity, families have put up their own rickety connections, forming a canopy of tangled wires that stretch out to the main road. Just a few streetlights flicker at night, leaving most of the slum in darkness. Jaipur city's sanitation workers do not come to remove trash, and residents are without toilets. As a result, a makeshift dump has emerged along the western edge of Ram Nagar that doubles as an open-air bathroom. Sewage seeps further into the settlement with each passing year, bringing with it the lingering smell of decay and burnt trash.

Two men, Varun and Rahul, have emerged from among Ram Nagar's 1,000 residents to become *basti neta*, or slum leaders. Their ability to read, write, and show courage before officials has made them focal points of resident efforts to demand development from the state. Due to his local popularity, Varun has even been extended a minor organizational position in one of India's national parties, the Bharatiya Janata Party (BJP), and in this capacity is expected to drum up local support for the BJP during elections. Over the past several decades, Varun and Rahul have made countless trips to government offices to fight for public services and push back against threats of eviction. Both men keep photocopies of the petitions they have written to officials. These documents, together with our many conversations about Ram Nagar's history, tell a story of relentless state neglect. One letter Varun shared with me, written to the Government of Rajasthan, captures the frustrated desperation of Ram Nagar's residents:

> We ... have to tolerate heat, cold, rain, and many other problems. We sell herbs, drive rickshaws, make swings, play drums, and make wooden trays ... We ... here for so many years, request the government for help. We do not get any attention and have been to offices many times and as a result, it has all become a headache. We request that Ram Nagar be rehabilitated, and wherever that is, we should get land titles. We poor people shall always be grateful.[1]

Just a kilometer east of Ram Nagar is Ganpati, a slum housing over 20,000 people. Like Ram Nagar, Ganpati was settled around 1980 and is located on government land. Residents of the two slums draw on common labor markets, lack formal land titles, and share the same state assembly and parliamentary constituencies, exposing them to identical politicians and election campaigns. Both settlements are the result of illegal squatting, culminating in dense, unplanned clusters of *jhuggies* (shanties) that are pieced together from wood, bricks, and corrugated metal.

Despite these similarities, Ganpati is significantly more developed than Ram Nagar in terms of its infrastructure and access to public services. Most of Ganpati's roads are paved and have cement grooves at their sides to remove wastewater. A drainage pipe runs along the front of the settlement, occasionally cleaned of silt by municipal workers. Piped water has been extended to large parts of Ganpati. Truck-fed tanks supplement the piped water – a crucial service during Rajasthan's melting-hot summer. No less than 414 streetlights keep the streets illuminated at night, and city sweepers sometimes come to collect waste. Sewers have been extended into the southern tip of Ganpati, though most residents use pit latrines or the sand dunes behind the settlement. The slum faces several vulnerabilities, a lack of sewers being the most pressing. Still, Ganpati has far surpassed Ram Nagar in its level of infrastructural development and access to public services.

These divergences are matched in their conspicuity by differences in the two settlements' political organization. Slum leaders with positions in party organizations – party workers – pervade Ganpati. Every alleyway seems to have at least one door marked with a party symbol, either the lotus flower of the BJP or open hand of the Indian National Congress

---

[1] Ram Nagar petition letter, June 1, 2006.

(INC), signifying that someone inside that home is a party worker. Ganpati has 147 party workers living and doing *netagiri* (leadership activities) in the settlement – six times more party workers per capita than Ram Nagar. These party workers are situated in defined party hierarchies that connect them to the highest strata of party leadership in the city. Drawing on these connections, Ganpati's party workers regularly make claims for public goods and services. The settlement's history is also punctuated with party-led protests to demand development. The results of this political organization are given physical form in the public goods and services that have flowed into Ganpati since its establishment.

The stark differences between Ram Nagar and Ganpati are not isolated. Instead, they represent puzzling disparities across India's vast population of urban slums. Despite a broader shared context of informality in housing and employment, entrenched forms of patronage politics, and state institutions that are often dismissive to the poor, India's slums are not uniformly marginalized in the distributive politics of the city. They exhibit dramatic variation in their capacity to organize and push the state to extend local public goods and services – piped water, paved roads, trash removal, sewers, storm drains, and streetlights. Such variation provokes a fundamental question in comparative political economy: Why are some vulnerable communities able to demand and secure development from the state while others fail?

The Global South is rapidly urbanizing.[2] Much of this demographic shift to cities is taking the form of sprawling slum settlements – crowded, low-income neighborhoods defined by their haphazard construction, weak or absent formal property rights, and disadvantaged position in the distribution of public services. More than 850 million people are estimated to live in urban slums worldwide. In sub-Saharan Africa, 213 million people – 62 percent of the urban population – reside in such conditions. South Asia is home to another 201 million slum dwellers, making up 35 percent of the region's urban population.[3] In India alone, a staggering 65 million people reside in urban slums,[4] exceeding the entire population of countries like Colombia, Italy, and South Africa.

---

[2] Half of the developing world's population currently lives in cities. By 2050, that percentage is projected to increase to 63.4 percent (United Nations 2015, pp. 204–205). Moreover, most future urbanization will take place in Africa and Asia: almost 90 percent of the estimated 2.5 billion additional people expected to live in cities between 2014 and 2050 will be located in those two regions (United Nations 2015, p. 1).

[3] These statistics are reported in UN-Habitat 2013, Statistical Appendix (p. 151).

[4] Government of India 2015, p. ix.

Understanding how slum residents organize and demand public services from the state, and the conditions under which such efforts are successful, is of global importance.

This book accounts for the variable success of India's slum residents in securing local public goods and services. I argue that the chief determinants of the provision of public goods and services can be found within the political organization of settlements and the degree to which they have been integrated into larger party networks in the city. Underneath the raucous surface of electoral politics in India's cities lies striking unevenness in the extent to which party worker networks have spread across slums – spaces commonly described as bastions of clientelistic politics, where parties are assumed to have local workers in place to generate support among poor voters. Studies of clientelism and distributive politics implicitly assume that party workers are uniformly present across localities, and when elections come, they are poised to sway voters and encourage turnout.[5] By contrast, I find wide variation in the density and partisan distribution of party workers across India's urban slums, with serious implications for the ability of residents to command state responsiveness.

Slums that have dense networks of party workers – large numbers of party workers, per capita, residing and operating in the settlement – are better positioned to demand development from the state than those with sparse or absent networks of party workers. Dense networks of party workers produce a degree of informal accountability because party workers must compete with each other to maintain and expand their personal following – the base of support upon which they attract patronage, rents, and party promotions. If a party worker fails to demonstrate efficacy in solving problems, residents can direct their support and requests for help to another party worker. Dense networks of party workers also provide residents with multiple points of connectivity to political elites and an organizational capacity for protest.

In probing the origins of party worker networks, this book reveals two deep determinants that guide their spread across slums. The first is a settlement's population, or the size of its "vote bank."[6] A slum's population shapes the electoral incentives of political elites to expend limited party resources and party positions. Moreover, residents of more populous settlements have greater incentives to enter the fray of slum leadership,

---

[5] For examples, see Stokes 2005, Nichter 2008, Camp 2015, and Larreguy et al. 2016.
[6] See Björkman 2014 on vote bank politics in urban India. See Breeding 2011 for a larger discussion on the concept and use of the term "vote bank" in Indian politics.

given the larger pools of local voters from which they can draw rents and launch their political careers. The importance of settlement population in driving local party organization has key implications for studies of distributive politics. It suggests that scholars must consider how community demographics shape party–voter linkages and the ability of residents to secure public goods and services. Poor voters do not make claims independently of space. Nor in the allocation of public services do politicians engage poor voters as individuals, untangled from the demographics of their neighborhoods.

The second factor guiding the spread of party worker networks is ethnic diversity. India's slums are richly and variably diverse along the lines of caste (*jati*), religion, and region (state) of origin.[7] Ethnic diversity tends to increase the fragmentation of informal leadership, as residents often prefer to support and turn to co-ethnic slum leaders for assistance.[8] Over time, parties seek to bring slum leaders into their fold to build electoral support, creating denser concentrations of party workers in ethnically diverse settlements. Provocatively, and cutting against the grain of a large literature in political economy that shows ethnic diversity dampening public goods provision,[9] this illuminates a pathway through which ethnic diversity can *positively* influence local public goods provision – through its impact on the formation of dense, competitive party worker networks. This suggests that scholars of ethnic politics should assess, alongside other mechanisms operating between ethnic diversity and outcomes in public goods provision, how ethnic diversity shapes the formation of local brokerage networks and, in turn, the ability of communities to organize and demand development from the state.

This book places much of its attention on the internal political organization of settlements because slum residents have significant political agency. We will see this includes not only autonomy in voting and claim-making but also the pivotal role of residents in producing the informal leaders who link them to the state. Understanding the political economy of development in slum settlements requires we depart from conventional frameworks that position the poor as locked in clientelistic relations with politicians in which the former passively react to top-down material

---

[7] On the use of the term "ethnic" to describe social identities such as caste, religion, and region in India, see Chandra 2004 and Chandra 2006.
[8] Auerbach and Thachil 2018.
[9] For overviews of this literature, see Habyarimana et al. 2009 and Singh and vom Hau 2016.

inducements.[10] We must also shift away from studying the supply of election-time handouts – cash, food, and liquor – to the sustained, bottom-up efforts of residents to secure public goods and services.[11] It is in the politics of everyday claim-making where we will find the factors that generate disparities in development across settlements.

India, the world's largest democracy and arguably most ethnically heterogeneous society, provides an important setting in which to examine the political economy of development in slums. Sixty-five million people, or 17 percent of India's 377 million city dwellers, reside in the country's slum settlements.[12] Within three decades, half of India's population will live in cities – a demographic trend now characterizing much of the Global South.[13] Concurrently, income and land inequality is sharp in India's cities,[14] with much of the poor residing in densely packed neighborhoods and working within a massive informal economy.[15] As urban India climbs past rural India in population, the manner in which the urban poor organize and interact with the state will increasingly shape the nature of democracy in the country.

This book rests on two years of fieldwork in the north Indian cities of Jaipur, Rajasthan and Bhopal, Madhya Pradesh. Between 2010 and 2012, I conducted fifteen months of ethnographic research in eight slum settlements – four each in Jaipur and Bhopal. These eight case studies provide a descriptive understanding of how residents solve day-to-day problems and make claims on the state, as well as afford comparative historical insights on the emergence of informal leadership, party organization, and the provision of public goods and services. This book's theoretical framework is inductively derived from this fieldwork. I then designed and administered an original survey to 2,545 residents across 111 slums in the same two cities. The resulting dataset allows me to quantitatively test the theoretical framework alongside key alternative explanations.

---

[10] Stokes 2005; Nichter 2008.
[11] On vote buying, see Schaffer 2007, Gonzalez-Ocantos et al. 2012, Kramon 2016, and Chauchard 2018. For broader discussions on political clientelism, see Kitschelt and Wilkinson 2007, Hicken 2011, Fox 1994, Fox 2012, and Weitz-Shapiro 2014.
[12] Government of India 2015, p. ix.
[13] On urbanization in India, see Sankhe et al. 2010; on urbanization in the Global South more generally, see Montgomery 2008 and United Nations 2015. See Auerbach et al. 2018 and Post 2018 for broad discussions on urban politics in the Global South.
[14] Kohli 2012, pp. 127–130; Motiram and Vakulabharanam 2012; Heller et al. 2015.
[15] On urban India's informal economy, see Gill 2009, Agarwala 2013, Breman 2013, Anjaria 2016, and Thachil 2017.

The remainder of this introductory chapter is organized into six sections. It first establishes the puzzle of uneven local public goods provision across India's slums and demonstrates the global reach of the puzzle. It then provides an overview of the book's theoretical framework and foreshadows its contributions to several literatures in the field of comparative politics. Next, the chapter defines the specific type of slum under study – squatter settlements – and introduces Jaipur and Bhopal. It then turns to the research design and data and concludes by mapping the remaining chapters.

## 1.1 THE PUZZLE OF UNEVEN PUBLIC GOODS PROVISION ACROSS SLUM SETTLEMENTS

Slums exhibit several shared economic and social characteristics stemming from their general position within India's cities that, taken together, make wide divergences in their access to local public goods and services puzzling. First, slums are archetypical examples of urban informality.[16] This is true with respect to housing as well as the vast informal economy in which most slum residents work. Second, relative to propertied middle-class neighborhoods, slums are low-income neighborhoods, where public services are frequently secured through political maneuvering, not appeals to programmatic rules.[17] Third, politicians unabashedly refer to slums as "vote banks" and see them as clusters of poor voters who can be attracted with the selective provision – or promise – of public resources. Yet, despite these commonly shared features, India's urban slums present startling variations in their access to public services. This section renders these broad brushstroke similarities before pivoting to describe inter-settlement disparities in development.

---

[16] It is important to note that just as the urban poor in India are not synonymous with the country's slum population, informality in India's cities is not limited to slums and their residents (Roy 2009; Bhan and Jana 2013). To provide just one example from my research sites, I encountered many middle-class neighborhoods in southern and western Jaipur that, despite planned layouts, gridded networks of streets, and upscale, multistory homes with cars parked out front, had not been approved by the Jaipur Development Authority and therefore had not been extended formal land titles.

[17] Benjamin and Bhuvaneswari 2001; Chatterjee 2004; Harriss 2005; Benjamin 2008; Das and Walton 2015.

## Informality in Employment and Housing

Residents of India's slums scratch out a living in an informal economy characterized by weakly enforced labor regulations, wage insecurity, and, for most, an absence of social benefits.[18] The jobs that compose the informal sector are as diverse as the people who work in it. Common jobs include auto-rickshaw drivers, welders, hawkers, butchers, carpenters, porters, domestic workers, street vendors, and unskilled construction laborers. Other informal-sector jobs are unique to specific regions. In Bhopal and Jaipur's slums, for instance, you will encounter gem cutters, marble masons, folk dancers, painters, and artisans who craft and perform with wooden puppets. Earning a living in the informal economy is uncertain and fiercely competitive.[19] It is also fraught with risk. If a worker becomes injured or sick, their family can plunge below – or fall deeper under – the poverty line. Some slum residents have salaried private jobs – call center operators, hotel cooks, and security guards, to name a few. Others work in the public sector, enjoying a modicum of economic security – for example, municipal sweepers, traffic police, and small-time government clerks. These formal occupations, however, are scarce and coveted.[20]

For many of India's slum residents, the uncertainty that accompanies work in the informal sector is compounded by informality in housing. India's slums are frequently enmeshed in webs of illegalities and regulatory ambiguities that stem from some combination of a lack of formal land property rights, an unauthorized presence on government or private lands,[21] and improvised, unsanctioned access to public services like water and electricity. Further, there are shades of gray between holding a land

---

[18] The percentage of "people in informal employment in non-agricultural activities" within India is estimated to be 84 percent (International Labour Organization 2013, p. xi).

[19] Thachil 2017.

[20] Only a small percentage (8.5 percent) of Auerbach and Thachil's 2,199 survey respondents across 110 slums in Bhopal and Jaipur held jobs that are conventionally seen as falling within the category of formal sector employment (school teachers, government workers, salaried private workers, and professionals like lawyers, engineers, and doctors). See the Appendix of Auerbach and Thachil 2018 for a detailed list of the informal-sector jobs that compose the sample.

[21] I am unaware of a nationwide figure for the percentage of slum households that lack land titles. Studies of individual Indian cities, however, document pervasive and multifaceted forms of informality in slum settlements. Krishna et al. 2018, for example, find a sliding scale of informality in Bangalore, where slum residents can have one of eighteen documents that signal a degree of rootedness on the land. The vast majority of the sampled households in this study (2,206 of 2,545 households) did not have full land titles.

title and facing total tenure insecurity. For instance, a lack of "notification" – official government recognition of a slum – can leave settlements more vulnerable to eviction than their notified counterparts.[22] Residents, moreover, keep a dizzying assortment of papers that signal some degree of rootedness on the land – ration cards, survey numbers, and electricity and water bills, for instance.[23] Heller and his coauthors argue that such gradations in tenure security within India's cities generate "differentiated" forms of citizenship.[24]

## Low-Income Neighborhoods

Based on a poverty line defined by monthly per capita consumption expenditures falling below Rs 1,407 (Rangarajan methodology), the Government of India estimated the urban poverty rate in the country in 2011/12 to be 102.5 million people, or 26.4 percent of the urban population.[25] Newspapers report that India's 2011 Socio-Economic and Caste Census puts 35 percent of urban households below the poverty line.[26] While these figures are slightly higher than the percentage of the urban population living in slum settlements (17 percent), it is important to note that not all poor people in India's cities reside in slums and not all slum residents experience poverty.[27] That said, slum settlements are frequently described as deprived, low-income catchments in India's cities, housing much of the country's urban poor.[28]

---

[22] Out of an estimated total of 33,510 slum settlements in India, the National Sample Survey Office (NSSO) found that 59 percent of slum settlements were not officially notified (NSSO 2014, Report 561, p. i). See Nakamura 2014 on slum notification in India.

[23] Das 2011; Srivastava 2012; Auerbach 2018. The NSSO found 58.5 percent of sampled slum households had ration cards, voter ID cards, or passports recording their residential address (NSSO 2014, Report 556, p. vi).

[24] "Differentiated citizenship" is a "system by which the state systematically assigns different levels of services to different categories of citizens based on their tenurial status" (Heller et al. 2015, p. 6). On inequality and citizenship in urban India, also see Chatterjee 2004, Heller and Evans 2010, and Das 2011.

[25] Government of India 2014.

[26] Nair 2015. The Socio-Economic and Caste Census measures the poverty line in a way that is distinct from the Rangarajan methodology (Nair 2015).

[27] On this point, see Gupta et al. 2009 and Bhan and Jana 2013. Some of the most vulnerable people in India's cities are not rooted in place but are instead transient, shifting around the city and between the city and countryside in search of work. On these "footloose" populations – for example, pavement dwellers and migrant laborers – see Breman 1996 and Thachil 2017.

[28] The Government of India's Statistical Compendium of Slums, for example, notes, "Income or capability poverty is considered, with some exceptions, as a central

In Jaipur and Bhopal, the average monthly household income per capita across the 111 slum settlements surveyed for this book is Rs 2,177 – using summer 2015 exchange rates, this amounts to roughly a dollar per person per day. Just under 80 percent of respondents have ration cards, providing subsidized food and fuel to citizens falling below a fixed income level. The average respondent has completed about five years of formal schooling. Thirty-eight percent of respondents do not have any formal education and 39 percent are illiterate, making a climb out of poverty exceedingly difficult.[29]

## Urban Popular Politics

Conditions of material poverty and informality are accompanied by high rates of political participation in India's slums.[30] Slum residents tend to vote in high numbers, earning them the title of "kingmakers" in the city. Of my survey respondents in 2012, 86.81 percent (1,671 of 1,925), for example, report voting in the last several elections. Beyond statistical estimates of electoral participation, politicians themselves see slums as clusters of poor voters that are crucial to win over.[31] Slum residents provide swelling crowds for rallies and are brought to the polls, en masse, during elections. They do so to engage in "vote bank" politics – a channel through which poor citizens use their numbers, as voters, to extract public resources from the state.[32] Chatterjee refers to this arena as "political society," where claims are made through popular politics, not

---

characteristic of slum areas" (Government of India 2015, p. 4). Similarly, Bag et al. (2016, p. 4) assert, "It is not necessary that the totality of the urban poor is living in the slums only, but definitely a dominant section of 'vulnerable and/or poor' population of a city finds their way into the slums." These descriptions are consistent with characterizations of slums as urban "poverty traps" (Marx et al. 2013).

[29] The 2011 Census reports that the nationwide literacy rate for slum dwellers is just over 84 percent (Government of India 2015, p. 34).

[30] Benjamin (2008, p. 724), for instance, estimated that 95 to 98 percent of slum dwellers in Bangalore voted in local elections. For comparative discussions on class and electoral participation in cities, see Holzner 2010 on Mexico; Resnick 2014 on Senegal and Zambia; and Nathan 2019 on Ghana.

[31] As one newspaper in Jaipur reported: "In slums the numbers of lovers of the BJP and INC are equal and their votes play an important role in elections, in the game of victory or defeat. So because of this both parties are working hard to get maximum votes from the slums. There're 2.5 *lakh* (250,000) voters in 205 bastis of the city" (Mohan Lal newspaper clipping dated September 7, 1999).

[32] Edelman and Mitra 2007; Bertorelli et al. 2014; Björkman 2014.

through appeals to citizen entitlements, legal procedures, and civil society.[33]

Examples of popular politics in India's slums abound. Parties distribute cash, food, and liquor in settlements before elections to encourage support and turnout.[34] Networks of political intermediaries assist slum residents in gaining access to state services, in the process collecting fees and generating popular followings that can be translated into crowds during elections.[35] State responsiveness to the needs of residents is often based on calculations of political expediency and the ability of residents to draw on various forms of popular politics like parties and protests to advance their material interests.[36] Public service provision in India's slums is, in short, largely mediated and politicized.

To summarize this section, India's slum residents – as a larger class in the city – broadly face material poverty, informality in housing and employment, capricious state institutions, and politicians who seek to take advantage of their vulnerabilities to extract electoral support. Mediated, often nonprogrammatic forms of distributive politics shape the arena in which slum residents demand public services. Underneath these overarching conditions, though, exists wide unevenness in access to public goods and services across slums. I now turn to describing that variation.

## The Unevenness of Development in India's Urban Slums

A recent nationally representative survey of India's slums reveals that large percentages of these settlements are deprived of local public goods and services.[37] Taps are the "major source of drinking water" in only 71 percent of sampled settlements; in others, residents rely on tube wells and bore wells, truck-fed tanks, or untreated sources such as lakes, rivers, and wells.[38] Sixty-six percent of sampled settlements have paved roads,

---

[33] Chatterjee 2004.
[34] Of my survey respondents in 2012, 37.51 percent (722 of 1,925) noted that parties distribute such handouts in their settlement during elections. This is likely an underestimate due to social desirability bias (Gonzalez-Ocantos et al. 2012). 1,075 respondents reported that election-time handouts are not distributed in their settlement and 120 respondents stated, "don't know" (with 8 missing observations).
[35] Harriss 2005; Jha et al. 2007; de Wit and Berner 2009; Berenschot 2010; Das and Walton 2015.
[36] Mitra 1988; Benjamin and Bhuvaneswari 2001; Chatterjee 2004; Jha et al. 2007; Banda et al. 2014; Das and Walton 2015.
[37] See NSSO 2014, Report 561.  [38] NSSO 2014, Report 561, p. ii.

69 percent have some kind of drainage system, and 29 percent have an underground sewer system. In 31 percent of the sampled settlements, "no latrine was used by most residents."[39] The municipality removes trash in just over half (62 percent) of sampled settlements, and a strikingly small percentage (24 percent) of sampled settlements had benefited from one of India's "slum improvement schemes" like the Jawaharlal Nehru National Urban Renewal Mission and Rajiv Awas Yojana.[40] The one service that nearly all settlements have some access to is electricity (93 percent),[41] though much of this is likely through illegal connections. It is important to note that these figures reflect binary measures of *some* presence of these goods and services. They neglect patchiness in access within settlements. Public service provision in India's slums is therefore grimmer than these statistics suggest.

These national figures render a broad picture of the state of public service provision in India's slums. Yet they are insufficiently disaggregated to capture intra-city variation. Surveys conducted in preparation for two urban development programs provide more fine-grained data on specific cities and, thus, bring us closer to observing uneven development across settlements.[42] Data from Jaipur and Bhopal, this book's two case study cities, show wide inter-settlement variation in paved road coverage, drainage, and access to water taps.[43] Data from Indore and Jabalpur, two cities in Madhya Pradesh, reveal gaping inequalities in access to streetlights, paved roads, water taps, and bathrooms.[44] And data from cities as diverse as Ahmedabad, Ludhiana, Nagpur, and Pune expose similar disparities.[45]

This book draws on even more granular measures of six development indicators: paved roads, sewers, streetlights, municipal trash collection, piped water, and government health camps (*sarkari chikitsa* camps). Table 1.1 presents descriptive statistics from a stratified random sample of 111 slums in Bhopal and Jaipur. The sampled settlements demonstrate

---

[39] NSSO 2014, Report 561, p. ii. The 2011 Census of India found that 66 percent of slum households have a "latrine facility within the premises." Within the 34 percent of households that do not have latrine facilities, 44.33 percent use public toilet facilities and 55.67 percent go to the bathroom in the open (Government of India 2015, p. x).
[40] NSSO 2014, Report 561, p. 45.    [41] NSSO 2014, Report 561, p. ii.
[42] These are Basic Services for the Urban Poor (BSUP) and Rajiv Awas Yojana (RAY).
[43] Bhopal and Jaipur RAY Datasets; Bhopal UN-Habitat Report 2007a.
[44] National Institute of Urban Affairs (NIUA) Indore Report 2008; Jabalpur UN-Habitat Report 2007b.
[45] NIUA Ahmedabad, Ludhiana, and Pune Reports 2008; CHF International Nagpur Slum Dataset.

TABLE 1.1 *Descriptive statistics of slum development indicators in Bhopal and Jaipur*

|  | Mean | SD | Minimum | Maximum |
| --- | --- | --- | --- | --- |
| Paved roads (%) | 70.05 | 37.74 | 0.00 | 100.00 |
| Streetlights per 1,000 residents | 5.73 | 5.40 | 0.00 | 25.22 |
| Water taps (%) | 42.05 | 37.50 | 0.00 | 100.00 |
| Sewer connections (%) | 27.10 | 33.53 | 0.00 | 100.00 |
| Municipal trash removal (%) | 42.41 | 26.05 | 0.00 | 100.00 |
| Government medical camps (%) | 24.43 | 16.90 | 0.00 | 95.00 |

*Note*: N = 111. Data from author surveys. *Paved roads* is the percentage of roads in a settlement that are paved. *Streetlights* is the number of streetlights in a settlement per 1,000 residents. *Water taps* and *sewer connections* are the percentages of survey respondents in a settlement who have household connections to piped water and sewer lines. *Municipal trash removal* and *government medical camps* are the percentages of survey respondents who state that these services are provided to their settlement.

tremendous variation in their access to local public goods and services. While some have paved roads, sewers, streetlights, trash collection, access to piped water, and periodic health camps, others have none of these goods and services and persist in the same squalor as the time of their founding decades before. Most slums lie somewhere between, exhibiting internal unevenness in public service provision.[46]

The local development outcomes under study in this book – the provision of paved roads, sewers, streetlights, piped water, trash collection, and medical camps – are commonly referred to as "local public goods," which serves as a "catch-all term used to refer to local public services and infrastructure."[47] These public services and infrastructure goods have "positive externalities" within the localities in which they are provided.[48] In India's urban slums,

---

[46] See Figures 1.1 and 1.2, respectively, for an example of an underdeveloped squatter settlement and an example of a squatter settlement with basic infrastructure and access to several public services.

[47] Post 2018, p. 123. For other examples of the use of this term in comparative politics and development economics, see Besley et al. 2004; Banerjee et al. 2005; Tsai 2007; Olken 2010; Baldwin 2015; Diaz-Cayeros et al. 2016; and Rao et al. 2017.

[48] See Tsai (2007, p. 5) on this feature of, and approach to local public goods. "Pure" public goods are those that are non-excludable and non-rival (Samuelson 1954; Tiebout 1967). The extent to which specific local public goods satisfy these two aspects of "pure" public goods varies by the good or service in question – some are more locally "high spillover" than others (Besley et al. 2004) – and the "relevant group of consumers" (Min 2015, p. 17) under study. Moreover, local public goods such as roads, streetlights, sewers, and storm drains can

FIGURE 1.1 An underdeveloped squatter settlement in Jaipur
*Note*: Author photograph (2011)

FIGURE 1.2 A squatter settlement with basic infrastructure in Bhopal
*Note*: Author photograph (2015)

public infrastructure and services like trash collection are usually provided by the state. This book, however, will also examine the provision of local public goods that are internally generated within settlements, by residents themselves, such as inter-household dispute resolution, the enforcement of informal property rights, and the pooling of money and labor for small-scale repairs to public infrastructure (for example, fixing public hand pumps, replacing broken taps on public water tanks, clearing public drains, and filling potholes on public streets).

Consistent with related studies, I use the terms "public goods and services," "public goods," and "public services" interchangeably in the following pages for ease of exposition.[49] Most often, I will leave off the word "local" as it is implied by this book's focus on the provision of public infrastructure and services in slum settlements. I will also sometimes use the terms "local development" and "community development" to refer to the outcomes under study. Development, of course, is a complex, multi-dimensional concept.[50] My use of the term in this book centers on a specific, albeit crucial facet of development dealing with the provision of local public goods. My use of the term also reflects how it is colloquially used on the ground in India's cities, where public infrastructure and services are forms of *vikas* (development) that residents demand from the state.

Before proceeding, it is worth stating plainly, beyond the sterile language of public goods provision, the stakes involved in slum residents' struggles to improve their neighborhoods. Without toilets and sewers, residents are forced to use sidewalks, street medians, and vacant areas within and around their neighborhood. The diseases that result from open defecation are many and serious, and have especially detrimental effects on infant and maternal health.[51] Furthermore, this says nothing about the implications of a lack of toilets for basic human dignity. An absence of piped water creates enormous hardships for residents, forcing them to rely on erratic water truck deliveries or rapidly depleting underground sources. Even in those settlements with pipes, water flows are often intermittent and unpredictable,[52] forcing residents to wait for long periods

---

be unevenly provided within neighborhoods, at times moving closer to the concept of local "club goods." A large empirical literature nevertheless refers to the types of local public infrastructure and services under study as "local public goods." See Min 2015 (pp. 16–24) and Lee 2018 for more detailed discussions on the varied use of the term "public good" in comparative politics and related fields, and the challenges of applying the theoretical ideal type to specific empirical examples on the ground.

[49] Tsai 2007, p. 5.   [50] Sen 1999.   [51] Padhi et al. 2015.   [52] Kumar et al. 2018.

each day to make sure they are able to fill their buckets and tanks, robbing them of time that could be spent engaging in more productive activities. Without paved roads and drainage, alleyways become thick pits of mud that are difficult to traverse by foot, scooter, or motorcycle. They also become breeding grounds for mosquitos, exposing residents to dengue and malaria. Without streetlights, alleyways are challenging to navigate at night. Infrequent trash collection generates heaps of solid waste that invite disease-carrying pests. Moreover, these mounds of garbage often accumulate in the few vacant places where local children can play. The local public goods under study in this book, in short, lie at the very core of resident dignity, health, and economic wellbeing.

## 1.2 PARTY WORKERS AND LOCAL DEVELOPMENT

Why are some settlements able to command state responsiveness while others fail? This book's argument centers on a pervasive type of political intermediary in urban India – slum leaders, especially those who are embedded within political party organizations. Before proceeding to the theoretical framework, I first define these actors and provide some descriptive scaffolding to situate them in the party organizations within which they operate.

### Slum Leaders and Party Workers

India's slum leaders are informal, nonstate actors. They are otherwise ordinary residents who live within settlements and face the same risks of eviction and underdevelopment as their neighbors. Political parties do not dispatch these individuals to live in slums. Instead, slum leaders squat on the land alongside other residents and build a local following afterward, by demonstrating an ability to get things done. The following chapters will show these figures engaging in an impressive range of problem-solving efforts. Slum leaders help residents obtain state-issued cards, resolve disputes, spread information about government programs for the urban poor, and spearhead efforts to fight eviction and claim public services. They are central features of local political life.

Many of India's slum leaders hold positions (*pad*) within party organizations. In this book, I refer to these party position-holding slum leaders as party workers (*karyakarta*). Party workers are paradigmatic examples of intermediaries, engaged in upward-facing forms of political mediation for residents and downward-facing forms of electoral mobilization for parties. Their party positions situate them in pyramidal party organizations that link them to political elites. Party workers operate at the core of this book's theoretical framework.

At face value, a focus on India's grassroots party workers is surprising. India's party organizations have long been described as weak and fleeting at the local level; that is, instead of relying on sturdy party organizations to sway voters and boost turnout, politicians must string together more ephemeral linkages with local elites to extend their influence downward into communities. For example, and in reference to precisely the same states under examination in this book, Krishna notes, "Parties are notoriously poorly organized in rural Rajasthan and Madhya Pradesh and in most other parts of India."[53] Kohli also describes India's parties, and the INC in particular, to be in disarray in the districts, generating an "organizational vacuum" at the local level.[54] Adding to what is now conventional wisdom, Manor writes, "Most of their [Indian politicians] parties possess only limited organizational strength. In particular, most fail to penetrate effectively downward below intermediate levels to the grassroots."[55]

In contrast to these accounts, party organizations in India's cities are structured and active during and between elections. The BJP and INC – the two parties in competition in Rajasthan and Madhya Pradesh – have tiered organizations in Jaipur and Bhopal that stretch from the humble polling booth president to committees at the ward, block, city, district, and state levels. Committee members at each of these tiers hold positions that relate them to others in the committee – president (*adhyaksh*), vice president (*up-adhyaksh*), secretary (*sachiv*), treasurer (*kosh-adhyaksh*), minister (*mantri*), and general member (*sadasya*). In addition to the main organizations, the BJP and INC have cells (*prakosht*) and wings (*morcha*) to organize specific groups of voters like women, Muslims, Scheduled Castes (the former "untouchables"), and slum dwellers. The hundreds of position-holders (*padadhikari*) that fill these committees fan out across the city and form the backbone of India's urban party organizations.

Party organizations are highly visible in India's cities. Party posters hang from walls and billboards, displaying party symbols and the headshots of local party workers next to national politicians. Party rallies hold

---

[53] Krishna 2007, p. 146.
[54] Kohli 1991. Other studies describe some subset of India's parties as organizationally weak (Bailey 1963, chapter 6; Manor 2005; Chhibber et al. 2014; Ziegfeld 2016).
[55] Manor 2010, p. 509.

up traffic and overwhelm public parks. Party headquarters are conspicuous, flag-draped buildings where political elites meet to oversee citywide party activities and rank-and-file workers gather to pass time and perform small tasks for their patrons. More modest locations for party work are strewn across India's cities as well, ranging from the private homes of politicians to tea stalls, tobacco stands, and roadside restaurants. These are the places of everyday *netagiri* where party workers trade in gossip and engage in politics.

Slums are inundated with the visual elements of party politics. Party flags flutter above the roofline of many settlements.[56] Party workers often have placards outside their homes listing their party and party position. In some settlements, iron signs are posted with the names of local party workers. Others have massive gates at their entrances, painted in party colors. In settlements like Ganpati, you can hardly find an alleyway that is not home to at least one party worker. These party workers, as the following chapters demonstrate, are engaged in daily forms of party work and resident problem-solving.

Descriptions of Indian party organizations as locally weak and limited in their activities to elections would thus come as a surprise to many of India's slum residents. While elections are moments of relatively intense mobilization, party workers are on the move between the votes as well, fueled by the many opportunities to take up local problems to expand their bases of public support. Political elites themselves readily acknowledge these acts of local problem-solving among party workers. One prominent INC politician in Jaipur explained: "They come to us and say, 'these are our problems, you have to sort it out ... this development should be done; this road work should be done; this water supply should be done; we [need] electricity; we [need] schools' ... [these issues are addressed] because of the ward president, the block president, the leaders of the slums. They generally solve these problems."[57] A narrow focus on election-time activities misses these bottom-up functions of party workers that are so crucial to the political economy of local development.

To provide a concrete example of a party worker, take Khan, a resident of a slum settlement not far from Jaipur's main train station. On most days, Khan can be found operating his small corner store (*kirana dukhan*), selling wheat, rice, soap, and other simple provisions. Residents widely

---

[56] See Figure 1.3 for an example of a party flag in a Jaipur squatter settlement.
[57] Interview with INC politician, Jaipur, July 13, 2018.

*Puzzling Disparities at the Margins of the City* 19

FIGURE 1.3 Party flag in a Jaipur squatter settlement
*Note*: Author photograph (2018)

acknowledge Khan as a slum leader and turn to him for help in gaining access to state services. Khan is also a Congress party worker. In this capacity, he is charged with mobilizing residents for the INC during elections and rallies. Khan is just one of nineteen party workers in his settlement (ten Congress party workers and nine BJP workers), all of whom perform similar tasks for residents and their parties.

In this book, I refer to a settlement's per capita number of party workers as the *density* of party workers. Figure 1.4 illustrates several outcomes

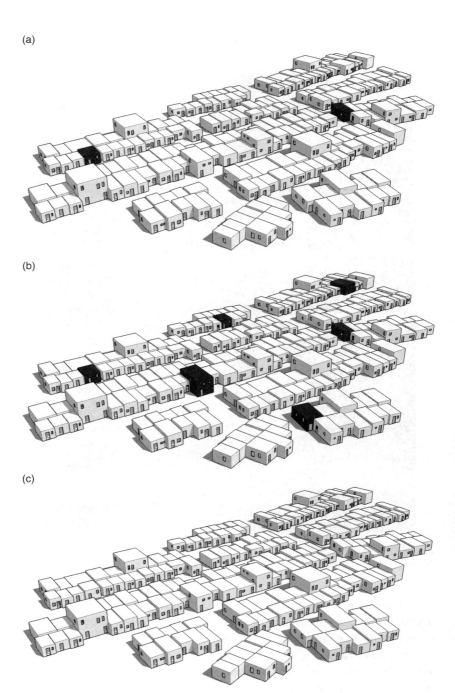

FIGURE 1.4 Three levels of party worker density in Kamal Nagar
*Note*: From top to bottom, these images depict situations of 2, 6, and 0 party workers per 200 households, respectively (party worker households shaded in dark gray). These numbers correspond to the average, maximum, and minimum number of party workers per 200 households across the 111 slum settlements surveyed for this book. Images drawn by Anthony Lavadera (2018).

in party worker density. The depicted settlement – let us refer to it as Kamal Nagar – is composed of 200 households, or roughly 1,000 residents. In the top image in Figure 1.4, Kamal Nagar has what I find to be the average party worker density in Bhopal and Jaipur's slums – 2 party workers per 200 households. Within this densely populated neighborhood, there are two slum leaders with party positions living right down the street, engaging in everyday acts of problem-solving for residents. In the middle image of Figure 1.4, we see a situation of six party workers in Kamal Nagar – the highest number of party workers per 200 households in my sample of 111 slum settlements. There are now four more party workers residing in Kamal Nagar, offering their intermediary services and competing with one another for a local following. Finally, we see in the bottom image in Figure 1.4 a situation in which there are no party workers. Residents are without a single party worker who can draw on their political connections in making claims for public services.

## Party Worker Density and Development

Some of India's slum settlements are pervaded with party workers. Residents in these areas have slum leaders with party connections who they can turn to for help in making claims. Some settlements have just a few party workers, while others are completely absent of them. Studies of distributive politics have overlooked variation in the presence and density of party worker networks across communities, and the resulting disparities in state responsiveness that face people residing in those communities.[58]

Slums with dense networks of party workers are well positioned to demand development from the state. In such settlements, competition among party workers for a popular following generates a degree of informal accountability that encourages development. Party workers who demonstrate efficacy in problem-solving and claim-making can build a large and loyal following. Those who are inactive risk seeing their base of support collapse and shift to another party worker. From above, parties can contribute to the production of informal accountability through top-down monitoring. Party workers who fail to perform or transgress on voters damage the party brand.

---

[58] In using the term *network*, I do not intend to evoke the literature on social network analysis. Instead, I use the term to underscore the face-to-face nature of the relationships among party workers who reside in the same settlement, as well as their direct, face-to-face linkages with party elites who are placed further up the ladder of party organization in the city.

When parties catch wind of this, they can sanction a worker by stalling promotion or taking away their position.

Dense networks of party workers further afford settlements with political connectivity. Through vertical party channels, workers can approach political elites to seek assistance with local problems. Such connections do not operate on abstract notions of co-partisanship. Instead, party workers cultivate close relationships with political elites. Armed with these connections, they can circumvent the daily queues of citizens that form outside the offices of politicians. And with their patrons' private contact details, party workers can bypass publicly listed numbers that are often defunct or ignored. Connectivity also manifests itself through the exchange of paper. Written petitions are common vehicles of claim-making in urban India.[59] Party workers have party letterhead stationery that signals the content of their claims should be taken seriously.

Dense networks of party workers also strengthen the mobilization capacity of settlements. Party workers take up resident problems in the effort to expand their personal following – and, by extension, the following of their party. They organize and accompany groups of residents to government offices to voice grievances and submit petitions. When settlement-wide problems arise, party organizations can be activated to mobilize residents for protest. Politicians descend on slums to be seen as responsive patrons, surrounded by their local workers who are tasked with rallying residents. Slums that lack dense networks of party workers face greater obstacles in attracting state responsiveness through these acts of group claim-making and protest.

In addition to revealing substantial inter-settlement variation in party worker density, this book documents unevenness in the partisan composition of those networks. In some settlements, party workers all belong to the same party, creating a situation of one-party dominance. In others, party workers represent several parties, generating partisan cleavages and divergent electoral interests among the slum's informal leaders. I argue that the presence of party workers from different parties has countervailing effects on public service delivery. On the one hand, it can improve development by intensifying political competition and thus boosting accountability and responsiveness. It also provides diverse partisan connections in India's fluid electoral landscape, ensuring that there are party workers with ties to the incumbent party at any given level of government. On the other hand, politicians are less likely to provide services to slums with multiparty worker networks, as rival party workers can undercut the

---

[59] Auerbach 2018.

politician's credit-claiming efforts. Partisan competition also creates incentives for rival party workers to undermine the other's claim-making efforts to consolidate their own electoral base of support, even to the detriment of local development.

## Why are Some Settlements more Flush with Party Workers than Others?

Why do party worker networks vary in their density and partisan balance across neighborhoods of the city that are commonly seen as universally fertile terrain for machine politics? India's urban slums offer important opportunities to comparatively trace the formation of party linkages through examinations of local histories. Most slum settlements in India are only several decades old. In the early stages of a settlement's emergence – after the initial influx of migrants on the land – squatters lack well-defined forms of informal leadership. The processes that give rise to slum leadership and party linkages unfold after the dust of squatting settles, in response to threats of eviction and underdevelopment. Many current residents were present during their settlement's initial formation and lived through changes in its physical and political development, affording researchers the chance to reconstruct the micro-histories of settlements.

The formation of slum settlements reveals two factors that generate unevenness in the density of party workers. The first is a settlement's population, or the size of its "vote bank," which shapes top-down incentives for parties to expend limited patronage, party positions, and campaign efforts. A unit of these resources has increasing marginal returns in relation to settlement population. Slum leaders residing in larger settlements are entrenched in areas with more voters and potential rally participants. It is more expedient to provide them limited network positions and patronage than slum leaders residing in smaller settlements. Similarly, a unit of party patronage, a party position, or a campaign event has greater reputational reverberations among voters in large settlements, giving political elites a bigger electoral bang for their buck.

Population also informs bottom-up incentives for residents to make a go at slum leadership. Engaging in slum leadership is more attractive in large settlements because there is a larger pool of voters to aspire to lead and, thus, harness as a source of rents, party patronage, and popularity on which to launch a political career. Such incentives in larger settlements generate higher concentrations of slum leaders and, in turn, more slum leaders for parties to bring into their organizations.

The second factor that produces unevenness in the density of party workers is ethnic diversity. Increasing levels of ethnic diversity – manifest in urban India as caste, religious, and regional (state) diversity – tend to generate denser concentrations of slum leaders. This is because residents frequently hold preferences to support and turn to co-ethnic slum leaders.[60] Over time, parties seek to bring slum leaders into their fold, producing denser networks of party workers in more diverse settlements. The contours of slum leadership, though, do not perfectly run along ethnic lines. Because of the importance of nonethnic criteria in shaping who becomes a slum leader – sufficient education to navigate government institutions and engage in written claim-making, connectivity to city officials, charisma, and tenacity, to name a few – most residents are without co-ethnic slum leaders.[61] And because of high rates of ethnic heterogeneity, most ethnic groups within settlements are too small to make demands on the state alone, encouraging them to look to non-coethnics for numbers and informal leadership. Therefore, while ethnic diversity tends to increase the density of slum leaders, it does not rigidly structure resident-slum leader ties. The market for a following of residents extends beyond a slum leader's own ethnic group, widening the arena of competition among slum leaders for local support.

### Shifting the Analytical Focus of Distributive Politics

This book departs from much of the literature on distributive politics along several fronts. First, it takes communities as the major unit of analysis, not individual voters, administrative units, or electoral constituencies. In the allocation of public services, politicians approach slum settlements as spatially defined areas that have distinct names, social groups, and collective problems that can be taken advantage of for electoral gain. Resident organization and claim-making erupts in response to settlement-specific problems, and the informal authority of slum leaders springs from resident support. Public services are extended to the whole or part of settlements and residents can consume them irrespective of their individual vote. Because of the social and political salience of the slum *settlement* in urban distributive politics – from the perspectives of both residents and political elites – it is the central unit of analysis in this book.

---

[60] Auerbach and Thachil 2018.
[61] See Auerbach and Thachil 2018 on the attributes that residents look for in their slum leaders.

When the individual voter is not the unit of analysis, studies of distributive politics tend to look at the allocation of public resources across formal political and administrative units – electoral constituencies and subnational units such as districts and states.[62] India's slums rarely coincide with the boundaries of administrative or electoral units. They are most often just a small part of even the most local unit of formal representation in cities – municipal wards – and share those wards with other neighborhoods with their own distinct demographics, partisan leanings, and degrees of formality. As such, this book joins an earlier wave of research on comparative urban politics that approached socially defined neighborhoods as the major unit of analysis.[63]

Second, this book looks beyond the study of election-time vote buying. It concentrates instead on bottom-up, routine forms of claim-making.[64] The slow grind of these efforts – mobilizing residents, writing petitions, and navigating state institutions – differs from episodic, top-down acts of vote buying. This is not to say that election-time party politics do not inform the allocation of public services. Instead, it is to argue that many of the most pressing problems that face slum residents do not wait for elections to present themselves. New arrivals need ration cards and voter IDs. Slums without public services engage in sustained efforts to get them. And in those settlements that have succeeded in such efforts, infrastructure deteriorates. Power lines fall, roads crumble, and drains clog. Municipal sweepers fail to show up. The need to solve collective problems is an ongoing reality in slum settlements, requiring a wider lens of analysis to capture the everyday claims that residents define and make from the ground up.

Third, this book probes a neglected form of political competition – competition among political intermediaries for a public following. Most slum settlements we will encounter in this book have multiple slum leaders who compete with each other – on an everyday basis – for a base of support among residents. This deviates from most studies of political intermediaries, which frequently overlook – both empirically and theoretically – the local presence of multiple brokers, and the implications of multifocal brokerage for distributive outcomes.[65] Everyday competition among political intermediaries, residing in the same localities, is distinct

---

[62] Chhibber and Nooruddin 2004; Vaishnav and Sircar 2013; Bohlken 2018.
[63] Gay 1994; Stokes 1995.
[64] On claim-making in rural India, see Corbridge et al. 2005 and Kruks-Wisner 2018.
[65] An important exception is Krishna 2002.

from the usual forms of competition studied by comparative political scientists – competition among candidates and parties during elections. This book shows how competition among slum leaders for a following generates incentives for them to be responsive to resident demands.

## Scope Conditions

The scope conditions of this book's theory are few and have broad geographic reach. Over the past several decades, the proliferation of slums in Africa, Asia, and Latin America has been nothing short of staggering.[66] For much of this population, formal property rights are insecure, employment is found in the informal sector, and public services are often accessed through complex networks of political intermediaries. Slum leaders have been documented across many cities in the Global South, spearheading claim-making efforts and serving as grassroots nodes of larger political networks.[67] Moreover, scholars have noted disparities in public services across slums in a wide range of countries. Gay, for example, highlighted uneven development across Rio de Janeiro's *favelas*.[68] Dosh encountered variation in public services in the *barrios* of Lima and Quito,[69] and others have described such variation in urban Argentina and Pakistan.[70]

The formal institutional environment under study in this book also resonates in many contexts outside of India. Within the last several decades, democracies across the Global South have undergone processes of political decentralization, creating elected subnational governments charged with some responsibilities over public service provision.[71] Multiparty competition marks many of these same democracies, including countries as diverse as Brazil, Ghana, and Mexico. While India's caste, linguistic, and religious diversity may be unique, ethnically diverse neighborhoods are common across a diverse range of cities in South Asia and sub-Saharan Africa.[72] The puzzle that stimulates this book, as well as the contextual features that shape distributive politics in India's cities – widespread informality, multiparty politics, decentralized and multitiered

---

[66] UN-Habitat 2013.
[67] Ray 1969; Cornelius 1975; Schoorl et al. 1983; Gay 1994; Auyero 2001; Marx et al. 2017.
[68] Gay 1994.   [69] Dosh 2010.   [70] Schoorl et al. 1983; Paniagua 2018.
[71] Crook and Manor 1998; Bardhan and Mookerjee 2006; Jayal et al. 2007; Auerbach et al. 2018.
[72] Schoorl et al. 1983; Marx et al. 2017; Nathan 2016.

# Puzzling Disparities at the Margins of the City

governance, and politicized forms of public service delivery – are therefore present in an expansive set of countries.

Some facets of this book's arguments and findings, however, will prove less applicable in certain contexts outside of India. First, the book's theoretical framework is fundamentally shaped by India's raucous, multi-party democracy. The politics of public goods provision in urban slums is likely to take on a distinct logic in autocratic regimes. Second, the state is not always the chief provider of local public goods.[73] In countries and cities where local public goods are mostly or entirely distributed by non-state providers, this book's emphasis on the state as the target of citizen claims will have less resonance. Third, highly centralized states will likely generate patterns of citizen-state relationships that differ from those in India's cities, where municipal governments and ward councillors are important institutions and actors in the politics of slum development. Fourth, this book's empirical and theoretical engagement with ethnic diversity, and the influence of ethnic diversity on local political organization, will prove less relevant in environments where ethnic diversity is absent or not a salient feature of the social environment. How residents of slums struggle to access public goods and services under these different conditions – and the factors that impact whether these efforts are successful – are open and important questions.

## 1.3 URBAN INFORMALITY AND THE STATE

This book's guiding questions evoke a rich literature on urban informality. Scholars in this multidisciplinary field have powerfully documented how the urban poor shape the politics and built space of cities. In a seminal book on the subject, Bayat describes how the "quiet encroachment of the poor" has come to define urbanization in Iran.[74] Holston's notion of "insurgent citizenship" illuminates the protracted struggles of Brazil's urban poor to demand inclusion in the city.[75] With a focus on India's cities, Benjamin and Bhuvaneswari's observation that slum residents use a "politics of stealth" to engage the state captures the fragmented, often nonprogrammatic ways the urban poor navigate and make demands on government institutions.[76]

---

[73] Cammett and MacLean 2014; Herrera and Post 2014; Post et al. 2017.
[74] Bayat 1997.
[75] Holston 2009. On citizenship and poverty in urban Brazil, also see Fischer 2010.
[76] Benjamin and Bhuvaneswari (2001, p. 68) define such "politics of stealth" as the "less visible political and administrative strategies that local groups, politicians, and lower level bureaucrats use to push an agenda that contradicts what is officially publicized."

Studies within this same line of research have examined how street vendors and migrant laborers carve out a living in cities.[77] Others investigate how slum residents covertly link themselves to water systems,[78] push back against eviction,[79] and make claims for public services,[80] often through nonstate intermediaries and other modes of popular politics.[81] These studies establish that the poor are far from passive actors in the city, persistently fighting to improve their lot through actions that are diverse in their form, scale, and structure.

This book takes the insights of this literature as foundational. The analytical orientations of these studies, however, tend to be bent toward describing broad patterns of urban politics, not to explain variation in political mobilization and public service delivery across neighborhoods. They are by design unable to capture the variety of organizational responses that slums have to the politics of cities, and why some have secured public services while others fail to. Slum residents, for example, use "stealthy politics" and elements of "political society" to engage the state.[82] Such concepts, though, are essentially constants across settlements and hence shed little light on the causes of inter-settlement disparities.

An early wave of studies in comparative politics examined the politics of urban informality in a variety of Latin American cities.[83] Scholars in this line of research investigated how slum dwellers use patron-client networks to improve local conditions and, in turn, how parties exploit such networks to cultivate popular bases of electoral support. This literature produced richly detailed case studies that described the political economy of slum settlements. These studies, however, lack comparison across a large and representative sample of settlements. Consequently, they are unable to reveal broader patterns of settlement organization and development.

A distinct literature in political economy investigates how the urban poor gain access to public resources,[84] use social networks to find employment,[85] develop inter-household trust,[86] and experience economic upward mobility.[87] Related studies examine the effects of land titling on

---

[77] Cross 1998; Anjaria 2016.   [78] Björkman 2015; Anand 2017.
[79] Weinstein 2014; Bhan 2016.
[80] Bapat and Agarwal 2003; McFarlane 2004; Kamath and Vijayabaskar 2014; Williams et al. 2015.
[81] Chatterjee 2004; Harriss 2005.
[82] Benjamin and Bhuvaneswari 2001; Chatterjee 2004.
[83] Ray 1969; Cornelius 1975; Collier 1976; Gay 1994; Stokes 1995.
[84] Harriss 2005; Jha et al. 2007.   [85] Mitra 2003; 2010.   [86] Carpenter et al. 2004.
[87] Lall et al. 2006; Krishna 2013.

household investments.[88] I extensively draw on this literature in the following chapters. These studies, however, do not seek to explain variation in public services across settlements. Their chief analytical focus on the individual and household limits the extent to which they can directly speak to the central questions guiding this book.

There are, of course, studies that do not specifically focus on urban slums but still offer important alternative explanations of community development. Several of these explanations center on top-down factors that shape politicians' incentives to provide public goods and services. These include the partisan leanings of residents (whether they are core, swing, or opposition voters);[89] the extent of electoral competition, which may lead incumbents to "overbid" in their public expenditures to chase every last vote;[90] and whether or not a slum is recognized by the state.[91]

Other studies sharpen their focus on intra-community factors that impact the ability of residents to advance their common interests. Key among those factors is social capital, or the extent to which residents trust and cooperate with one another;[92] settlement population, and its influence on collective action;[93] ethnic diversity, which scholars have argued has deleterious effects on cooperation and public goods provision;[94] and the strength of formal land property rights.[95]

The puzzle that animates this book thus sits at the intersection of several large and multidisciplinary literatures. Each of the alternative explanations highlighted above will be examined in the chapters that follow. We will find them silent or limited in their ability to explain variation in public service provision across India's slums, compelling us to look elsewhere for answers.

## 1.4 WHAT IS A SLUM?

The urban poor reside in a wide range of housing conditions. The term "slum" is used to describe many of these conditions: derelict old-city neighborhoods, construction-site housing, post-eviction resettlement camps, squatter settlements, and once-peripheral villages that have been engulfed by city sprawl. The common use of "slum" to describe these

---

[88] Field 2005; Galiani and Schargrodsky 2010.
[89] Cox and McCubbins 1986; Stokes 2005; Nichter 2008; Calvo and Murillo 2013.
[90] Sáez and Sinha 2010.   [91] Nakamura 2016.
[92] Bowles and Gintis 2002; Krishna 2002; Narayan and Pritchett 1999.   [93] Olson 1965.
[94] Alesina et al. 1999; Besley et al. 2004; Habyarimana et al. 2009.
[95] de Soto 2003; Field 2005.

different housing arrangements largely flows from the amorphous nature of official definitions of the term.[96] For example, in reference to Andhra Pradesh but with relevance throughout India, Naidu notes, "Students with a textbook notion of slums would be quite bewildered by the range of housing conditions which constitute a 'slum area' under the Andhra Pradesh Slum Act."[97] Similarly, Roy writes, "The idea of a generic informal housing ... fails to examine the varied conditions under which housing is acquired and negotiated. An obvious case is the difference between Calcutta's slums and squatter settlements, the former with regularized rights to land, and the latter with tenuous and revocable claims to residence. In both instances, rights and claims have to be negotiated and maintained, but the parameters within which such contestations take place are drastically different."[98]

As Krishna and his coauthors argue, "Little is gained (and much is lost) by considering slums as a homogenous category of settlements."[99] Indeed, because slums vary in their legality, historical origins, and social integration in the city, researchers must define and differentiate among the types of settlements under study. For example, Mathur and Bhatnagar separate old-city slums in Jaipur – crumbling residential areas within the walled city – from their more recent squatter settlement counterparts.[100] In Bhopal, Risbud and Agnihotri make a distinction between slums in the old city and the hundreds of squatter settlements outside of it, as well as distinctions among squatter settlements, unauthorized colonies, and resettlement areas.[101] Studies of other Indian cities use similar classifications of informal, low-income settlements.[102]

---

[96] UN-Habitat (2006b) defines a slum household as "a group of individuals living under the same roof in an urban area who lack one or more of the following: Durable housing of a permanent nature that protects against extreme climate conditions; sufficient living space, which means not more than three people sharing the same room; easy access to safe water in sufficient amounts at an affordable price; access to adequate sanitation in the form of a private or public toilet shared by a reasonable number of people; security of tenure that prevents forced evictions." India's Census (see Census of India 2013 and the Slum Areas Improvement and Clearance Act 1956) defines slums as "residential areas where dwellings are in any respect unfit for human habitation by reasons of dilapidation, overcrowding, faulty arrangements and design of such buildings, narrowness or faulty arrangement of streets, lack of ventilation, light, or sanitation facilities or any combination of these factors which are detrimental to safety, health, and morals."
[97] Naidu 2009, p. 205.    [98] Roy 2002, p. 49.    [99] Krishna et al. 2014, p. 2.
[100] Mathur 1996; Bhatnagar 2010.    [101] Risbud 1988 and Agnihotri 1994.
[102] For example, Singh and de Souza note (1980, p. 7), "in Delhi there are basically two types of slums: (i) the indigenous *katras* [old city slums], many of which date back to the time before the city became the British capital in 1911, and (ii) the more recent

This book focuses on *squatter settlements* – unplanned, low-income neighborhoods that are constructed by residents in an unsanctioned and haphazard manner.[103] Squatter settlements lack formal property rights at the period of their establishment and are often located on environmentally sensitive areas such as riverbeds, mountainsides, and landfills, or along highways, drains, and railroad tracks. They spread across India and many other countries in the Global South in the second half of the twentieth century.[104] The shared origins of squatter settlements in conditions of illegality, informality, and underdevelopment, as well as their relatively recent proliferation, afford unique leverage in comparatively tracing the formation of informal leadership, political linkages, and public service provision.

FIGURE 1.5 A squatter settlement in Jaipur
*Note*: Author photograph (2012)

unauthorized housing areas, including squatter settlements [*jhuggi-jhopprie* settlements]." See also Schenk 2001 and Dupont and Ramanathan 2008.

[103] UN-Habitat (1982, p. 15) defines squatter settlements as "mainly uncontrolled low-income residential areas with an ambiguous legal status regarding land occupation; they are to a large extent built by the inhabitants themselves using their own means and are usually poorly equipped with public utilities and community services ... The land occupied by squatter settlements is often, but not always, further from the city center than is the case with slums ... The land is often occupied illegally, while in many other cases the legality of occupation is complicated or unclear." See Figure 1.5 for a photograph of a Jaipur squatter settlement.

[104] UN-Habitat 1982, p. 15.

For ease of exposition, and to conform to the colloquial use of the term by residents and officials in India's cities, I use the terms "slum," "settlement," and "squatter settlement" interchangeably to refer to the localities under study.[105] Squatter settlements, however, are the specific empirical focus of this book.

### Ethnic Diversity in India's Slums

India's slums are home to impressive ethnic diversity along several dimensions. The first dimension is subcaste (*jati*): hierarchically arranged ethnic groups for which there are hundreds in India. Over 300 *jati* populate the 111 slum settlements surveyed for this book. The average settlement has a remarkably high *jati* fractionalization score of 0.80 (with a one standard deviation of 0.15), meaning that two randomly selected residents, in the average settlement, have an 80 percent chance of belonging to a different *jati*.[106] A large percentage of respondents belong to the Scheduled Castes (SCs): a composite social category that includes caste groups that have faced the worst forms of discrimination and marginalization associated with the caste system. Thirty-four percent of respondents are SC – considerably higher than Bhopal and Jaipur's city-level percentages.[107] All strata of castes, though, are represented in the sampled settlements, including "high"-caste Rajputs, Banias, and Brahmins.

The second dimension is religion, which in Jaipur and Bhopal most prominently includes Hindus and Muslims, with a small percentage of Jains, Sikhs, and Buddhists.[108] In the average sampled settlement, the probability that two randomly selected residents belong to different religions is 0.17, with a one standard deviation of 0.17. Only 37 percent of sampled settlements (41 of 111) are homogeneous in terms of religion. Most settlements, then, have some degree of multireligious representation, and in most cases this diversity emerges from Hindus and Muslims living alongside one another in the same settlement. The prevalence of

---

[105] In addition to using the English term "slum," residents in Bhopal and Jaipur refer to these settlements as *kachi bastis* and *jhuggi jhopris*. See Weinstein (2014, pp. 8–11) on the historical and contemporary use of the term "slum."

[106] On the measurement of the ethnic fragmentation scores presented in this section, see Chapter 6.

[107] Jaipur's population is 12.9 percent SC. Bhopal's population is 13.5 percent SC (Jaipur and Bhopal 2011 District Census Handbooks).

[108] Of the survey respondents, 74 percent are Hindu and 24 percent are Muslim.

such diversity is remarkable given the recent history of Hindu-Muslim riots in Jaipur and Bhopal.

The third dimension is regional. India's slums are frequently home to residents who have migrated from different states in the country. Only 24 of the 111 sampled settlements have sampled households from just one state, and in all such cases that state is either Rajasthan or Madhya Pradesh. Most settlements are multiregional, with migrant families from states like Bihar, Chhattisgarh, Haryana, Maharashtra, Punjab, Uttar Pradesh, and West Bengal. The average settlement has a regional (state) fractionalization score of 0.28 with a one standard deviation of 0.22. Such diversity brings distinct languages and cultures into the social fabric of slum settlements. And this says nothing of sub-state regional identities (for instance, the Bhojpuri-speaking areas of Bihar and Uttar Pradesh), which also carry social weight.

Ethnographic studies of India's slums also describe these as remarkably diverse places.[109] Datta aptly captures this feature of India's slum settlements: "It is in its slums and squatter settlements that India's social diversity is truly reflected."[110] As I will argue in the following chapters, this social diversity is largely the result of a scarcity of urban land for squatting and preferences among poor migrants to be close to a family member or village contact who can help them get set up with housing and employment in the city. Such constraints and preferences push migrants of various ethnic groups into the same crowded settlements.

## Slum Settlements as Social and Spatial Units

India's slums are officially enumerated as distinct, named settlements. It cannot be assumed, though, that their borders are socially relevant. Nor can it be assumed that politicians see slum residents as voters located in distinct settlements. It is essential to establish the weight of slum settlements in distributive politics, from the point of view of both residents and politicians.

To assist in this discussion, Figure 1.6 presents a Google Earth image of slum settlements in a southern area of Bhopal. Each of the roughly seventy gray polygons is a named settlement with its own history, ethnic groups, and level of access to public goods and services. Dense living conditions and shared threats are centripetal forces, deepening the social relevance of settlements among residents. Slum leaders emerge from among the ranks of ordinary residents and are rooted in local social networks. Their

---

[109] Mathur 1996; Jha et al. 2007.   [110] Datta 2012, p. 753.

FIGURE 1.6 Squatter settlements in southern Bhopal

*Note:* Google Earth, DigitalGlobe Image (2019). Each of the gray polygons in the figure is a named and spatially distinct squatter settlement. The area of the city shown in the image is approximately seven by four kilometers. For reference, the largest gray polygon in the upper-middle area of the figure has roughly 15,000 residents. The gray polygons were created using the polygon drawing tool in Google Earth.

informal authority is largely circumscribed by their settlement's boundaries. The settlement is thus a key unit of collective action and claim-making.

From above, politicians look across their constituencies and see slums as geographically defined and named settlements with particular characteristics; clusters of poor people whose problems they can champion in seeking votes. Residents and slum leaders come to them from specific settlements with claims for locally consumed goods and services. Politicians seek to build linkages with these slum leaders because the latter have the ear of local voters. Slum settlements are therefore fundamental units in the distributive politics of India's cities.[111]

## 1.5 STUDY SETTINGS AND RESEARCH DESIGN

The cities of Jaipur, Rajasthan and Bhopal, Madhya Pradesh provide the research settings for this book. These two cities share many characteristics that make them an appropriate pairing. They rank closely in terms of population – with three million and two million inhabitants, respectively – and are the capitals of their respective states.[112] Jaipur is currently divided into ninety-one municipal wards and Bhopal is divided into eighty-five wards. Both were princely states before Independence in 1947 – Jaipur a Hindu princely state and Bhopal a Muslim princely state – with dilapidated old cities (*purana shehar*) at their core and more recent sprawl in the peripheries. In Rajasthan and Madhya Pradesh, the two major parties in competition are the BJP and INC. Jaipur and Bhopal are also situated in north India's Hindi-speaking belt, composed of a group of states with comparatively low human development indicators. Thus, much is held constant by looking at slum settlements across these two cities, allowing us to dissect the factors that drive variation in public service provision across settlements.

Studies of India's urban slums overwhelmingly concentrate on a handful of megacities. Yet most of India's slum residents do not live in Bangalore, Delhi, Hyderabad, Kolkata, and Mumbai. Instead, they live in a constellation of relatively small and medium-sized cities spread

---

[111] Other studies of urban slums similarly approach the urban neighborhood as an informally defined social and political unit (Ray 1969; Suttles 1972; Cornelius 1975). Ray, for example, argues in his study of Caracas, "Each barrio is a small political arena with leaders and followers, and a constant interplay between groups of different allegiances" (Ray 1969, p. 10).

[112] Based on the 2011 Census, Jaipur and Bhopal have populations of 3,046,163 people and 1,798,218 people, respectively (Government of India 2015, p. 107).

throughout the country. These smaller cities tend to have lower levels of state capacity than their megacity counterparts. As Davis notes, "If megacities are the brightest stars in the urban firmament, three quarters of the burden of future world population growth will be borne by faintly visible second-tier cities and smaller urban areas."[113] Jaipur and Bhopal represent these "faintly visible second-tier cities" that characterize urbanization in India and other emerging economies.

My fieldwork in Jaipur and Bhopal, conducted over a total of twenty-four months between 2010 and 2016, unfolded in two interrelated phases. The first phase was qualitative, involving fifteen continuous months of interviews, archival research, and ethnographic fieldwork in eight case study squatter settlements. The second phase was centered on survey work. I briefly describe these two phases below, leaving more detailed discussions for their respective empirical chapters.

### Qualitative Research Design and Data

A pressing task at the start of my fieldwork was to decide how to select case studies from the roughly 600 slum settlements across Bhopal and Jaipur. While this phase of the fieldwork was foremost meant to be exploratory and inductive, case selection nevertheless required a degree of structure that would allow me to isolate potentially important explanatory variables that could be tested with survey data from a larger sample of settlements. I therefore sought to hold constant demographic and political variables that were not of immediate theoretical interest, leaving space to assess other factors that might impact political organization and public service provision.

In each city, I first selected a state assembly constituency.[114] I chose these constituencies, Johri Bazar and Bhopal South, for several reasons. First, they exhibit large numbers of slums but are also home to middle-class neighborhoods and commercial areas, providing a mix in their class composition. Johri Bazar and Bhopal South, moreover, are situated outside the old cities, removing the possibility of selecting old city slums, which fall outside the population of squatter settlements. By selecting

---

[113] Davis 2007, p. 7.
[114] One case study settlement in each city was divided from the other three after the 2008 state elections, placing them in a new state assembly constituency in 2009 – a year prior to the start of my fieldwork. Case study settlements shared the same state assembly constituency for twenty-eight years in Jaipur and thirty years in Bhopal.

settlements within the same state assembly constituency, I hold constant exposure to the same state politicians and election campaigns, as well as local labor market conditions.

Next, I stratified slums in Johri Bazar and Bhopal South into population quartiles, and then purposefully selected four – one in each quartile – to hold constant settlement ages, landownership categories, and an absence of formal property rights. In addition to population, the settlements vary in their ethnic compositions and locations in different municipal wards. They otherwise all "started" around the same time and under the same local conditions, facilitating comparative historical research.

Ethnography allowed me to observe spontaneous events – flooding, evictions, rallies, and intermittency in water supply – and resident responses to them. Everyday conversations yielded many of my most valuable interviews. These took place not only in residents' homes but also in public places where people gather to trade gossip – tea stalls, temples, and around water tanks. I listened to residents' migration stories, how they interact with slum leaders, and the strategies they use to secure public services. Ethnography further pointed me to informal leaders and helped me build a rapport with them.[115] Much of my ethnographic fieldwork was historically bent, centered on tracing the local emergence of informal authority, the formation of party linkages, processes of claim-making, and the provision of public services. These efforts proved essential in uncovering causal mechanisms, establishing the sequencing of events, and tracing the direction of causality.[116]

Outside the eight case study settlements, I interviewed politicians and officials to probe the logic of their responsiveness to slum residents' demands, as well as how parties extend their organizational networks into slums. I also gathered a range of materials from government archives, including laws pertaining to slums, municipal election data, historical photographs of settlements, constituency maps, and government surveys of slums.

Invaluable sources of historical data were the troves of materials that slum leaders keep on their public engagements – petitions, community meeting notes, newspaper clippings, photographs of protests and rallies, correspondence with officials, and various forms of political ephemera like party posters, manifestos, and pamphlets. Many of these documents

---

[115] The names of residents, slum leaders, and case study settlements in this book have been changed to ensure the anonymity of research subjects.
[116] On comparative historical analysis, see Mahoney and Thelen 2015.

stretch back to the earliest years of the settlements. These informal archives are useful in reconstructing the histories of settlements – areas from which documents rarely make their way into conventional archives. Because they are locally generated and kept, they allow for settlement-level comparisons.[117] I photographed or photocopied several thousand of these informal archival documents across the eight case study settlements and draw on them extensively in the following chapters.

### Survey Research Design and Quantitative Data Collection

Based on my qualitative findings, I designed and administered an original survey across a stratified random sample of slums in Jaipur and Bhopal. The survey was intensive and multistaged. I first gathered official lists of slums[118] and then isolated squatter settlements through a combination of field visits, interviews with officials, and inspections of satellite images. The final sample frames totaled 115 squatter settlements in Jaipur and 192 in Bhopal. Settlements were stratified into population quintiles and city areas and then 72 were randomly selected across the two cities. The eight case study settlements were also surveyed, bringing the total to 80 settlements. Using satellite images, settlements were divided into clusters of roughly twenty contiguous households. Similar to a design in which every $n^{th}$ household is sampled along a street, households were sampled across each of the clusters to deliberately maintain approximate distances. Sampled households were marked on the satellite images and assigned to enumerators. I accompanied the survey teams on a daily basis to ensure the integrity of the sampling protocol. In 2012, this resulted in 1,925 respondents across 80 settlements. An additional 620 residents across 31 settlements were surveyed in 2015,[119] increasing the sample size to 2,545 respondents and 111 settlements.

This study required other forms of quantitative data collection, the most prominent of which was constructing an accurate census of party workers across the 111 settlements. I enumerated party workers by triangulating official party membership rosters gathered from party organizations, resident survey responses, and most importantly, interviews with local party workers in the sampled settlements. I uncovered a total of 663

---

[117] On the collection and use of informal archival materials, see Auerbach 2018.
[118] These lists include both officially recognized and nonrecognized settlements. The total number of slums was 273 and 375 in Jaipur and Bhopal, respectively.
[119] The 2015 survey was conducted with Tariq Thachil.

# Puzzling Disparities at the Margins of the City

party workers across the 111 settlements. To my knowledge, this is the first study to comprehensively enumerate party workers across a large and representative sample of communities.

I created community asset maps with satellite images and traverse walks to accurately measure several development indicators. A research assistant and I crossed every alleyway in the 111 settlements to note the exact location of streetlights and paved roads. Along with the survey data, this produced a total of six development indicators – paved roads, streetlights, trash removal, household piped water, household sewer connections, and government medical camps. These six indicators represent the primary outcome variables under examination in this book. The resulting quantitative dataset – built from surveys, archival research, and mapping work – allows me to statistically examine the relationship between party worker networks and public service provision while assessing the relative impact of alternative explanations.

## 1.6 ORGANIZATION OF THE BOOK

The remainder of this book is organized into seven chapters. Chapter 2 situates the book in the context of a rapidly urbanizing India. It describes India's demographic shift to cities and towns since Independence in 1947 and the concurrent proliferation of slum settlements. The chapter further outlines the formal institutions of governance in India's post-decentralization cities and the sources of public finance that are used to provide services to slums. It then goes on to delineate the mediated and politicized environment in which slum residents seek access to public services. The chapter ends with a description of the organizational structures of the BJP and INC in Bhopal and Jaipur.

Chapter 3 presents the theoretical framework. It explains why settlements with dense networks of party workers are better positioned to demand public services than those with thin or absent party worker networks. The discussion is set around the three mechanisms that undergird this relationship: political connectivity, mobilization capacity, and the informal accountability generated by competition among party workers for a following. The chapter further considers the implications of having party workers affiliated to competing parties, which I argue has several countervailing influences on public service delivery. Next, the chapter takes a step backward in the sequencing of events and asks why settlements vary in the density and partisan balance of their party worker networks. I will argue that two variables – settlement population and ethnic diversity – shape bottom-up incentives for residents to engage in party work and top-down incentives for parties to extend their organizational networks.

Chapter 4 examines the book's main protagonists – India's slum leaders. I first draw on my ethnographic fieldwork and survey data to explore the strategies that residents use to claim public services. I find that India's slum residents primarily orient their collective action toward the state, in the presence of informal slum leaders, to improve local conditions. The chapter then establishes the pervasiveness of slum leaders and their central place in local distributive politics. Next, it describes how slum leaders climb into positions of informal authority, the material incentives that motivate them to make this gritty political ascent, and the diverse problem-solving activities they perform for residents. I then argue that slum leaders must demonstrate efficacy in problem-solving to build a following – the base upon which they collect rents, attract party patronage, and seek party promotion. The chapter subsequently describes the subset of slum leaders who have become party workers, absorbed into party organizations and given positions within their hierarchies.

Chapter 5 presents historical narratives from eight case study settlements – four from Jaipur and four from Bhopal. The narratives trace the emergence of informal authority, party linkages, and public service delivery in each settlement, from the initial period of squatting to the present. In addition to demonstrating the mechanisms underpinning the book's theoretical framework, the narratives help to address issues of historical sequencing and causality.

Chapter 6 quantitatively tests the theoretical framework with survey data from 111 squatter settlements. To preview the main results, I find that party worker density is positive and statistically significant in its association with paved road coverage, streetlight coverage, municipal trash removal, and the provision of government medical camps. These findings hold when controlling for a wide range of potential confounders and are robust to several model specifications and post-estimation tests. Read alongside my qualitative findings, these statistical relationships provide further evidence that denser networks of party workers are associated with higher levels of public service provision.

Chapter 7 examines the formation of party worker networks and the reasons why they vary so remarkably across settlements. The chapter presents quantitative evidence that key drivers of variation in party worker density are settlement ethnic diversity and population. It then takes one additional step backward, probing why settlements vary in their populations and levels of ethnic diversity in the first place. I find that local features of the urban geography and constraints over where poor migrants settle influence slum size and ethnic diversity, providing analytical leverage in explaining their impact on party organization and, in turn, public service provision.

Chapter 8 concludes. It revisits the substantive and theoretical motivations of the book and provides a brief summary of its main findings. The chapter then expands on the contributions of the book to our understanding of democracy and development in India and other rapidly urbanizing countries in the Global South, and subsequently discusses the book's implications for the design and implementation of community-driven development programs.

2

# Setting the Stage

## Governance and Political Parties in Urban India

There is a wrought iron signboard in Rajiv Nagar, firmly cemented in the ground between a butcher shop and one of the slum's busiest entrances. In rich hues of emerald and saffron, the signboard displays the name of the area member of the legislative assembly (MLA), Uma Shankar Gupta, and declares his use of public funds to improve the local drainage system – infrastructure that Rajiv Nagar's residents have long demanded from their elected representatives. Prior to the installation of gutters and pipelines, Bhopal's monsoon rains inundated large parts of Rajiv Nagar, exposing residents to a murky mix of rainwater and sewage, as well as a relentless barrage of mosquitos. The signboard now stands as an immovable reminder of Gupta's patronage and affiliation to the BJP.

Ten kilometers to the northeast of Rajiv Nagar is Bheem Nagar, central Bhopal's largest slum. The settlement blankets a sprawling hill, making the provision of water difficult without a complex assemblage of pipes and motorized pumps. While visiting Bheem Nagar in 2011, I encountered a crowd of residents gathered on a particularly steep alleyway. The ward councillor had financed a water pipeline and was attending the inauguration ceremony – an important act of credit-claiming in India's three-tiered system of elected government. Donning a garland of canary yellow marigolds and surrounded by a group of Bheem Nagar's INC workers, the councillor distributed *ladoos* (a sweet) to residents while a Hindu priest blessed the settlement.

The politicized nature of public service provision in India's slums is given overt, physical form in these everyday symbols and performances.[1]

---

[1] See Figure 2.1 for an example of local credit-claiming through the use of signboards and Figure 2.2 for a common image of political graffiti in Bhopal's slum settlements.

# Governance and Political Parties in Urban India

FIGURE 2.1 Sign declaring roadwork funded by MLA and councillor, Bhopal
Note: Author photograph (2015)

What otherwise might be routine acts of governance – mechanically flowing from a set of programmatic rules – are instead the result of clamorous and protracted exchanges between residents and officials in which the latter have considerable discretion in the timing and outcome of their decisions. In this setting, slum residents must actively demand public services from the state, and muster what political influence they can to strengthen their claims. What formal institutions of governance in India's cities attract these claims? And through what channels do slum residents seek to command state responsiveness?

This chapter sets the stage for the remainder of the book, providing essential context on governance and political representation in India's cities. It starts by sketching recent trends in India's urbanization and the concurrent proliferation of slums in the country. It then outlines the formal institutional landscape in Indian cities. Many of these institutions were created or strengthened during India's decentralization reforms in the early 1990s, creating new focal points of local governance around which slum residents make claims. The chapter then provides a brief overview of the government policies and programs that have targeted slums since Independence in 1947, as well as other sources of public finance that are used to extend public services to

FIGURE 2.2 Political graffiti in a Bhopal slum settlement
Note: Author photograph (2015)

slums. The chapter concludes with a description of how parties are organized in Bhopal and Jaipur and how their networks of workers connect residents with political elites. This lays the groundwork for the next chapter, which puts party workers at the center of the book's theoretical framework.

## 2.1 INDIA AT HOME IN ITS CITIES AND TOWNS

The Global South is undergoing a seismic demographic shift to its cities.[2] Roughly half of the developing world's population now lives in cities, and by 2050 that number is set to approach 63.4 percent.[3] India, though a laggard relative to other emerging economies like Brazil and China, is hurling toward being a country mostly at home in its cities.[4] At the start of

---

[2] For an overview of urbanization in the developing world, see Montgomery 2008 and United Nations 2015.

[3] United Nations 2015, p. 205. While much of this expansion can be attributed to migration from the countryside, most of the developing world's urbanization is fueled by natural population growth within cities (Montgomery 2008, p. 763).

[4] A location is defined as urban by the Census of India if it has at least 5,000 people, a density of at least 400 people per square kilometer, and "at least 75 percent of the male main working population engaged in non-agricultural pursuits." These places are referred to as

the twentieth century, 10 percent of India's population lived in cities. The last century saw a threefold increase in that percentage.[5] Urban India stands at 377 million people as per the 2011 Census, or 31 percent of the total population. By 2050, this figure will approach 50 percent.[6] Signaling this shift, the 2011 Census was the first to capture larger absolute population growth in cities versus the countryside.[7]

At least fifty-three cities in India now have populations of more than one million people.[8] Several boast populations that approach or exceed ten million, surpassing the entire populations of countries like Honduras, Jordan, and Sweden. With populations of roughly three million and two million people, respectively, Jaipur and Bhopal rest in the upper tier of Indian cities but are still considerably smaller than the megacities of Bangalore, Chennai, Delhi, Hyderabad, Kolkata, and Mumbai. Below India's million-plus cities is an expansive constellation of smaller cities and towns.[9]

India's million-plus cities are undergoing arresting transformations in their economies and built space. Business towers, apartment buildings, and shopping malls increasingly define the skyline. Flyovers darken the narrow, once-congested lanes below them and metro systems and rapid bus transit lanes snake their way through the urban landscape. Municipalities are wired and staffed with personnel trained in e-governance technologies. Cities like Bangalore and Hyderabad have become nodes of global capital and innovation, producing a burgeoning middle class with consumption patterns similar to their counterparts elsewhere.[10]

---

census towns. There are also statutory towns, which are notified by states as areas with a municipal government. There were 3,894 census towns and 4,041 statutory towns in India in 2011. A final class of cities are urban agglomerations, which "must consist of at least a statutory town and its total population ... should not be less than 20,000." There were 475 such urban agglomerations in 2011 (2011 Census of India, Provisional Population Totals, Urban Agglomerations and Cities).

[5] Sivaramakrishnan et al. 2006, p. 27. Estimates of India's urban population are contested. See Bhagat 2011 and Kundu 2011 on the challenges of estimating India's urban population.

[6] See United Nations 2015, p. 207.   [7] Bhagat 2011, p. 10.

[8] 2011 Census of India, Provisional Population Totals, Urban Agglomerations/ Cities.

[9] Just over 40 percent of urban India's population is estimated to live in cities below 100,000 people (Denis et al. 2012, p. 56). A sizable portion of India's urban growth between the census periods of 2001 and 2011 took place in these smaller cities and towns (Pradhan 2013).

[10] On India's middle class, see Fernandes 2006.

While more modest in scale, such changes have touched Jaipur and Bhopal as well. The former is now replete with luxury apartment buildings, car dealerships, upscale restaurants, shiny commercial centers, and middle-class neighborhoods that barricade themselves with gates and security guards. In addition to a new airport and ring road, a metro system and a series of flyovers have been constructed in Jaipur, all painted in the city's famous shade of pink. Even in more humble Bhopal there are signs of such changes, ushered in with the construction of DB City Mall in the late 2000s, the city's first "modern" shopping mall. The "aesthetics of world-class cities" has powerfully shaped the expansion of India's metros.[11]

Despite constituting only a third of the population, India's cities now produce 63 percent of the country's gross domestic product (GDP), compared to 45 percent in 1990.[12] The Modi government, like the United Progressive Alliance (UPA) government before it, has identified the important role of cities in the economy and has accordingly given them considerable policy attention, at least relative to governments in the pre-liberalization period (pre-1991),[13] when India's cities were largely sidelined next to investments in the countryside.[14] The Jawaharlal Nehru National Urban Renewal Mission (JNNURM), executed in the mid-2000s during the first Congress-led UPA government, threw substantial resources at India's cities.[15] After the 2014 parliamentary elections, the BJP government's Atal Mission for Rejuvenation and Urban Transformation (AMRUT) has taken up this mantle, aiming to boost investments in urban capital projects.

Alongside these investments and transformations in India's cities lie daunting challenges in governance and poverty alleviation. India's cities exhibit high rates of economic inequality, environmental degradation, crumbling infrastructure, sprawling slum settlements, and a vast informal

---

[11] Ghertner 2015.
[12] Barclays Emerging Markets Research 2015, p. 4. A much-cited McKinsey report estimates that by 2030, India's cities could contribute more than 70 percent of the country's GDP (Sankhe et al. 2010, p. 13).
[13] On India's economic liberalization in the early 1990s, see Jenkins 2000 and Kohli 2006.
[14] As Bhan et al. (2014, p. 83) state, "Historically, the Indian welfare state has largely been rurally imagined. Programs of social security in India – ranging from enabling and rights-based entitlements to basic transfers seeking to prevent destitution – have been and remain focused on rural poverty and vulnerability, with budget allocations that reflect such priorities." See Varshney 1998 on the political influence of the countryside in post-Independence India.
[15] See Kundu 2014.

economy that provides little security for those who work in it.[16] The Government of India's Rangarajan Expert Group estimated that 102.5 million city dwellers in the country (26.4 percent of the urban population) lived below the poverty line in 2011/12, with consumption expenditures of less than Rs 1,407 per person per month – at that time, an amount of roughly a dollar per person per day.[17] While India has seen a steady decline in poverty rates since the 1970s, this drop has been slower in cities than in rural areas.[18] As Mishra and Dasgupta conclude in a recent government report, "Increasing urbanization has also been accompanied by urbanization of poverty in India."[19]

## 2.2 THE PROLIFERATION OF URBAN SLUMS

Slums are among the most visible manifestations of material deprivation in urban India. One does not need to travel to far-flung corners of cities to find slum settlements. Even casual movement around India's cities will reveal dense clusters of shanties with slapdash brick siding and roofs made from tarp, thatch, or corrugated steel. Slums are wedged beside middle-class neighborhoods, shopping malls, and luxury hotels; along railroad tracks and riverbeds; at the base of mountains; and on the edges of cities where construction labor is in high demand. Slum residents are integrated into local informal economies as domestic workers, factory workers, auto-rickshaw drivers, hawkers, street vendors, construction laborers, and a variety of other jobs that make up India's swollen informal sector. Slum settlements, and the many people who call them home, are central to the social and economic life of Indian cities.

The 2011 Census of India estimated that sixty-five million people reside in slums. This figure is likely an underestimate. A 2010 Ministry of Housing and Urban Poverty Alleviation report projected that the slum population would reach ninety million in 2011,[20] and an earlier estimate by the United Nations (UN) Development Program projected India's slum population to be well above one hundred million by 2010.[21] Even taking the lower bound of 65 million, though, India's slum population is nothing short of massive,

---

[16] See Kohli 2012; Motiram and Vakulabharanam 2012; Bhan and Jana 2015; Heller et al. 2015.
[17] Government of India 2014, pp. 4–5.   [18] Mishra and Dasgupta 2014, pp. 5–6.
[19] Mishra and Dasgupta 2014, p. 6.   [20] Government of India 2010.
[21] UN-Habitat 2006b, p. 193.

making up a large portion of the 850 million people living in slums worldwide.[22]

India's slum population is unevenly distributed across states and cities.[23] Among India's major states, the average percentage of urban residents living in slums is 15.70 percent, with a one standard deviation of 9.01 percentage points.[24] At the top of the list is Andhra Pradesh,[25] with 36.10 percent of its urban population residing in slums. Kerala, at the bottom, has just 1.27 percent of its urban population living in slums. Behind Andhra Pradesh are Chhattisgarh and Madhya Pradesh, with 31.98 and 28.35 percent, respectively, of urban residents living in slums. Rajasthan lies closer to the average, with 12.13 percent of its urban population residing in slums.

India's municipal corporations with million-plus populations also significantly vary in the percentages of their residents reported to live in slums.[26] Jabalpur sits at the top of the list in terms of the percentage of residents living in slum settlements (44.71 percent). At the other end, Dhanbad (in the state of Jharkhand) is reported to have just 1.23 percent of its residents living in slums. Jaipur and Bhopal sit in between, with 10.62 percent and 26.68 percent, respectively, of their populations in slums.[27] More broadly, out of the 4,041 statutory towns in the Census of 2011, 2,543 (63 percent) towns report the presence of slums.[28] Remarkably, less than half of India's slum population can be found in India's municipal corporations with million-plus populations.[29]

As discussed in the previous chapter, the term "slum" homogenizes a range of urban poverty pockets that are otherwise distinct in their

---

[22] UN-Habitat 2013, p. 151.
[23] See Government of India 2015 (p. 101) for the state-level data presented in this paragraph. Also see Census of India Primary Census Abstract for Slums.
[24] These states and union territories are Jammu and Kashmir, Himachal Pradesh, Punjab, Chandigarh, Uttarakhand, Haryana, Delhi, Rajasthan, Uttar Pradesh, Bihar, Assam, West Bengal, Jharkhand, Orissa, Chhattisgarh, Madhya Pradesh, Gujarat, Maharashtra, Andhra Pradesh (now Andhra Pradesh and Telangana), Karnataka, Kerala, and Tamil Nadu.
[25] The 2011 Census was conducted before Andhra Pradesh split into Andhra Pradesh and Telangana.
[26] See Government of India 2015 (p. 107) for the city-level data presented in this paragraph.
[27] In absolute population terms, the Census of 2011 records 323,400 people living in Jaipur's slums and 479,699 people living in Bhopal's slums.
[28] Government of India 2015, p. 125.
[29] 25,099,576 people are reported to live in slums in municipal corporations with million-plus populations, out of a total of 65,494,604 people living in slums across India (Government of India 2015, p. 108).

historical origins, degree of legality, and social integration in the city.[30] This book focuses on squatter settlements, which are spontaneous, low-income areas constructed by residents in a haphazard and unsanctioned manner. Because the Census of India does not distinguish among different types of urban poverty pockets, it is difficult to estimate the percentage of India's slum population that lives in squatter settlements. City-specific studies, though, suggest squatter settlements make up very large portions of slums. In Delhi, for instance, Heller and his coauthors note that 2.5 million people (14.8 percent of the *total* city population) live in *jhuggi jhopris*, or squatter settlements.[31] In Jaipur and Bhopal, I estimate that just under half of the slums in the two cities are squatter settlements.

## 2.3 GOVERNANCE IN THE POST-DECENTRALIZATION INDIAN CITY

What is the formal institutional environment within which India's slum residents struggle to improve local conditions? Like many countries in the Global South, India has undergone a process of political decentralization, generating local governments that have become arenas of electoral competition.[32] The 74th Constitutional Amendment (1992) mandates that states devolve a list of political powers to municipal governments. Prior to the 74th Amendment, most municipalities rarely, if ever, held elections, and did relatively little in the way of governance.[33] State governments and urban improvement trusts largely oversaw the functioning of cities.[34] The 74th Amendment states that municipal elections should be held once every five years,[35] with seats

---

[30] As Roy observes, "The term slum remains an inadequate shorthand for what is the sheer heterogeneity of urban political economy: the diversity of informal and paralegal property arrangements, the dense economies of work and livelihood, the complex formations of associational life and popular politics" (Roy 2014, p. 138).

[31] Heller et al. 2015, p. 5.

[32] On decentralization in India, see Bardhan and Mookherjee 2006 and Raghunandan 2017.

[33] As the 74th Amendment states in it's opening paragraph, "In many States local bodies have become weak and ineffective on account of a variety of reasons, including the failure to hold regular elections, prolonged supersessions and inadequate devolution of powers and functions. As a result, Urban Local Bodies are not able to perform effectively as vibrant democratic units of self-government."

[34] This continues to be the case in many, if not most, of India's cities, where development authorities dwarf municipalities in their fiscal and technical capacities.

[35] In Jaipur and Bhopal, the first post-decentralization elections were held in 1994, with the former electing councillors across seventy wards and the latter across sixty-six wards. At

reserved for women and the Scheduled Castes and Scheduled Tribes.[36] It further outlines eighteen responsibilities for municipalities to undertake. These tasks include sanitation, water provision, land regulation, the construction and maintenance of roads and bridges, and slum development. In practice, most municipalities lack the resources to engage in all of these tasks,[37] resulting in the continued prominence of state-level agencies like urban development authorities (*vikas pradhikaran*).[38]

In India's post-decentralization cities, slum residents have multiple nodes of governance around which to make claims. These include three tiers of elected government at the municipal, state, and national levels. The two most important elected representatives for slum residents are ward councillors and MLAs, the former directly elected members of the municipal council and the latter directly elected members of the state legislative assembly (*vidhan sabha*). Ward councillors are the most accessible to residents given the relatively small sizes of their constituencies: the average ward populations in Jaipur and Bhopal are 39,557 and 25,689, respectively.[39] As of 2018, there are ninety-one municipal wards in Jaipur and eighty-five wards in Bhopal. MLAs have substantially more resources and political clout than ward councillors, though they have larger constituencies – in Rajasthan, for example, roughly 350,000 people – making direct engagement with them more challenging. Attesting to the relative accessibility of ward councillors, 51.32 percent of the slum residents I surveyed in 2012 could correctly name their councillor, while 31.64 percent could correctly name their MLA. Members of parliament (MPs), with roughly 2.5 million constituents,[40] are too distant (in terms of the magnitude of their constituency size) to be common targets of slum residents' claims.

the height of my fieldwork in 2011 and 2012, there were seventy-seven wards in Jaipur and seventy wards in Bhopal.

[36] See Bhavnani 2009 and Jensenius 2017 on electoral quotas in India.

[37] Describing the weak financial condition of India's municipalities, Sharalaya writes, "India's annual per capita spending on cities stands at a measly US $50. The corresponding figures for China and UK are about $362 and $ 1,772, respectively. The financial health of Indian cities is in such a pathetic state that several urban local governments have to rely on state governments to fund even basic operational expenses like employee salaries" (Sharalaya 2017).

[38] See Baud and de Wit 2008 and Ruet and Lama-Rewal 2009 for excellent overviews of municipal governance in India.

[39] Author calculations based on 2011 Census data. For a foundational study on India's municipal councillors, see Oldenburg 1976.

[40] Vaishnav and Hintson 2019.

Beyond elected representatives, slum residents target nonelected officials across a wide variety of government departments. The Public Health Engineering Department (PHED), overseeing water supply, is a frequent aim of slum residents' claims. In addition to the central office, service extension offices are spread throughout the city, absorbing much of the traffic of petitions. Other important public institutions include the Public Works Department, which, among other things, oversees roads; the Municipal Sanitation Department; and the Electricity Department. In short, slum residents' claims are splintered across a range of elected representatives, bureaucrats, and government departments in the city.

### Sources of Public Finance for Slum Development

India's central government has implemented a series of policies and programs since 1947 that target urban slums for public services.[41] The Slum Improvement and Clearance Act of 1956, the first major central policy on the subject, outlines a protocol for slum "notification." The act specifies that states and cities can acknowledge areas as slums, in the process granting them a degree of tenure security through protection from unannounced eviction.[42] What constitutes a slum in the act is broadly defined: a settlement that is "in any respect unfit for human habitation; or [by] reason of dilapidation, overcrowding, faulty arrangement and design of such buildings, narrowness or faulty arrangement of streets, lack of ventilation, light or sanitation facilities, or any combination of these factors, are detrimental to safety, health, or morals."[43] Researchers have described the process of notification, in practice, as discretionary and politicized.[44]

The Environmental Improvement of Urban Slums Scheme of 1972 extended the Slum Act by outlining a process of service delivery to those areas that have been notified, alongside a rule that beneficiary settlements

---

[41] For an overview of these policies and programs post-1947 and prior to the mid-2000s, see Durand-Lasserve and Royston 2002 and Batra 2009. For a discussion on urban poverty alleviation efforts in the 2000s, see Government of India 2009 and Mathur 2014. See Gooptu 2001 on colonial-era governance and poverty in urban India.

[42] See the Slum Improvement and Clearance Act of 1956. As Banerjee notes, "Notification of an area as a slum under the Act, in itself, implies secure tenure, as residents cannot be evicted without the approval of the competent authority" (Banerjee 2002, p. 39).

[43] Slum Improvement and Clearance Act of 1956.    [44] Risbud 2009, p. 180.

not be evicted for at least ten years to justify the investment.[45] The program was limited to twenty cities in India, including Jaipur and Bhopal, and then extended in spirit under the Seventh and Eighth Plans (mid-1980s–late 1990s) as the Urban Basic Services for the Poor Program and the National Slum Development Program (NSDP).[46] The impact of these programs was negligible. For example, in several major cities in Madhya Pradesh, NSDP transfers, local uptake, and coverage across settlements were described by UN-Habitat's Water for Asian Cities Program as "limited."[47] NSDP was further portrayed as politicized, riddled with corruption,[48] and "rarely used for construction activities aimed at providing better access to basic services."[49] The Valmiki Ambedkar Awas Yojana of 2001, designed to upgrade housing and sanitation in slums, had a similarly narrow impact. The same UN-Habitat report on Madhya Pradesh noted that "under various VAMBAY schemes operating in the state a total of 6062 dwelling units have been covered and 170 toilet seats (only 2.8 percent of the total dwellings units constructed) have been provided."[50]

In the early 2000s, the Indian government enacted several urban development programs that were unprecedented in their financial scope.[51] JNNURM, a multiyear development initiative to improve infrastructure and governance in cities, had a section on urban poverty alleviation and slum upgrading – Basic Services for the Urban Poor (BSUP). Jaipur and Bhopal were among the cities included in JNNURM. Following JNNURM are Rajiv Awas Yojana (RAY) and AMRUT, the first executed under the Congress-led UPA government and latter under the Modi government. RAY was unique from its predecessors in its emphasis on formal property rights: slum residents on sensitive lands should be moved and given land titles elsewhere, and those on nonsensitive lands should be settled *in situ* with land titles.[52] Similar to JNNURM, AMRUT is a broad-based program for urban development.

Jaipur and Bhopal have received funding from these central programs. The limited scope of funding in the face of expansive slum populations,

---

[45] Banerjee 2002, p. 39.   [46] Mishra and Dasgupta 2014, p. 8.
[47] UN-Habitat 2006a, p. 16.
[48] "[NSDP] funds are mainly used for construction of roads. Officials at the implementing agencies and monitoring bodies were of the view that this was because the maximum kickbacks from contractors are available in the road sector" (UN-Habitat 2006a, p. 17).
[49] UN-Habitat 2006a, p. 17.   [50] UN-Habitat 2006a, p. 12.   [51] Batra 2009, p. 33.
[52] On the historical precursors to this emphasis, see Banerjee 2002 and Risbud 2002.

however, has meant that only small fractions of settlements in the two cities have benefited from them. This is exacerbated by the fact that significant amounts of funding do not make their way down to the local level; nationally, less than half of JNNURM funds were released by the central government as of 2012, and it is estimated that 10 percent or less of the projects were finished as of 2012.[53] The slow grind of governance means that many projects are left idle or are canceled over time.[54] For instance, the use of BSUP funds for north Jaipur's Sashtri Nagar slums are years behind schedule; only the foundations of resettlement apartments were visible in the summer of 2015, years after project approval. A newspaper article captures the generally dismal state of slum development in Jaipur:

Only 10 of 308 slums in the city have benefitted from the Slum Development Policy under the public-private partnership mode 2012. These 10 slums are in the process of being provided in-situ rehabilitation in multistory flats. All other slum dwellers in the city still live in precarious conditions, with not even basic facilities like safe drinking water. On Monday, a large group of about 1,000 slum dwellers gathered near the state assembly to protest the continued absence of services in their areas. They demanded proper rehabilitation as provided for under the Pradhan Mantri Awas Yojana [Prime Minister Housing Program].[55]

Broadly reflecting this reality, the NSSO's 2012 national slum survey found that only 24 percent of India's slums had benefitted from "welfare schemes like JNNURM and RAY."[56]

Other central programs for the urban poor provide employment and job training. Nehru Rozgar Yojana, enacted in the late 1980s, sought to improve job opportunities for the urban poor through micro-enterprise

---

[53] Mishra and Dasgupta 2014, p. 15. Risbud provides an example of how the funds that reach settlements are fractions of what are allocated in budgets. Describing one Bhopal settlement, Risbud writes: "Until 1980, no improvements were carried out by any agency ... The first improvements were provided in the settlement around 1982–1983 when the Slum Board released Rs. 62,000 for improvement, under the Environmental Improvement Scheme. Of this Rs. 32,301 were actually spent by the Municipal Corporation for providing one road, two taps and eleven electric poles" (Risbud 1988, pp. 37–38).

[54] An Asian Development Bank report on the Urban Water Supply and Environmental Improvement in Madhya Pradesh Project provides an illustration of such delays: "The project completion was delayed by four years and three months, mainly due to (i) the time taken by the urban local bodies and state government to decide which components to execute using JNNURM and UIDSSMT funds, which were available by the end of 2005; (ii) uncertainty about the escalation of material prices; and (iii) a shortage of contractors due to a sudden increase in construction activities" (Asian Development Bank 2016).

[55] Thomas 2017.   [56] NSSO 2014, Report 561, p. iii.

training and employment in public construction projects. Swarna Jayanti Shehari Rozgar Yojana (SJSRY), enacted in 1997, similarly aimed to provide job training to the urban poor. The impact of SJSRY has been negligible.[57] In Rajasthan, an evaluation of SJSRY found the program to be an unambiguous failure: only 0.02 percent of slum residents in the sampled cities (including Jaipur) had been exposed to the program. This was in part due to a lack of interest among officials in implementing the program.[58]

There are state-level programs targeted at slums as well.[59] Among the most notable of these is Arjun Singh's 1984 Patta Act, which provided hundreds of thousands of slum residents in Madhya Pradesh temporary land titles for one or thirty years, depending on the environmental sensitivity and ownership of the land. Another example from Madhya Pradesh, Ayodhya Basti Yojana, was implemented in the 2000s to improve conditions in the state's slums. This program benefitted a paltry six settlements in Bhopal.[60] Madhya Pradesh Urban Services for the Poor, funded by the United Kingdom's Department for International Development in the 2000s, and Project UDAY, funded by the Asian Development Bank in the 2010s, also sought to improve access to public services in a limited set of slums in Bhopal, Gwalior, Indore, and Jabalpur.

Elected representatives at the municipal, state, and national levels receive discretionary budgets ("area development funds") that can be drawn on to finance development in their constituencies.[61] Expenditures data I collected provide many examples of area development funds being used in slums. For example, in 2002, the councillor of ward 65 spent Rs 4.6 *lakh* to pave streets in Sanjay Bhatta and Rs 1.69 *lakh* the following year to install pipes in Vijay Nagar, two slums in northern Jaipur. In 2002, the councillor of ward 30 spent Rs 3.11 *lakh* to improve

---

[57] Mishra and Dasgupta 2014, p. 19. With a focus on Bangalore, Ramanathan writes, "The citywide SJSRY platform provided little tangible benefit to the poor in terms of public service outcomes or governance outcomes" (Ramanathan 2007, p. 677).
[58] Tewari 2002.
[59] See the chapters on Indian states in Durand-Lasserve and Royston 2002.
[60] UN-Habitat 2006a, pp. 26.
[61] Jaipur's councillors were allocated roughly Rs 20 to Rs 25 *lakhs* in 2011, and can receive more based on "needs" and their "political skills" (interview with Jaipur Municipal Corporation official, March 18, 2011). Alignment with the party in power in the municipality can help attract more resources, though ward councillors from the opposition party can overcome such problems if they are assertive and hardworking (interview with mayor of Jaipur, April 4, 2011). For a study on the politics of spending these funds at the level of the parliamentary constituency, see Keefer and Khemani 2009.

FIGURE 2.3 Ward councillor overseeing drainage work in a Jaipur slum
Note: Author photograph (2011)

drainage in Jaipur's Jawahar Nagar slum.[62] In 2011, Babu Lal Gaur and Uma Shankar Gupta, two Bhopal MLAs, allocated Rs 0.5 *lakh* and Rs 2 *lakh* to repair a well in Vallabh slum and pave a road in Aaradhana slum, respectively.[63] While the use of these funds must be approved (by the district collector for MLAs and the city commissioner for councillors), their distribution unfolds through calculations of political expediency.[64]

Slum residents, as noted above, also make claims directly on government departments. Political intervention in these efforts is often crucial. In an interview with the head engineer of a waterworks department in Jaipur, I asked if and how political intervention is important to the responsiveness of state agencies to citizen claims. He responded that, without political involvement, applications usually "wander" in the office and are then sent back to lower levels for reassessment. He said that

---

[62] Nagar Nigam Area Expenditure Reports, Jaipur, 2000–2004.
[63] Vidhan Sabha Area Expenditure Reports, Bhopal, 2008–2011.
[64] See Figure 2.3 for an image of a municipal councillor overseeing work funded by his area development funds.

contact from a politician is necessary to move things along. Bureaucrats have incentives to entertain these requests for their own professional advancement. Rigid or defiant bureaucrats face political transfer to undesirable locations and departments.[65]

In sum, a string of programs at the central and state levels has been implemented for public service provision in India's slums. Jaipur and Bhopal have been included in these central programs as well as those enacted in their respective states. Their cumulative impact, however, has been limited and uneven due to inadequate resources and politicized distribution.[66] The discretionary funds given to elected representatives add to the mix of resources available for the provision of public services; yet these too come up short in addressing the many demands emerging from slum settlements. Slum residents can directly petition government departments for public services, though political intervention is often necessary to boost the chances of state responsiveness. In the political economy of India's cities, not all claims can be addressed, and those that are addressed are frequently the result of political maneuvering.

## 2.4 DISTRIBUTIVE POLITICS IN INDIA'S SLUMS

The previous two sections outlined the formal institutions of governance in India's cities, as well as the diverse sources of public funding available for development in slum settlements. How, though, do residents access these institutions and resources? What shape does that politics take? Establishing these contextual parameters is essential, as it suggests where to look for the drivers of uneven development. This section argues that distributive politics in India's slums is largely nonprogrammatic and mediated. The following chapters will illustrate these elements of local politics in India's cities in detail with ethnographic and survey data.

First, the provision of public services in India's slums is, in part, nonprogrammatic, meaning that the formal rules do not always determine how resources are allocated in practice.[67] This should not suggest that formal

---

[65] Interview with water engineer, Jaipur, June 14, 2011.
[66] Following an assessment of finances available for slum development in Madhya Pradesh, a UN-Habitat report (2006a, p. 79) noted, "It is evident that the resource allocations for development in slum areas out of various development funds, which are untied in nature, are small. Even expenditures for slum development by the municipal corporations are not significant."
[67] To provide just one example, the Government of Rajasthan has failed to act on a high court order to extend public services to Kathputhli, a slum in Jaipur: "In an order of

rules are always and completely disregarded, thus rendering them useless for understanding patterns of development. Instead, it suggests that there is wiggle room generated by political interventions and citizen-state negotiations that explain much of the uneven public service provision documented in the following chapters.[68] Eligibility does not automatically mean access. And a lack of eligibility can sometimes be overcome with sufficient political pressure. The impact of politicized distribution on uneven public service delivery is exacerbated by scarce resources, high public demand, and officials who are stretched thin and must make daily decisions over who and where to give their attention.

The Indian state has long been described as largely discretionary and politicized in its responsiveness to citizen claims, especially those of the poor. Ahuja and Chhibber refer to the state in India as "capricious" – "a state whose treatment of the poor is largely arbitrary, ad hoc, and often disrespectful."[69] Herring describes the "embedded particularism" of the Indian state, where the actions of officials are shaped by particularistic social and political pressures.[70] Gupta ethnographically documents the "blurred lines" that exist between state and society in India, highlighting the tortuous and bribe-riddled negotiations that unfold between citizens and state officials in everyday local governance.[71] With an empirical focus on Bangalore, Benjamin and Bhuvaneswari describe the local state as "porous," capable of being penetrated and influenced with sufficient political force. In this environment, they argue that access to state institutions and resources requires "stealthy politics."[72] Chatterjee influentially argues that the poor cannot simply point to entitlements of citizenship but must instead fight to improve their conditions through various forms of popular politics – for example, the use of political intermediaries and protests.[73]

---

August 11, 2015, the Rajasthan High Court had asked the government, in three months, to provide facilities like better roads and toilet facilities to residents of Kathputhli Nagar. It is now 2017, and those orders have not been complied with" (Thomas 2017).

[68] Reflecting on this point, and with reference to a Delhi slum, Banda et al. (2014, p. 12) write, "Residents' everyday lives are shaped by negotiations with various state actors and frontline bureaucrats for fundamental needs ... [They] do not approach the state as citizens with rights, nor even as clients of a patronage regime. They approach the state as supplicants in a woefully unbalanced bargaining equation."

[69] Ahuja and Chhibber 2012, p. 392.   [70] Herring 1999.   [71] Gupta 1995; Gupta 2012.
[72] Benjamin and Bhuvaneswari 2001.
[73] Chatterjee 2004. Chatterjee (2008, p. 57) asserts, "Those in political society make their claims on government, and in turn are governed, not within the framework of stable constitutionally defined rights and laws, but rather through temporary, contextual and unstable arrangements arrived at through direct political negotiations." In diverse

An example of nonprogrammatic forms of distributive politics in Jaipur is the existence of – and provision of public services to – squatter settlements on *Van Vibhag* (Forest Department) lands, which are not sanctioned for residential or commercial purposes. During an interview with a Forest Department official in Jaipur, I asked how much of the *Van Vibhag* land in east and north Jaipur has come to be inhabited by squatters. He explained that such squatting is allowed, and the extension of services to these squatters persists, because of "political interference." Reflecting on the ability of politicians to flaunt the Forest Department's authority and provide services to squatters on *Van Vibhag* land, he went on to say that "votes are important and these are vote banks … during elections, anything is possible."[74] Water officials similarly point to "vote bank politics" in explaining how piped water has been extended to many of Jaipur's squatter settlements on *Van Vibhag* land.[75]

A second dimension of the politics of public service delivery in India's slums is that it is frequently mediated. India's slum residents are highly pessimistic about their ability to command the attention of officials alone: only 12 percent of my survey respondents believed they would get attention if they individually approached a politician or public official for assistance.[76] As a consequence, slum residents frequently turn to nonstate political intermediaries to help them access state institutions and resources. As one slum resident in Jaipur put it, "The public can't solve these problems (paved roads and sanitation) themselves, that's why we are dependent on [slum leaders]. It is like a chain link – we are connected to the slum leader, who is connected to a bigger leader, who in turn is connected to an even bigger leader. When we complain to the slum leaders, they complain to the higher officials on our behalf. That's how work gets done because we don't have direct contact with [higher officials]."[77]

A sizable literature documents the use of intermediaries in India, both within cities and in the countryside.[78] Harriss, for example, finds in a large

---

contexts in India, scholars have encountered slippage between those who are eligible for public welfare programs and public services and those who actually receive them (Banerjee et al. 2012; Sukhtankar 2016; Kruks-Wisner 2018).

[74] Interview with Forest Department official, Jaipur, July 12, 2018.
[75] Interviews with waterworks officials, Jaipur, July 12 and 13, 2018.
[76] Survey respondents across the eighty settlements surveyed in 2012 were asked: "If you went to a politician or government official by yourself, would you receive attention or be ignored?"
[77] Interview with resident of Baba Ramdev slum, July 2017.
[78] Reddy and Haragopal 1985; Oldenburg 1987; Manor 2000; Hansen 2001; Krishna 2002; Corbridge et al. 2005; Witsoe 2012. For studies on political intermediaries outside

citizen survey in Delhi that the urban poor are significantly more likely to turn to intermediaries for help than middle-class and wealthy citizens.[79] Wiebe, de Wit, and Jha et al. document the prominent place of India's slum leaders as agents of resident-state mediation.[80] Berenschot, reflecting on his fieldwork in Ahmedabad, asserts, "Political mediation is so deeply entrenched in the procedures, policies and habits that guide the daily functioning of state institutions that we can speak of a 'mediated state.'"[81]

## 2.5 PARTY ORGANIZATIONS IN BHOPAL AND JAIPUR

Within the political context just described, the chief "institutions in the middle" operating between India's slum residents and the state are party organizations.[82] Set against the backdrop of extant studies on Indian politics, this role for parties cannot be assumed. India's parties have long been described as organizationally weak at the local level.[83] Such accounts, though, mostly flow from studies of rural India. In this section, I describe the structure of party organizations in Bhopal and Jaipur, laying the groundwork for the theoretical framework presented in the following chapter.

In Jaipur and Bhopal, the major parties in competition are the INC and BJP. These parties are organized in a similar pyramidal fashion in the two cities. At the most grassroots level is the booth, where both parties have a president and a small team of workers in place who can be drawn on to persuade voters and build turnout. One level higher than the booth is the municipal ward. In each ward, a committee (*samiti*) is formed and given the responsibility to oversee party activities.[84] Committees include a president (*adhyaksh*) as well as positions for vice presidents (*up-aadhyaksh*), secretaries (*sachiv*), treasurers (*kosh-adhyaksh*), ministers (*mantri*), and members (*sadasya*). Above the ward, the parties slightly diverge. The INC

---

of the Indian context, see Stokes et al. 2013, Holland and Palmer-Rubin 2015, and Larreguy et al. 2016.
[79] Harriss 2005.   [80] Wiebe 1975; de Wit 1997; Jha et al. 2007.
[81] Berenschot 2010, p. 885.
[82] "Institutions in the middle" is a term coined by Krishna (2011) to describe intermediaries in rural India.
[83] Kohli 1991; Krishna 2007; Manor 2010; Ziegfeld 2016.
[84] As my first segment of fieldwork was concluding in 2012, there were discussions within the BJP to do away with ward committees and push this organization further downward, toward the booth, to strengthen local organization. Party workers, however, were still claiming to have organizational positions at the ward level in 2016, suggesting this reform had not yet been fully implemented.

is divided into blocks – two blocks for each state assembly constituency. In 2012, Jaipur had twelve blocks and Bhopal had ten blocks. Instead of blocks, the BJP has *mandals*, which correspond to the boundaries of state assembly constituencies. Above the block and *mandal* are the district and state, composed of well-known figures who hold considerable political sway. All of these higher tiers of party organization have their own committees within their respective areas, structured and staffed in the same ways as the ward committees.

Both parties also have *morchas* (wings) and *prakoshts* (cells) to organize various interest groups. In the BJP, there are six *morchas*: for women (*Mahila Morcha*), youth (*Yuva Morcha*), farmers (*Kisan Morcha*), Scheduled Castes (*SC Morcha*), Scheduled Tribes (*ST Morcha*), and "minorities" (*Alpsankhyak Morcha*). A Rajasthan state secretary of the BJP estimated that there are between thirty-six to thirty-nine *prakoshts* in the BJP, including cells for businessmen, engineers, doctors, and lawyers.[85] Most relevant is the cell for slum residents in Rajasthan and Madhya Pradesh, referred to as the *Kachi Basti Prakosht* in the former and the *Jhuggi Jhopri Prakosht* in the latter. The hierarchical structure of the *morchas* and *prakoshts* generally follow the rest of the organizational structure of the party, with the exception that positions do not exist at the booth, and for the slum cells there are sometimes positions at the settlement level (*basti pramukh*). In addition to workers in the main party organizations, the most common cells and wings I encountered were the Slum Cell, Youth Wing, Scheduled Caste Wing, and Minority Wing.

There are thousands of BJP and INC rank-and-file party members in Jaipur and Bhopal.[86] In the BJP, these members are divided between primary members and "active members," the latter of whom have been members for at least three years, attend events, and subscribe to party publications. They are eligible to hold posts in the organizational hierarchy: "Any person who will be taking any position in the organization, from the ward to *mandal* to the state then the nation, should be an active member."[87] The INC also has a large body of rank-and-file workers, but to my knowledge it does not distinguish between primary and active

---

[85] Interview with BJP state secretary, Jaipur, February 15, 2011.
[86] For example, a 2010 official party document I collected in Jaipur put the INC membership in the city at 107,076 people. For reference, Jaipur has a total population of 3,073,350 people (Census of India 2011).
[87] Interview with BJP state secretary, Jaipur, February 15, 2011. See BJP Constitution 2012, p. 4.

members.[88] Becoming a member of either party is not particularly taxing – one must pay an entrance fee and, at least on paper, agree to abide by the party constitution.[89] Because of this low bar, and incentives for parties to inflate their numbers, citywide estimates of rank-and-file party members must be approached with skepticism.[90]

Above the fray of rank-and-file party members are those who possess committee positions (*pad*) at the various levels described above. These position holders (*padadhikari*) make up a small portion of the larger pool of party members. Committee members at the *mandal* level for the BJP, for instance, are limited to a specific number. As per the 2012 party constitution, this number should range between thirty and sixty members depending upon the population of the state.[91] There are roughly 350,000 people living in a *mandal* area in Jaipur and Bhopal, and so those who make their way into these committees are a selective group. Committees of the BJP *morchas* and *prakoshts* face similar upper bounds in membership.[92] The INC generates an upper bound – though less defined than that of the BJP – for the size of committees at the ward, block, city, and district levels by tying their membership to individuals coming up from subordinate committees, which are spatially demarcated.[93]

Party membership rosters I collected for Jaipur's Vidhyahar Nagar assembly constituency in 2011 provide an illustration of how the INC is structured. The total number of common rank-and-file INC members listed in the constituency was 13,590. The constituency is broken into two blocks, Vidhyahar Nagar and Jhotwara, with 4,773 rank-and-file members in the former and 8,817 rank-and-file members in the latter. Vidhyahar Nagar block has sixty committee members. To provide an example of a ward, Ward 63 in Vidhyahar Nagar has fourteen ward-level committee members.[94]

---

[88] The INC constitution does state, "A person who has been a member for at least three years shall only be eligible to be elected as a delegate or an office bearer of any Congress Committee" (INC Constitution 2010, p. 3). This approximates the BJP's status of an "active member."
[89] INC Constitution 2010; BJP Constitution 2012.
[90] Chubb describes the membership base of the Christian Democratic Party in southern Italy in a similar fashion. She noted that regular membership of the *tesserati* was inflated and, in some cases, even falsified, and was thus an unreliable measure. The position holders at various levels of the Christian Democratic machine – like their counterparts in the INC and BJP – are more defined and limited (Chubb 1982).
[91] BJP Constitution 2012, pp. 6–7. BJP organizational rules I collected in Jaipur in 2016 stated that there should be sixty-one total members of a *mandal* committee in Rajasthan.
[92] BJP Constitution 2012, pp. 31–32.   [93] INC Constitution 2010, pp. 12–16.
[94] I thank the District Congress Committee of Jaipur for generously providing this information.

Organizational positions in the party hierarchy are limited, competitive, and sought after, as they signal political connectivity and social prestige, and invite party patronage during elections.[95] The many perks of these positions would diminish if they endlessly proliferated across the city. This would cheapen the positions and discourage members to work for party promotion. Moreover, if organizational positions limitlessly spread, it would weaken the ability of the party to monitor the activities of its workers.[96] Indeed, when asked if these positions can balloon in an unchecked way, a retired city president of the INC in Jaipur noted that most committees had a small number of members (five to seven), and that there could not be a "jumbo jet" to hold a large mass of position holders. He explained that it is important to have smaller, active groups of *padadhikari* who know one another and are loyal to their superiors.[97] For similar reasons, a senior BJP official in Jaipur noted that keeping the committees small and select is important.[98]

The compulsion of party elites to generate their own factions also pushes back against an excess of position holders. Party elites prefer to have "direct touch" with the appointed workers below them to foster trust and allow for some oversight of their activities.[99] Those at higher rungs of party organizations have incentives to keep the networks below them manageable and known to maintain factional interests. Allowing an unrestrained expansion of position-holders within a committee would run counter to efforts to keep networks close and dependable.[100]

---

[95] A BJP member in Ahmedabad, for example, told Ward Berenschot that despite twenty-five years of service to the party he has not been given an organizational position. He explained that this is due to the fact that "there is much competition within the BJP because the party is big" (Berenschot 2011, p. 390).

[96] See Stokes et al. 2013 and Larreguy et al. 2016 on the compulsions of parties to monitor their workers.

[97] Interview (with Tariq Thachil) with former city president of the INC, Jaipur, May 28, 2016.

[98] Interview (with Tariq Thachil) with city president of the BJP, Jaipur, June 6, 2016.

[99] Interview (with Tariq Thachil) with former city president of the INC, Jaipur, May 28, 2016.

[100] Bailey makes a similar point on the importance of personalized relationships in party network expansion in India, and the influence this has on keeping these networks limited in size: "The fact that the party machine is composed of many relatively autonomous parts in the control of individuals, is not an accident. A structure of relationships based on self-interest and calculation cannot exceed a limited size; every link ... has to be forged by hand, and cannot be mass-produced in the manner of links in a movement which is based on moral considerations" (Bailey 1963, p. 156).

Party organizational networks extend into many slum settlements. Indeed, ethnographic studies have widely documented the presence of party-affiliated slum leaders in India. Jha and his coauthors described informal leaders with party affiliations in Delhi's slums.[101] Wiebe and de Wit encountered such figures living and operating in the slums of Chennai.[102] Studies of slums in Ahmedabad, Bangalore, Pune, and Vijayawada also mention the presence of these actors.[103] While these studies establish the presence of party-affiliated slum leaders, they come short of providing a systematic account of the party structures in which these actors are embedded. Moreover, they overlook unevenness in the density of these party worker networks across slums, and the implications of such variation on state responsiveness. I take up these themes in the next chapter.

## 2.6 CONCLUSION

This chapter laid a descriptive foundation for the remainder of the book. It positioned the study in an India that is increasingly at home in its cities and towns. It then detailed the spread of slums in India and asserted that a substantial portion of the country's sixty-five million slum residents live in squatter settlements – the specific type of slum under study – which are defined by their unsanctioned, spontaneous growth and initial absence of infrastructure and formal property rights.

A constellation of officials and elected representatives are the targets of slum residents' claims for public services. Foremost among them are ward councillors, MLAs, and the many local officials that staff municipal and state government departments in cities. Since India's Independence in 1947, a number of public programs have been enacted to provide public services to slum settlements. Discretionary area development funds for elected representatives add to the pot of resources available for slum development. Yet the sheer scale of India's slum population, combined with inadequate resources and politicized distribution, have limited the impact of these programs and budgets and generated uneven development across settlements.

Slum residents cannot passively wait for the state to extend public goods and services. They must actively and boisterously demand them from elected representatives and government institutions that are often dismissive and moved by political intervention. Slum residents frequently

---

[101] Jha et al. 2007. [102] Wiebe 1975; de Wit 1997.
[103] Bhatt and Chavda 1979; Rao and Rao 1984; Rao 1990; Schenk 2001.

make such claims with the assistance of slum leaders, many of whom are party workers embedded in larger party organizational networks. Party organizations fan out across the city and connect street-level party workers to political elites through their hierarchical networks. The following chapter will place party workers at the center of the book's theoretical framework.

# 3

# How Party Worker Networks Impact Local Development

India's urban slums exhibit striking variation in their levels of infrastructural development and access to public services. Why are some settlements able to demand and secure development from the state while others fail? This chapter presents a two-stage theory of local political organization and development. The first stage centers on explaining variation in public service provision across settlements. I will argue that such divergences emerge because not all slums are equally positioned to organize and make claims on the state through party worker networks. The second stage takes a step backward and accounts for why party workers vary in their presence and density across settlements in the first place. I will argue that two demographic variables – settlement population and ethnic diversity – guide much of their uneven spread across slums.

## 3.1 COMPETITION, CONNECTIVITY, AND MOBILIZATIONAL CAPACITY

Political parties in Bhopal and Jaipur, as described in the previous chapter, have hierarchical organizations that connect street-level workers to the most influential party elites in the city.[1] Similar party structures have been found in a wide range of contexts outside of India. Indeed, scholars have documented the organization and activities of party machines in a variety of urban contexts. Early studies focused on cities in the United States, where poor European migrants, settled in working-class neighborhoods, were provided with jobs

---

[1] See Figures 3.1 and 3.2 for example signs that list local party workers in Bhopal's slum settlements.

66 *Demanding Development*

FIGURE 3.1 Party sign listing local Congress workers, Bhopal
*Note*: Author photograph (2012)

and public services in exchange for their political support.[2] Tammany Hall in New York City epitomized this form of politics, where the Democratic Party tasked its ward bosses to persuade voters through the distribution of targeted

[2] Gosnell 1937; Mushkat 1971, and Erie 1988.

*How Party Worker Networks Impact Local Development* 67

FIGURE 3.2 Party sign listing local BJP workers, Bhopal
*Note*: Author photograph (2012)

patronage. Party machines thrived in several major American cities for decades, with their height during America's Gilded Age (the late nineteenth century) and the first decades of the twentieth century.

Contemporary studies of machine politics predominantly concentrate on parties in Latin America. The Peronist Party in Argentina and the Institutional Revolutionary Party (PRI) in Mexico stand out as prominent examples.³ These parties have historically extended their influence downward through networks of party workers who are responsible for drumming up support during elections, frequently through the distribution of particularistic goods.

Despite a wealth of scholarship on party machines, little empirical or theoretical attention has been paid to the spread of party worker networks across city neighborhoods and the consequences of uneven local party organization on the wellbeing of residents – especially the poor, who often depend on political intermediaries to gain access to state resources.⁴ This book reveals startling unevenness in the presence, density, and partisan distribution of party workers across India's slums. Some settlements are flush with party workers who are arranged in defined hierarchies that link them to the highest strata of party leadership in the city. Others have only a few party workers, while others exhibit a total absence of them. I refer to this variable as the *density* of party workers, measured as the per capita number of party workers in a settlement.

This section presents the first stage of the book's theoretical framework, in which I argue that settlements with dense networks of party workers are better positioned to demand and secure development from the state than those in which party workers are sparse or absent. Three mechanisms undergird this relationship. I discuss each of these mechanisms in turn and draw on my qualitative fieldwork to provide illustrations of how they operate on the ground.

## Competition for a Following

A first mechanism linking the density of party workers with outcomes in local public goods provision is competition among party workers for a following, which pushes them to be active claim-makers or else risk seeing their base of popular support shift to another party worker. Studies of clientelism often cast the relationship between brokers and clients as rigid and uncontested. This description may characterize brokers or patrons that rely on hereditary titles or brute coercion to maintain their authority.⁵ In such settings, clients have limited room to circumvent the broker in accessing the state, and the latter faces little competition from

---

[3] See Auyero 2001; Levitsky 2003; Greene 2007; Magaloni 2008; Herrera 2017.
[4] Harriss 2005; Jha et al. 2007.
[5] Examples include colonial-era *zamindars* and post-Independence upper-caste landlords in parts of rural north India (Weiner 1967; Brass 1965).

other brokers within his or her locality. This lack of competition suggests that the broker's status, as such, is untethered to their performance in satisfying client demands.

In stark contrast, India's slums are multi-focal brokerage environments marked by intense competition among party workers for a following.[6] The presence of multiple party workers gives residents room to maneuver in choosing whom to seek help from and follow. The ability of residents to turn elsewhere for assistance is a sanctioning mechanism that keeps party workers in check. Party workers who secure public services and expeditiously help residents with their problems surpass those who drag their feet or fail to demonstrate efficacy in problem-solving. Slums are information-rich environments, abuzz with gossip. If word spreads that a party worker is ineffective or transgressive, that worker will take a reputational hit that diminishes their local following. They will take on colorful titles: wastes (*baekar*), thieves (*chor*), and a slew of far more abusive names. The rumor mill of a slum is constantly in motion and can make any moment a referendum that can sap a party worker of his or her following.

Illustrating the link between a party worker's problem-solving credentials and level of public support, Harish, a BJP worker in Ganpati settlement in Jaipur, explained why some party workers have larger followings than others. He stressed the importance of knowledge about urban officialdom and the ability to extract public resources:

People who are less popular do not have any knowledge. Some don't know the Jaipur Development Authority, Jaipur Municipal Corporation, or Electricity Board ... they don't know about government policies. And, even if they do, they have a hard time getting them. They don't know where officers sit, where the mayor's office is, where the police commissioner's office is ... And they don't know that the collector sits in the collectorate, Vasundhara sits in the Vidhan Sabha ... People like us are so knowledgeable that we can meet a minister; we can meet the mayor too ... [So] that's what makes them less popular.[7]

I went on to ask Harish for an example of a slum leader losing support after a more effective slum leader emerged. He turned to the story of his own political ascent in Ganpati:

---

[6] In an early study of clientelism, Scott (1977) described a continuum in the degree of agency that clients hold in relation to their patrons. At one extreme, clients are tied to their patrons through dependency and coercion. At the other extreme, clients can voluntarily enter and exit relations with patrons. Patrons compete with one another for a following and hold little coercive capacity over clients. The relationship between slum residents and slum leaders (as political brokers) leans strongly toward the latter extreme.

[7] Interview with Harish, Ganpati, June 7, 2016.

Yes, there is an example of one leader who people stopped following after I came to the slum because I knew more than him ... I knew everything about the system; whether you go to the Public Health and Engineering Department, Jaipur Municipal Corporation, Electricity Board, Jaipur Development Authority, or collectorate. I knew how to solve all the problems related to these departments. Hence, that leader became less popular.[8]

Slum leaders could attempt to use violence to stamp out competition and force residents to fall in line. Yet I observed little such violence. And in those instances where I heard rumors of thuggish behavior, it was associated with the decline of the slum leader. Sachin, an ex-party worker in Bhopal's Rudra slum, provides an example. Sachin was once the most famous INC worker in Rudra. However, as he consolidated his authority, he became increasingly brash and aggressive toward residents. His following crumbled to the point where he was kicked out of the INC and banished from his local caste association. Many residents in Rudra attribute their current support for the BJP to Sachin's spoiling of the INC brand.

From above, party elites have incentives to monitor and sanction party workers – and they do. Workers are the local face of the party. Acts of extortion, corruption, or violence reflect poorly on the party brand. As one BJP MLA in Jaipur put it, "[We] talk to the common people and [ask], is this man is doing a good job? If they tell us that, no, he always takes money from us whenever we ask for help, we kick him out."[9] During his tenure, one ex-city president of the INC claimed to have removed fifty-nine party workers for either not working diligently for the party or engaging in "anti-social" activities that gave the party a bad name.[10] After asking if and how party elites can monitor workers, the head of the BJP's slum cell in Madhya Pradesh told me:

See, I am from the top, from the state level. In a slum, I will have a chief (*pramukh*) who will watch the other local workers. It's his job to monitor the local workers. Every worker monitors every other worker, and so this is how we get to know what is going on from the top to the bottom. If someone is doing wrong things, we'll try to teach them. If that doesn't work, we will kick them out of the organization.[11]

---

[8] Interview with Harish, Ganpati, June 7, 2016.
[9] Interview with BJP MLA, Jaipur, February 11, 2012.
[10] Interview (with Tariq Thachil) with former Congress city president, Jaipur, May 31, 2016.
[11] Interview with head of the BJP's slum cell in Madhya Pradesh, Bhopal, October 3, 2011.

The ex-city president of the INC mentioned above described a similar process of monitoring party workers:

We send five or so workers that we trust to an area, unannounced, to see how local workers are behaving. We talk to people in the area and have conversations about the workers, and ask what is going on, are the workers listening, and how honest they are.[12]

Harish discussed what monitoring looks like through a party worker's eyes:

Parties watch workers in the community. Now, how do they do this? By seeing our work. Suppose my party gave me a task to complete and I'm unable to do it. They get to know I'm not a good worker. Or if the party didn't give me a task, but I should have done it on my own, but couldn't. The party will think I'm not a good worker. And so they kick that person out and appoint someone else. Our party makes a team that goes through booths and checks workers' work. That team gives feedback to the big people in the party.[13]

Party elites also directly observe local party workers when they visit settlements for rallies and social events. To provide an example: a state-level BJP politician insisted that I attend a rally he organized in one of north Bhopal's many slums. Upon my arrival, I found BJP flags fluttering in the wind, gravy-laden vegetables and bread being distributed to residents, and long red mats being unfolded so that people could comfortably sit, eat, and listen to speeches. The politician handed children food in paper bowls and put *tikkas* on their foreheads. Once the crowd settled in, a Hindu priest conducted a prayer alongside the BJP politician and his six local party workers. These six party workers were responsible for organizing the event. Such tasks allow politicians to evaluate the diligence of party workers and their capacity to mobilize residents.[14]

In short, party workers are kept on their toes, both by residents and party elites. This is especially true in settlements with multiple party workers, where they must compete with one another for resident support. This mechanism of competition-generated responsiveness should extend to other settings in which brokers must vie for the same pool of voters. Studies of South Asia's countryside, for example, have pointed to similar dynamics. Krishna writes, "Villagers are not bound to any particular

---

[12] Interview (with Tariq Thachil) with former Congress city president, Jaipur, May 31, 2016.
[13] Interview with Harish, Ganpati, June 7, 2016.
[14] Field notes, Bhopal, October 5, 2011.

[broker], and [brokers] who are effective and honest in their dealings attract a sizable following among their fellow villagers. But villagers are watchful and wary. Alternative [brokers] are available in most villages, and any hint of cheating or diminished effectiveness can result in a transfer of allegiance by a majority of villagers."[15] Shami finds in rural Pakistan that village patrons have greater incentives to provide local public goods when they face competition from intermediaries outside the village.[16] Outside the context of South Asia, Acemoglu and his coauthors find that increasing numbers of ruling families in Sierra Leone's chiefdoms generates greater competition among them for the position of paramount chief, creating higher levels of accountability and improved regional development.[17]

Studies of informal leadership in Latin American slums also point to the risk of resident defection if leaders fail to perform. In his study of squatter settlements in Mexico City, Cornelius writes: "[The] cacique's position can be quickly undermined by particularly flagrant financial indiscretions and abuses of authority, or by his failure to meet certain standards of performance ... he must strive continually to legitimize his claim to leadership."[18] Cornelius goes on to argue, "The cacique's responsiveness to the preferences of his followers seems to vary directly with their ability to perceive alternatives to his leadership."[19] Burgwal describes similar dynamics in his study of a Quito squatter settlement, where he finds leaders maintaining their informal position only when they are "useful" to clients.[20] Koster and de Vries write in their study of Recife's *favelas*: "[Leader] is a severely fought for position, one for which a reputation has to be cultivated. Community leaders are known to make efforts for the community, do personal favors for people, and thoroughly know the community's history and current problems."[21]

To summarize, competition among party workers in settlements with dense networks of these figures pushes them to work harder to maintain and grow their following. Settlements with few or no party workers have less competitive brokerage environments, reducing incentives for party workers to be active in problem-solving. A degree of accountably trickles down from above too, as party elites have incentives to select and promote

---

[15] Krishna 2007, p. 148.  [16] Shami 2012.  [17] Acemoglu et al. 2014.
[18] Cornelius 1975, p. 143.  [19] Cornelius 1975, p. 153.  [20] Burgwal 1996, p. 157.
[21] Koster and de Vries 2012, p. 88.

those slum leaders who have a large following. Slum leaders without party positions are less subject to such top-down oversight.

## Political Connectivity

A second mechanism linking the density of party workers with outcomes in local public goods provision is political connectivity. Party workers, embedded in party organizational networks, can draw on their face-to-face connections with political elites to push the state to extend public services. In the cacophony of claim-making that emanates from slums, having such direct connections to elites amplifies voice and increases political leverage over the officials in charge of specific public services.

As one party worker in Bhopal put it, "Politicians are the ones running the government, appointing people. So, when you become part of a party, then you can meet the government officers easily ... it helps me get things for my community."[22] Similarly, a state-level BJP officer in Jaipur described the difference between someone who simply supports the party versus a position holder: "He (the politician) will not recognize him (the rank and file supporter) by name; if you [have a position], it will be easier to recognize you."[23] A slum leader in Jaipur offered yet another statement on why having party connections is so useful in securing public services:

It is necessary to have good connections with the party. That is how development happens. When you have good connections with the party, you tell them, "we have an electricity problem"; you can write to your party or MLA for development ... Then, the MLA will write a letter on his letterhead to the electricity department regarding the problem; our problem then gets resolved immediately. And if there is an issue regarding the road the MLA writes a letter to the Jaipur Municipal Corporation and they pass the tender to fix the road.[24]

A visit to a politician's office provides an intimate look at political connectivity in action. A common scene is a small group of party workers sitting around the politician, discussing local politics and passing time.[25] Such close, daily proximity to power gives party workers direct channels of claim-making. They enjoy priority over the hundreds of other constituents vying for the politician's time. Political connectivity is also

---

[22] Interview with party worker in Rudra, Bhopal, July 2012.
[23] Interview with BJP state secretary, Jaipur, February 15, 2011.
[24] Interview with Harish, Jaipur, June 7, 2016.
[25] See Figure 3.3 for an example of a meeting location for local BJP workers and politicians in Bhopal.

FIGURE 3.3 Local BJP office, Bhopal
*Note*: Author photograph (2015)

revealed through the use of party stationery – an important part of a party worker's claim-making toolkit. These business cards and letterheads bear the party symbol, name of the worker, his or her position, and often the name of a prominent area politician. Party workers flash business cards to signal their connectivity and use party letterheads to write petitions for local development.

Officials across a range of government departments – the Water Works Department, Municipal Sanitation Department, Public Health and Engineering Department – pointed to the role of political interference in pushing them to prioritize certain citizen demands over others. One chief sanitation inspector in Jaipur, for example, said that a phone call from the ward councillor or MLA makes him get to work on a project faster, cutting the time of having a sanitation team dispatched to an area from a month to a week or less. If he doesn't comply, the councillor or MLA will complain to his superiors, or, even worse, might push for him to be transferred out of Jaipur.[26] A high-ranking doctor in the Public Health Department in Jaipur similarly noted that politicians sometimes interfere

---

[26] Interview with chief sanitation inspector, Jaipur, July 12, 2018.

FIGURE 3.4 Congress party rally, Jaipur
Note: Author photograph (2011)

in where and when government medical camps are held in slums.[27] Through their ties with politicians, party workers can exert this kind of influence on those officials with the authority to provide public services.

Party workers go to great lengths to show off their political connectivity. They hang placards on their front doors with their party symbol and position. They decorate their walls with framed pictures of themselves alongside prominent politicians and keep newspaper clippings that mention their acts of "social work." When politicians visit their neighborhood, party workers jostle to stand beside them, hoping that they will later find themselves on TV or in the local newspaper.[28] Party workers also craft banners with their headshots next to those of well-known politicians and hang them in public places. Those on Facebook post digital versions as well.

The importance of political connectivity in commanding state responsiveness is a long-documented theme in the study of Indian politics.[29]

---

[27] Interview with Rajasthan Health Department official, Jaipur, July 27, 2018.
[28] See Figure 3.4 for a photograph of an INC rally with an area MLA surrounded by his party workers.
[29] de Wit 1997; Hansen 2001; Véron et al. 2003; Corbridge et al. 2005; Berenschot 2011; Chidambaram 2012.

Capturing the thrust of this literature, Véron and his coauthors write, "Poverty and powerlessness are the fate of those who lack political connections."[30] So too is the frequent fate of settlements that lack political linkages to the state.

### The Role of Opposition Party Workers

The importance of political connectivity begs the question of what party workers can do when their party is out of power at any given level of elected government. Are such party workers forced to sit on their hands until the next election, or can they deploy other tactics and use other channels to solve residents' problems, thereby preserving their local followings?

India's three-tiered system of elected government, as well as its nonconcurrent elections and frequent party turnover in both constituencies and legislative bodies, generate outlets for party workers who are cut off at one level to draw on other channels to make claims. Consider the mixed partisan environment surrounding Saraswati slum in Jaipur: during my fieldwork in 2012, the ward councillor belonged to the Congress, the BJP held the majority of seats in the municipal council, and the mayor belonged to the Congress. The MLA belonged to the BJP, the Congress held the majority of seats in the state legislative assembly, and the chief minister belonged to the Congress. In this setting, both Congress and BJP workers have partisan ties with elected representatives that can be leveraged in acts of claim-making. And this says nothing about nonelected party elites in the city who can exert some pressure on officials to extend public services.

Party workers with few or no co-partisans in power can also take on the role of the opposition party. At times, this opposition manifests as protests, with effigies burnt and chants wishing the downfall of the incumbent. Other times, opposition pressure takes quieter forms, through spreading rumors of an incumbent's neglect toward the settlement. Take, for example, the distribution of a poster in a Jaipur slum that scolded the area BJP MLA (Figure 3.5). The poster rhetorically asks the MLA a series of questions, including "where did you spend your funds?" and "why haven't you fulfilled even a single promise you made?" These actions allow opposition party workers to raise public grievances, pushing incumbent politicians to do something or else face mounting public scorn.

Political elites also continue to assist party workers and organize protests even when they are out of power. Doing so is critical to maintain and expand

---

[30] Véron et al. 2003, p. 5.

FIGURE 3.5 Poster criticizing an MLA, Jaipur, mid-1990s
*Note*: Poster courtesy of Mohan Lal Lakhiwal

their electoral following for the following election. Former elected representatives often have ties with bureaucrats that were forged during their time in office. Bureaucrats know that these politicians may return to office someday, giving the latter some leverage over the machinery of the state even after losing an election. Illustrating this point, a two-time Congress MLA in Jaipur who lost in 2013 told me, "Politics is not a one day game ... it is a game of being in regular touch with the assembly constituency, the workers, and voters. For the last five years I'm not in power; in any case, I'm in regular touch ... they come to me and I go there to sort out problems." I then asked if this sorting out of problems is more difficult when he is out of power. He agreed it is more difficult, but that work can still get done through his personal ties with bureaucrats: "If I go for any type of work to an officer ... generally those officers give respect because they know which leaders have a good image ... in that case our works are done."[31]

---

[31] Interview with former INC MLA, Jaipur, July 13, 2018. For a broader discussion on acts of constituency service by legislators in India, see Bussell 2019.

Slum leaders, of course, can directly appeal to bureaucrats for specific public services. For example, a waterworks official, if convinced, can ensure a negligent water tanker driver shows up on time. That same official can have a broken tube well fixed or a replacement tap attached to a faulty water tank. The zonal sanitation inspector can, at his or her discretion, dispatch sweepers to an area to remove solid waste. Political intervention helps to push along such actions, though slum leaders can and do make direct appeals to state functionaries.[32] For instance, Jagdish, a slum leader in Jaipur's Saraswati settlement, visited the zonal water engineer during my fieldwork to request that the engineer fix a broken hand pump, install a water tank, and drill a new bore well.

In short, co-partisan linkages between party workers and elected representatives facilitate the former's demands for development. Party workers without a co-partisan in power at one level of government, however, are not completely muted in their claim-making efforts. India's multitiered system of government, frequent party turnover, and bureaucracy provide a plethora of opportunities for opposition party workers to try to access state resources. Opposition party workers can also change roles to that of the protestor, pushing incumbent politicians to respond to local needs or risk losing the support of voters.

## A Capacity to Mobilize for Protest

A third mechanism linking the density of party workers with outcomes in public service delivery is the capacity to mobilize for protest. Party workers coordinate with one another to organize residents to flood the streets. In instances of intense problems like an impending eviction, party elites will be called to the settlement. Alternatively, residents are bussed to protests held at government buildings – the state legislative assembly building, collectorate, or municipal headquarters – to voice their grievances and hear speeches from area politicians. To provide an illustration from Bhopal:

Due to apathetic attitude of BHEL [Bharat Heavy Electricals Limited] administration, people living in the area have been infested with the infrastructural problems. [Slum] cell of Madhya Pradesh Congress has warned the BHEL administration that if problems of these areas would not be sorted out soon, the cell will stage a dharna (protest) in front of the residence of BHEL executive director ... Residents of BHEL jhuggi (slum) area have been suffering from various problems such as lack of proper

---

[32] Interviews with Fool Chand and Berwa, Ganpati, Jaipur, July 13, 2018.

## How Party Worker Networks Impact Local Development 79

FIGURE 3.6 Congress slum cell protest, Bhopal, mid-1990s
*Note*: Photograph courtesy of Mangal Singh

drainage facilities ... and shortage of water taps ... a lack of such facilities have been spreading various disease.[33]

Underdevelopment and threats of eviction provide rich opportunities for parties to harness a slum's *lokshakti*, or people power, to expand and invigorate their electoral following. The larger party organization in the city, alongside its network of local party workers in a settlement, can be mobilized to demand development and push back against eviction. During interviews, politicians sometimes referred to this as a settlement's "agitation power."[34] An example of a political elite threatening protest to push officials to deliver public services:

The residents of Durga Nagar met and concluded that in order to address the problem of mud in the neighborhood, around three to four trucks of bricks are required. Please arrange for this. In addition, the settlement does not have any bathrooms. We request that you construct a community bathroom. These demands should be met immediately. Otherwise, residents will hold a *dharna* (demonstration) outside your office.[35]

---

[33] Undated English-language newspaper clipping; given its content, I place the article in 1998. Bharat Heavy Electricals Limited (BHEL) is a public manufacturing company that owns a large area of land in eastern Bhopal.
[34] See Figures 3.6 and 3.7 for pictures of protests by slum residents.
[35] Letter from area MLA to Bhopal Municipal Corporation, September 14, 1993.

FIGURE 3.7 Jawahar Nagar slum protest, Jaipur, early 1980s
Note: Photograph courtesy of Alice Garg

Jaipur's former mayor, pointing to the importance of protests in slum development, provided a telling analogy: "Only a crying baby gets its mother's milk."[36] Settlements with dense networks of party workers are better able to organize residents and galvanize larger, citywide party organizations to hold protests in the name of local development.

## 3.2 THE PARTISAN DISTRIBUTION OF PARTY WORKERS

In slums with dense networks of party workers, the electoral compulsions of political parties, material self-interest of party workers, and needs of residents converge to generate an incentive structure that encourages development. Party workers have incentives to secure public services in the effort to maintain and expand their public following. Dense party worker

---

[36] Interview with former mayor of Jaipur, April 4, 2011.

networks also strengthen a settlement's capacity to mobilize for protest and provide political connectivity that can be leveraged in dealings with politicians and officials. What, though, are the implications of having party workers from different parties living and competing in the same settlement? How, if at all, might this impact local public goods provision?

The presence of party workers with different partisan ties adds a unique dynamic to the nature of competition among them for a following. Multiparty representation among party workers generates competition across partisan lines and, therefore, might increase the responsiveness of party workers to resident demands. On this point, one slum leader in Bhopal described how interparty competition among slum leaders is beneficial to local development: "Having many leaders and many parties helps the slum because it creates a pressure of competition. That will make people have to do better. Because now I am worried that if I don't do well, I will lose supporters."[37] Moreover, having slum leaders affiliated with different parties provides multipronged partisan linkages in a context marked by frequent party turnover at the municipal, state, and national levels. If a seat changes party, residents can shuffle behind a party worker from the incumbent party, taking advantage of his or her political connectivity.

My fieldwork, however, presented several reasons to be less optimistic about the influence of partisan competition among party workers in a settlement. Party organizations can soften some of the negative externalities associated with intraparty competition among their party workers through shared electoral interests and hierarchical discipline. Multiparty networks lack such mechanisms across party lines. Competing party networks have incentives to undermine each other's efforts in mobilizing residents to improve local conditions. While rumors are the everyday artillery in these confrontations, violence is also sometimes employed.[38] The presence of multiparty networks can serve to fragment the leadership of slums, dampening the scale of collective action and, in turn, the provision of public services.

---

[37] Interview with Shaarad, Rudra, Bhopal, January 17, 2017.
[38] For example, in Jaipur's Pahari settlement, local INC supporters pelted a group of BJP supporters with stones: "Some people started throwing rocks at BJP candidates and BJP workers and broke the windows of the Maruti van in which Kali Charan Saraf was sitting. Flags and party banners that were on the vehicles were also destroyed"(first incidence report dated 1993, kept by a Pahari slum leader).

Politicians articulated a second reason why the presence of party workers with different partisan affiliations can undermine local development. I asked a BJP MLA in Bhopal why elected representatives prioritize some slums over others in the allocation of public resources. He replied, "Where did you get good votes? The other factor is your workers, if they are strong, if they are able to convince you, you give work priority to that place." I asked him to clarify what he meant by "good votes." He responded, "Where you get majority votes, those areas automatically get priority."[39] A BJP MLA in Jaipur echoed this same sentiment: "Wherever [the politician] gets more votes, more supporters, that will be his priority area."[40] These statements are consistent with the logic of core targeting, evidence of which has been documented in studies of distributive politics in India and elsewhere.[41] Camp, for example, finds in Argentina that "parties over-invest in neighborhoods where they already have strong support."[42]

The composition of party workers in a settlement is a potential way for politicians to estimate the partisan leanings of that settlement. The presence of rival workers might signal that the settlement is not fully committed. It means that rival workers are attempting to undermine the politician's reputation, steal votes, and take credit for development projects.[43] If politicians observe opposition workers in a settlement, they might allocate projects to more loyal areas.[44]

The following letter, written by an INC slum leader in Bhopal, illustrates this point:

This is to inform you that [this area of the city has] been subject to discrimination on account of political reasons. BJP politicians are ignoring public issues [here], including neglecting basic responsibilities like cleaning initiatives ... On account of these politicians' attitudes toward residents [of this area], the latter are deprived of other necessities, like clean water,

---

[39] Interview with BJP MLA, Bhopal, July 7, 2012.
[40] Interview with BJP MLA, Jaipur, July 26, 2012.
[41] Nichter 2008; Calvo and Murillo 2013; Dunning and Nilekani 2013; Min 2015; Bohlken 2018.
[42] Camp 2015, p. 17.
[43] Residents recognize the compulsions of credit-claiming among politicians. One resident in Jaipur (interview in Bapu Nagar slum, July 2017), for example, said, "For any development work that they do, they want recognition. They expect the residents of the slum to then vote for them, participate in their rallies or demonstrations."
[44] See Schneider (forthcoming) for a study on the extent to which local politicians can "guess" the partisan leanings of villagers in rural Rajasthan.

sewers, drainage, pensions, etc. The lives of residents here have become appalling.[45]

Politicians are eager to expend resources in ways that lend themselves to credit-claiming.[46] Steering resources to slums that are mostly or exclusively home to co-partisan party workers increases the odds that residents will learn about the politician's efforts – through word of mouth, ribbon-cutting ceremonies, and the tagging of infrastructure with signs and graffiti.

There are, consequently, reasons to anticipate that the presence of party workers with different partisan affiliations has multiple, cross-cutting effects on the provision of local public services. The following chapters will assess the relationship between the partisan distribution of party workers and outcomes in local development.

## 3.3 WHY PARTY WORKER NETWORKS VARY ACROSS SETTLEMENTS

The construction of informal leadership in India's slums, as I will show in Chapter 4, is bottom-up. In a context of pervasive risks, residents gravitate toward those in their settlement who possess qualities that signal an ability to get things done – literacy, some formal education, connectivity to city officials and political elites, and more nebulous qualities like charisma and boldness. For those who aspire to engage in *netagiri*, informal authority is earned through entrepreneurial sweat. Village-based hierarchies and hereditary titles mean little in India's slums, populated by migrants from different regions and ethnic groups who do not share preestablished forms of authority. Moreover, parties do not dispatch party workers to live in slums. Nor can they indiscriminately crown residents as locally influential figures.

The establishment of linkages between slum leaders and political parties happens in one of several ways. During elections, candidates visit slums to give speeches and distribute handouts, in the process becoming acquainted with local slum leaders. In other cases, slum leaders repeatedly approach politicians for help solving problems, hardening into a political linkage over time. One MLA in Bhopal explained this process to me:

If someone has guts to lead certain people, if he has guts to come to the MLA and the concerned officers for work and raise a voice for their problems, then he automatically becomes leader of the slum ... it lies in him only, in the person.

---

[45] Gandhi Nagar committee documents, September 25, 2000.   [46] Harding 2015.

What we do if we see that this man is good, and he is interested in development and is a reasonable person, and doesn't put unreasonable demands in front of you, we try to push him, to help him, to make him come up, if he is of our thinking, our principles, we promote him.[47]

Parties, of course, have paramount agency in the top-down extension of party positions and patronage. Organizational positions are limited and coveted. Hundreds of party supporters in any given corner of the city want positions but there can be only one president and a limited number of members in a committee – at the booth, ward, block, district, and state levels. The scarcity of party positions precludes the possibility that these networks can endlessly proliferate. Otherwise they cease to hold value – access to patronage, social prominence, and political connectivity – and undermine the ability of parties to monitor workers and engender loyalty.

Despite claims of bottom-up elections, higher party officers, in practice, appoint most individuals to positions. As one former Congress MLA in Bhopal described, "When you see the parties, the committee is made from the top down."[48] In allocating positions to slum leaders, political elites are, in large part, interested in the size of an individual's following. This, as Szwarcberg has shown in the Argentine context, can be observed during rallies and elections.[49] India's slum leaders similarly lead groups of residents to protests and rallies, flaunting the influence they have within their settlement.

Politicians see slum residents as "kingmakers." They know that the same unit of effort exerted in slums has higher electoral returns than in secure, middle-class neighborhoods. These latter areas already have basic public services. A state-level party officer in Madhya Pradesh described this rationale. He pointed in the direction of a wealthy colony in Bhopal, and said that "there, only 25 or 30 percent of people will vote. They will not decide the outcome of the election. Instead, 80 to 90 percent of people vote in slums, and so they are the kingmakers."[50]

Parties extend their networks into slums to generate local nodes of partisan influence that can promote the party and mobilize turnout. A member of the BJP's district slum cell in Bhopal explained this electoral calculation. He stated, "There are over 300 slums in Bhopal, and in some neighborhoods, there might be between 2,000 and 3,000 shanties. To get these votes, the BJP needs workers operating in the slums."[51] Settlements,

---

[47] Interview with BJP MLA, Bhopal, July 7, 2012.
[48] Interview with former INC MLA, Bhopal, September 30, 2011.   [49] Szwarcberg 2015.
[50] Interview with state-level BJP officer, Bhopal, October 3, 2011.
[51] Interview with BJP district slum cell member, Bhopal, October 8, 2011.

however, are not uniformly enmeshed in party organizational networks. Instead, party workers are uneven in their presence and density across slum settlements. What generates this variation? I argue that two variables guide the spread of party worker networks: settlement size and ethnic diversity.

## Settlement Size

Political parties face resource constraints in fighting elections and building organizational networks to boost local support and turnout. Not every vote can be fought for with equal amounts of attention, money, and vigor. Only a finite number of positions can be allocated among the thousands of rank-and-file party supporters in the city. Parties and their candidates must therefore make decisions in where to allocate resources. Broadly, as a class of neighborhoods, slums receive significant attention in the organizational efforts of parties. Yet, hundreds of slums dot the landscape in India's cities, and the sea of informal leaders residing in these settlements want party positions and patronage. Not all of their demands can be met.

A major consideration in the allocation of party patronage and organizational positions is the population of settlements. A unit of party resources expended in a larger settlement has higher electoral returns than in a smaller one. To understand why, we must think about slums the way politicians do – as named, spatially defined, and socially relevant neighborhoods that have distinct demographics. Slum residents are not an undifferentiated mass of voters who organize and make demands for public services independently of space. Instead, resident mobilization, claim-making, and slum leadership emerge within settlements to improve settlement conditions. Explaining outcomes in local political organization thus requires pivoting from the individual as the central unit of analysis to considering the neighborhood-level variables that make some settlements more attractive than others for party investments in network building.

In the allocation of scarce party positions, it is more advantageous to give positions to slum leaders in larger settlements rather than those in smaller settlements. As a high-ranking BJP officer asserted: "In politics, there are only voters. Where to get these votes, then? Wherever there are many voters, the party will send people there to take people into the party."[52] A popular slum leader in a large slum is able to potentially deliver a bigger crowd of voters, and thus is able to command greater consideration in the allocation of party positions and patronage.

---

[52] Interview with BJP district slum cell member, Bhopal, October 14, 2011.

Consider the Congress *Kachi Basti Prakosht* (slum cell) in Jaipur. The state president of the *Prakosht* took it upon himself to designate *basti pramukhs*, or slum chiefs, in a relatively small number of Jaipur's settlements. The twenty-nine selected slums are among the very largest in Jaipur. In an interview with him, I inquired why those particular twenty-nine slums were chosen out of the several hundred settlements in the city. At first, he said to provide development. I then asked, don't all of Jaipur's slum settlements require such attention? He went on to say that these slums are a priority for the party. I asked him to elaborate. He stated that they are large slums, and thus electorally crucial.[53]

A slum leader in Bhopal, commenting on the importance of slum size, gave a pertinent analogy. He said, "To an MLA, a small slum is like a scooter. You wouldn't really want to go far on it, and it only requires a little gas. A big slum is like a large four-wheeler. It is something you want to take far and requires a lot of gas, tune-ups, and attention."[54] The extension of party organizational networks into larger slums, then, helps to fuel the engines of large "vote banks."

The privileged position of slum leaders in large settlements is related to Schaffer and Baker's concept of "persuasion buying," which suggests that parties target individuals with large social networks for scarce patronage, taking advantage of the "cascade effect" they offer through their wide social networks. Schaffer and Baker argue that targeting these "opinion-leading epicenters" afford "greater potential yield ... because [they] can create a 'social multiplier.'"[55] While the actual following of a slum leader is difficult to directly observe,[56] politicians are well aware of the size of a slum leader's settlement, and thus can glean the upper bound of a slum leader's potential following. Granting positions to slum leaders in larger settlements, therefore, has greater positive externalities because of the expansive numbers of voters who surround them.

---

[53] Interview with state president of the INC's slum cell, December 31, 2010.
[54] Interview with Rudra slum leader, Bhopal, September 23, 2011.
[55] Schaffer and Baker 2015: 1094.
[56] Rally attendance can be an effective way for patrons to observe the followings of brokers (Szwarcberg 2015). Rallies, however, are only episodically held (and do not necessarily coincide with the timing of party position allocations), and the turnout ability of individual brokers is often confounded by the fact that multiple brokers from the same neighborhood arrive with crowds together. The size of the neighborhood for which a slum leader makes claims, and word of his or her popularity in the settlement, suggests the upper limits of that slum leader's potential following and is therefore a useful heuristic that political elites can use in prioritizing among slum leaders.

Top-down efforts by parties to spread their organizational networks must be met by an eager group of slum leaders, ready to join a party and transform their followings into votes. There are bottom-up factors related to settlement population that generate such eagerness among slum leaders. Because the authority of slum leaders is largely circumscribed by the boundaries of their settlement, the size of a slum is often the extent to which a slum leader can build a following. Thus, a settlement with 5,000 residents presents a larger pool of potential followers than one of 800. More potential followers means more opportunities to attract fees from people who require assistance with problems. Since a slum leader's following is the currency of exchange for party patronage and promotion, a larger potential base of support increases material incentives to engage in leadership activities. Having public support in a large settlement also presents a compelling case for slum leaders when jostling for party tickets to fight in municipal elections.[57] Increasing settlement population thus expands incentives for residents to enter the fray of slum leadership.

In sum, parties disproportionately extend their organizational networks into populous slums. The logic is simple: "Our main strategy is that those [places] that have more voters, we have to capture them."[58] Small slums are marginalized in these efforts; they have fewer voters, and, hence, less attention is given to them in the spread of party organizational networks. Disproportionately greater party attention paid to larger slums is also met with an eager set of slum leaders. Standing before bigger potential support bases, residents in large settlements have more incentives to jump into the rowdy world of slum leadership. These top-down and bottom-up forces combine to produce denser party worker networks in more populous slums.

### Ethnic Diversity and Party Network Formation

India's urban slums exhibit rich and variable levels of ethnic diversity along the lines of caste, religion, and region of origin. From villages in South Asia to cities in Uganda and the United States, studies have found a negative association between ethnic diversity and public goods provision.[59] I find no such association in India's slums. Instead, I argue

---

[57] In 2011, the average population of a municipal ward in Jaipur was 39,557 (2011 Census of India, Jaipur District Handbook). In Bhopal, it was 25,689 (2011 Census of India, Bhopal District Handbook). Informal leaders in large slums can thus launch a plausible run for municipal councillor just by consolidating support within their settlement.

[58] Interview with INC worker, Bhopal, November 21, 2011.

[59] Alesina et al. 1999; Banerjee et al. 2005; Khwaja 2009; Habyarimana et al. 2009.

and show in subsequent chapters that ethnic diversity is *positively* related to party worker density; suggesting this, in turn, is a pathway through which ethnic diversity can have a positive influence on local public goods provision. To understand why, we must consider how ethnic diversity shapes the emergence of informal hierarchy in slum settlements.

In the initial stages of a squatter settlement's formation, informal leadership is nascent and unsettled. Squatters in India do not typically blanket the land *en masse*, in a matter of hours or days, with strong internal leadership and linkages with political elites. This is not to suggest that outside actors are uninvolved in settlement formation. Squatters can be encouraged by politicians to set up their shanties on vacant lands. Politicians also shield them from eviction to build local bases of support. The fragmented, gradual nature of squatting in India, though, means that early forms of informal leadership are largely constructed from scratch. Schoorl et al. make this point in their study of Karachi's slums: "*Bastis* of this type mostly come about without much organization. Often, their inception is marked only by a smaller cluster of families just settling on a vacant piece of land, without payment and without much planning ... However, very soon, the dwellers organize themselves strongly in order to resist government's attempts to evict them, to improve their settlement and to request certain facilities from the government."[60] Based on fieldwork in Mumbai, Lynch argues that ethnic diversity further contributes to the "newness" of slum leadership: "Given such heterogeneity there are few traditional leaders and principles of organization to which all give assent and respect. Some other form of organization ... than that of caste *panchayats* and leaders is necessary to overcome and incorporate this heterogeneity."[61]

Scholars have found that co-ethnicity can facilitate cooperation and political organization.[62] As such, we would expect that more ethnically diverse settlements tend to feature more slum leaders per capita because local ethnic groups will often generate their own narrow forms of informal leadership. Speaking to this point, a Bhopal politician described the nature of slum leadership in a nearby settlement: "There, someone is Buddhist, someone is Muslim, someone is Rajput, and someone is Brahmin. All castes are there ... so there are many leaders."[63] A veteran resident in that same settlement recalled that leadership first emerged in smaller *mohallahs* (blocks), which tended to be more

---

[60] Schoorl et al. 1983, p. 47.   [61] Lynch 1974, p. 1667.
[62] See, for example, Bowles and Gintis 2004 and Corstange 2016.
[63] Interview with former INC MLA, Bhopal, November 21, 2011.

ethnically homogenous than the slum as a whole.[64] More systematically, Tariq Thachil and I find experimental evidence that slum residents in Bhopal and Jaipur do often prefer to support co-ethnic slum leaders.[65]

Yet, there are several factors that push back against ethnicity rigidly determining the contours of informal authority. First, some ethnic groups in a settlement will lack members who possess the qualities that make for effective slum leadership, compelling them to look outside their narrow group for effective problem solvers.[66] The self-described rise of one slum leader in Bhopal illustrates this point: "See, in the beginning, people from my group supported me most. But then other groups saw the support I was getting from my own group. And they thought, he must be doing something well, so then I started getting people of other *jatis* (castes) coming to me."[67] Second, given high rates of local ethnic diversity, many local ethnic groups lack the numbers to go at claim-making alone. When problems arise, the importance of "people power" encourages residents to collectively act with non-coethnics, under slum leaders who can galvanize a large crowd. Third, everyday exposure and shared problems erode some of the relevance of co-ethnicity in shaping resident-slum leader linkages. Indeed, scholars have noted the faded importance of ethnicity in India's slums. Datta, for example, observed a "cosmopolitan neighborliness" in a Delhi slum.[68] Rao described similar dynamics in a Pune slum: "Although the character of Wadarwadi slum is multi-ethnic, inter-ethnic relations do not pose any serious problem ... the spirit of cooperation in multi-ethnic Wadarwadi slum is quite high."[69] For these several reasons, a one-to-one match between slum leaders and ethnic groups is uncommon.

To summarize, more ethnically heterogeneous settlements tend to produce more crowded nodes of informal leadership, which, over time, become denser party worker networks as parties seek to absorb slum leaders into their organizations. Yet, while residents may hold preferences for co-ethnic slum leaders, these preferences are not rigidly determinative of who the former support given the centrality of nonethnic criteria in

---

[64] Interviews with Rudra slum leader, August 28, 2011 and October 20, 2011.
[65] Auerbach and Thachil 2018.
[66] These qualities can include literacy and some formal education, charisma, and occupational connectivity to local government officials. See Auerbach and Thachil 2018 on the characteristics that shape who becomes a slum leader.
[67] Interview with Shaarad, Rudra, Bhopal, January 17, 2017.
[68] Datta 2012. See Kapur 2017 for a larger discussion on how urbanization in India is reshaping social identities and social cleavages.
[69] Rao 1990, p. 121.

effective slum leadership. And, because of the importance of signaling "people power" in making claims on the state, residents look to non-coethnics in their settlement for numbers and effective leadership. Hence, while ethnic diversity tends to increase the density of informal leadership, it does not fully define linkages between residents and slum leaders. There are residents to attract beyond a slum leader's own ethnic group, increasing the scope of competition among slum leaders for followers.

## 3.4 CONCLUSION

In this chapter, I argued that dense networks of party workers strengthen the capacity of slum settlements to demand and secure development from the state. Competition among party workers over a local following motivates them to be more active in problem-solving than they otherwise would be if their informal authority were unchallenged. Dense networks of party workers further bolster the organizational capacity of settlements to push the state to extend local public goods, as well as provide residents multiple points of political connectivity through which they can make claims on the state. Settlements that are thin or absent of party workers are more likely to be marginalized in the distributive politics of the city.

Distinct from the density of party workers in a settlement is the partisan distribution of those workers. I argued that the impact of multiparty networks on development can cut in both directions. On the one hand, competition between workers of different parties might increase responsiveness to resident demands because losing followers to opposition party workers can harm one's own party's electoral prospects. Moreover, in India's competitive, three-tiered democracy, where party turnover in elected seats is common from election to election, it is useful for residents to have diverse partisan linkages through their local party workers. On the other hand, multiparty competition can generate perverse incentives for rival party workers to undermine each other's organizational efforts. And from above, politicians may be less likely to extend public services to slums with multiparty networks because rival workers might undermine the politician's credit-claiming efforts.

The chapter next explained why settlements vary in the density of their party workers. First, I argued that parties disproportionately allocate party positions to slum leaders in large settlements. Moreover, and from the bottom-up, residents in more populous settlements have greater incentives to engage in slum leadership because they have a larger potential pool of followers from which to extract rents and party patronage. This generates a larger supply of slum leaders with whom parties can extend organizational positions. Second, I argued that increasing levels of ethnic heterogeneity tend to generate denser concentrations of slum leaders, which, over time, become denser networks of party workers.

The following two chapters descriptively ground the theoretical framework in context. Drawing on qualitative fieldwork and survey data, Chapter 4 describes the emergence and activities of India's slum leaders. It also draws on a census of 663 party workers across 111 slums to establish wide inter-settlement variation in the density and partisan distribution of party workers. Chapter 5 then presents historical narratives from eight squatter settlements. These narratives provide comparative, analytically driven accounts of the emergence of informal authority, the formation of party linkages, and the provision of local public goods.

# 4

## India's Slum Leaders

Shyam's tea stall is nestled beside a narrow and unmarked entrance to Ganpati settlement. The ramshackle stall is a bustling hub of social exchange. Residents gather to trade gossip, watch the news on Shyam's grainy television, and reinvigorate themselves with *chai* and *bidis* (hand-rolled cigarettes). The tea stall is also a focal point of problem-solving in Ganpati. When Shyam is not serving tea and selling cigarettes, he is acting as a *basti neta*, or slum leader, assisting residents in securing ration cards and voter IDs, resolving disputes, and writing petitions to one of Jaipur's many government departments. Shyam has built a large following through these activities. And as a member of the INC, he is expected to transform this support into votes during elections.

Shyam represents a widespread class of political actors in India's cities. Situated in an informal space between residents and the larger political currents of the city, slum leaders like Shyam are influential actors in urban distributive politics. They are centers of what Javier Auyero refers to as "problem solving networks."[1] For residents, slum leaders spearhead efforts to resist eviction and demand public goods and services. For political elites, they are entrenched in vote-rich neighborhoods. As such, slum leaders are positioned to sway voters, organize rallies, and encourage turnout during elections. This intermediary position can be lucrative, providing slum leaders with opportunities to attract party patronage and a daily stream of fees from residents seeking their help. Slum leadership also offers a pathway of political upward mobility through the ranks of party organizations and, for

---

[1] Auyero 2001.

the most successful of slum leaders, a party ticket to fight in municipal elections.

This chapter describes India's slum leaders, the main protagonists of the book. It begins by examining the strategies that slum residents use to improve local conditions and establishing the prominent role of slum leaders in those efforts. The chapter then shifts to describing the pervasiveness of slum leaders, how they emerge within settlements, and the pivotal role of resident choice in that emergence. It goes on to outline the diverse set of activities that slum leaders perform for residents, as well as the material and political motivations for engaging in these activities. The chapter next turns its attention to an important subset of slum leaders – party workers – who have been absorbed into political parties and given positions in their hierarchical organizations. The chapter concludes with a presentation of data from a census of party workers I conducted across 111 squatter settlements in Bhopal and Jaipur, which unearthed substantial inter-settlement variation in the density and partisan distribution of party workers.

## 4.1 DEMANDING DEVELOPMENT IN INDIA'S SLUMS

How do slum residents struggle to improve their neighborhoods? My fieldwork revealed three broad strategies that slum residents use to secure public goods and services. The first is internal self-provision, without the resources and technical assistance of the state. The second and third – group claim-making and settlement protest – look to demand resources from the state, and differ from one another in their degree of contentiousness and scale of resident participation. In practice, residents combine these strategies, hedging their bets in the face of often-dismissive government institutions. I observed the three strategies during my ethnographic fieldwork and then measured their frequency across the eighty settlements surveyed in 2012 (see Chapter 6 for details on the survey).

### Internal Self-Provision

The first strategy used by slum residents to improve local conditions is internal self-provision, without the assistance of the state.[2] I encountered many such efforts in my fieldwork. Residents collected money to fix water

---

[2] See Houtzager and Acharya 2011 on the concept of citizen "collective self-provisioning," with reference to such acts in São Paulo and Mexico City.

taps, replace streetlight bulbs, and fill potholes after the monsoon rains. Residents came together to dig channels to remove wastewater in areas without drainage, sweep waste into areas designated for trash, and repair electricity lines after storms knocked them down. Some residents pooled their resources and labor for more ambitious ends. For instance, in Jaipur's Saraswati settlement and Bhopal's Durga Nagar settlement, residents collected money to have a bore well and drainage pipe installed, respectively. In Jaipur's Rajiv Nagar settlement, residents collected money to build a one-room schoolhouse and pay for a private teacher.[3]

Of the 1,925 residents (across eighty settlements) surveyed in 2012, 30.75 percent (592 of 1,925) stated that people in their settlement had engaged in acts of internal self-provision.[4] Of these 592 respondents, 386 (65.20 percent) reported that slum leaders were at least sometimes involved in organizing these efforts. Internal self-provision, then, is common, and when residents engage in these activities, slum leaders are often involved. Yet, for many of the most essential local public goods, the resources and technical expertise of the state are required.[5] I now turn to the two primary strategies that slum residents use to demand development from the state.

## Group Claim-Making

A second strategy is group claim-making. This strategy involves petitioning politicians and government officials for public services.[6] Its group-based footing is important because it signals *lokshakti* (people power) – a crowd

---

[3] Field notes and interview with Rajiv Nagar slum leader, Jaipur, October 20, 2010.
[4] Survey respondents were asked: "Sometimes people are able to get together and improve their community without the help of the government. In this slum, have people ever collected money or organized to fix something, build something new, or generally improve the community?" Of the 1,925 respondents, 1,306 reported that residents in their settlement had not engaged in acts of internal self-provision and 23 respondents stated, "I'm not sure" (with 4 missing observations). In the average settlement, 28.51 percent of respondents noted that residents in their settlement had engaged in internal self-provision (with a one standard deviation of 17.53 percentage points).
[5] Capturing the limits of internal self-provision, and the frequent need to look upward to the state to provide public services, one resident in Jaipur recollected: "We collected money from residents and tried to clean the drain ourselves but it did not work because it is an expensive task. We had to approach a politician" (interview with Bapu Nagar resident, Jaipur, July 2017).
[6] Cornelius (1975, p. 188) also encountered group claim-making in Mexico City's *barrios*: "The most commonly used strategy among the poor in Mexico City is that of forming a committee or delegation of community residents to visit the office of an official and present a formal request for assistance."

of residents who can use their numbers to push bureaucrats and politicians to address their problems. Group claim-making differs from internal self-provision in its positioning toward the state. And it falls short of the contentiousness and scale of resident participation that defines settlement-wide protest, the third strategy discussed below. Group claim-making was the most common strategy I observed during my fieldwork. An urgent problem would arise: a streetlight burnt out, a drain was spewing sewage, or the monsoon rains washed away part of a road. In response, a group of residents would visit a politician or official. Usually, after a few hours of waiting, the group would be given the chance to ask for assistance.

The struggle for water in Saraswati illustrates the practice of group claim-making. Piped water has not been extended to the eastern part of the settlement. To provide residents with water, a public truck comes five or six times a week to fill a single 5,000-liter PVC tank. In the height of summer 2012, the number of water deliveries to Saraswati dwindled. When the truck did come, timings varied widely – anytime in the morning or afternoon. This forced residents, and women and children in particular, to sit for long hours by the tank, preventing them from engaging in more productive work or attending school.[7] Desperate, a group of twenty-five to thirty women visited the ward councillor to demand daily water supply at a fixed time.

80.21 percent of respondents (1,544 of 1,925) reported that residents of their settlement gather in groups to meet officials;[8] 51.95 percent (1,000 of 1,925) said they have *personally* been involved in these efforts within the past twelve months.[9] As with internal self-provision, group claim-making is often conducted in the presence of slum leaders.

[7] Field notes, Saraswati, November 30, 2010.
[8] Survey respondents were asked, "Do people in this slum ever gather together in groups to meet political leaders (the ward councillor, MLA, or MP) or government officials to ask for development or solve a problem in the slum?" 327 respondents reported that residents in their settlement do not engage in group claim-making and 53 respondents replied, "I don't know" (with 1 missing observation). In the average settlement, 80.54 percent of respondents reported that residents engage in group claim-making (with a one standard deviation of 16.04 percentage points).
[9] 884 respondents said that they had not personally participated in group claim-making in the past twelve months (with 41 missing observations). Participation in group claim-making is not limited to men, nor are residents from historically marginalized castes or Muslim residents excluded. Indeed, 48.27 percent of female respondents (433 of 897), 53.53 percent of Scheduled Caste respondents (372 of 695), 50.35 percent of Scheduled Tribe respondents (71 of 141), and 52.67 percent of Muslim respondents (237 of 450) reported having personally participated in group claim-making within the previous twelve months.

64.51 percent of those respondents who acknowledged group claim-making (996 of 1,544) reported that slum leaders were at least sometimes involved in those efforts. Slum leader involvement includes galvanizing residents, writing petitions, and leading discussions with officials. Beyond adding numbers to the crowd, residents support slum leaders in a variety of ways, including collecting money for letterhead stationery and transportation to government offices.[10] In some instances, slum leaders go alone to request help, carrying petitions with resident signatures and fingerprints. Officials – water engineers and sanitary inspectors, for example – often told me that residents come in groups and that slum leaders accompany them and do much of the talking.[11]

### Settlement Protest

A third strategy is settlement protest. These events are contentious, initiated for the purpose of drawing attention to the slum's problems through public disruption. Protests involve much larger segments of a settlement than acts of group claim-making. In some instances, hundreds or even thousands of residents will forgo their daily wages to go out into the city to block roads, march on government buildings, and burn effigies of politicians who have neglected them. The following newspaper article illustrates a protest conducted by a settlement in Jaipur:

> Around 1,500 [slum dwellers] came to the state assembly building this afternoon to protest and make demands. Many women and children were also in the protest. First, the protestors reached the circle and had a meeting with [the ward councillor and slum leaders]. They were planning to meet the chief minister to inform him about their problems ... The slum leaders gathered at the main door of the assembly building and declared they would block the road.[12]

A total of 735 respondents (38.18 percent) acknowledged that their settlement had engaged in protests to improve local conditions[13]

---

[10] For example, in Bhopal's Durga Nagar settlement, residents collected money to pay for letterhead stationery so that their slum leader could write petitions: "The settlement council called for a meeting in which it informed members that an amount of Rs 5 was collected from all 278 homes. Out of the total amount collected, Rs 465 was spent on letterheads and other office stationery. The remaining Rs 925 is with the council treasurer" (Durga Nagar committee documents, October 5, 2006).
[11] Interviews with water engineers and sanitation inspectors, Jaipur, July 27, 2018.
[12] Mohan Lal newspaper clipping, Jaipur, undated.
[13] Survey respondents were asked: "Have people here ever participated in a public protest to get development for the slum, like roadblocks, picket lines, or a demonstration?" 1,160 respondents reported that residents in their settlement had not engaged in protests and 21

(29.66 percent, or 571 of 1,925 respondents, claimed to have been personally involved in protests[14]). Of those 735 respondents, 582 (79.18 percent) stated that slum leaders were involved in at least some of the protest events. The involvement of parties is also noteworthy: 449 of the 735 respondents (61.09 percent) claimed that parties were involved in organizing protests at least "some of the time."

To summarize, India's slum residents tend to seek local development in groups and position their collective action toward the state. They often engage in these efforts under the guidance of slum leaders. Acts of internal self-provision are not absent, though they are relatively uncommon vis-à-vis struggles to secure local public goods and services from the state. This is not necessarily due to a lack of cooperation. Rather, many local public goods require substantial resources and technical expertise. Efforts to improve local conditions are consequently oriented toward the state.

## 4.2 THE PERVASIVENESS OF INFORMAL LEADERSHIP

Slum leaders are pervasive features of political life in many cities of the Global South.[15] This is certainly true in India's cities. In Bhopal and Jaipur, as well as during more limited research trips to Delhi, Indore, Mumbai, Nagpur, Pune, and Surat, I found slum leaders to be nothing short of widespread – an element of local politics that can almost be

---

respondents replied, "I don't know" (with 9 missing observations). In the average settlement, 32.76 percent of respondents noted that residents had engaged in protests (with a one standard deviation of 20.34 percentage points).

[14] 1,333 respondents had not personally participated in settlement protests (with 21 missing observations). 28.87 percent of female respondents (259 of 897), 31.08 percent of Scheduled Caste respondents (216 of 695), 30.50 percent of Scheduled Tribe respondents (43 of 141), and 29.33 percent of Muslim respondents (132 of 450) reported having personally participated in settlement protests.

[15] Much of the seminal work on slums and their informal leaders focuses on cities in Latin America. For classic studies in this literature, see Ray 1969, Cornelius 1975, and Perlman 1976, who study these figures in Caracas, Mexico City, and Rio de Janeiro, respectively. More recent contributions include Gay 1994, Burgwal 1996, and Stokes 1995, who examine slum leaders in Rio de Janeiro, Quito, and Lima, respectively. In sub-Saharan Africa, scholars have documented slum leaders in Accra (Paller 2014; Morrison 2017), Lagos (Barnes 1986), and Nairobi (Marx et al. 2017). In South and Southeast Asia, scholars have encountered slum leaders in Bangkok (Lee 1998; Carpenter et al. 2004), Dhaka (Banks 2008), Karachi (Schoorl et al. 1983), and Lahore (Shami and Majid 2014).

assumed. Even a quick chat with residents at a local *chai* stand will start to expose the contours of informal leadership. Slum leaders who are party workers make this task even easier: many display their party symbol and rank on placards hanging outside of their homes, leaving little ambiguity about their role in the slum. During interviews, party workers would often produce party stationery, photographs of rallies, and newspapers documenting their "social work," all to flaunt their political status.

To capture the prevalence of these figures, I asked survey respondents whether or not there are slum leaders living and operating in their settlement.[16] Across the full sample of 111 slums, 74.83 percent of respondents (1,903 of 2,545) acknowledged slum leadership.[17] In the average settlement, 70.26 percent of respondents confirmed the presence of these actors (with a one standard deviation of 23.79 percentage points). Only in 3 of the 111 settlements did not a single respondent indicate the presence of a slum leader. Respondents across the 111 settlements provided approximately 1,150 slum leader names, and nearly all settlements (103 of 111) had more than one named slum leader. Not only are India's slums saturated with informal leaders, but that informal leadership is usually multifocal.

Prior research on India's slums supports the assertion that slum leaders are part and parcel of settlement politics. Scholars have documented the presence and activities of these actors across a wide collection of cities – Delhi,[18] Chennai,[19] Bangalore,[20] Kolkata,[21] Mumbai,[22] Patna,[23] and Pune.[24] The actors at the center of this book's theoretical framework thus operate in cities throughout India and the Global South more broadly.

## 4.3 THE CONSTRUCTION OF INFORMAL LEADERSHIP

A slum leader's position is informal, without state sanction. Slum leaders do not face formal elections, term limits, or codified rules that delineate

---

[16] Respondents were asked: "In some slums there are people that do leadership activities. I'm not talking about the ward councillor or MLA. I'm talking about smaller community leaders that live inside the slum. These leaders go by several names, like slum leader (*basti ka neta* or *pradhan*), slum president (*basti ka adhyaksh*), headman (*mukya*), or party worker (*party karyakarta*). They are usually prominent people in the community. Are these kinds of people in this slum?"

[17] 586 respondents denied the presence of a slum leader in their settlement and 54 stated, "I'm not sure" (with 2 missing observations).

[18] Jha et al. 2007; Datta 2012; Snell-Rood 2015.  [19] Wiebe 1975; de Wit 1997.

[20] Kamath and Vijayabaskar 2014.  [21] Roy 2002.  [22] de Wit 2017.

[23] Rains et al. 2019.  [24] Rao 1990.

## India's Slum Leaders

their responsibilities.[25] Stripped of their title they are just ordinary residents. How, then, does a slum *resident* become a slum *leader*?

A first and analytically important feature of this process is that slum leaders emerge from the pool of residents. Parties cannot parachute their people into settlements and expect residents to fall in line.[26] Not once in two years of fieldwork did I encounter a party dispatching someone to live in a settlement and engage in leadership activities. Parties, moreover, cannot arbitrarily tap a resident and expect that person to immediately command authority. Slum leaders attract a following themselves by demonstrating efficacy in problem-solving.[27] Political connections can, of course, deepen and expand a slum leader's following, in large part because it strengthens their ability to secure public resources.[28] But it is a slum leader's own entrepreneurial sweat in taking up resident problems that underpins his or her popularity within the settlement. It is precisely this rootedness and self-stitched reputation that makes slum leaders attractive to parties.

In India's ethnically diverse slums, where residents have migrated from a mix of villages and states and belong to an assortment of caste (*jati*) groups, village-based hereditary titles and other rural forms of informal authority have little social currency. Just as parties cannot impose informal authority on settlements, a resident cannot simply proclaim to be a slum leader based on their prior status in their village of origin. Slum leaders attract a following because they are able to get things done in the city. This capability often stems from attributes such as literacy, a modicum of education, and bureaucratic connectivity through low-level municipal

---

[25] For a larger discussion on the concept of informal institutions, see Helmke and Levitsky 2004. Also see Ostrom 1990 for a seminal study on the role of local informal institutions in facilitating collective action and generating public goods.

[26] This is not unique to India. Burgwal (1996, p. 82) notes in his study of Quito's squatter settlements that, "[Core] leaders ... were *local leaders*. They were not imposed on the Cooperative by supra-local forces and they were more than merely representatives of the party or union. They led the land invasion, were squatters themselves and experienced the same hardships as the settlers, and probably even more."

[27] Ray describes a similar feature of slum leadership in Caracas: "Unlike the political bosses in the rural areas who gain ascendency over the campesinos but who are not campesinos themselves, the cacique rises out of the midst of the very people over whom he exercises authority" (Ray 1969, p. 60).

[28] On this point, a slum leader in Bhopal remarked, "Let us say that I rise with public support. If the party gives me a task and I do it well, I get a higher organizational position, and this will help me get problems solved faster and this gets me more public support. So in this way public support and party positions are connected to one another" (interview with Shaarad, Rudra, January 17, 2017).

jobs.[29] It also stems from more nebulous characteristics like charisma and courage before officials. Reflecting on the weight of efficacy in problem-solving relative to "traditional" sources of authority, one MLA explained: "In slums, the system of caste and creed is not there. It is needs based."[30]

Informal leadership in slums is also multifocal and competitive, with multiple slum leaders residing within the same settlement and vying with each other for public support. Across the 111 settlements, respondents provided an impressive 1,170 slum leader names. The average number of named slum leaders per settlement was 10.54, with a standard deviation of 11.93. In most slums there are numerous slum leaders offering their services, giving residents room to maneuver in choosing whom to seek help from and follow. If a slum leader fails to perform, residents can shuffle behind another slum leader, eroding the former's following and the material and political benefits it affords.

Competition among slum leaders is an ongoing reality, with resident support for a slum leader subject to quick reversal if that slum leader fails to perform. This unsettled state allows for dramatic shifts in the distribution of public support across the slum leaders of a settlement. One slum leader's success in bringing in a new paved road, gutter line, or streetlight can boost their popularity, sapping the following of another slum leader. Similarly, rumors that a slum leader is growing complacent in problem-solving or engaging in acts of extortion or violence can deflate that leader's following, pushing residents elsewhere. Slum leadership, moreover, is not limited to a fixed set of residents over time. New aspirants can enter the fray and seek to push aside an existing slum leader.

Because of the presence of multiple slum leaders, and resident agency in selecting whom they seek help from and follow, residents are pivotal actors in the construction of slum leadership.[31] My fieldwork uncovered two primary ways that residents select slum leaders. The first is through discrete events in which a group of residents throw their support behind a slum leader. These moments are often a response to a collective threat – eviction or total underdevelopment. Some communities select their leaders in public meetings in which residents vote with their hands or voices.

[29] Auerbach and Thachil 2018.   [30] Interview with BJP MLA, Jaipur, July 26, 2012.
[31] Resident agency and choice in selecting slum leaders also exist in settlements that emerge through large-scale, preplanned land invasions, which are commonly documented in Latin America (Collier 1976; UN-Habitat 1982; Gilbert 1998). Scholars have described land invasion settlements as competitive brokerage environments, where new challengers emerge to compete with established slum leaders, and residents are able to select who they turn to for assistance (Ray 1969; Gay 1994; Burgwal 1996).

In other instances, residents deliberate and come to a consensus over who is best fit to lead. Remarkably, some settlements organize informal elections with makeshift ballots and campaigns. Of the 1,903 respondents across the 111 settlements who recognized slum leadership (out of 2,543 total respondents), a remarkable 941 respondents (49.47 percent) reported that their slum leaders were selected in community meetings or through informal elections.[32] Ethnographies of slums in India and Latin America have uncovered similar instances of informal elections.[33]

The second pathway is more decentralized and fluid, with individual residents deciding whom to approach with their problems. These assessments are made on an everyday basis, and aggregate into a distribution of support for slum leaders. Kiran's rise in Bhopal's Rudra slum illustrates this second pathway. Kiran was never informally elected or chosen in a group meeting, though he enjoys a large following. He rose to prominence through acts of claim-making, organizing cultural events, and holding training sessions to teach residents how to cut hair – his own vocation. You will often find Kiran sitting on an iron stool at a *chai* shop in Rudra, discussing politics and giving advice to residents. Kiran's status as a slum leader is likely to persist as long as he continues to solve local problems.

To summarize, informal leadership in India's slums is competitive and unsettled. It is also multifocal, with most settlements home to more than one slum leader. Slum leadership is constructed from the bottom-up through resident-driven selection. Those who amass a following and gain the status of slum leader are otherwise ordinary residents, living with their families and confronting the same hardships as their neighbors. The eight case study squatter settlements presented in the following chapter will provide detailed qualitative evidence for each of these descriptive elements of slum leadership.

## 4.4 THE PROBLEM-SOLVING ACTIVITIES OF SLUM LEADERS

What services do slum leaders offer slum residents? My fieldwork uncovered a wide range of activities conducted by slum leaders, most of

---

[32] Respondents were asked: "In some slums, leaders are chosen through informal elections, and in others there is a big meeting where everyone sits and decides the leader through discussion. Were leaders here in this slum chosen by residents in these kinds of ways?"
[33] Ray 1969; Mathur 1996; Gay 1990; Jha et al. 2007.

which can be divided into two categories: (1) helping residents secure private goods that are consumed at the household-level and (2) spearheading claim-making efforts for local public goods and services. In this section, I describe the activities that compose these two categories and provide statistics on their relative frequency.

Slum leaders face a regular stream of residents seeking their assistance with individual and household-specific problems. The most prevalent of these requests are for help in obtaining government-issued documents like voter IDs, ration cards, and below-the-poverty-line (BPL) cards. Ration cards and BPL cards are essential for residents to access food at subsidized prices, as well as other public services for the poor. Other requests include mediating access to widow and handicapped pensions, postal savings accounts, and caste certificates. When residents become entangled in police cases, slum leaders can leverage their connections to reduce fines or jail time. Slum leaders refer to these activities as "social work".

In addition to these run-of-the-mill requests, residents seek the help of slum leaders with a wide array of idiosyncratic problems, a few examples of which are provided below. These are excerpts of letters directed at officials, composed by slum leaders on behalf of residents:

> I am a poor woman and I feed my three small children by doing hard work. On February 28 my 10-year-old son was crossing the road and suddenly a man struck him with his truck. He died. After the incident, the truck driver sped away. I request that you catch the driver as soon as possible and punish him as per the law. I hope you will bring justice. I hope I will get relief from a state fund or the chief minister's fund ... I am helpless after losing my son.[34]

> Rocks fell [from the mountain] and ... 15–20 pigs died ... Because of these pigs I was able to secure my daily wages and food. For years ... we were engaged in the trading of pigs and that is how we were able to run our life. None of my family members are employed. Also my son ... took a loan from Punjab National Bank for these pigs, which he paid back to the bank on time. Therefore, sir, we request that you dispatch orders to provide financial help.[35]

These activities often cast slum leaders in the role of *dalaal*, or "fixer." However, in contrast to images of shadowy backroom brokerage, most acts of "fixing" unfold in public spaces. A common sight during my fieldwork was a slum leader sitting at the local *chai* shop or *kirana dukhan*

---

[34] Letter to district collector, written by a slum leader in Ganpati on behalf of a resident, Jaipur, February 28, 1982.
[35] Letter to state authorities, written by a slum leader in Pahari on behalf of a resident, Jaipur, undated.

(general store), in front of his or her house, or outside a temple or mosque, discussing an issue with a resident.

The second cluster of activities that slum leaders perform for residents centers on making claims for shared public goods and services. A sample of the hundreds of petitions I collected from slum leaders gives a sense of the varied public services for which they fight:

> We have a huge problem of water and electricity [and] it is very dark at night. People are scared of going out from their houses at night because of thieves. So, therefore, we request that you resolve our problems as soon as possible and allot (regularize) our slum here. We slum dwellers hope something will happen soon ...[36]

> Sir ... roads are damaged and dirty in our slum and always full of muddy water. It is so much so that a disease called cholera is spreading and the whole slum is paralyzed because of this dirt ... the mentioned road is 700 feet long and 30 feet wide. Please kindly make this road so that we can get rid of these life-taking diseases.[37]

> The residents of the slum want to thank you for repairing the hand-pump. There is an additional request now. We have a water tank with a capacity of 3,000 liters ... but it does not have a lid and sometimes dirt and lizards get into the tank. We have lots of problems because of this. We request that you kindly arrange for a lid.[38]

> The roads have not been cleaned and there are a lot of mosquitos. In some of the lanes the water is overflowing due to improper drainage ... the gutters are blocked due to garbage on the roads, and residents find it hard to walk.[39]

Other activities include organizing community events during religious and national holidays, leading efforts to build community temples or mosques, resolving disputes between neighbors, and collecting funds for residents who are sick or lost a family member. For example, a slum leader in Bhopal's Durga Nagar organizes a festival in the settlement for Durga Puja. A few kilometers away in Rudra Nagar, a slum leader regularly organizes religious programs at a temple he helped to construct. In 2015, this same slum leader pushed the MLA to release funds for the construction of a community center, which has since become a center of social life in Rudra Nagar. These activities boost a leader's *namcheen*, or social prominence.

In sum, slum leaders provide a range of services for individuals and groups. To gauge the extent to which residents approach slum leaders for

---

[36] Letter from a slum leader in Pahari to a Rajasthan state minister, Jaipur, undated.
[37] Letter from a slum leader in Parvatpuri to the Jaipur Development Authority, undated.
[38] Letter from a slum leader in Saraswati to government officials, Jaipur, undated.
[39] Letter from slum leaders in Ganpati to the ward councillor, Jaipur, 2005.

help, survey respondents who acknowledged informal leadership (1,903 out of 2,545 respondents) were asked if they or someone in their family had gone to a slum leader to seek assistance.[40] Of those who acknowledged informal leadership in their settlement, 48.19 percent (917 respondents) said "yes." That percentage drops to 36.03 if we include those respondents who do not acknowledge slum leadership. This reported frequency is likely to be an underestimate, as residents who went to a slum leader but did not resolve the issue may dismiss the contact. In fact, in some interviews during my fieldwork, a resident would initially tell me that there are no informal leaders in their settlement, only to later acknowledge that there *are* slum leaders, and he or she has even tried to seek their help, but the effort was in vain. The figure also excludes activities that slum leaders engage in for groups of residents. Residents can benefit from these efforts without having directly met with a slum leader.

I asked those respondents who reported having visited a slum leader to describe the nature of the help requested.[41] The most common reason was to secure voter IDs, ration cards, or BPL cards (52 percent of the stated reasons). The second most common reason was to ask the slum leader for help in making claims for local public goods (48 percent). Other less common reasons included finding employment, starting a bank account, assisting with police cases, resolving disputes, and getting electricity connections.

Residents can, of course, be aware of the general activities of their slum leaders even if they have not personally approached one of them for help. To measure the scope of problem-solving activities performed by slum leaders, I asked survey respondents whether or not slum leaders in their settlement engage in twelve distinct activities, each observed during my qualitative fieldwork. Tables 4.1 and 4.2 provide descriptive statistics at the respondent and settlement levels.

Among the most common activities performed by slum leaders are making demands on politicians for local public goods and helping residents secure voter IDs, ration cards, and BPL cards. Just over 45 percent of respondents in the average settlement noted that their leaders engage in these two activities.

---

[40] Respondents were asked, "Have you or anyone in your family ever gone to a slum leader for help?"
[41] Respondents could name multiple issues for which they sought help from a slum leader. These data are from the 2012 survey (in which 683 of 1,925 respondents reported that they or someone in their family had visited a slum leader for help).

TABLE 4.1 *Slum leader activities: resident level*

| Slum leader activity | Mean (%) |
|---|---|
| Help residents obtain state-issued cards | 51.67 |
| Organize money collections | 30.14 |
| Organize settlement meetings | 35.25 |
| Stop anti-social activities in settlement | 42.00 |
| Resolve disputes in settlement | 48.25 |
| Help residents deal with the police | 47.74 |
| Petition state officials for public services | 48.41 |
| Organize religious and social events | 47.23 |
| Help residents meet politicians and officials | 41.45 |
| Spread information about public programs | 26.21 |
| Alert media to settlement problems | 15.44 |
| Demand public services during elections | 59.33 |

Note: N = 2,545. This table presents the percentage of survey respondents who reported that slum leaders in their settlement engage in the given activity. Respondents who did not acknowledge slum leadership or stated "don't know" with respect to the given activity are coded as 0.

At the other extreme, respondents infrequently reported their slum leaders bring problems to media outlets. Respondents also infrequently reported that their slum leaders collect money to improve local conditions, or spread information about government programs and services for the poor. The remaining activities lie somewhere in between – resolving disputes, helping with police cases, calling meetings to discuss problems, and organizing cultural events.

## 4.5 THE ELECTORAL ACTIVITIES OF SLUM LEADERS

As political intermediaries, slum leaders, and party workers in particular, also engage in electoral activities. Primary among these activities is organizing rallies for candidates during elections. These events are brimming with fanfare, accompanied with food, speakers blasting music, ceremonial garlands for key guests, and a lineup of speeches by candidates and their local party workers. Nearly all of the survey respondents in 2012 (94.49 percent, or 1,819 of 1,925 respondents) reported that politicians visit their settlement during elections to give speeches and engage in door-to-door canvassing

TABLE 4.2 *Slum leader activities: settlement level*

| Slum leader activity | Mean (%) | SD (%) | Min (%) | Max (%) |
| --- | --- | --- | --- | --- |
| Help residents obtain state-issued cards | 47.10 | 23.63 | 0.00 | 100.00 |
| Organize money collections | 26.18 | 18.35 | 0.00 | 80.00 |
| Organize settlement meetings | 32.27 | 21.26 | 0.00 | 90.00 |
| Stop anti-social activities in settlement | 38.91 | 23.53 | 0.00 | 96.43 |
| Resolve disputes in settlement | 44.19 | 24.76 | 0.00 | 100.00 |
| Help residents deal with the police | 43.25 | 24.39 | 0.00 | 100.00 |
| Petition state officials for public services | 46.11 | 20.25 | 0.00 | 100.00 |
| Organize religious and social events | 41.56 | 22.47 | 0.00 | 100.00 |
| Help residents meet politicians and officials | 39.08 | 19.37 | 0.00 | 80.00 |
| Spread information about public programs | 24.92 | 15.46 | 0.00 | 70.00 |
| Alert media to settlement problems | 15.18 | 13.58 | 0.00 | 60.00 |
| Demand public services during elections | 55.65 | 23.12 | 0.00 | 100.00 |

Note: N = 111. This table presents settlement-level descriptive statistics after calculating the percentage of respondents in each settlement who reported that slum leaders in their settlement engage in the given activity. Respondents who did not acknowledge slum leadership or stated "don't know" with respect to the given activity are coded as 0. The denominator for each settlement is the number of respondents in that settlement.

(*jansampark*) to be in direct touch with the public.[42] Among those who acknowledged slum leaders in their settlement and stated that politicians visit during elections (1,428 respondents), 90.34 percent (1,290 respondents) said that slum leaders mobilize resident attendance for these events.[43]

I also asked those respondents who acknowledged slum leaders in their settlement if the latter (a) approach them to suggest who to vote for during

---

[42] 82 respondents reported that politicians do not visit their settlement during elections and 15 respondents were "not sure" (with 9 missing observations).
[43] Respondents were asked: "Do leaders in your slum try to gather residents to attend these candidate speeches?" 120 respondents reported that their slum leaders do not organize these events and 13 respondents were "not sure" (with 5 missing observations).

elections[44] and (b) hold community meetings to discuss which party to vote for during elections.[45] 69.31 percent of those respondents (1,030 of 1,486 respondents) confirmed that slum leaders attempt to personally persuade them about whom to vote for[46] and 52.83 percent (785 of 1,486 respondents) confirmed that their slum leaders organize community meetings to discuss which candidate to vote for.[47] Slum leaders thus widely attempt to engage in voter persuasion. As one resident in Jaipur noted, "[our slum leaders] tell us we should vote for those [politicians] who have helped in getting our work done. We also have to go to rallies, if time permits." Another resident remarked, "They want us to vote for whomever they recommend; they want us to go wherever they tell us to go."[48]

Studies of clientelism anticipate that slum leaders distribute election-time handouts to "buy" votes or turnout.[49] My interviews with slum leaders and politicians confirmed that parties do often spread around small amounts of cash, liquor, and food during elections. A ward councillor in eastern Jaipur, for example, detailed how he distributed wheat, meat, clothing, money, and liquor in his constituency's slums. He added that party workers are the ones who physically hand these goods out to voters.[50] To capture a more systematic picture of this activity, I asked respondents: "During elections, sometimes parties give out things to voters like money, liquor, clothes, or food. Does this happen in your settlement?" 37.51 percent of respondents (722 of 1,925) noted that such handouts are distributed in their settlement during elections. This is likely an underestimate given the social desirability bias surrounding vote buying efforts.[51]

---

[44] Respondents were asked: "During elections, do leaders in your slum approach you to suggest which party to vote for?"
[45] Respondents were asked: "During elections, do leaders in your slum organize community meetings to discuss which party to vote for?"
[46] 446 respondents said that slum leaders do not attempt to personally persuade them and 5 respondents were "not sure" (with 5 missing observations).
[47] 665 respondents said that slum leaders do not hold community meetings to discuss who to vote for and 24 respondents were "not sure" (with 12 missing observations).
[48] Interview with resident of Baba Ramdev slum, Jaipur, July 2017.
[49] Stokes 2005; Nichter 2008; Stokes et al. 2013.
[50] Interview with ex-ward councillor in Jaipur, June 16, 2011.
[51] Gonzalez-Ocantos et al. 2012. 1,075 respondents reported that the election-time distribution of handouts does not happen in their settlement. 120 respondents stated that they "don't know" if such activities occur in their settlement (with 8 missing observations).

## 4.6 MOTIVATIONS TO ENGAGE IN SLUM LEADERSHIP

Slum leaders engage in the activities outlined above because they bring concrete material and reputational rewards. While residents sometimes refer to this flow of material rewards as *bhrashtachar*, or corruption, slum leaders see fees and patronage as compensation for their time in helping residents with problems – and parties with quenching their thirst for votes. *Netagiri* is a vocation, and for many slum residents, it represents a path of upward mobility paved with political connections.[52]

There are several related motivations for engaging in slum leadership. The first is the money associated with acts of problem-solving. Solving the day-to-day problems of residents can be a profitable source of fees for slum leaders who can get things done. One resident in Bapu Nagar in Jaipur, for instance, described his transaction with an informal leader in his settlement: "I gave him my file (for an electricity connection). He must have pulled some strings. I had to pay Rs 1,000 but my work was done."[53] As another example, one slum leader in Ganpati settlement in Jaipur said that he fetches between Rs 500 and 1,000 for helping secure a ration card.[54]

A second motivation to engage in slum leadership is party patronage. Engaging in party work during elections can be lucrative, albeit more episodic than the fees derived from everyday problem-solving. Slum leaders that are able to signal a large following are poised to gain access to party patronage in exchange for the election-time mobilization of those followers. A slum leader in Jaipur boasted that during one election, he was able to make Rs 30,000 – an amount equal to almost six months of income for most of his neighbors. An INC worker in Ganpati said that parties often spend Rs 10,000 to 20,000 to bring a slum leader into their camp. These incentives can go up to a *lakh* (Rs 100,000) depending on the importance of the slum leader, and might involve gifts of liquor and fancy dinners out in the city.[55] Handouts such as cash, liquor, and food also pass through the hands of slum leaders, giving them privileged access to the spoils of electoral competition.

---

[52] See Jeffrey 2010 on India's large unemployed youth population in cities, who often turn to local politics as a matter of "time-pass" as well as an opportunity to make connections that can potentially be parlayed into more gainful and regular employment.
[53] Interview with resident of Bapu Nagar, Jaipur, July 2017.
[54] Interview with a slum leader in Ganpati, Jaipur, April 17, 2011.
[55] Interview with Suresh in Ganpati slum, Jaipur, February 4, 2011.

Improving one's social standing in the settlement is a third motivation for slum leaders. Resolving disputes, organizing community events, and demanding public services improve a slum leader's *namcheen*, or social prominence. Slum leaders are not bashful about spreading word of these activities to boost their reputations as active problem solvers. They carefully archive and display newspaper articles in which they are mentioned engaging in acts of leadership. Slum leaders decorate the walls of their homes with pictures of themselves standing next to famous politicians. They mark their front doors with their name, rank, and party symbol. These are efforts to visually signal their informal authority.

Fourth, the motivation to improve one's settlement for its own sake should not be underestimated. Slum leaders live within settlements and seek a higher quality of life for themselves and their families. They too want paved roads, public schools, waste removal, and clean drinking water. In addition to being local leaders, they are neighbors, parents, and friends. These social ties can spur problem-solving activities for reasons beyond the material benefits that accompany them.[56]

## 4.7 SLUM LEADERS AS PARTY WORKERS

In India's slums, party workers (*karyakarta*) are a subset of slum leaders who have been absorbed into parties and given positions within their organizational hierarchies (described in Chapter 2). A principal data collection task for this book was to accurately build a census of party workers across the sampled slum settlements. There were two inclusion criteria for enumerating party workers. First, the individual had to be a party member with a position (*pad*) in either the main body or an organizational cell or wing.[57] Any committee level from the booth to the national level was acceptable (position-holders (*padadhikari*) in slums usually do not hold positions above the ward and block levels). Slum leaders who were only party supporters, or rank-and-file members without positions in a party organization, were not included in the list of party workers.

---

[56] Tsai 2007.
[57] At levels above the booth, this includes committee members who have been allocated the positions of president (*adhyaksh*), vice president (*up-adhyaksh*), secretary (*sachiv*), minister (*mantri*), treasurer (*kosh-adhyaksh*), and member (*sadasya*). During my fieldwork, all of the booth-level workers I encountered were booth presidents. This is likely due to the fact that booth committees only meaningfully expand beyond the booth president during elections. For this reason, at the booth level, only booth presidents were taken within the sample of party workers, as this position is locally important, limited to one individual, and sought after for individuals seeking to move up in the party organization.

Second, the individual had to live *within* the settlement. While outside party workers are, of course, involved in local politics, an analytically important division exists between those living within settlements and their external counterparts whose presence is episodic and fixed on election-time mobilization.[58] The former are embedded in local social networks and face the same risks as their neighbors. They can be appealed to on the basis of shared problems. This is what makes slum leaders so attractive to parties and political elites – their rootedness in settlements. Illustrating this point, one slum resident in Jaipur remarked, "They are one of us; they are like us so they understand the problems we face."[59]

I identified party workers across the sampled slums by triangulating several sources of information. First, I collected available party membership rosters from party offices. These lists were often aggregations of information provided by lower party committees, and were highly uneven in their quality, availability, and comprehensiveness. When possible, I gathered rosters directly from slum leaders, which sometimes came in the form of posters or party stationery. Second, I asked survey respondents to identify informal leaders in their settlement, which provided valuable, slum-wise lists that I used to locate party workers. Third, and most important, were the interviews I conducted in all of the sampled settlements with party workers to fill out the lists and ensure their completeness. Together, these efforts resulted in a comprehensive list of 663 party workers across the 111 sampled settlements.

Studies of distributive politics often implicitly assume that political brokers are uniformly present across the space under study. In contrast, I find the per-capita number of party workers to be highly unequal across settlements. I measure the variable *party worker density* as follows:

$$\text{Party Worker Density} = \left(\frac{w}{\text{population of slum}}\right) \times 1,000,$$

where $w$ is the number of party workers living in a settlement.

---

[58] Cornelius makes a similar distinction in his study of poor settlements in Mexico City: "The cacique ... emerges from the community over which he exerts his influence, and his following is confined to the residents of that locality. Moreover, his political activity must be oriented primarily to local issues and concerns ... he must be contrasted with individuals who function only as local agents or representatives of the government, political parties, labor unions, or other organizations whose activity is oriented in some degree toward the local community but whose primary concerns are clearly supralocal" (Cornelius 1975, p. 142).

[59] Interview with resident of Baba Ramdev slum, Jaipur, July 2017.

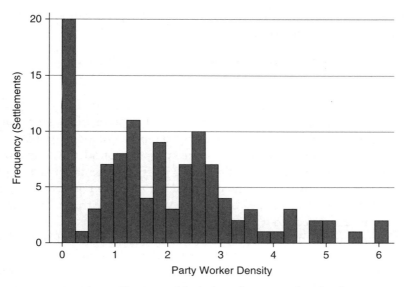

FIGURE 4.1 Frequency histogram of party worker density

The average settlement has just under 2 party workers per 1,000 people, with a one standard deviation of 1.47 party workers. Twenty of the 111 settlements are absent of party workers, while the most saturated settlements have approximately 6 party workers per 1,000 people.[60]

Two party workers per 1,000 people is significant. In a tightly packed cluster of 200 shanties,[61] the presence of two party workers means that there are two individuals with vertical party linkages – living down the street, if not next door – that residents can turn to for help. In slums with the highest levels of party worker density (around 6 party workers per 1,000 people), there are 4 additional party workers in that congested space providing problem-solving services – and competing for a following.

Distinct from party worker density is the partisan distribution of those workers. Party workers within a settlement can all belong to the same party, creating a local situation of one-party dominance. Or, several parties can be represented, giving the contours of slum leadership defined

---

[60] See Figure 4.1 for a frequency histogram of party worker density.
[61] There are approximately five people per household in India's urban slums (Census of India 2013).

partisan cleavages. I measure the balance of party representation among the party workers of a settlement as:

$$\textit{Party Representational Balance} = \left(\frac{1}{\sum p_j^2}\right) - 1$$

where $p$ is the proportion of party workers in the slum from party $j$.[62] Because Jaipur and Bhopal exhibit two-party competition, scores are bound between 0 and 1, with a score of 0 representing one-party dominance and a score of 1 representing a 50–50 split. Considering only those slums *with* party workers (91), the average party representational balance score is 0.42, with a one standard deviation of 0.40. Forty settlements have party workers from just one party. At the other extreme, five settlements have a perfect 50–50 representational split.[63]

To provide examples, take Satnami, a slum settlement in Bhopal that houses 2,000 people. Satnami is flush with BJP workers (nine workers) but does not have a single INC worker. Shiv Nagar, another slum settlement of 2,000 people in Bhopal, has a less-tilted distribution. It has three INC workers

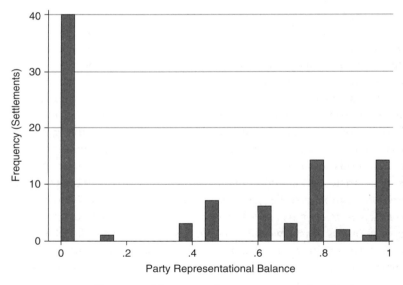

FIGURE 4.2 Frequency histogram of party representational balance

---

[62] This measure was adapted from Laakso and Taagepera's (1979) measure of effective number of parties.
[63] See Figure 4.2 for a frequency histogram of party representational balance.

and six BJP workers. While the BJP's workers are numerically dominant, the INC nevertheless has a foothold. Finally, consider Harijan slum in Bhopal, a settlement of 1,600 people. There are five INC workers and four BJP workers in Harijan, creating a partisan distribution among local party workers that is nearly evenly split.

India's urban slums therefore exhibit significant variation in the presence, density, and partisan balance of their party workers. This unevenness has gone largely unnoticed and unexamined in studies of distributive politics. The previous chapter argued that variations in party worker density and party representational balance have powerful consequences for public service provision. The next three chapters examine the causes and consequences of these divergences in the spread of party worker networks.

## 4.8 CONCLUSION

This chapter sketched the emergence and activities of India's slum leaders, the actors at the center of the book's theoretical framework. It established that slum leaders are widespread and frequently engaged in acts of local problem-solving. Slum leaders help residents obtain government documents and other forms of paperwork that allow residents to dig in their heels in the city and access public services. They lead efforts to petition and protest the state for public services. The benefits that accrue to effective slum leaders are many, including fees for assisting residents, party patronage, and the popular followings that fuel party promotion.

The position of slum leader is informal and underpinned by resident support. Keeping up a popular following is an ongoing task, as other slum leaders – and new waves of aspirants – are working to wrestle it away. Indeed, this chapter demonstrated that informal leadership in India's slums is fragmented and contested. The multifocal and competitive nature of slum leadership defines the relationship between residents and slum leaders – one that gives the former agency in shaping the nodes of local political brokerage.

An important subset of India's slum leaders are those who have secured positions within party organizations, situating them within larger party networks in the city. My census of party workers shows that these actors are highly uneven in their presence, density, and partisan distributions across settlements. I now turn to my ethnographic fieldwork in eight squatter settlements to provide comparative accounts of the uneven rise of party worker networks and the consequences of this unevenness for local public goods provision.

# 5

# Views from the Ground

## Historical Narratives from Eight Squatter Settlements

This chapter presents findings from my qualitative fieldwork in eight squatter settlements. I present these eight case studies as historical narratives, each of which traces the emergence of informal authority, the formation of party linkages, and the provision of local public goods from the initial period of squatting in that settlement to the present. The narratives illuminate the three mechanisms connecting the density of party workers with outcomes in local development: political connectivity, organizational capacity, and competition among party workers for a following, which pushes party workers to show efficacy in problem-solving. They provide insights into historical sequencing in the political organization and development of squatter settlements – insights that I draw on in the following two chapters to address concerns of reverse causality. Finally, the narratives shed light on the claim-making activities of slum leaders and demonstrate the political agency that slum residents exercise in India's cities.

The role of the case studies in my fieldwork was primarily exploratory – to understand, from the bottom-up, how slum residents organize and demand development from the state and to identify, in an inductive and comparative fashion, the factors underlying success or failure in those efforts. This fieldwork also informed the design and implementation of my survey, allowing me to assess, in the following two chapters, whether the patterns observed in the eight case studies hold across a larger, representative sample of squatter settlements in Bhopal and Jaipur. The case studies were selected to hold constant variables that were not of immediate theoretical interest – settlement age, land ownership category, official notification status, and electoral constituency – affording me a deeper

## Historical Narratives from Eight Squatter Settlements 115

look into the factors that produce disparities in local public goods provision across settlements.[1]

The narratives are based on fifteen months of ethnographic research; interviews with residents, slum leaders, and political elites; research in municipal and state archives; and engagement with several thousand paper documents produced and preserved by slum leaders, including petitions for public services, notes from neighborhood association meetings and political party meetings, newspaper clippings, photographs of public events, and political ephemera like party pamphlets and posters. These informal archival materials[2] often go back to the earliest years of the settlements in the 1970s and 1980s, providing a close look at how residents have organized and made demands on the state over time.

I triangulate among these rich and diverse sources of data to craft the historical narratives below. Such triangulation is essential, as the insights gained from each type and source of data are incomplete. The churn of migration in squatter settlements, as well as social and environmental shocks – fires, flooding, landslides, riots, and eviction drives – generate significant variation in residents' length of stay, splintering the content and depth of interviews. Slum leaders exaggerate their own importance in the history and development of settlements. The troves of paper materials they keep, moreover, exhibit gaps and biases, as important events may not have been documented and not all materials – petitions, photographs, and notes from community meetings – are assembled and preserved. These collections are also curated, in part, to demonstrate the prominence and problem-solving efforts of the slum leader.[3] Slum leaders' informal archives therefore provide valuable, albeit partial and biased insights into settlement histories. To address these inferential challenges, and arrive at more textured understandings of the histories of these complex

---

[1] See Chapter 1 for a more detailed discussion on the selection of the eight case study settlements.

[2] I refer to the troves of historical paper materials produced and preserved by India's slum leaders as informal archives. See Auerbach 2018 for an article-length discussion on the collection and use of informal archival materials. See Tarlo 2001 and 2003 on conducting historical research on the urban poor in India through ethnography and research in local archives. Also see Gupta 2012 on the politics of official paperwork in everyday governance in India.

[3] Slum leaders retain these paper materials for several reasons. First, they are public in nature and crafted to solve collective problems. Petitions are kept for future reference and may be drawn upon in cases where services are not provided. Second, many slums face land disputes and so slum leaders keep documents in the event that they are needed during court cases. Third, slum leaders keep paper records of their problem-solving activities as physical evidence of their informal authority.

social spaces, each narrative is the product of sustained fieldwork and iterative, back-and-forth movements among ethnography, interviews, and archival research.

The following two sections organize the narratives by city. Each section begins with a brief description of the local context in which the four settlements in that city are situated; the key similarities and differences of those settlements; and the values that each settlement takes along the two variables at the center of this book – party worker density and community development – to foreground how it inductively contributed to the theoretical framework. I conclude the chapter by distilling a set of broader comparative observations.

## 5.1 JAIPUR CASE STUDIES

The four case study settlements in Jaipur – Ram Nagar, Saraswati, Pahari, and Ganpati – are located within a 5-kilometer radius of one another and were settled between the mid-1970s and 1980. They shared the same state assembly constituency until 2008 (Johri Bazar), at which time new delimitation boundaries placed one in Bagru assembly constituency and the others in Adarsh Nagar assembly constituency. The four settlements draw on the same local labor markets, are officially "notified" (recognized) as slums, and are located on lands administered by the Forest Department, with smaller areas within them administered by the Jaipur Development Authority (JDA) or Jaipur Municipal Corporation (JMC). They exhibit demographic differences – in particular, their population sizes and levels of ethnic diversity – and have been located in different municipal wards since 1994.

This corner of Jaipur, like much of India, has witnessed considerable party turnover since the 1970s. The Janata Party held Johri Bazar assembly constituency in the late 1970s. Following the resurgence of Indira Gandhi in 1980, the Congress won back the constituency until it fell to the BJP in 1985. The following two decades were marked by an oscillation between an INC politician, Taqiuddin Ahmed, and a BJP politician, Kali Charan Saraf. The four settlements' municipal wards, as well as the mayor's seat and majority party in the municipal council, have swung between the INC and BJP since the first post-decentralization municipal elections in 1994. The Jaipur case studies have thus been exposed to city and state representatives from both parties since their establishment.

Squatters were initially drawn to eastern Jaipur for jobs in the construction of Jawahar Nagar, Malviya Nagar, and Raja Park, three middle-class neighborhoods. The active stone quarries that lined Jaipur's mountains in the 1970s and 1980s presented another source of employment. Besides jobs, the floods that struck this part of Rajasthan in the early 1980s pushed many poor, displaced families from within and outside of Jaipur into the expanding slums of the city's eastern and northern periphery, further contributing to population growth in the four case study settlements.

Before proceeding, it is useful to first broadly characterize the four Jaipur case study settlements as they relate to this book's central variables – party worker density and local development – so that readers can anticipate how they compare to one another and how they informed the theoretical framework. Ram Nagar and Saraswati exhibit the lowest levels of party worker density among the four Jaipur settlements (see Table 5.1). They also have the lowest overall community development scores. Pahari and Ganpati, on the other hand, are highly saturated with party workers. They also have higher community development scores than Ram Nagar and Saraswati. As noted above and in Table 5.1, the four settlements differ in several respects. The following chapter will control for these variables with quantitative data from 111 squatter settlements.

## Ram Nagar

The 1,000 residents of Ram Nagar are wedged between a government building and a middle-class neighborhood in eastern Jaipur. Squatters settled Ram Nagar in 1980 after having been removed twice from other lands – once to clear space for the 1982 Asian Games[4] and once by a Muslim community that objected to them residing on a local *kabristan* (cemetery).[5] Two castes make up a majority of Ram Nagar's population: the Singiwals, a Scheduled Caste from Rajasthan, and the Gonds, a Scheduled Tribe from Maharashtra and Madhya Pradesh. Smaller sections of Ram Nagar are home to migrants from Bihar, Gujarat, Haryana, and Punjab. Residents sell herbal medicines, drive auto-rickshaws, weave bamboo threshers, perform musical acts, and hold carnivals in nearby neighborhoods. Children collect waste that can be resold.

Officials from the adjacent government building have long been hostile to Ram Nagar's residents. The former erected a wall in the 1990s to

---

[4] Some squatters were given plots outside the city following the Asian Games eviction, in an area called Paldi Meena (interview with Ram Nagar residents, April 22, 2011).
[5] This second eviction involved physical violence between the squatters and Muslim community, culminating in some of the squatters' shanties being burnt to the ground (interview with Ram Nagar resident, April 14, 2011).

TABLE 5.1 *Jaipur case studies*

|  | Ram Nagar | Saraswati | Pahari | Ganpati |
|---|---|---|---|---|
| **Party workers** | | | | |
| Party workers | 1 | 1 | 12 | 147 |
| Party worker density | 1.07 | 0.33 | 2.49 | 6.17 |
| **Development outcomes** | | | | |
| Paved roads (%) | 0.00 | 37.44 | 100 | 90.30 |
| Streetlights per 1,000 residents | 8.53 | 11.53 | 2.9 | 17.39 |
| Household water taps (%) | 0.00 | 0.00 | 80.95 | 29.96 |
| Sewer connections (%) | 0.00 | 0.00 | 30.95 | 0.88 |
| Trash removal (%) | 0.00 | 3.85 | 29.27 | 16.37 |
| Government medical camps (%) | 50.00 | 38.46 | 57.50 | 49.10 |
| Primary development index | −1.28 | −0.81 | 1.09 | 0.90 |
| **Settlement-level characteristics** | | | | |
| Population | 938 | 3,036 | 4,827 | 23,811 |
| Year of establishment | 1980 | 1980 | 1978 | 1976 |
| Notification status | Notified | Notified | Notified | Notified |
| Percent Muslim | 0.00 | 0.00 | 76.19 | 9.78 |
| Percent SC/ST | 90.00 | 76.92 | 14.29 | 61.33 |
| Caste (*jati*) fractionalization | 0.66 | 0.90 | 0.88 | 0.95 |
| Religious fractionalization | 0.00 | 0.00 | 0.36 | 0.18 |
| Region (state) of origin fractionalization | 0.58 | 0.33 | 0.39 | 0.18 |

*Note:* The primary development index, described in more detail in Chapter 6, is derived from principal component analysis conducted across all 111 sampled settlements. This index is calculated using the component with the highest eigenvalue, which is positively related to all six development indicators.

prevent further encroachment, creating what is now a hard line between the settlement and government building.[6] In a separate line of attack, the head administrator of the government building wrote a total of thirty-four

---

[6] The officials assert that they own the land on which Ram Nagar is settled. Administrative documents, however, attest to the fact that Ram Nagar is located on Forest Department land: "That land belongs to the Forest Department. Therefore, in this matter our department cannot do anything" (letter from the state government to Rajesh, August 13, 1991). "The land on which the slum is settled is owned by the Forest Department and in the master plan it is used by the [government building]" (letter from the Jaipur Development Authority to the Government of Rajasthan, 2000).

letters between 1983 and 2004 to various government departments trying to have Ram Nagar evicted.[7] The officials also found allies in the middle-class neighborhoods surrounding Ram Nagar. The president of one of those neighborhoods described Ram Nagar to me as a "nuisance."[8] Explaining the slum's continued presence on the land, he remarked, "Illiterate people make for good voters in India."[9] Ram Nagar's residents know that their status as poor, active voters anchors them in place.[10] Forest Department officers, for example, attempted to remove the settlement in the late 1990s. Residents successfully appealed to Kali Charan Saraf, the area MLA, to stop the eviction.[11] Saraf stopped another eviction attempt in the early 2000s, during Ashok Gelhot's first term as chief minister.[12] For this protection, residents "pray for Saraf's long life."[13]

Upon arriving in Ram Nagar in the early 1980s, residents faced a total absence of public infrastructure and services.[14] In response, two people came forward to organize residents: Rajesh and Varun. Rajesh's seventh-grade education separated him from his mostly illiterate neighbors and propelled him into the position of slum leader. His authority was further hardened in the late 1980s when he was invited on stage with Kali Charan Saraf and introduced as Ram Nagar's leader.[15] Varun gained popularity within his caste group (the Gonds) because of his relatively high education and confidence in dealing with officials. He also had the support of an influential Gond leader in Jaipur.[16] Varun is recognized as a slum leader across Ram Nagar, though his influence is limited mostly to the Gonds.[17]

---

[7] Letter written by the head administrator of the government building, September 29, 2004.
[8] "The residents of [middle-class neighborhood] will be thankful if the government shifts this slum of criminals and illegal squatters, who are from outside the state and make illegal alcohol, steal, engage in prostitution, and do other anti-social behaviors ... the government should remove the slum before the public goes crazy" (letter from middle-class colony president to Jaipur Development Authority, undated).
[9] Interview with ex-president of middle-class association, Jaipur, May 9, 2011.
[10] Interview with Ajit, Ram Nagar, April 22, 2011.
[11] Interviews with Rajesh, Ram Nagar, December 3, 2010 and April 19, 2011.
[12] Interview with Rajesh, Ram Nagar, February 18, 2011.
[13] Interview with Ram Nagar residents, April 22, 2011.
[14] Interview with Ram Nagar resident, April 23, 2011.
[15] Interview with Ram Nagar's residents from Haryana, April 23, 2011.
[16] Interview with Ram Nagar resident, April 15, 2011.
[17] For instance, the residents from Haryana (twenty-five families) are aware of Varun's status as slum leader but consider Rajesh to be *their* slum leader. Rajesh helped them obtain ration and voter ID cards. He also accompanies them to the ward councillor several times a year to demand roads, drainage, and land titles (interview with Ram Nagar's residents from Haryana, April 13, 2011).

Both leaders perform a range of problem-solving activities. Rajesh stores residents' ration cards and helps keep them up-to-date. He also assists widows in applying for widow pensions,[18] and has brought an employment program to the slum that involves building rickshaws having pedal-generated electricity. Rajesh put an end to several illegal activities in Ram Nagar and demanded a replacement for a negligent schoolteacher. He also facilitates access to government health programs.[19] Varun fought for a primary school in the early 2000s. After much effort, a one-room schoolhouse was constructed.[20] He further demanded (unsuccessfully) that Gonds be included in Rajasthan's official list of tribes. Both leaders demonstrate awareness of government programs and provide information to residents. Rajesh and Varun have spent countless hours in government offices and have sent dozens of letters demanding public services:

We are poor people who sell herbs and raise our children. In this changing world, our business does not do well. We are not settled. Neither the central or state governments have done anything for our progress. With all the difficulties we are facing, we request that we get some facilities and land ... Why is the state government treating us like a step on a staircase?[21]

The BPL survey has never been conducted here. We humbly request you to do this survey and help us miserable people. Help make us participants in this state program so that we too can benefit. Our blessings are with you.[22]

Our slum was settled in 1980–1981. Our people have not been given *pattas* (land titles). We have sent many letters to chief ministers but never received an answer. *Pattas* are being distributed in every slum of Jaipur but we are not on that list. Moreover, before this, many politicians came and assured us that we will get *pattas*. But we did not get them. So, we humbly request you, respected sir, to give us *pattas*.[23]

Varun and Rajesh are involved in election-time voter mobilization. During elections, they encourage residents to vote for the BJP and

---

[18] Field notes, Ram Nagar, April 25, 2011.  [19] Field notes, Ram Nagar, June 13, 2011.
[20] Varun wrote to the chief minister: "The state government has not opened a temporary primary school for our children. But when we heard the announcements of the state government concerning primary schools we became full of hope. Sir, we request you to please dispatch orders to open a primary school here. We all will be thankful for your help" (Varun's letter to the chief minister, August 22, 1996).
[21] Letter to the local self-governance minister, March 19, 1996.
[22] Letter from Rajesh to city zonal commissioner, July 29, 2003. The ward councillor weighed in on this issue: "The people of Ram Nagar need BPL cards. They currently have ration cards. They should be selected to get BPL cards as soon as possible. What is the problem?" (letter from ward councillor to the Government of Rajasthan, written sometime between 2009 and 2011)
[23] Letter from Rajesh to the chief minister of Rajasthan, undated (likely 2003).

accompany residents to rallies and the polls. Rajesh admitted that during elections he is offered between Rs 15,000 and 20,000 – three to four months of income for most residents of the settlement – to deliver Ram Nagar's votes. He said that he does not take this money but does take food and liquor to distribute among Ram Nagar's residents, which he accepts only from the BJP.[24]

Varun is the head of a *jati panchayat* (caste association) in Ram Nagar – a small group of men that engage in dispute resolution among the Gonds. The *jati panchayat* was active during my fieldwork. For instance, I entered Ram Nagar one day to find a large group of residents congregated in the temple. A violent conflict between a husband and wife threatened to invite police intervention. The husband and wife aired their grievances in front of the *jati panchayat* with heightened emotion. The woman charged her husband with physical abuse and excessive drinking. The husband accused his wife of neglecting household chores. Varun and the *jati panchayat* heard both sides, deliberated, and decided the punishment: the husband was forced to end his abuse or be banished from Ram Nagar. He additionally had to pay the *jati panchayat* a fine for lost wages.[25]

Rajesh also led a *jati panchayat* for Ram Nagar's Singiwals.[26] During one of my visits, I found Rajesh surrounded by twenty residents. A Singiwal man had taken money out of a rotating savings group without recording it. The group argued over how much money he took and how to resolve the issue.[27] During a separate fight over money between a nephew and uncle in the settlement, it was decided that the nephew needed to pay the *jati panchayat* Rs 1,100 for lost wages and that the case would have to be shifted to the larger *jati panchayat* in their village.[28]

---

[24] Interview with Rajesh, Ram Nagar, April 15, 2011.
[25] Other punishments were on the table. One punishment would have been to shave the head of the person at fault. There are also fines that can "go up to a *lakh*." One of the worst punishments, according to Varun, is that the guilty party is required to buy cigarettes for the *jati panchayat* and sit among them as they smoke. This suggests that what they did was so bad that no fine can fit the crime (field notes, Ram Nagar, May 9, 2011). On caste associations in India, see Rudolph and Rudolph 1984.
[26] When fights break out between Gonds and Singiwals, each *jati panchayat* sends representatives to meet their counterparts and work through the issue (interview with Ram Nagar residents, April 17, 2011). Residents estimated that this happens six to eight times a year (field notes, April 21, 2011).
[27] Field notes, Ram Nagar, February 17, 2011.
[28] Field notes, Ram Nagar, April 16, 2011.

Another organization in Ram Nagar, created in the early 2000s but defunct by the time I started my fieldwork, was the *Ram Nagar Vikas Samiti* (Ram Nagar Development Committee). Rajesh served as the president and Varun served as the vice president. The remainder of the committee (seventeen members) drew from multiple caste groups in the settlement. The committee letterhead displays the lotus flower of the BJP, conveying the partisan preferences of the committee. Rajesh said that he started the committee to spread around the responsibility of leadership. He noted that the committee initially met two or three times a month, but participation later declined and then ceased altogether.[29]

Rajesh and Varun, working together and separately, have exerted considerable effort to improve conditions in Ram Nagar.[30] Yet, despite their positions of informal authority in a poor "vote bank," the two have been largely dismissed in the distributive politics of the city. For two decades of support for the BJP, Rajesh has only been given a minor organizational position at the ward level. Varun has not been given a party position. Consequently, Ram Nagar lacks much in the way of political connectivity. Parties have never organized Ram Nagar's residents to protest for public services. Residents have not attempted to organize protests either, which Varun attributes to Ram Nagar's small population and lack of "people power." In explaining this, he told me, "our understanding level is low, our population strength is low, and we are afraid."[31]

The ward councillor acknowledged Rajesh and Varun's efforts to improve Ram Nagar, narrating how they often come to her for help with ration cards, as well as asking for roads and drains. Sometimes the two leaders do this alone, and sometimes they bring groups of residents. Reflecting on the slum's lack of paved roads, she said that the houses in Ram Nagar are too close for paved roads. After I noted that other slums are arranged in the same way but have paved roads, she said she was not sure why Ram Nagar only has dirt roads but that she did not have enough funds to pave them.[32]

In its thirty years of existence, the public services that have been extended to Ram Nagar are negligible. Rajesh secured a small handful of communal water taps from Kali Charan Saraf in the mid-1980s. Saraf then extended a few electricity connections in the

---

[29] Interview with Rajesh, Ram Nagar, December 3, 2010.
[30] In the late 2000s, these joint efforts came to an end. Varun told me that Rajesh said, "I will take care of my *samaj* (social group) and you take care of your *samaj*" (interview with Varun, Ram Nagar, May 8, 2011).
[31] Interview with Varun, Ram Nagar, June 12, 2011.
[32] Interview with Ram Nagar's ward councillor, April 18, 2011.

1990s.[33] Ashok Parnami, Ram Nagar's MLA between 2008 and 2018, provided some additional water taps, which residents demanded prior to the 2008 elections.[34] A few streetlights have also been placed in Ram Nagar, though most of the settlement is left in the darkness at night.

Other than shared water taps, electricity connections, and a few streetlights, the needs of Ram Nagar's residents remain unmet. Roads are unpaved and without drains. Residents are forced to dig makeshift channels in the dirt to establish some semblance of drainage. The municipality rarely collects solid waste. Instead, residents throw garbage in what has become a trash dump flanking the western edge of the slum. Without public or private toilets, residents resort to open defecation. Shortly after the 2008 state elections, Rajesh wrote to the area MLA: "Sir, we request you ... to provide roads, drainage pipes, land titles, and bathrooms, and settle the slum in an organized way ... You said earlier that roads and drainage would be given through your development fund."[35] Nothing has been done. Children in Ram Nagar confront the same challenges that faced their parents.

## Saraswati

Saraswati is situated at the base of the mountain range in eastern Jaipur, bordered by forestland to the east and an industrial area to the south.[36] Migrants first settled Saraswati in the late 1970s to work as laborers in the local stone quarries. As the settlement became more established, families began to join the laborers to work in nearby neighborhoods and factories. Saraswati's population now stands at just over 3,000 people. Residents mostly hail from Rajasthan, though small pockets of the settlement are home to migrants from Bihar, Uttarakhand, Uttar Pradesh, and West Bengal. The settlement is remarkably diverse in terms of caste. All residents are Hindu, though regional differences among residents have generated a rich mosaic of small temples.

---

[33] Interview with Rajesh, Ram Nagar, May 30, 2011; interview with Varun, Ram Nagar, June 12, 2011.
[34] Interview with Varun, Ram Nagar, June 12, 2011.
[35] Letter from Varun to the area MLA, 2008.
[36] Saraswati's historical narrative was previously published in my article "Neighborhood Associations and the Urban Poor: India's Slum Development Committees." *World Development* 96 (2017): 119–35. I include it here with permission from Elsevier.

For the first fifteen years of the settlement's existence, Bilu, a labor contractor with ties to the INC, engaged in leadership activities alongside a small committee of residents.[37] As the "don" of the area, Bilu informally represented the settlement before the police and officials.[38] Older residents say that Bilu's contributions to the development of Saraswati were minimal. In a decade and a half, he was only able to secure a hand pump. In the same conversations, residents described Bilu's illicit activities.[39] According to current residents, Bilu used the settlement for the production and storage of country liquor (*desi daru*), which was sold to local laborers. Further, Bilu collected rents from workers and controlled who could enter the settlement and construct shanties.

Given his control over employment, Bilu's authority could not easily be challenged. His reign came to an end in the mid-1990s, though, when the High Court of Rajasthan closed mining activity in the mountains. Bilu left the area, creating a void in leadership. Many residents stayed, realizing that there was a shortage of jobs in their villages.[40] Between 1996 and 2006, resident collective action was fluid and isolated to distinct sections of the settlement.

[At that time] few people were living here. So, for instance, when they had a water problem five to ten people would meet and collect some funds and try to fix the problem by making a bore well or other water facilities.[41]

In the mid-2000s, pockets of the settlement began to develop nascent forms of informal leadership. In the northern part of the settlement, Prem engaged in leadership activities. Prem was a driver for an official, and through this connection he managed to secure a paved road and a water tank. Meanwhile, a young, ambitious schoolteacher named Jagdish, whose father was a contractor in the settlement,[42] was growing in popularity in the center of Saraswati. In the east, Sharma, a Brahmin, served as an informal leader.[43] Other residents engaged in fleeting acts of leadership during this period, though only enough to be mentioned in passing.

---

[37] Interview with Saraswati resident and past member of Bilu's group, April 27, 2011.
[38] Interview with Bilu, Jaipur, January 9, 2011.
[39] Interviews with Saraswati residents, January 6 and April 28, 2011.
[40] Interview with Saraswati resident, December 6, 2010. An older resident, Banwari, estimated that roughly half the families left after the mines were closed (interview with Banwari, Saraswati, April 27, 2011).
[41] Interview with Jagdish, Saraswati, September 2010.
[42] Interview with Jagdish, Saraswati, September 26, 2010.
[43] Sharma was fifty-one at the time of my fieldwork and worked as a small-time water contractor, making Rs 6,000 a month. He is educated up to the tenth grade.

Informal leadership in Saraswati became more defined in the face of eviction. In the mid-2000s, the Forest Department began to clear encroachments in the area. The community was thrown into panic. Without strong political connections, residents first reached out to a shopkeeper just outside the slum who was a position-holding member of the BJP. The shopkeeper was briefly made president of Saraswati and began to approach the BJP MLA for help.[44] Residents wrote letters to newspapers to spread awareness about the planned eviction.[45] With the help of the MLA, the Forest Department temporarily stalled the eviction.

Uncertainty over the possibility of eviction persisted. In the winter of 2007, concerned residents decided that someone from the slum must be president of Saraswati, someone who could unite the community.[46] A group of residents listed eligibility criteria: candidates must be at least twenty-one years old, be "mentally balanced," want to improve local welfare, not have a criminal background, and have at least a primary education. Further, candidates needed to promise to take action against "anti-social" residents, maintain public spaces, prevent further encroachments into the forest, and not use foul language. The president of the settlement would be "suspended or punished" if they were found to break these rules.[47]

Three residents came forward: Jagdish, Prem, and Prabhu. A community meeting was held to discuss the needs of the settlement and the conditions of granting informal authority. Roughly 150 people were in attendance. It was decided that the president should be well educated, knowledgeable about the government, and confident when dealing with politicians. Prabhu, a truck driver, soon after abandoned the race.[48] The choice came down to Jagdish or Prem.

Residents and the two candidates decided that an informal election with secret ballots should be held. All residents over the age of eighteen were asked to participate. Police were invited to oversee the ballot counting. The municipal and state representatives were also invited:

On January 8th, 2008, an election will be held for the post of president of Saraswati with the consent of residents and for the purpose of progress, development, and stopping anti-social activities. Therefore, we request you, sir,

---

[44] Interview with Gupta, Jaipur, January 12, 2011.
[45] Interview with Jagdish and Sharma, Saraswati, November 16, 2010.
[46] Interview with Mahvar, Saraswati, January 18, 2011; interview with Prem, Saraswati, May 21, 2011.
[47] Saraswati committee documents, 2007.
[48] This was because of Prabhu's illiteracy and growing rumors of his intentions to seek personal benefits from the position (interview with Jagdish, Saraswati, January 9, 2011).

to accept our proposal of being the chief guest ... The people of the slum hope you will give us your valuable time.[49]

Almost 800 residents voted on January 8, 2008 – a majority of Saraswati's adult population.[50] With 458 votes, Jagdish defeated Prem, who received 317 votes.[51] Several factors explain Jagdish's victory. Prem had developed a reputation for land-grabbing and engaging in *dadagiri*, or forceful, intimidating behavior.[52] In contrast, Jagdish had opened a tutoring center in his house, led two savings groups for women, started a youth group to clean public areas,[53] and taught in a local NGO school. Jagdish's "social work" and education are well known.[54] He also had the support of Sharma, thereby holding two of the three areas of the slum. The other Berwas (Jagdish's caste) in Saraswati supported him, though this could have only taken Jagdish so far, given the high level of caste diversity in Saraswati.[55] Both Jagdish and Prem openly supported the BJP, and so partisan preferences could not have been the deciding factor.

Following the election, Jagdish formed a small development committee to assist him with leadership activities.[56] The committee held a public ceremony in which they promised to work diligently and honestly to improve Saraswati. Committee members drafted nineteen rules regarding resident social conduct, as well as specific rules for future committee members, such as a minimum age for participation and education requirements. The aims of the committee were ambitious: the advancement of education, cleanliness, cooperation, and development. Among their first tasks was to push back against eviction:

---

[49] Saraswati committee documents, January 6, 2008.
[50] A substantial portion of Saraswati's population is under the age of eighteen – residents who were not eligible to vote in the informal election.
[51] Saraswati committee documents, January 2008.
[52] Interviews with Saraswati residents, December 29, 2010; January 18, 2011; March 29, 2011.
[53] The youth group, the Bajrang Yuva Mandal, started in March 2007 as a savings group. They also fixed water tanks and put in speed breakers on several of Saraswati's streets (interview with Mandal member, Saraswati, January 2, 2011).
[54] Interviews with Saraswati residents, November 17, 2010 and January 16, 2011.
[55] Interviews with Saraswati residents, January 16 and May 29, 2011. Jagdish believed that the Meenas did not support him or the election because of caste discrimination toward Berwas. There were Meenas on Jagdish's development committee, though. As one Meena committee member told me, "casteism" is not a problem in the committee, though there is some "casteism" in the community (interview with Meena, Saraswati, January 16, 2011).
[56] I asked Jagdish if Kali Charan Saraf had encouraged the informal election. He said "no ... our voice was not being heard by the government. It was our slum's idea to make a development committee for our development" (interview with Jagdish, email correspondence, March 18, 2017).

We wrote a letter to the area [MLA] and called the district forest officer ... [the forest officer] told us that the slum will not be evicted and everyone got permission to make houses outside the Forest Department's boundary wall. In this, the development committee played an important role.[57]

Around this time, Jagdish became a booth-level president for the BJP. He was an attractive local leader to win over given his following in Saraswati. I asked Jagdish to describe his relationship with the BJP:

AA: Can you tell me about your history with the BJP?
Jagdish: When I was in 9th grade ... many people were not able to fill forms. At that time, I was not from any party and I wanted to help the poor. There was a water problem here. We struggled with the Water Department and ended up getting a water tank and a hand pump. I felt then that it was necessary for me to make an alliance. Kali Charan Saraf had a hold on this area. After seeing his determination, I got excited and I started working for the BJP. Through him, problems in our area concerning water and lights were solved. Several times I became a BJP polling agent. Like that, I met party people and put the problems of the area in front of them ... for the development of my area I became a party worker ...
AA: What are your responsibilities for the BJP?
Jagdish: To participate in party meetings. And at the time of elections, deliver voter IDs and make booth arrangements ... I also discuss the party's new policies with people in the slum ... [and] check voter lists ... After this, I discover how many voters are in our area.[58]

Jagdish engaged in a variety of activities through the committee and his connections with the BJP. These included requesting water tanks, bore wells, streetlights, and hand pumps. He also helped residents to obtain ration cards, caste certificates, and pensions, and worked to bring in job training programs.[59] Many of Jagdish's activities were in reaction to spontaneous problems. For example, in December 2010, I encountered a group of women who had discovered a broken water tap. The women approached Jagdish to address the problem.[60] A month later, in a separate

---

[57] Interview with Jagdish, Saraswati, August 19, 2011. While total eviction was avoided, smaller conflicts persisted. For instance, in 2011, forest officers ventured into Saraswati to inspect rumors of new encroachments. In the darkness of night, squatters had erected several shanties. When I entered Saraswati the following week, the homes had been destroyed. Desperate, the squatters sat in the rubble and discussed where to find shelter.
[58] Interview with Jagdish, Saraswati, August 19, 2011. Indeed, residents reported that Jagdish suggests to them how to vote (interview with Bhil, Saraswati, December 29, 2010; interview with Suraj, Saraswati, May 28, 2011).
[59] Interviews with Saraswati residents: November 14, 2010; December 2, 6, 22, and 29, 2010; January 2 and 11, 2011. Interview with Jagdish, Saraswati, August 19, 2011; field notes, Saraswati, December 2, 2010.
[60] Field notes, Saraswati, December 22, 2010.

incident, a resident visited Jagdish to complain that a forest officer had fined him Rs 4,500 for extending his home beyond the boundary wall. Jagdish said that he wrote a letter to the local newspapers to put pressure on the Forest Department to stop harassing residents.[61]

Other examples of Jagdish's claim-making activities are found in the many petitions he has written to improve conditions in Saraswati:

The people of Saraswati have, since last year, been suffering from a scarcity of water. At times we have to go to the factories and sometimes to the cremation grounds for water. When we go to the water works they tell us that the level of water in the ground is very low. There is no water in the hand pumps ... we are in trouble.[62]

We have been neglected and that is why it is hell to stay here. But because of you certain things have been done. Sir, when you were honored on January 18th, 2008, you told us that before the elections a sewer line would be provided. But, until now, nothing has been done. Therefore, we request you to please solve this problem.[63]

We kindly request a public toilet. Because there are no toilets here now people urinate near the water tank or on house walls. The streets and drains are not clean and we have a lot of mosquitoes. Therefore, we request you to kindly make arrangements for cleanliness.[64]

Residents were not uniformly satisfied with Jagdish's efforts. In the eastern and northern parts of Saraswati, unpaved roads and water shortages generated disappointment. Jagdish himself acknowledged more could be done.[65] He expressed frustration with having limited time to spend on leadership activities. He blamed the budget constraints of the MLA and councillor, too.[66]

Residents sometimes approached government officials without Jagdish's assistance. For example, Sruthi, a widow in Saraswati, frequently gathered groups of women to go to the water department and lodge complaints about water shortages. The women even locked the official's door once and would not release him until he took actions to improve the water situation.[67] During a separate event, a resident collected thumbprints from neighbors and submitted a handwritten

---

[61] Field notes, Saraswati, January 8, 2011.
[62] Saraswati committee documents, undated.
[63] Saraswati committee documents, March 30, 2008.
[64] Saraswati committee documents, September 3, 2009.
[65] Interview with Jagdish, Saraswati, March 14, 2011.
[66] Interview with Jagdish, Saraswati, January 3, 2011.
[67] Interview with Sruthi, Saraswati, November 17, 2010.

application for a new hand pump.[68] In yet another instance, residents in the north section of Saraswati took pictures of a clogged drain and sent it to the Jaipur Municipal Corporation.[69]

Toward the end of my fieldwork in Saraswati, Jagdish began to travel outside of Jaipur for work. As a result, by 2015, he completely ended his leadership activities. Meanwhile, three new aspirants came forward – a Brahmin shopkeeper, a Scheduled Caste schoolteacher, and a Scheduled Caste municipal sweeper. The shopkeeper, a college-educated thirty-six-year-old, was extended the position of booth president for the INC. He estimates that ten to fifteen people approach him every month for help with problems. His tenure as an INC worker began with a major victory: he secured a paved road and drain, funded by the ward councillor's development funds.

Relative to Pahari and Ganpati, the following two Jaipur case study settlements, party worker density in Saraswati has been and continues to be low. There has been only a single party worker operating in the settlement at any given time. Neither Saraswati's residents nor its leaders mentioned engaging in protests during interviews, suggesting, like in Ram Nagar, a history of weak mobilization capacity and a lack of party interest in organizing residents.

Saraswati's access to public services is, relative to most of the other case study settlements, low. Only 37 percent of the settlement's roads are paved. Water is scarce, especially in the eastern part of the settlement where residents rely on water trucks. Sewers have not been extended, forcing those without pit latrines to go to the bathroom in the open. Thirty-five streetlights keep parts of Saraswati illuminated at night, but they are thinly spread throughout the settlement. Trash is rarely removed and the city drain that runs through Saraswati is always clogged, emitting a rotten stench. A resident likened the paltry level of public services to "a small seed in a hungry camel's mouth" (*unt kae muh mae jira*).[70]

## Pahari

Pahari is located between a transport depot and the imposing cliffs of Jaipur's eastern mountains.[71] Its 5,000 residents are predominantly north

---

[68] Field notes, Saraswati, November 30, 2010.
[69] Field notes, Saraswati, March 29, 2011.
[70] Interview with Jitendra, Saraswati, December 29, 2010.
[71] Pahari's historical narrative was previously published in my article "Informal Archives: Historical Narratives and the Preservation of Paper in India's Urban Slums." *Studies in*

Indian Muslims. Pahari, however, is not homogeneous; a number of Muslim castes populate the settlement,[72] and nearly one-fifth of Pahari's residents migrated from Uttar Pradesh. Residents from Uttar Pradesh are mechanics, butchers, and textile workers, while residents from Rajasthan are mostly artisans and gem cutters. Indeed, the morning hours in Pahari are characterized by the sounds of grinding gemstones, hammered metal, buzzing sewing machines, and the smells of freshly cut chicken, mutton, and fish.

Squatters settled Pahari in the late 1970s to work in the local stone quarries.[73] A number of threats quickly surfaced. Paramilitary troops stationed in the area harassed residents.[74] On two occasions, fires destroyed part of Pahari, and several other times, the municipality sent bulldozers to evict residents, leaving behind piles of stones and plastic tarps.[75] Vulnerabilities stemmed from the physical environment as well. Rockslides often damaged shanties and injured residents, and water runoff from the mountain inundated the low-lying sections of the settlement.

During this period, a group of residents under the leadership of two men, one Muslim and one Hindu, began to organize residents. Funds were collected to pay for their leadership activities – the costs of traveling to government buildings and the fees associated with official paperwork. These two slum leaders engaged in dispute resolution and worked to curb illegal activities. Based on documents from the time, they also managed the distribution of land and enforced informal property rights. Residents note, however, that suspicion grew over how funds were spent. The two slum leaders, moreover, were unable to secure public services. Their legitimacy began to erode:

> The members present in the meeting decided to have elections to choose new leaders, because the current leaders, one year after the establishment of the committee, could not do much regarding water and allotment of land titles. The working style of the committee was not effective.[76]

---

*Comparative International Development* 53 (2018): 343–64. I include it here with permission from Springer Nature.

[72] As one resident stated, "We are one religion, but *Khuda* (God) also made different *samaj* (social communities) too" (interview, Pahari, June 7, 2011).

[73] Interview with Majid, Pahari, May 30, 2011. The first wave of squatters migrated from nearby villages or from Jaipur's walled city (interview with Majid, Pahari, May 30, 2011).

[74] A letter from Pahari residents to an official noted, "A close encounter between the [troops] and the Muslim community has occurred and it is spreading feelings of mistrust" (January 1, 1991). These tensions lifted when the troops left in the mid-1990s (interview with Singh, settlement adjacent to Pahari, June 6, 2011).

[75] Interview with Majid, Pahari, May 30, 2011.

[76] Pahari committee notes, early 1980s.

## Historical Narratives from Eight Squatter Settlements 131

In the early 1980s, a Congress politician started to visit Pahari to help residents.[77] The settlement presented a growing "vote bank" in which to build electoral support.[78] Older residents remember that Uttam, the Congress leader, would regularly visit. Under his guidance, a development committee was created, the *Pahari Kachi Basti Vikas Samiti*. The stationery of the committee was adorned with the spinning wheel, a symbol of Gandhi and the Congress. Residents were invited to a clearing behind the slum to elect a president. In lieu of ballots, residents raised their hands in support of their candidate.[79]

Several current slum leaders in Pahari maintain the committee's documents. This includes the minutes of committee meetings, lists of informal community rules, and petitions for development. These rules have not persisted in their enforcement to the present day, and the extent to which they were followed earlier is unclear. Still, they provide insights into how Pahari's leaders initially sought to govern the slum:

> Women cannot come to meetings unless they are widows or helpless ... Personal problems must be resolved in the meetings so there are no fights. On empty land, delayed construction should be completed within 15 days – otherwise the land and structure will be given to someone else who has nowhere to live.[80]

> It is decided that every month Rs 5 will be taken from each shanty ... [If] someone does not deposit the money there is penalty of Rs 5 ... and this money will be used for slum development. Those who have new possessions and those who are not members will pay Rs 105 for the temple and mosque and Rs 15 to become a member [of the slum] ...[81]

> (1) Nobody will play cards on the road or at an intersection; (2) nobody will speak vulgar language: (3) it should not happen that there is a fight and ten people are beating one person ... (4) keep the roads wide, if possible.[82]

---

[77] Several letters demonstrate Uttam's involvement in the settlement: "In Pahari a common meeting was held in which getting water taps and electricity was discussed. The meeting was held under the guidance of Uttam and the president ... for the facilities of water and electricity we have been given a time when the chief minister will see our situation. This will happen on Sunday at 7" (August 17, 1980). Another letter stated: "Pahari is settled below the mountain. We came to you for help on July 19, 1981 and you assured us that we will get help soon ... The only things we have are forms from the state office that were brought by Uttam, which we filled and have submitted to the district collector but we have not yet received anything from his office" (letter to the chief minister, 1981).

[78] Documents I examined that were provided by Uttam's family recall stories of him fighting for development and keeping peace between Hindus and Muslims (letter to Rajasthan's Congress Committee, September 20, 1993).

[79] Interview with Yamin and Ram Babu, Pahari, June 4, 2011.

[80] Pahari committee meeting notes, June 15, 1980.

[81] Pahari committee meeting notes, July 15, 1980.

[82] Pahari committee meeting notes outlining rules, July 16, 1996.

In *Pahari*, those who sell their shanty must pay a Rs 500 fee that will be used for the mosque and temple. The slum has decided this unanimously. The current *imam* on mosque land will stay here as long as he teaches *namaz* (prayer) and if he does not he will leave the slum and a new *imam* will take his place ...[83]

Money collected from residents went toward committee activities and the construction of the mosque and temple.[84] The committee maintained accounting books on its revenues and expenditures.[85]

The committee continued from the early 1980s until the late 1990s with varying levels of activity. The president changed at least four times because of leadership fatigue, a leader shifting out of the slum, and, in one case, accusations of corruption. Residents described an important meeting in the 1980s to elect a new president. Khan, the winner, was selected because he was educated and bold.[86] During another election in the 1980s, 700 to 800 people sat in the back of the settlement to decide on a new president.[87] Residents raised their hands and made Abdul president.[88] Regardless of changing leadership at the helm, letters and committee notes provide evidence that the development committee was engaged in problem-solving activities:

Because of continuous rain our shanties are damaged and people have no place to live. However, our slum has not received any help from the state. In our temple and mosque there isn't light. We don't even have streetlights and because of this our daughters, wives, and daughters-in-law cannot go out at night. Thieves roam in the dark.[89]

300 families live here and yet there is only one water tap. Water comes at 11PM or not at all. We have requested [your help] several times but nothing has happened ... each day our wives and daughters go to [a nearby colony] to fetch water. While they collect water, many people tease [them]. We request you to please stop this problem ...[90]

We don't have any arrangements for cleaning. We have so much mud that people cannot live happily ... Water is always collecting in potholes and we do not have drains for the water ... because of the dirt, mosquitoes are multiplying and diseases are spreading. Please place the orders to make a drain and road ...[91]

---

[83] Pahari committee meeting notes, October 12, 1980.
[84] Interview with Ali, Pahari, June 6, 2011.
[85] Pahari committee meeting notes, undated.
[86] Interview with Yamin, Pahari, June 26, 2011.
[87] Pahari's leaders disputed the size of each other's election meetings (interview with Abdul, Pahari, June 17, 2011).
[88] Interview with Abdul, Pahari, June 3, 2011.
[89] Letter to the chief minister of Rajasthan, July 20, 1982.
[90] Letter to the chief minister of Rajasthan, October 10, 1980.
[91] Letter to the chief minister of Rajasthan, undated.

Pahari's slum leaders also addressed individual problems:

The power wires pass right above my house and every day we fear that children might get shocked ... these wires can be removed by putting up a 2.5 to 3 foot pole ... my family can be saved from being shocked if you do this ...[92]

Today, April 13, 1997, a meeting was called with the members of the development committee. The meeting was called because of the petition of Rafeeq and Ahmed. It was decided in the meeting: the trolley was stolen and so Ahmed should give Rafeeq Rs 2,285 for the trolley and Rs 500 for rent of the trolley. That is a total of Rs 2,785.[93]

The Hindu-Muslim riots that shook Jaipur in the early 1990s powerfully influenced the demographic composition of Pahari. During interviews, residents stressed that attackers came from the outside. I heard stories of residents hiding neighbors and forming patrols.[94] Despite these efforts, Pahari's Hindus moved to the southern tip of the settlement and established their own enclave after the riots. They felt they would be safer in a Hindu-majority settlement.

Also in the early to mid-1990s, migrants from Uttar Pradesh came to Pahari, many for training in gem cutting. In their villages of origin, a dam had disrupted their fishing trade, forcing them to look elsewhere for work. The group estimates that they have 150 to 200 households in Pahari, making them one-fifth of the community. Despite their numbers, though, the group expressed feelings of marginalization. One resident stated that they are only given attention during elections, and then they must "follow [the politicians] around like dogs." Others said that their children were denied schooling and that they struggle to obtain ration cards.[95] Given their locally marginalized status, residents from Uttar Pradesh have organized themselves to improve conditions in their section of Pahari.

The influence of Uttam and the use of the committee waned in the 1990s as Pahari's slum leaders became independently tied to parties, built their own personal followings, and competed with one another for local prominence.[96] Describing this process of authority building, one of Pahari's current slum leaders stated, "If someone knows how to lead and work in politics, to the public, he will be king."[97] While a majority of Pahari's leaders joined the INC, the BJP also made inroads. Pahari's BJP workers cite the hard work of

---

[92] Letter to an engineer of the Electricity Department, May 5, 2001.
[93] Pahari committee meeting notes, April 13, 1997.
[94] Interview with Pahari residents, June 27, 2011.
[95] Interview with residents from Uttar Pradesh, Pahari, June 4, 2011.
[96] Interview with Yamin and Ram Babu, Pahari, June 4, 2011.
[97] Interview with Yamin, Pahari, June 26, 2011.

Kali Charan Saraf and the neglect of the INC toward its "Muslim vote bank"[98] for why they joined the BJP.

Twelve party workers live and operate in *Pahari*. Ten of them belong to the INC and two to the BJP. Residents say that Pahari's twelve party workers actively compete with one another for a base of support in the settlement.[99] For example, while they both promote the INC, Khan and Abdul are highly competitive and belittle each other's contributions to Pahari.[100] The origins of their animosity began with a conflict over the location of a water pipeline. Around 1992, a water pipeline was sanctioned for Pahari. Abdul wanted it to start near his end of the settlement. However, other leaders, including Khan, wanted the work to start on their end, near the mosque. They told Abdul that his area is too close to the Hindus, and so they should start the work in the Muslim area. Abdul persisted, causing a rift between the two leaders.[101] Not long after the pipeline incident, residents accused Abdul of taking substantial amounts of money for helping with ration cards, undercutting his public following.

Though less prominent than Khan and Abdul, other INC workers operate in Pahari and have their own personal followings. For example, Yamin, a mechanic and INC block *maha mantri* (minister), had by the start of my fieldwork worked for the INC for thirty years.[102] Majid, one of the oldest residents in Pahari, similarly engages in INC party work. Khan's son, Faisal, had also entered into party politics during my fieldwork, taking on the position of ward president of the Youth Congress Committee. The other INC workers have varying levels of influence in Pahari, and each works to move up in the party hierarchy by cultivating their reputation for getting things done.

A senior BJP worker, Rasooq, came to Pahari in the early 1980s.[103] His position during my fieldwork was the ward vice president of the BJP. The only other BJP worker in Pahari is Jakeer, who works under Rasooq. Jakeer is the ward president for the BJP's "minority wing". Rasooq and Jakeer are tasked with gathering crowds, putting up posters, and

---

[98] Interview with Jakeer, June 2, 2011.
[99] Interview with Pahari residents, May 31, 2011.
[100] Interview with Khan, Pahari, November 10, 2010. Khan was a member of the civil defense force and received an award from the district collector for helping people in Pahari get ration cards. Having completed schooling up to the tenth grade, Abdul is more educated than Khan and owns a gem-cutting business that employs several residents.
[101] Interview with Abdul, Pahari, June 17, 2011.
[102] Interview with Yamin, Pahari, June 4, 2011.   [103] Field notes, Pahari, June 3, 2011.

promoting the BJP during elections.[104] Competition across party lines occasionally generates conflict in Pahari. For instance, during a visit in the 2000s, Kali Charan Saraf and his local BJP workers had rocks thrown at them – an attack instigated by Pahari's INC workers.

Pahari's party workers provide residents with vertical political connectivity. Armed with party stationery, Pahari's party workers have produced a flurry of petitions to improve local conditions. INC workers regularly meet with the ward councillor to discuss local problems, and the BJP leaders have close ties with Kali Charan Saraf and Ashok Parnami, the latter of whom was the area MLA from 2008 to 2018.

Pahari's residents have been able to attract a high level of local public goods – substantially higher than in Ram Nagar and Saraswati. Public infrastructure – paved roads, streetlights, piped water, and drains – were provided to Pahari in the mid-1990s, after party worker networks emerged in the settlement. Public water taps came earlier, in the late 1980s and early 1990s.[105] Roads were paved after the municipal election of 1994. According to Rasooq, Kali Charan Saraf and the ward councillor at the time funded the roads.[106] Taqiuddin (an INC politician) then extended the roads in the early 2000s, after he beat Saraf for the state assembly constituency seat.[107] All of the roads in Pahari are now paved and many have cement drains to remove rainwater. The majority of residents have their own water taps. The people of Pahari, however, have not had all of their needs met. Some sewers were constructed in the settlement after the 2008 state assembly elections,[108] though most of Pahari is still without them. Streetlights are sparsely placed in the settlement, making it difficult to move about at night. Trash removal is also a problem, especially at the settlement's entrance where a mound of festering garbage is seemingly always present.

### Ganpati

With over 20,000 residents, Ganpati is among the largest slums in Jaipur. Migrants hail from a variety of states – Bihar, Madhya Pradesh, Uttar Pradesh, West Bengal, and, of course, Rajasthan. Ganpati's Hindu

---

[104] Interview with Rasooq, Pahari, June 2, 2011.
[105] Interview with Pahari residents, May 31, 2011; interview with Rasooq, Pahari, June 2, 2011.
[106] Interview with Rasooq, Pahari, June 2, 2011.
[107] Interview with Majid, Pahari, May 30, 2011.
[108] Interview with Rasooq, Pahari, June 2, 2011.

residents, which make up a majority of the settlement, represent all strata of the Hindu caste hierarchy. A sizable Muslim population also resides in Ganpati, particularly around the mosque in the northern part of the settlement.[109] Residents engage in occupations typically associated with the urban poor: auto rickshaw drivers, construction workers, butchers, rag pickers, hawkers, and recyclers. Cottage industries can be found in Ganpati as well, producing everything from toasted biscuits to wedding invitations.

Ganpati emerged on the sand dunes of eastern Jaipur in the late 1970s. Many of the early residents worked as construction laborers in a nearby middle-class neighborhood. At that time, small roving gangs operated in different sections of Ganpati, selling empty plots to squatters and then shifting to other vacant lands to continue lining their pockets. Predation also came from the police and forest department, whose officers looked the other way as long as they were given *ghus* (bribes). Local politicians saw Ganpati not as a population to squeeze for money, but as a new "vote bank" from which to extract electoral support.[110]

Informal leadership quickly emerged in the face of underdevelopment. As in the other case study settlements, these figures were not placed in Ganpati by parties but instead migrated like other residents and became slum leaders after demonstrating an ability to get things done. Mamta, a Congress politician in eastern Jaipur, began to travel to the settlement in the early 1980s to build ties with Ganpati's nascent leaders. With their help, she mobilized residents for protests and engaged in other forms of "social work."[111] Anish, Mamta's right-hand man in Ganpati, sat at the top of the Congress network during this period.[112] Anish was an active problem-solver. To provide just two examples from his many meeting notes and petitions:

---

[109] The imam of the mosque noted that parties approach him to ask for support from local Muslims during elections (interview with Ganpati imam, February 16, 2011).
[110] Interview with Harish and Manoj, Ganpati, January 29, 2011; interview with Dattar, Ganpati, April 26, 2011. One resident said that the gangs charged Rs 500 for a plot in the early 1980s (interview with Ganpati resident, May 28, 2011).
[111] Interview with Ganpati resident, May 28, 2011.
[112] A letter written by Anish to the area MLA in the mid-1980s illustrates his local prominence at that time: "Our development committee is for all and works for all. There are seven hills here and this committee is working for the development of the slum and with your help and support and the hard work of the committee good things are happening in Ganpati."

President of the slum development committee, Anish, will hold a meeting. Heads of [all sections] of the slum will attend. Things that will be discussed are the shortage of water in summers, fighting among residents, and how to improve settlement conditions.[113]

We request that you resolve our problems: (a) People are dying because the water supply is insufficient ... (b) The problem of electricity is so much that we spend whole nights in darkness ... some anti-social people roam around at night and can get away with anything ... We have already written many letters to the government about these problems. Still we poor people do not get any justice.[114]

Meanwhile, Kali Charan Saraf began to cultivate ties with a separate group of Ganpati's slum leaders. One of his main men, Singh, built a committee of roughly twenty people in Ganpati, erecting the foundation of what would become the local BJP network.[115] Partisan competition between the INC and BJP networks was and is intense. To win Ganpati is to win the ward (and much of the state assembly constituency), and so the spoils for popular slum leaders in Ganpati are abundant.

Today, party worker networks percolate into all corners of Ganpati. Party workers are eager to advance the interests of residents – and, in the process, their own status and material wellbeing. The ward councillor lives within the settlement. A history of sustained "social work" propelled her family to local fame and, ultimately, a BJP ticket. The BJP first approached the councillor's husband, the source of the family's social prominence. There was an electoral reservation for women in the ward in 2009 and she was given the party ticket. The husband, however, is the de facto ward councillor. He goes to the municipality to engage in representative work and helps people make ration cards, voter IDs, and below-the-poverty-line (BPL) cards in a quasi-official capacity.[116]

The BJP ward president sits toward the apex of the local BJP network. Beneath him, dozens of BJP workers with assorted positions extend the reach of the party to every corner of the settlement. I interviewed Manoj, a former BJP ward president, on a handful of occasions. Manoj's leadership activities began in the year 2000. He explained that he became a leader in Ganpati because of his social work, decent education (eighth-grade pass), and confidence in dealings with officials. After demonstrating a popular following, Kali Charan Saraf selected him as BJP ward

---

[113] Letter to area police station, April 27, 1987.
[114] Letter from Anish to the chief minister of Rajasthan, undated.
[115] Interview with Singh, Ganpati, October 16, 2011.
[116] Interview with ward councillor, Ganpati, January 15, 2011.

president. In this capacity, Manoj regularly organized meetings of the BJP workers to discuss local problems, often with the BJP ward councillor in attendance.[117] These meetings allowed BJP workers to bring problems from their areas of Ganpati to the attention of the ward councillor. For instance, on December 20, 2006, BJP workers met with the ward councillor to discuss problems with mosquitos and the need for drainage, sewer lines, road repairs, and more frequent trash collection.[118] In his role as BJP ward president, Manoj also helped residents get ration cards, organize protests, and petition the state for public goods and services.[119] One resident even told me that Manoj helped his family get money from an uncooperative bank teller by accompanying them to the bank with a wooden rod (*lathi*).[120] Some examples of Manoj's petitions:

There is no water pipeline in [a section] of Ganpati and therefore the slum is suffering problems. People have to go to [the nearby middle-class neighborhood] to fetch water and while crossing the road people are scared of accidents. Please provide 200 feet of pipeline.[121]

Cleaning work is not being done. We went to the sanitation office many times but did not get a helpful reply ... the ward is very dirty. Please take action quickly.[122]

Today in the slum a general meeting was held and it was decided that the slum should be rehabilitated. We have been told so many times that it will be rehabilitated but nothing has happened. We request that this been done soon or else residents will organize a strike in front of your house.[123]

Manoj's close relationship with Kali Charan Saraf provided him a bridge to non-elected officials and a wide array of political elites in the city. This connectivity is illustrated in a letter that Saraf wrote to the chief minister of Rajasthan on behalf of Manoj:

---

[117] Entries from the party's ward committee meetings illustrate this: "Today, November 25, 2005, there will be a meeting at 6:00pm. All BJP workers are supposed to be present." "On April 25 at 6:00pm ... an important meeting will be held at the ward level. All of the workers of the ward (office bearers, members of different wings and cells and their office bearers) must attend and grace the meeting. In the meeting Saraf and the ward councillor will be present." "Today, April 22, 2009, ward members have called a meeting at 7:00pm. The MLA of the area, Ashok Parnami, and the ward councillor will be present."
[118] BJP ward meeting notes, December 20, 2006.
[119] Interview with Manoj, Ganpati, January 25, 2011.
[120] Interview with Ganpati resident, May 20, 2011. On the role of "muscle" in Indian politics, see Hansen 2001 and Vaishnav 2017.
[121] Letter from Manoj to Jaipur's mayor, November 15, 2008.
[122] Letter from Manoj to ward councillor, August 28, 2005.
[123] Letter from Manoj to Kali Charan Saraf, August 28, 2005.

Manoj, BJP ward president of Ganpati, has attached a memo asking for Ganpati to be rehabilitated in a planned fashion. Ganpati is the largest slum in my constituency ... there are problems with meeting basic needs and people in the slum are forced to live a hellish life ... take action immediately.[124]

Manoj explained to me that slum leaders spend so much time on problem-solving activities because if they do not, they fall out of favor with the public and, thus, fall out of favor with the party.[125] Other party workers in Ganpati expressed similar sentiments.[126] During elections, they can then say, "Remember I helped you. Now support my party."[127]

The current BJP ward president, Niraj, owns a small general store in the center of Ganpati and has a BA from a college in Alwar, a nearby district. During his childhood, Niraj was active in the *Rashtriya Swayamsevak Sangh* (a Hindu nationalist social organization affiliated with the BJP); he says this inspired him to do "social work." He was also a college *Akhil Bharatiya Vidyarthi Parishad* (ABVP) president (the BJP's student wing), which then launched him into the BJP's *Yuva Morcha* (Youth Wing). So began Niraj's climb up the party hierarchy.[128] Like Manoj, his predecessor, Niraj noted the importance of routinely solving local problems to stay popular. The party "keeps an eye" on party workers like him to ensure they are strengthening and not undermining the party brand.[129]

The BJP also has party workers belonging to its organizational cells and wings in Ganpati. Phool Chand, the *pramukh* (chief) of the BJP slum cell, sits atop an eleven-person committee. Among his most proud accomplishments is helping to organize a group of 10,000 residents to demand a government survey in 2002. On a more daily basis, he helps people obtain various government-issued cards and solve water problems.[130] The *Yuva Morcha* and *Mahila Morcha* (Women's Wing) also have a local presence. The ward president of the *Yuva Morcha*, armed with a high school degree, has two-dozen men under him, spread throughout the settlement. He meets with the MLA roughly ten times a month to discuss local problems.[131] Suvita, his counterpart in the *Mahila Morcha*,

---

[124] Letter from Kali Charan Saraf to Vasundhara Raje, September 23, 2005.
[125] Interview with Harish and Manoj, Ganpati, January 29, 2011.
[126] Interview with Pariya, Ganpati, April 4, 2011; interview with Phool Chand, Ganpati, June 28, 2011.
[127] Interview with Ganpati resident, May 20, 2011.
[128] Interview with Niraj, Ganpati, February 4, 2011.
[129] Interview with Niraj, Ganpati, February 4, 2011.
[130] Interview with Phool Chand, Ganpati, January 28, 2011.
[131] Interview with Darmendra, Ganpati, February 13, 2011.

oversees her own committee. Her committee is tasked with mobilizing women for the BJP during elections.[132]

The INC network, despite not having a co-partisan councillor or MLA during my fieldwork in 2011, was still active. The ward president, Rathik, is a college-educated schoolteacher. In narrating his rise to power in Ganpati, he noted that in 1993 he helped 250 people secure BPL cards in the southern part of the settlement, and that he vigorously fought for water pipelines. He is in charge of dozens of other INC workers of varying ranks that are spread throughout the settlement.

The INC's organizational wings and cells have also penetrated Ganpati. For example, Berwa, a general store owner, serves as the ward president of the INC slum cell. In the event that government officials are unresponsive to his claims, Berwa contacts Bhati, the state president of the INC slum cell, to ask that he put pressure on those officials.[133] A smaller network of Youth Congress workers also exists in Ganpati, with a young Muslim resident in charge at the ward level.

These are examples of just a handful of Ganpati's 147 party workers – roughly 6 per 200 households – all of whom aspire to climb up their party hierarchies and expand their bases of public support. These workers afford Ganpati's residents multiple points of political connectivity. An excerpt from the BJP ward committee's notes exemplifies such connectivity:

Today, a meeting will be held with the entire group of workers. Ward members [of the BJP] will lead the meeting and the agenda will concern development work. A team will be formed and the ward councillor will play the leading role in the group (December 19, 2005).

The ease with which area politicians know the names of Ganpati's slum leaders further attests to the close ties between the two sets of actors. For example, Ganpati's second ward councillor (from 1999 to 2004) invited me to go on a walking tour of the settlement with him.[134] He effortlessly went through the names of dozens of slum leaders with whom he had direct connections.

---

[132] Interview with Suvita, Ganpati, February 13, 2011.
[133] Interview with Berwa, Ganpati, January 18, 2011.
[134] During the walk, the councillor described some of his accomplishments while in office. He was proud of a large protest that he organized in front of the Jaipur Development Authority to address the many traffic accidents that were occurring in front of Ganpati. He also secured permanent water tanks for Ganpati, pushed roadwork in the settlement forward, and processed 1,800 BPL cards for residents (field notes, Jaipur, June 16, 2011). One slum leader in Ganpati estimated that this councillor spent Rs 10 lakh on his own election (interview with Phool Chand, Ganpati, June 28, 2011).

# Historical Narratives from Eight Squatter Settlements

When major threats confront Ganpati, party workers organize residents for protest. Residents have engaged in protests for water, electricity, land titles, roads, drainage, and speed bumps after children died playing on the busy road in front of the settlement. The following newspaper excerpts illustrate the role of parties in these protests:

> Under the leadership of [a] former minister and BJP leader ... slum dwellers organized a traffic jam at [Ganpati] bypass to protest about various issues ... The gathering was addressed by BJP workers and [local municipal councillors]. They demanded repairing the roads, discontinuation of heavy vehicle movement, removing biases in development work, and resettling [Ganpati] in an organized way at the same spot. The gridlock continued from 10 am until 2 pm ... Police officers tried to appease the BJP leaders who were organizing the traffic jam. But the hundreds of people who were jamming the traffic opened the roads only after the meeting was over.[135]

> Around 1500 people of Ganpati slum came to the state assembly building this afternoon to protest and raise demands. Many women and children were also in the crowd. First protestors reached Jaleb circle and assembled under the guidance of the ward councillor. They were planning to meet the chief minister to inform him about their problems.[136]

Party workers compete with one another for a following. Partisan competition across rival networks, however, is particularly intense. Each network seeks to undermine the other. In response to the protest described above, Congress workers distributed a pamphlet to weaken the BJP's mobilization efforts:

> A few BJP leaders, with a personal selfish motto, are misleading the people with deceptive statements, whereas in their eight years of rule, they neither got the [road] repaired even once, nor did they work toward the planned settlement of slum dwellers. So much so, they collected money from you for this purpose but did nothing concerning this issue, which is not fair ... Congress has always promoted development. Block Congress Committee, [Ganpati] asks that you not be fooled by these people.

A newspaper article on protest activity in Ganpati described similar forms of interparty contention:

> BJP and Congress are in confrontation on the issue of blocking the road in front of Ganpati. BJP has announced plans to jam the road on January 11th whereas Congress has opposed such action. The BJP president of the ward said the road

---

[135] *Dainik Navajyoti*, January 12, 2002.
[136] Mohan Lal newspaper clipping, undated, though given its content I place it in the late 1990s.

would be blocked from 10am on Friday morning, under the leadership of ex-MLA Kali Charan Saraf. The block Congress president and Congress ward councillor argue that the state government has sanctioned Rs six *crores* for the construction of a new road and that BJP leaders are obstructing the development work by misleading the people.[137]

This is not to say that partisan competition among Ganpati's party workers undercuts every protest. For example, the ward president of the BJP told me that the public water utility declared in 2010 that water would only be available for one hour every two days. He estimated that 10,000 people flooded the streets that night to block the road. The INC and BJP both spread word of the protest through their networks.[138]

Ganpati's uneven topography makes it a challenging place to provide public infrastructure and services. Nevertheless, given its enormous population of voters and army of active party workers, it has secured a high level of local public goods. Nearly all roads are paved[139] and streetlights keep a majority of the alleyways lighted.[140] Every morning, water is provided through community taps.[141] No fewer than thirty-six water tanks supplement the piped water.[142] A drainage channel has been constructed in front of the settlement to remove wastewater, and municipal sweepers periodically clean it of silt. Sewers were extended to the southern tip of the settlement in the early 2000s, though this construction work stalled after the 2008 state assembly elections.

---

[137] *Pariya* newspaper clipping, January 10 (year not provided, but I place it in the mid-2000s).

[138] Interview with Niraj, Ganpati, February 4, 2011.

[139] Paved roads came bit by bit (interview with ward councillor, June 12, 2011). In the south and central parts of Ganpati, streets were paved in 1994 (interview with Bengali residents, Ganpati, October 16, 2010). In the north, roads were paved in the late 1990s (interview with Ganpati shopkeeper, November 15, 2010; interview with Kallu, Ganpati, February 11, 2011; interview with Dattar, Ganpati, April 26, 2011).

[140] Kali Charan Saraf provided electricity in the late 1980s (interview with Ganpati resident, May 28, 2011). The streetlights came later, in the early 1990s (interview with ward councillor, Ganpati, June 12, 2011).

[141] A veteran slum leader said that Kali Charan Saraf organized residents in the early to mid-1980s to break pipelines in nearby middle-class neighborhoods to siphon water. He offered his protection and instructed them to tap into the electricity grid as well (interview with veteran slum leader, Ganpati, April 26, 2011). Water pipelines were extended into Ganpati in June of 1994 before the first municipal election. Kali Charan Saraf attended the inauguration of the pipelines (interview with ward councillor, Ganpati, June 12, 2011).

[142] This system of water tanks started in the late 1990s (interview with ward councillor, Ganpati, June 12, 2011).

## 5.2 BHOPAL CASE STUDIES

The four case study settlements in Bhopal – Gandhi Nagar, Tulsi Nagar, Durga Nagar, and Rudra – are situated within a five-mile radius of New Market, one of the city's busiest commercial areas, and were settled in the 1970s during a booming expansion of the city's squatter settlements.[143] The four settlements were all part of Bhopal South state assembly constituency until 2008, at which time three remained in Bhopal South assembly constituency and one was placed in Narela assembly constituency. They share the same local labor markets, have been officially "notified" as slums, and are located on lands administered by the *nazul* (revenue) department. The four settlements emerged on green-field sites void of local public infrastructure and services. Further, residents across the four settlements continue to lack full land titles (*patta*), though many have been given temporary titles through the 1984 Patta Act, described below.

The Janata Party ruled Madhya Pradesh and Bhopal South assembly constituency during the earliest years of the settlements' formation. Following the 1980 state elections and up to the point of my fieldwork, the state government and Bhopal South assembly constituency have shifted between the INC and the BJP. The four settlements have been located in different municipal wards since the first post-decentralization municipal elections in 1994. These wards have also, over time, swung between the INC and the BJP.

Several events unfolded in the 1970s and 1980s that continue to impact Bhopal's slum residents. In the late 1970s, Madhya Pradesh passed the Slum Improvement and Clearance Act, paving the way for the Slum Clearance Board – tasked with slum development and the "rehabilitation" of evicted residents[144] – and programs for public service delivery in the state's slums. As in other Indian cities, these programs were insufficiently resourced and bent by politicized distribution.[145] In 1984, Arjun Singh and the state legislative

---

[143] "In the eleven years between 1973 and 1984, Bhopal's squatter population saw a ninefold increase. In 1984 there were 163 squatter settlements occupying 320 hectares and housing 31,277 households or about 178,000 people, roughly 26.5 percent of the city's population" (Mitra 1988, p. 9). A smaller group of construction workers and squatters set up shanties in Rudra Nagar in the 1960s, though they were mostly evicted and resettled soon after to make space for a sanctioned building (Risbud 1988).

[144] See Agnihotri 1994 on the Madhya Pradesh Slum Clearance Board.

[145] Risbud (1988, p. 77) provides several examples of how resources for slum development in Bhopal were meager and misused: "Amounts sanctioned to the Municipal Corporation for improvements are diverted (for payment of salaries etc.). Similarly,

assembly passed the Patta Act, giving temporary land titles to thousands of slum dwellers in Madhya Pradesh.[146] Addressing the legislative assembly, Singh declared: "[Slum dwellers] shall no longer be the dispossessed and forgotten citizens of this state but shall have a legal right to their hearth and homes, a right which the power of the state shall protect and promote to the fullest extent possible."[147] Single-point electricity connections were also provided to many of the slums benefitting from the temporary title program, including the four case study settlements.[148]

Less than a year after the announcement of the Patta Act, the Union Carbide factory exploded, releasing a toxic cloud of chemicals that killed several thousand of Bhopal's residents. The social and environmental aftermath of the Union Carbide factory explosion, as well as the corruption that plagued the distribution of post-disaster aid, still haunts the city. The four case study settlements were not in the immediate vicinity of the factory, though the toxic gas spread toward their general area of the city.[149]

Before moving on to the Bhopal case study narratives, I first describe the four settlements in terms of their levels of party worker density and access to local public goods (see Table 5.2) – the explanatory and outcome variables, respectively, at the core of the book's theoretical framework. Gandhi Nagar represents the least developed of the Bhopal case studies. It also has a relatively low party worker density score. At the other end, Rudra has the highest community development score, as well as the highest party worker density among the four Bhopal case study settlements. Tulsi Nagar represents a middling case, with an

---

because it has so many functions, the Environment Improvement does not get priority. Agencies like the Development Authority are not interested in small work." "Records of the Slum Department showed that three community latrines were provided in Shiv Nagar, but in fact, no latrines were found on the site, and only excavations for the proposed latrines existed" (Risbud 1988, p. 76).

[146] On the Patta Act, see Risbud 1988, Mitra 1988, and Agnihotri 1994. Banerjee (2002, p. 47) estimates that 150,000 temporary *pattas* were granted across Madhya Pradesh under the 1984 Patta Act.

[147] India Today, May 15, 1984.

[148] See Mitra 1988 on the Patta Act and the provision of the one-point electricity connections.

[149] On the Bhopal Gas Tragedy, see Basu 1994, Lapierre and Moro 2002, and Hanna et al. 2005.

TABLE 5.2 *Bhopal case studies*

|  | Gandhi Nagar | Tulsi Nagar | Durga Nagar | Rudra |
|---|---|---|---|---|
| *Party workers* | | | | |
| Party workers | 1 | 3 | 1 | 24 |
| Party worker density | 1.39 | 2.62 | 0.82 | 5.07 |
| *Development outcomes* | | | | |
| Paved roads (%) | 71.47 | 100 | 95.1 | 96.75 |
| Streetlights per 1,000 residents | 6.96 | 11.33 | 2.47 | 5.49 |
| Household water taps (%) | 0 | 12.5 | 0 | 34.62 |
| Sewer connections (%) | 0 | 12.5 | 75 | 34.62 |
| Trash removal (%) | 37.50 | 46.67 | 41.67 | 65.30 |
| Government medical camps (%) | 25.00 | 13.33 | 25.00 | 38.46 |
| Primary development index | −0.89 | 0.01 | 0.14 | 0.64 |
| *Settlement-level characteristics* | | | | |
| Population | 718 | 1,147 | 1,214 | 4,734 |
| Year of establishment | 1978 | 1972 | 1978 | 1976 |
| Notification status | Notified | Notified | Notified | Notified |
| Percent Muslim | 0 | 0 | 8.33 | 23.08 |
| Percent SC/ST | 100 | 75 | 33.33 | 36.54 |
| Caste (*jati*) fractionalization | 0.86 | 0.70 | 0.86 | 0.95 |
| Religious fractionalization | 0.22 | 0.30 | 0.15 | 0.38 |
| Region (state) of origin fractionalization | 0.53 | 0.60 | 0.63 | 0.55 |

*Note*: The primary development index, described in more detail in Chapter 6, is derived from principal component analysis conducted across all 111 sampled settlements. This index is calculated using the component with the highest eigenvalue, which is positively related to all six development indicators.

above-average level of party worker density and an average level of community development. Durga Nagar's community development score exceeds what the theory would expect, given a relatively low party worker density score. We will see that Durga Nagar's low party worker density score is due to its most influential slum leader, Joshi, shying away from holding a party position because he works as an official in the local government – despite being a BJP supporter and exploiting connectivity to BJP political elites.

## Gandhi Nagar

Gandhi Nagar sits in a shallow basin between a busy road and a middle-class neighborhood in central Bhopal. Since emerging in the 1970s, the settlement has grown into a dense cluster of shanties housing approximately 800 people, and has expanded to the limits of the basin, right up to the edge of the road and the wall separating Gandhi Nagar from the middle-class neighborhood. A 2004 eviction drive cut Gandhi Nagar's population by a quarter, removing a section of the settlement located on a strip of land on the opposite side of the road. Despite the eviction, Gandhi Nagar remains ethnically diverse, home to a handful of Hindu castes as well as Buddhists and a few Muslim families. The numerically dominant castes are Bastors and Bangees, the former of whom weave thatch baskets and make bamboo scaffolding within the settlement. Most residents have moved from rural parts of Bhopal district or the adjacent district of Sehore.

Gandhi Nagar formed a neighborhood development committee in the late 1970s to fight eviction and petition the state for public goods and services. The committee was tied to the Congress's *Jhuggi Jhopri Maha Sangh* (Grand Slum Organization) led by Ishwar Singh Chouhan and P.C. Sharma – two of the most storied politicians in the history of Bhopal's slums. Committee documents provide a long list of efforts to improve Gandhi Nagar, stretching from the association's inception in the late 1970s to the mid-2000s:

The contractor responsible for the construction of the drainage system in Gandhi Nagar is engaging in illegal practices that will compromise the drainage system. He is not using the required quantities of cement and sand, and the way the drains are designed will lead to flooding. When we asked the contractor to correct this, he bullied us, including using foul language and threatening to stop the work. We request that this be investigated, and the drains be made correctly.[150]

This is to inform you that the poor residents of Gandhi Nagar have been deprived of essential ration items, such as sugar, for the last two months.[151]

On account of heavy rains in the past few days, several houses in Gandhi Nagar have been extensively damaged. The flooding has destroyed our meager things, such as food, utensils, and clothes. Although houses were flooded for three to four days no one from the government deemed it necessary to survey the damage. This cruel attitude adopted by the BJP government has saddened and angered residents. We request that you conduct a survey of the damage and provide compensation.[152]

---

[150] Letter from Gandhi Nagar residents to official, January 24, 2003.
[151] Letter from Gandhi Nagar president to Arif Aqueel, minister of food, May 23, 1999.
[152] Letter from residents of Gandhi Nagar to district collector, August 2006.

# Historical Narratives from Eight Squatter Settlements 147

There have been at least three presidents of the committee over the past three decades, each selected in a large community meeting: Varma, Soni, and Wasim – a Hindu, a Buddhist, and a Muslim, respectively.[153] Soni, the second president whose tenure lasted from 1984 to 1992, worked closely with Ishwar Singh Chouhan and P.C. Sharma during the mid-1980s, particularly at the height of Arjun Singh's *patta* distribution.[154] P.C. Sharma's involvement in Gandhi Nagar was further cemented during Bhopal's Hindu-Muslim riots in the early 1990s, when he visited the settlement to distribute food after nearly two weeks of an intense, citywide curfew. Soni's informal authority was reasserted twice during this period through community meetings. He was also made a local INC consultant (*salahakar*). Soni boasted during one interview that he helped organize a crowd of residents to visit Arjun Singh and demand a ticket for P.C. Sharma to fight in the assembly elections. With a look of disappointment, Soni told me that P.C. Sharma did not return the favor to Gandhi Nagar's residents after he received the ticket and won the election. P.C. Sharma provided only a few water taps and a hand pump.[155] Soni admitted that, despite his struggles to develop Gandhi Nagar over the course of a decade, he was not able to improve local conditions:

To get something you have to struggle hard, and I have done that, but there are very few things I have gotten after working so hard.[156]

By the time I started my fieldwork in Gandhi Nagar, the development committee had been defunct for several years. Judging by the poor conditions of the settlement, the committee was unsuccessful in its claim-making efforts.

---

[153] Interview with Gandhi Nagar resident, August 28, 2011.
[154] Interview with Soni, Gandhi Nagar, August 29, 2011. Soni is originally from Maharashtra and moved to Bhopal in the late 1960s to work as a laborer in a dam construction project. He is literate (with a fourth-grade education), separating him from many of his neighbors.
[155] Several committee documents show the effort that Gandhi Nagar's residents exerted to support P.C. Sharma, in the hopes that such support would yield improvements in the community: "The residents of Gandhi Nagar organized a meeting, where they invited ... P.C. Sharma. In the meeting, residents discussed their problems and presented demands ... the construction of drains, improved electricity supply, addressing issues related to hygiene and mosquitoes, and providing employment to poor individuals from the Dalit community. P.C. Sharma assured residents that he would try his best to do the needful. Residents applauded and thanked him" (Gandhi Nagar committee documents, March 26, 1995).
[156] Interview with Soni, Gandhi Nagar, August 29, 2011.

Gandhi Nagar has not developed strong nodes of local party leadership. Despite more than a decade of electoral support for the INC, the settlement has never had an INC worker. Only one BJP worker lived and operated within the settlement during my fieldwork – a young, twenty-five-year-old Bastor named Tejas, who served as the BJP's booth president. Tejas is literate but only educated to the third grade, preventing him, in his own words, from securing a steady job. Tejas explained to me that he joined politics because as a child he would see politicians come to Gandhi Nagar to distribute small amounts of money, bottles of liquor, and other cheap things in an effort to buy votes. He wanted people to work together and demand meaningful forms of development, not accept such gifts. Tejas also had a mentor, a local politician who won the 2004 municipal election in Tejas's ward. After his mentor won the election, Tejas's own star as a slum leader and BJP worker rose.

Tejas has built a small following in the settlement by helping his neighbors apply for ration cards, BPL cards, handicapped pensions, and widow pensions. He successfully engaged in these activities despite, in his opinion, older leaders in the settlement trying to "pull him down" out of jealously.[157] Tejas noted that he typically meets the ward councillor five or six times a month to discuss Gandhi Nagar's problems.[158] When BJP politicians come to campaign in the settlement, Tejas is in charge of encouraging residents to attend the event.

While residents participated in several rallies organized by the *Jhuggi Jhopri Maha Sangh* in the 1980s and 1990s, Gandhi Nagar does not have a history of protests to raise awareness about their problems.[159] Since his more recent rise to prominence in Gandhi Nagar, Tejas has not mobilized residents for protests either. In this respect, Gandhi Nagar is similar to Ram Nagar and Saraswati in Jaipur, which also lack histories of contentious mobilization.

Gandhi Nagar possesses the lowest level of public infrastructure and services of the four Bhopal settlements. Only a single alleyway is paved, connecting the main road to a small Hindu temple. The remainder of the settlement has either dirt pathways or makeshift cobblestone streets, both

---

[157] Interview with Tejas, Gandhi Nagar, July 10, 2012.
[158] Interview with Tejas, Gandhi Nagar, August 29, 2011.
[159] Interview with Soni, Gandhi Nagar, August 28, 2011.

of which flood during even light rains, turning the entire settlement into a cesspool. The settlement is without bathrooms and proper drainage, forcing residents to use an empty plot of land across the street. Most residents collect water from public stand posts. The density of streetlights in Gandhi Nagar is adequate – five streetlights have been placed in different areas of the settlement. The city occasionally removes trash on the main road, though daily sweeping is mostly left to residents.

During a 2017 trip to Bhopal, I discovered that the residents of Gandhi Nagar had recently been evicted and their homes demolished. Only the small Hindu temple remained, surrounded by a field of damaged trees, crushed bricks, and remnants of housing materials too bent and rusted to justify being taken away by the evicted squatters. A few loiterers standing beside the temple told me that residents had been shifted to a resettlement area on the outskirts of the city. They were unaware of what would be constructed on top of the rubble.

## Tulsi Nagar

Tulsi Nagar blankets a small hill in central Bhopal. To its south and east are post-eviction resettlement colonies, to its west is a state government building, and to its north is a major road. Tulsi Nagar's nearly 1,200 residents are Buddhist and Hindu. The presence of Buddhists is particularly conspicuous: at the slum's entrance is a Buddhist temple and a statue of Ambedkar dressed in his familiar navy blue suit and round, black spectacles.[160] Three quarters of Tulsi Nagar's residents are from Madhya Pradesh while the rest are from Rajasthan, Bihar, and Uttar Pradesh. Large caste groups in Tulsi Nagar include Chamars, Kolis, and Shafers, as well as forty Brahmin families.

Squatters came to Tulsi Nagar in the 1970s to work in a nearby stone-crushing site. The settlement at that time was a "jungle," totally absent of public infrastructure and services.[161] Residents regularly faced eviction drives by the state government.[162] To combat this, they eagerly welcomed new squatters to increase the number of shanties in the settlement, making eviction attempts more difficult.[163] The stone-crushing

---

[160] Buddhist residents collected money and had the temple and Ambedkar statue built in 1989. The former cost Rs 9,000 and the latter cost Rs 3,000 – significant sums of money at that time (interview with Gagbae, Bhopal, September 14, 2011).
[161] Interview with Tulsi Nagar resident, September 5, 2011.
[162] Interview with Tulsi Nagar resident, October 1, 2011.
[163] Interview with Manish, Tulsi Nagar, September 6, 2011.

machines closed in the early 1970s, but were then bought by the state government and reopened. They closed again in 1975 and subsequently became owned and operated by residents.[164] At the time of my fieldwork, the stone-crushing work had long since ceased and residents had turned to a wide range of other informal-sector jobs.

One of the stone crushers, Manish, was instrumental in settling laborers in Tulsi Nagar.[165] He was also active in organizing laborers at the stone-crushing site under the tutelage of Bhopal's famous Communist Party leader, Shokat Ali.[166] The Communist Party's decline in Bhopal at that time, though, meant that it was not a viable path of political upward mobility for Manish. His career in politics would instead take him into the ranks of the INC.[167]

Manish quickly ascended the INC's hierarchy and become the district president of the *Jhuggi Jhopri Prakosht* in the 1990s.[168] Interviews, newspaper articles, and photographs show that Manish was a firebrand organizer, fighting for better access to local public goods and services, security from eviction, and housing for the poor.[169] He was also not shy to flex his muscles. Among the most famous stories about Manish in Tulsi Nagar

---

[164] Two hundred residents ran the cooperative (interview with Manish, Tulsi Nagar, September 15, 2011).

[165] Interview with Kamal, Tulsi Nagar, October 2, 2011.

[166] Photographs I collected of Ali's organizational work in Bhopal show him with a large and loyal following of laborers. He was famous for carrying around an axe in public and frequently saying, "If someone kills me, just take off my turban, wrap my body in it and burn me on the spot."

[167] Interview with Manish, Tulsi Nagar, September 15, 2011.

[168] In one of his most proud political moments, Manish had the opportunity to speak to Sonia Gandhi in Delhi about his work for the INC: "President of Jhuggie-Jhopdi cell of State Congress [Manish] with office-bearers of the cell and district unit presidents apprised the All India Congress Committee president Ms. Sonia Gandhi, general secretary Oscar Fernandes, general secretary-in-charge of MP Tariq Anwar, convener Ghulam Nabi Azad, general secretary Miera Kumar, secretary SC Vats and secretary Ramesh Chennithala of the activities and achievements of the cell in Delhi" (undated newspaper clipping, though given its content I place it in the late 1990s or early 2000s). In another event celebrating Digvijaya Singh's plan to extend land titles to slum dwellers in Madhya Pradesh (like Arjun Singh), Manish had the opportunity to introduce Singh before a large crowd: "President of the slum cell, [Manish], welcomed the chief minister with garlands and by lighting a lamp" (undated newspaper clipping, though given its content I place it in the early 2000s).

[169] A newspaper clipping that Manish kept described one of these organizational efforts: "The Madhya Pradesh Congress Committee *Jhuggi Jhopdi Prakosht* will hold a *dharna* (protest) against anti-encroachment at the commissioner's office at 11am on Thursday. The *dharna* will be led by *Prakosht* president [Manish]" (undated, though given its content I place it in the year 2000).

recounts the time that he stood up to a local gang leader who was terrorizing residents. As the story goes, Manish menacingly approached the gang leader with a machete and demanded he leave and never return to Tulsi Nagar. The gang leader folded his hands in respect of Manish's bravery and thereafter left Tulsi Nagar.[170]

Manish's ascent in the INC put him into direct competition with Ishwar Singh Chouhan, who similarly sought to build a citywide reputation for spearheading political mobilization in slums. Chouhan's reputation and political influence in Bhopal, however, ultimately dwarfed Manish's. This put Manish at odds with a Tulsi Nagar-based block president of Chouhan's *Maha Sangh*, Kamal. Kamal told me in an interview that Chouhan had visited him in Tulsi Nagar several times to see and discuss local problems. Kamal admitted, though, that Chouhan's contributions to the development of Tulsi Nagar were modest.[171] Even two decades after the height of the factional competition between Manish and Kamal, the two are competitive with each other.

Looking to transform his sizable base of support within Tulsi Nagar into a formally elected position, Manish fought in three municipal elections. He had to do so twice as an independent candidate, however, because other INC workers beat him out for the party ticket due to intra-party politics with Chouhan's faction. Manish lost all three elections, dimming his once-bright political star.

A second organization in Tulsi Nagar, distinct from Manish's INC work, was the *Dalit Sudharan Samiti* (Dalit Improvement Committee). Dhruv, a resident of Tulsi Nagar, started the committee in 1983.[172] Its stated purpose was to unify and develop Tulsi Nagar, as well as to secure an English-medium school for local children. Residents at that time believed the committee would make their petitioning efforts more legitimate in the eyes of officials.[173] Committee members were selected in a community meeting for their "working ability."[174] After registering the committee, members called a meeting of residents to discuss the

---

[170] Interview with Manish, Tulsi Nagar, October 2, 2011.
[171] Interview with Kamal, Tulsi Nagar, October 2, 2011.
[172] Dhruv's son told me that his father was one of the original stone crushers in Tulsi Nagar before securing the job as a government clerk. He suggested his father's education and government job were attractive leadership qualities to residents (interview with Dhruv's son, Tulsi Nagar, September 15, 2011).
[173] Interview with a Tulsi Nagar resident, September 11, 2011.
[174] A participant estimated that 100 people attended the meeting (interview with Lila, Tulsi Nagar, September 14, 2011). That participant also noted that Dhruv was an attractive candidate because he was better educated and had a government job.

priorities of the committee.[175] Dhruv and his successor, Sharma, were both small-time government clerks, the former in the Education Department and the latter in the Forest Department.[176] After Dhruv passed away in 1996, and the following two presidents proved ineffective, 150 to 200 residents met to decide a new president.[177] Pavan, a construction worker, was selected. At the time of my fieldwork, the committee had been inactive for several years.

Pavan keeps several thick folders of his meeting notes and copies of petitions. Judging from our conversations and his impressive informal archive of materials, the development committee had been active for nearly two decades.[178] To provide an example of the committee's petitions:

> We residents of Tulsi Nagar request that individual toilets be provided in this area; also, there is no proper access to drinking water, and so the pipeline near the [government building] should be extended to provide tap water.[179]

Yet, despite sustained fights for roads, drainage, and the school, the committee experienced few victories.[180] On this point, a resident who moved to Tulsi Nagar in August 1989 – at the height of the committee's work – described the area at that time as undeveloped (*kacha*), with the houses made of stone, bamboo, and plastic tarps. The roads were unpaved and only two hand pumps had been provided to residents.[181] Development came to Tulsi Nagar after the committee had disbanded, when party worker networks took root within the settlement.

The Brahmins of Tulsi Nagar arrived in the 1970s, mostly from Rewa District in Madhya Pradesh. Soon after their arrival, they worked with Manish and the Buddhist residents to collect money to have a well built.[182] Relations between the two groups, however,

---

[175] Interview with Pavan and Lila, Tulsi Nagar, September 16, 2011.
[176] Sharma operated the phone and made photocopies (interview with Raju, Tulsi Nagar, September 22, 2011).
[177] Interview with Lila, Tulsi Nagar, September 14, 2011. There was one other president selected after Sharma (Sahari), but Pavan noted that president's tenure lasted only for a few months. Pavan said that Sahari was selected because he was a government employee and owned a car, facilitating the committee's claim-making efforts (interview with Pavan, Tulsi Nagar, September 16, 2011).
[178] Interview with Pavan and Lila, Tulsi Nagar, September 16, 2011.
[179] Tusli Nagar petition to the area MP, undated (given the content of the petition, I place it in the late 1990s).
[180] Interview with Lila, Tulsi Nagar, September 14, 2011.
[181] Interview with Gagbae, Bhopal, September 14, 2011.
[182] Interview with Sharma, Tulsi Nagar, October 1, 2011.

have periodically soured. In the late 1990s, for example, a Buddhist resident jumped in the drinking well to bathe. A fight between 150 Brahmins and Buddhists erupted, with the Buddhists claiming that the Brahmins only took offense because of caste discrimination.[183] Two of Tulsi Nagar's Buddhist leaders, moreover, asserted that they were not able to secure a community school because of caste discrimination – they believed that the Brahmins did not want "lower"-caste children to become educated and so they did not help fight for the school.[184] Some Brahmin residents retorted that the Dalit association excluded them from participating in community governance.[185] Despite these episodic flares of conflict, Hindus and Buddhists in Tulsi Nagar generally coexist peacefully and attend each other's social events. For instance, on Ambedkar Day, both groups collect funds for a large community festival.[186]

For the past two decades, a handful of party workers in Tulsi Nagar have served as focal points of local problem-solving. Manish's daughter was, at the time of my fieldwork, the ward *maha mantri* (minister) for the Youth Congress. Two female BJP workers also live in Tulsi Nagar. One of them, Lila, is in her mid-fifties, has a second-grade education, and, like most of her neighbors, is Buddhist. Lila has a position as the block *maha mantri* for the BJP's slum cell.[187] She has helped residents acquire ration cards, drains, and paved roads, and attributes these successes to her connections with BJP politicians. The other BJP worker, Chhavi, is a district-level member of the BJP's women's wing and performs the same tasks as Lila.[188]

Tulsi Nagar has a significantly higher level of infrastructural development and access to public services than pre-eviction Gandhi Nagar. All of the settlement's roads are paved and most have above-ground drainage. Cobblestone roads were first provided in the mid-1990s and paved roads were provided in 2007 and 2008.[189] Residents report irregular trash removal. There are fifteen to twenty community taps in the settlement. Tulsi Nagar is without underground sewers, though some of the houses have their own latrine pits. Streetlights line the roads, but most are broken or erratically flicker at night.

[183] Interview with Brahmin resident, Tulsi Nagar, September 22, 2011; interview with Buddhist resident, Tulsi Nagar, September 22, 2011.
[184] Interview with Pavan and Lila, Tulsi Nagar, September 16, 2011.
[185] Interview with Chotae Lal, Tulsi Nagar, September 19, 2011.
[186] Interview with a group of Brahmin residents, Tulsi Nagar, September 16, 2011.
[187] Interview with Lila, Tulsi Nagar, September 14, 2011.
[188] Interview with Chhavi, Tulsi Nagar, September 16, 2011.
[189] Interview with Manish, Tulsi Nagar, October 11, 2011.

## Durga Nagar

Squatters from what is now the state of Chhattisgarh settled Durga Nagar in the mid-1970s.[190] Currently, 65 percent of the settlement's 1,200 residents are from Chhattisgarh, with the remainder hailing from Bihar, Madhya Pradesh, and Uttar Pradesh. Durga Nagar is also diverse in terms of caste: one can find residents from the Sahu, Raekwar, Gupta, Raut, Keer, Manjhi, Kewath, and Kashyap castes, among others. Durga Nagar is predominantly Hindu, though there are a handful of Muslim families as well. Religious life for Hindu residents revolves around a local Durga temple. A placard on the temple declares that Babu Lal Gaur, one of Bhopal's most famous BJP politicians and former chief minister of Madhya Pradesh, inaugurated the temple on July 16, 1979. Durga Nagar's population expanded after the temple was constructed.[191]

City roads and middle-class neighborhoods encase all sides of Durga Nagar. In the mid-1980s, Durga Nagar's residents also found themselves in close proximity to another squatter settlement: after Arjun Singh's announcement that slum settlements in Madhya Pradesh would be considered for temporary land titles, a group of squatters hurriedly set up a cluster of shanties across the street and claimed to have long been part of Durga Nagar in an attempt to benefit from the land title distribution. The squatters even went as far as to steal Durga Nagar's signboard and erect it on their side of the street. The Bhopal Development Authority evicted these new squatters in the late 1980s.[192]

In 1982, the fifty to sixty families living in Durga Nagar created a neighborhood association called the *Chhattisgarh Mazdoor Sangh* (Chhattisgarh Laborer Association).[193] The *Sangh*'s aims were to unite residents, fight for better wages from labor contractors, demand public services, and fight eviction.[194] Joshi, the current president, told me that the initial spark for organizing the committee was an abusive local contractor for whom many residents worked. The first committee president, Rama, described how the committee struggled for water, electricity, drainage,

---

[190] One of the original squatters, who came to Durga Nagar in 1978, said that there were only ten shanties when he arrived (interview with Charan Lal, Durga Nagar, October 10, 2011).
[191] Interview with Durga Nagar resident, November 20, 2011.
[192] Interview with Joshi, Durga Nagar, September 30, 2011.
[193] Focus group with Durga Nagar residents, November 19, 2011.
[194] Interview with Joshi, Durga Nagar, August 27, 2011; focus group with Durga Nagar residents, November 19, 2011.

## Historical Narratives from Eight Squatter Settlements 155

and sanitation.[195] They met almost weekly to deal with rampant problems. At that time, Durga Nagar was a cluster of shanties in a small field, void of public infrastructure and services.[196] Rama was able to secure a few water taps, but they were soon ripped out of the ground after the state government discovered that the water was contaminated.

The *Sangh* crafted rules of conduct for committee members, including how they should be compensated for their committee work. For example, during settlement-wide meetings, a committee member is sent to gather residents; that person is paid Rs 20 for carrying out the task.[197] Rules were also created for ordinary residents. If a family leaves Durga Nagar, they are asked to pay the committee Rs 151, which will be used for the committee's operating costs. The *Sangh* has also fined people for fighting, and periodically collects Rs 30 from households for electricity and Rs 50 for water. These informal user fees are then passed along to the public utility.

The president of the *Sangh* has changed several times. The first president's tenure was short, lasting just a few years. Biswa, the second president, moved from Chhattisgarh in the mid-1970s to work as a construction laborer. He was selected by a group of residents in the mid-1980s to be president, though his tenure, much like that of his predecessor, was brief. Biswa admitted that despite his efforts to improve Durga Nagar, the present local public goods and services in the settlement came long after his term as president.[198]

Following these leadership changes and one other short-lived presidency, Joshi, a Brahmin resident, took the helm. Joshi works as a small-time clerk in a state government office. This position may not command much respect among his work colleagues, but in Durga Nagar it represents a valuable connection to the state. Residents also noted Joshi's relatively higher education as a reason why he makes for a good leader.[199] His position as the committee president was reasserted on several occasions during the 1990s and 2000s. Once, Shelender Pradhan, the area MLA in the mid-1990s, was invited to reinvigorate the *Sangh*.[200] Pradhan said, "If I can speak, I think [Joshi] will be a good

---

[195] Interview with Rama, Durga Nagar, November 19, 2011.
[196] Focus group with Durga Nagar residents, November 19, 2011.
[197] Interview with Durga Nagar resident, September 3, 2011.
[198] Interview with Biswa, Durga Nagar, October 1, 2011; focus group with Durga Nagar residents, November 19, 2011.
[199] Interview with a resident of Durga Nagar, September 10, 2011.
[200] Interview with Joshi, Durga Nagar, September 20, 2011.

president. What do you all think? You should choose someone who will work for you."[201] After declaring their continued support for Joshi, residents selected other committee members. The committee changed again in 1996 because Joshi grew frustrated with inactive members. He was elected yet again as Durga Nagar's president in the summer of 2006 and was still in the position during the summer of 2016.[202]

Slum leadership in Durga Nagar during the 1980s and early 1990s leaned heavily toward the INC and the *Jhuggi Jhopri Maha Sangh*.[203] Even Joshi, who would later become a staunch BJP supporter,[204] initially had strong ties with Ishwar Singh Chouhan and P.C. Sharma. The incentives to foster close connections with the *Maha Sangh* were powerful: it was aligned with Arjun Singh's faction of the INC. Ishwar Singh Chouhan and P.C. Sharma would draw on Durga Nagar's residents for rallies. In return, Durga Nagar's slum leaders would visit the two politicians for help in claiming local public goods and services.[205] These efforts, however, yielded little more than electricity connections.

Joshi has stored three decades of community meeting notes, petitions for public services, and correspondence with politicians and officials, demonstrating the considerable effort that he and the committee have exerted to improve the settlement. To provide just a few examples:

We have been residing in Durga Nagar since 1977–78. In spite of written assurances provided by the former chief minister, our problems have not been resolved. We face a lack of land titles, bathrooms, ration cards, relief from the Gas Fund, and electricity connections. We request that the aforementioned issues be addressed.[206]

The water pump located in Durga Nagar has been broken for the last twenty days. Although we lodged a complaint with the required department ... nothing has been done to fix it. The residents of Durga Nagar have had to scavenge for water. We request that you address this issue.[207]

---

[201] Interview with Joshi, Durga Nagar, September 20, 2011; Durga Nagar committee materials, September 17, 1993.
[202] Durga Nagar committee documents, August 27, 2006.
[203] Focus group with Durga Nagar residents, November 19, 2011; interview with Joshi, Durga Nagar, September 20, 2011.
[204] Joshi has not accepted an organizational position within the BJP because he sees it as a conflict of interest with his government job. Nevertheless, Joshi was an outspoken BJP activist during my fieldwork and engaged in many of the same electoral activities as a party worker. Residents, moreover, see Joshi as a BJP worker, despite his lack of a position.
[205] Interview with Charan Lal, Durga Nagar, October 10, 2011.
[206] Durga Nagar petition to the area MLA, December 27, 1985.
[207] Durga Nagar petition to the Bhopal Municipal Corporation, August 9, 1989.

## Historical Narratives from Eight Squatter Settlements 157

This is to inform you that the drain flowing from the government quarters and the main drainage pipe in the area are choked with debris. They are overflowing and bringing dirty water into our settlement. This has led to a steep increase in the number of mosquitoes and diseases here. It is our urgent request that you clean the sewers and drains so that residents can be healthy.[208]

The residents of our slum have been using the bathrooms at the [government building]. Last evening, however, they barricaded the office grounds with barbed wire, depriving us of the only sanitary space available. Residents have no option now but to use the roadside. This is problematic and takes away our dignity, especially for our women. We urgently request you make the space available again or construct community bathrooms.[209]

I asked Joshi to describe his strategy for claiming public services. Joshi replied that, if the problem concerns the Bhopal Municipal Corporation (BMC), he first goes with a group of residents to the ward councillor. If the ward councillor is unhelpful, he goes up one rung to the area MLA. If that fails, he goes directly to the concerned government department to submit petitions, hoping for a response despite a lack of political intervention.[210]

In addition to making claims for public services, Joshi engages in a wide range of other activities to improve the lives of residents. He has fought off two major eviction attempts – the first in 1987, when the state government wanted to build a public school on the land, and the second time in 1994, when the state government wanted to build a small healthcare center. Joshi is heavily engaged in the social life of Durga Nagar, overseeing events in the local temple and community center. He also helps to maintain social order. Joshi estimated having resolved nineteen fights among residents during his time as president.[211] Further, Joshi led an effort to collect money (Rs 230 per household) to install a drainage pipe.[212] He additionally organizes collections for sick neighbors and pregnant women needing to travel to the hospital.

Dhari, a high-school-educated BJP booth president, lives just down the street from Joshi.[213] Residents describe Dhari's activities as mostly

---

[208] Durga Nagar petition to health official at the Bhopal Municipal Corporation, 1994.
[209] Durga Nagar petition to state official, February 5, 1991.
[210] Interview with Joshi, Durga Nagar, September 30, 2011.
[211] Interview with Joshi, Durga Nagar, August 3, 2011.
[212] Interview with Joshi, Durga Nagar, August 27, 2011; interview with Durga Nagar resident, November 19, 2011.
[213] Interview with Dhari, Durga Nagar, October 7, 2011.

centered on organizing local turnout for BJP rallies. Buses are sent to Durga Nagar and residents who come along are given food. About 100 to 200 people from the settlement usually participate.[214] Dhari confirmed these accounts, stating his main responsibilities are to canvass for the BJP and encourage turnout. Between 2008 and 2012, he estimated having gathered residents for six or seven BJP rallies.

Durga Nagar has attracted higher levels of infrastructural development and access to public services than Gandhi Nagar. Most of the roads are either paved or laid with cemented cobblestones. In 1994, the MLA and the ward councillor provided the first stone road in the settlement.[215] That same ward councillor provided metered electricity connections. Uma Shankar Gupta paved most of the roads in 2005.[216] A water tank was placed in front of Durga Nagar in the late 2000s – prominently tagged by the ward councillor – and eleven community taps are strewn throughout the settlement. Durga Nagar also has a covered community center, provided by Uma Shankar Gupta. The Bhopal Municipal Corporation occasionally removes trash placed at the entrance of the settlement. Otherwise, residents must clean in front of their own homes. Two streetlights keep small sections of Durga Nagar lit at night.[217]

## Rudra

Rudra is located along a winding creek in central Bhopal.[218] Over the last four decades, the settlement has become a dense mass of shanties and tangled alleyways – the product of hundreds of squatters constructing their homes in a haphazard fashion. Rudra is now home to roughly 5,000 people. Most residents work in the informal sector – auto-rickshaw drivers, welders, painters, hawkers, and construction workers. The caste makeup of Rudra is highly diverse. With Hindus, Muslims, and Buddhists and migrants from Chhattisgarh, Madhya Pradesh, Maharashtra, and Uttar Pradesh, Rudra is also impressively heterogeneous in terms of religion and region of origin.

---

[214] Interview with Durga Nagar resident, September 10, 2011.
[215] Field notes, Durga Nagar, August 27, 2011; interview with Durga Nagar resident, November 20, 2011.
[216] Field notes, Durga Nagar, August 27, 2011.
[217] In June 2011, Joshi secured replacement bulbs through the ward councillor.
[218] Rudra's historical narrative was previously published in my article "Neighborhood Associations and the Urban Poor: India's Slum Development Committees." *World Development* 96 (2017): 119–35. I include it here with permission from Elsevier.

# Historical Narratives from Eight Squatter Settlements 159

Rudra was a barren field when squatters first settled the land in the 1970s.[219] The first wave of squatters established clusters of shanties along the creek. Older residents describe the organization of Rudra then as spatially fragmented, with each cluster producing nascent leadership that dealt with disputes, police aggression, and water collection.[220] The settlement also faced a barrage of eviction threats, pushing a handful of residents into slum leadership.[221] These early slum leaders were not party workers and lacked strong political connections.[222]

Around 1980, as the population of Rudra began to steadily increase and eviction threats mounted, a group of residents met to organize a development committee. A Brahmin resident, Shukla, became president without competition. Shukla estimated that 500 to 600 people were involved in the meeting and explained that he commanded authority because people saw him as honest, hardworking, and knowledgeable about government programs. Further, he was a government clerk, providing an important degree of connectivity to the state, and had built goodwill by distributing ayurvedic medicine.[223] An older resident of Rudra noted, "We people took a step and put all of our responsibility in [Shukla's] hands ... He was an important asset for us because he was working in [a government building], and so if there was information or news about the slum, he would be the first to know and tell us."[224]

Shukla and the committee members successfully registered the committee. Letterhead stationery, stamps, and accounting books were purchased and members gathered to discuss their plans of action. An emblem was created for the letterhead stationery – three equally sized shanties with a mosque and Hindu temple immediately behind them, signaling interfaith unity. The first entry in the minutes of the committee describes the founding moment:

---

[219] A small group of construction workers and squatters inhabited the land in the 1960s but were removed for housing construction (Risbud 1988). The population of squatters in Rudra rebounded and expanded in the 1970s.
[220] Interviews with residents of Rudra, August 28 and September 1, 2011.
[221] Risbud 1988, p. 42.
[222] Interview with Samir, Rudra, August 28, 2011. Samir noted that his father made the initial suggestion to unite the small leaders under a common organization of 25 to 30 people but others disputed this narrative. His father narrated the same story to me (interview with Rahman, Rudra, September 1, 2011).
[223] Interviews with Shukla, Bhopal, August 29 and September 3, 2011.
[224] Interview with a resident of Rudra, September 4, 2011.

160                      *Demanding Development*

Today, on October 14, 1980, *Rudra Kalyan Vikas Sangh* held a meeting ... the *Sangh* was made and the naming of the organization was completed. As the founder, [Shukla] has been given responsibility including registering the organization.[225]

The archival documents I collected from the development committee show an organized, active, and ethnically diverse body. Members represented a wide array of caste and religious groups.[226] The committee took up a range of issues facing the settlement, from encouraging peaceful relations among residents to demanding public goods and services. A selection of letters exemplifies the committee's activities:

Today ... an *Eid* celebration was arranged in which the president of Rudra and the brothers of other areas met with love and courtesy ... The program started with Hindu and Muslim brothers hugging each other and congratulating each other for *Eid*.[227]

Under the guidance of the president, a committee meeting started in which decisions were unanimously taken. The chief minister will be informed about our problems ... like water, electricity, land titles, and shanties that have not yet been surveyed ... Roads and drainage should be provided to all of Rudra.[228]

A unanimous decision was taken that a formal complaint will be made to the electricity department that Rudra's lights do not work ... The full provision of lights should be made and the pending drainage work should be completed.[229]

Periodic committee elections were held throughout the 1980s.[230] Shukla's authority, for example, was reaffirmed during a large community meeting in 1983, in response to the threat of eviction.[231] However, the elections were mostly to reassert Shukla's leadership. Shukla noted that the committee members did not change during this period.

Another committee was created in Rudra in the early 1980s. Like Shukla, the president of this second committee, Rana, worked at the time as a clerk in a government office. Similar to Shukla, Rana claimed to have organized the committee to push back against eviction and demand development.[232] Rana described how a large meeting was held in his section of Rudra in the early 1980s. Rana, a member of a marginalized caste, was selected as the president, and he asked residents

[225] Shukla committee documents, October 14, 1980.
[226] Interview with Shukla, Bhopal, September 3, 2011.
[227] Shukla committee documents, February 8, 1981.
[228] Shukla committee documents, April 20, 1988.
[229] Shukla committee meeting notes, November 5, 1988.
[230] Interview with Shukla, Bhopal, August 29, 2011.
[231] Interview with a Rudra resident, September 2, 2011.
[232] Interview with Rana, Rudra, November 16, 2011.

interested in joining the committee to step forward. The crowd then decided who would best fit each position.[233]

Rana stressed in several interviews that his committee, the *Rudra Shetriya Jhuggi Jhopri Samiti* (Rudra Area Slum Committee), began free from party ties and persisted in that state for four years. It was not until the efforts of his committee made their way into the local news that the INC, and Ishwar Singh Chouhan and P.C. Sharma in particular, approached the committee to establish an alliance. "They said OK, you want development and you have a committee, why don't you join our *Maha Sangh*. We will have more people power then."[234]

Rana, like Shukla, has archived an impressive amount of paperwork – several hundred letters, meeting notes, photographs, and newspaper clippings – showing the activities of the committee. The committee worked to improve the same issues as Shukla's committee:

Respected [area politicians] ... please come to our [area] and flow the river of development ... help the poor with roads, water, electricity, and toilets ...[235]

Because of the dark, many people ... fall down in the drain. I even fell in the drain when I was putting up a poster for the state elections. Accidents can happen anytime. Therefore, place orders to install 10 or 12 streetlights.[236]

We have been requesting a small office for many years. This way poor people, minorities, and Scheduled Castes and Scheduled Tribes can visit the office and seek your [the MLA] assistance. You should visit the office every week or at least every 15 days. Through this you can hear the poor and kindly help.[237]

Shukla and Rana competed intensely with one another for prominence. They were both mutually dismissive of the other's achievements and also dismissive of the three other development committees that were mentioned during my interviews in Rudra.[238] For at least two of these

---

[233] Interview with Rana, Rudra, September 23, 2011. Subsequent committees were chosen through elections: "The [Rudra] committee elections will be held on April 17, 1981. This is the first time that office-bearers of the committee will be decided through elections; in the past, office bearers have been selected through consensus among committee leaders" (Rana newspaper clipping, March 31, 1981).
[234] Interview with Rana, Rudra, November 16, 2011.
[235] Rana committee documents, November 5, 1988.
[236] Rana committee documents, undated.
[237] Rana committee documents, September 17, 2002.
[238] In a study conducted in the mid-1980s (Risbud 1988, p. 44), this multifocal organizational environment was described as follows: "Four organizations are operative in the settlement with clearly demarcated territories. All the settlement's leaders belong to the ruling party, the Congress-I, and have contacts with the MLA and councillor. Therefore

committees, their dismissiveness appears justified – I was only able to uncover documents for one of those three other committees. One of the committees was called the *Jhuggi Jhopri Ekta Samiti*, which had ties to a federation created by Moti Lal Vora, a factional leader in Madhya Pradesh's Congress Party.[239] The other committees enjoyed only a flash of activity, failing to take root among a larger group of residents. Even for Shukla and Rana's more active and prominent development committees, resident satisfaction in the 1980s appeared to be mixed, with some complaints of corruption and ineffectiveness in improving local conditions.[240]

The development committees in Rudra are no longer active. Shukla left Rudra in the mid-1990s. In addition to his deteriorating health, the BJP's rise to power in Bhopal contributed to the erosion of Rana's committee. In 2012, the INC had a handful of workers in Rudra (eight party workers), outsized by a larger and more active BJP network (sixteen party workers). Party worker networks have spread into Rudra and absorbed local leaders into their organizational hierarchies. These networks initially coexisted and overlapped with the committees. The party worker networks, though, have outlasted and spread beyond the committees.

Jhatav, a BJP worker in Rudra, noted that slum leaders in the settlement started to drift toward party politics in the mid-1980s and competition among them for public support intensified thereafter.[241] The BJP network in Rudra especially grew in strength in the 1990s. Jhatav remarked that the BJP workers are competitive with each other for a following, but when it comes to the electoral interests of the party, they work together.[242] The ward councillor relies on these BJP workers to be his eyes and ears in the settlement. He noted that residents come to him with household problems, but the BJP workers in Rudra visit him to discuss larger problems regarding infrastructure and public services.[243]

At the very top of the BJP network in Rudra is Shaarad, who was born in the settlement and is now forty-five-years old. His parents moved from Gwalior and were among the first in Rudra to join the BJP. They encouraged Shaarad to join the *Rashtriya Swayamsevak Sangh* (RSS), a Hindu nationalist organization, contributing to his affinity for the BJP.[244]

there are no conflicts among them ... [The] organizations have been corresponding with various officials and leaders and have sent 181 letters so far to various officials."
[239] Interview with Rahman, Rudra, October 20, 2011.   [240] Risbud 1988, p. 46.
[241] Interview with Jhatav, Rudra, September 1, 2011.
[242] Interview with Jhatav, Rudra, September 1, 2011.
[243] Interview with Rudra ward councillor, August 28, 2011.
[244] On the RSS, see Jaffrelot 1998.

Shaarad is now the vice president of the BJP's slum cell in Bhopal. Armed with a law degree, he is among the most educated residents in Rudra, making him a particularly effective problem-solver.

Jhatav, positioned just below Shaarad in the Rudra BJP hierarchy, moved to the settlement in the mid-1970s to be close to New Market, where his family could sell vegetables. Although he never received a formal education, he moved up through the party organization because of his leadership abilities. He started in the 1990s as the *mandal* (block-level) secretary for the BJP's youth wing. He then became the *mandal* president, followed by the district vice president of the BJP's wing for Scheduled Castes.

Jayesh is another prominent BJP worker in Rudra with whom I spent considerable time. Jayesh's father moved to Bhopal from Uttar Pradesh, looking to escape intense discrimination toward Dalits in their village of origin. His father got a job as a sanitation worker in the city. Jayesh studied to the first grade and at the age of sixteen started informal leadership activities in Rudra. He has helped residents start saving groups and teaches people how to cut hair – his own vocation. He is also highly active in a settlement temple for Dalits.[245]

Why are there relatively fewer INC workers in Rudra? Samir, an INC worker, explained that this is because of the larger rise of the BJP in city and state politics over the past few decades. He argued that before the mid-1990s Rudra was an INC stronghold.[246] Exemplifying the shift in popularity from the INC to the BJP, his father was a popular INC leader within Rudra in the 1980s but quickly fell from prominence in the 1990s during the rise of the BJP. Samir's simple interpretation of this political decline was that, "naturally, people do not follow others who are not powerful."[247]

A related story is the rise and fall of Sachin, who was a major INC worker in Rudra in the 1980s. Sachin moved to Rudra in the early 1970s and became active in Shukla's development committee. He was a butler for Arjun Singh, fetching the chief minister tea, water, and food.[248] Through this rare connection, his stock rose considerably in Rudra. Residents, however, noted that Sachin grew physically and verbally aggressive. Because of this behavior, he lost his following in Rudra and was removed from his local caste association and the INC. Watching the

---

[245] Interview with Jayesh, Rudra, September 3, 2011.
[246] Interview with Samir, Rudra, August 28, 2011.
[247] Interview with Rahman, Rudra, September 1, 2011.
[248] Interview with Sachin, Rudra, September 2, 2011.

bullying behavior of Sachin pushed many of the younger residents in Rudra toward the BJP.[249]

Photographs of Rudra in the late 1970s and early 1980s suggest that it had little beyond a handful of water taps and electricity poles. Risbud's 1988 study on Bhopal's slums described Rudra as a "large settlement" and one "without improvement."[250] Shaarad claimed that stone roads and a few electricity connections were extended in 1985 but it was not until Shelender Pradhan came to power as the area MLA in the early 1990s that paved roads came to Rudra.[251] Rahman, the retired INC leader, and his son Samir said the same,[252] though Jayesh argued that the roads were dirt until 1994, at which time they secured paved roads and drains from the MLA's development funds.[253] These differences are likely a result of intra-settlement variation in when infrastructure and public services were provided.

Rudra's level of infrastructural development and access to public services is high. Nearly 100 percent of the roads are paved or laid with cemented cobblestone. Streetlights illuminate many of the alleyways at night and networks of water pipes wind through the settlement. A majority of surveyed residents in Rudra (65 percent) report that the municipality removes trash and 35 percent report having sewer connections. A large community center was constructed in 2014, funded by the MLA's area development fund.

## 5.3 COMPARATIVE OBSERVATIONS

Several comparative observations flow from the eight case studies. First, residents deploy an impressive range of group-based strategies to improve their settlements. Some of these efforts fall squarely in the category of internal self-provision. Residents collected money and pulled their own labor to dig drains, clean alleyways, fix electrical wiring, replace water

---

[249] Interview with Jayesh, Rudra, October 20, 2011.
[250] Risbud 1988, p. 41. Risbud (1988, p. 43) also noted the presence of ten paved roads, though it is not clear what *percentage* of the settlement had paved roads at that time.
[251] Interview with Shaarad, Rudra, August 28, 2011.
[252] Interview with Rahman and Samir, Rudra, September 1 and 5, 2011. Rahman also noted that the Gas Tragedy Relief Fund helped pay for some of this development. The ward councillor in 2011 estimated that the money allocated to Rudra from the Relief Fund was Rs 85 *lakh*, though it is unclear how much of that made its way into the settlement (interview with Rudra's ward councillor, September 4, 2011).
[253] Interview with Jayesh, Rudra, September 3, 2011. Jayesh's father said that *farshi* (cobblestone) roads and drains were extended in the second half of the 1980s but the rest of Rudra's infrastructure subsequently came through funds provided by the Bhopal Municipal Corporation and area MLAs (interview with Jayesh's father, Rudra, September 4, 2011).

taps, fill potholes, and construct temples and mosques. Yet many of the most essential local public goods and services – sewers, paved roads, storm drains, streetlights, and regular trash collection – require considerable resources and technical capacity. As such, residents turned to the state to demand them. The historical residue of this active claim-making is evidenced by the stacks of written petitions that slum leaders produce and preserve, many of which are cited above.

In addition to acts of internal self-provision and group claim-making, residents of Ganpati, Pahari, and Rudra periodically engaged in thunderous protests to demand public goods and services. Among the eight settlements, these three settlements are those with the largest populations as well as dense networks of party workers who can rapidly organize residents for protests. Without these population numbers and organizational capacity, settlements like Ram Nagar, Gandhi Nagar, and Saraswati lacked such histories of protests.

Each narrative depicted the instrumental role of slum leaders in local problem-solving. These informal actors performed an impressive range of activities for residents. They foremost made claims on the state for local public goods and services. These efforts typically took the form of group-based claim-making, with slum leaders writing petitions, collecting signatures, and organizing residents to travel to government offices to voice grievances and submit petitions. Slum leaders also organized festivals, resolved disputes, enforced informal property rights, and helped residents with more idiosyncratic, household-specific problems.

Residents of the case study settlements selected their slum leaders in a variety of ways. In Saraswati, this took place through an informal election with makeshift ballots. In other settlements, residents held large meetings to discuss who was best fit to lead, illustrated in the cases of Durga Nagar, Pahari, Gandhi Nagar, and Rudra. Residents raised their hands as an expression of support, like in Pahari, or sat behind their preferred leader, like in Gandhi Nagar. Other slum leaders built a following more iteratively and quietly by attracting residents with their reputations for getting things done, represented by slum leaders like Rajesh, Niraj, and Shaarad in Ram Nagar, Ganpati, and Rudra, respectively. Regardless of the process of selection, residents were pivotal in constructing the grassroots nodes of political brokerage in their settlements. Parties did not impose slum leaders on settlements from above. Instead, slum leaders in the case study settlements are everyday residents who built followings through their own entrepreneurial sweat.

In each of the eight settlements, slum leaders competed with one another for a following. Their public followings were tied to their ability to solve problems. Incompetence, thuggish behavior, or the emergence of a more effective slum leader was associated with a decline in popularity. Indeed, the narratives provide examples of slum leaders quickly losing their followings. In Saraswati, this unfolded in an informal election, where one slum leader, Prem, lost in large part because of his reputation for *dadagiri* (dominating behavior) and because his opponent, Jagdish, was better educated and seen to be more committed to improving local conditions. In Rudra, a violent party worker was ostracized by residents and stripped of his position in the INC. In Pahari, Abdul's status as slum leader was diminished due to accusations of corruption.

The presence of party workers with different partisan affiliations generated a distinct form of political competition in Pahari, Ganpati, Tulsi Nagar, and Rudra. Assessing the direction of partisan competition's impact on public service delivery, however, is difficult because it involves several mechanisms that run counter to one another. The case studies produced examples of partisan competition among party workers undermining efforts to improve local conditions. In Pahari, heated interparty competition led to stone throwing. In Ganpati, competing party networks sought to deflate the mobilization efforts of the other, even when those efforts were initiated to improve local conditions. Interviews with political elites, cited in Chapter 3, also suggest that politicians prefer to target partisan strongholds that are saturated with co-partisan workers. These qualitative findings suggest that the presence of party workers with different partisan affiliations might be harmful for efforts to secure public services.

At the same time, the case studies produced examples of opposition party workers sparking protests and holding incumbent politicians accountable in the name of local development. The presence of party workers from different parties also ensures that residents have political linkages regardless of the party in power at any given level of government. This was illustrated in the case of Saraswati, where the appointment of the local shopkeeper to the position of INC booth president allowed residents to press the INC ward councillor to provide a paved road and drains, a request that would have proved more difficult for Jagdish, a BJP supporter. Partisan competition among party workers, therefore, generates reasons to believe it can be both beneficial and harmful to public service provision. I examine this relationship quantitatively in the following chapter.

## Historical Narratives from Eight Squatter Settlements 167

All of the case study settlements formed one or more development committees (*vikas samitiyaan*). These associations overlapped in their membership with party worker networks but were distinct organizational templates for collective action and petitioning. As I discuss in detail elsewhere, such neighborhood associations are common in the slums of Jaipur and Bhopal.[254] Because all eight settlements formed development committees, the formation and use of these associations alone cannot explain divergences in public service provision. Nevertheless, these associational activities are important, as they challenge depictions of these spaces as too riddled with clientelistic politics for such associational life.[255]

While all eight settlements produced informal slum leadership, the density and partisan balance of their party workers varied tremendously. Ganpati, Pahari, and Rudra Nagar are awash with party workers. For every 200 households in these settlements, there are 6.2, 2.5, and 5.0 party workers (147, 12, and 24 total party workers), respectively. Residents in these settlements have multiple party workers in their immediate area, jostling with one another for their support. In Ram Nagar, Gandhi Nagar, and Saraswati, party workers are sparse, with just a single party worker in each settlement. Durga Nagar and Tulsi Nagar exhibit more middling levels of party worker density. As shown in the previous chapter, many slum settlements are missing party workers altogether, meaning that residents are without slum leaders who can exploit defined party connections to advance local development.

Settlements with dense networks of party workers – Ganpati, Pahari, and Rudra – have the highest levels of infrastructural development and access to public services.[256] These settlements have the party machinery to forcefully make claims and organize protests. Competition among party workers is especially intense in these settlements given the many spoils that accompany being a popular party worker in a large settlement. Conversely, settlements like Ram Nagar, Gandhi Nagar, and Saraswati have weak party connectivity manifest in a single party worker. These

---

[254] For an extensive discussion on India's slum development committees, see Auerbach 2017. See Wade 1988 for a seminal study on informal committees and local development in rural India.
[255] Harriss 2007.
[256] An exception is Durga Nagar, which has a higher community development score than its level of party worker density would suggest. This lower measure of party worker density is partially due to Joshi's hesitance to take on a BJP position because of his government job.

settlements do not have histories of protests, and their informal leaders possess little in the way of strong party ties. They also represent the most undeveloped of the eight settlements. There are, as Tables 5.1 and 5.2 show, other moving variables across the eight settlements. Population in particular appears to be correlated with outcomes in public service provision. The regressions in the following chapter will control for these and other theoretically important covariates and find substantial evidence of a positive relationship between party worker density and local development.

Finally, the case studies provide insights into historical sequencing in the physical formation, political organization, and development of squatter settlements – insights that reduce concerns of reverse causality and selection bias. Specifically, the eight case studies show the common origins of squatter settlements in a state of total underdevelopment, ameliorating concerns that the first waves of squatters self-selected into areas with particular levels of public service provision. They demonstrate that slum leaders emerge from within the ranks of ordinary residents and do not rove among settlements to either offer their services in deprived areas or enjoy better access to public services in more developed settlements. The narratives show that local public goods and services were overwhelmingly extended, if at all, in the mid-1990s onward, after the demographic makeup of settlements had already been largely established and patterns of slum leadership had taken root. I elaborate on these key aspects of historical sequencing in the political organization and development of squatter settlements in the following two chapters.

# 6

# Party Workers and Public Goods Provision

## Evidence from 111 Settlements

In the preceding chapters, I have argued and demonstrated qualitatively that slum settlements with dense networks of party workers are well positioned to demand and secure development from the state. In such settlements, party workers must intensely compete with one another for a following, pushing them to signal efficacy in problem-solving or risk losing their personal base of public support. Dense networks of party workers further provide settlements with political connectivity and an organizational capacity to mobilize for protest. I also argued that the presence of party workers from different parties has countervailing effects on public service provision. On the one hand, it can intensify competition and push party workers to be more active claim-makers. It additionally offers residents diverse partisan linkages – an asset in India's fluid electoral landscape. On the other hand, it can create perverse incentives for rival party worker networks to undercut each other's mobilization efforts – even to the detriment of local development – and signal to political elites that rival party workers are busy undermining their reputation and attempting to take credit for development projects, reducing incentives for political elites to provide local public goods.

This chapter quantitatively examines the book's theoretical framework alongside several alternative explanations. Drawing on data from 111 squatter settlements in Bhopal and Jaipur, it conducts a series of correlative analyses to assess whether the patterns of political organization and development uncovered in the eight case study settlements are reflected in a larger, representative sample of squatter settlements in the two cities. Read alongside my qualitative findings, the statistical results below provide compelling evidence that denser networks of party workers are broadly associated with higher levels of infrastructural development and access to public services.

I begin the chapter by describing my survey design and quantitative data. I then introduce the variables, present the statistical results, and establish the robustness of the findings to several alternative model specifications and post-estimation tests. I will show that settlements with denser networks of party workers have, on average, better access to local public goods and services. I conclude by delving into the historical formation of squatter settlements to address concerns of selection bias and reverse causality. The following chapter pushes further on themes of historical sequencing, investigating the deeper factors that shape political organization in India's squatter settlements.

## 6.1 SURVEY DESIGN AND DATA

The statistical analyses below rest on an original survey conducted with 2,545 residents across 111 squatter settlements. The survey was intensive and multistaged in its design and implementation. First, to generate a comprehensive sample frame of slums in Bhopal and Jaipur, I gathered lists of slums from government departments in the two cities.[1] The total numbers of listed slums in Bhopal and Jaipur were 375 and 273, respectively.

These official lists do not differentiate among various types of urban poverty pockets and therefore required truncation to isolate squatter settlements. Several settlement types had to be removed: resettlement colonies, villages located within city boundaries, and old-city neighborhoods. Dilapidated old-city neighborhoods are not squatter settlements.[2] Resettlement colonies are established following evictions, with homes arranged in coherent plots and residents granted land titles and sanctioned

---

[1] In Jaipur, I gathered lists from the Jaipur Municipal Corporation, the Jaipur Development Authority, and PDCOR, a consulting firm that conducted a survey of Jaipur's slums for the Government of Rajasthan. In Bhopal, I gathered lists from a local UN-Habitat office and the Urban Administration and Development Department, Government of Madhya Pradesh, the latter of which was produced for Rajiv Awas Yojana. These lists include slums that are officially recognized and those that are not, offering a sample frame that does not suffer from the coverage bias that faces studies of only officially recognized slums.

[2] Slums are "run-down housing in older, established, legally built parts of the city proper. Slum buildings are mostly old and poorly maintained … in many cases, considerable areas of the old parts of cities in the Middle East and Asia are occupied by substandard housing" (UN-Habitat 1982, p. 14). Other studies of Jaipur and Bhopal treat old-city slums as distinct from squatter settlements (Risbud 1988; Bhatnagar 2010).

access to public goods and services. Further, and consistent with the Census of India, I only included squatter settlements with over 300 residents (sixty to seventy households).[3] Housing clusters that stray below this size cease to constitute a settlement.

In Jaipur, there are listed slums that have gone through processes of regularization and gentrification, including the demolition of shanties, reorganization of roads, and allocation of housing plots and public spaces. Others were never slums, but are resettlement colonies, planned and propertied neighborhoods that have become dilapidated over time, or planned middle-class "societies" that are awaiting approval from the Development Authority. These latter settlements are often referred to as "unauthorized colonies" and are common in India's cities.[4] They do not exhibit the features of squatter settlements and were accordingly excluded from the sample frame.[5]

I identified squatter settlements by their distinctive physical features – unplanned, densely populated, and amorphously shaped neighborhoods with tangled and narrow networks of alleyways – using Google Earth images and field visits.[6] Interviews with officials, government surveys, and prior studies of slums in Bhopal and Jaipur provided supplemental information.[7] The quality and availability of public services did not inform my identification of squatter settlements. Rather, the defining criteria of inclusion were that the settlement originated through squatting and maintains a distribution of homes and roads that exhibit a continued lack of any coordinated or centralized planning. To avoid mistakenly removing a squatter settlement, any ambiguous settlements were left in the sample frame and required a field visit if randomly selected.

---

[3] I consolidated nineteen squatter settlements into contiguous units because they were arbitrarily divided into smaller sections during government surveys. For instance, Durga Nagar in east Bhopal is one larger settlement but was divided into three sections. I merge it in the sample frame, as residents recognize it as one settlement.

[4] On Delhi's unauthorized colonies, see Heller et al. 2015.

[5] After a mapping and survey exercise of slums in Jaipur, Singhi (1997, p. 6) found 101 "clusters of poor people" despite the official list of 172 slums at the time. Many of the settlements that remain on government lists of slums no longer – or never did – exhibit the qualities of urban poverty pockets.

[6] See Figure 6.1 for an example of the narrow alleyways commonly found in squatter settlements.

[7] These studies include Risbud 1988, Mitra 1988, Agnihotri 1994, Singhi 1997, and Bhatnagar 2010.

FIGURE 6.1 Common image of a narrow alleyway in a Bhopal squatter settlement
*Note*: Author photograph (2011)

The final list of squatter settlements totaled 115 in Jaipur and 192 in Bhopal. I stratified these settlements into population quintiles and divided cities into three areas of roughly equal size to maximize variation in local labor markets, landownership categories, political representation, and electoral competition. In 2012, I randomly sampled thirty-one settlements across the areas and population quintiles in Jaipur and forty-one settlements across the areas and population quintiles in Bhopal. I also surveyed the eight case study settlements, resulting in a total of 80 sampled settlements. In 2015, an additional 31 settlements were sampled (16 in Jaipur and 15 in Bhopal), bringing the total number to 111 settlements.[8]

Some randomly selected settlements had been evicted, while I found others to be non-squatter settlements upon arrival.[9] One settlement in Jaipur was located on a military base and access would have been

---

[8] The 2015 survey was conducted with Tariq Thachil. See Figures 6.2 and 6.3 for city ward maps that show the location of the 111 sampled settlements. I thank Julie Radomski for creating these maps.

[9] I discovered upon inspection that four settlements had been evicted. See Figure 6.4 for an example of one of those evicted settlements. In Bhopal, I could not locate a small handful of settlements. Most likely, this was because the settlements had been evicted or had become regularized to the point that they were unidentifiable as squatter settlements and were no longer recognized by area residents as such.

*Party Workers and Public Goods Provision* 173

FIGURE 6.2 Ward map of Jaipur with location of sampled settlements

prohibited. For these reasons, sampled settlements were visited before sending in the survey teams to ensure they had not been evicted and fit the category of squatter settlements. If the initially selected settlement was evicted, could not be located, or fell outside the category of squatter settlements, a new one was randomly sampled. This close, context-driven sampling process ensured that all of the sampled settlements fell within the population of interest.

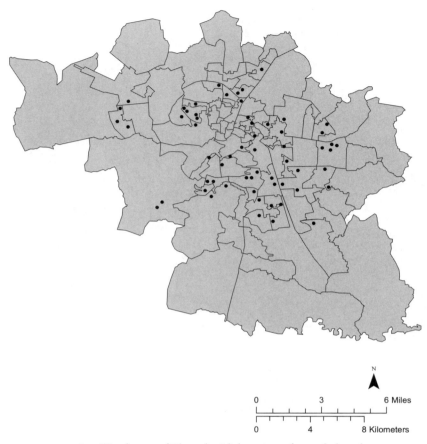

FIGURE 6.3 Ward map of Bhopal with location of sampled settlements

### Sampling Households within Settlements

The next stage of the survey design involved sampling households. Slums are poorly documented spaces. Accurate, up-to-date household rosters do not exist. As such, I could not rely on extant survey data or voter rolls to provide reliable sampling frames for any given settlement. Sampling every $n$th household by linearly traversing a street is also infeasible, as these areas do not have coherent roads but rather dizzying networks of unmarked alleyways. Random walks from landmarks would be fraught with problems as well (in many settlements, it is not clear what would constitute a unique, recognizable landmark). Some areas of squatter settlements are considerably more difficult to access than others (e.g., up the

FIGURE 6.4 The remaining rubble of an evicted slum, Bhopal
*Note*: Author photograph (2015)

sides of mountains, on sand dunes, and in drainage basins), potentially biasing the sample toward those living on main roads or other more easily accessible places. I therefore employed a spatial sampling technique that used satellite images to ensure a representative sample of households.

I created Google Earth satellite images for the sampled settlements and divided them into clusters of roughly twenty households. I then arbitrarily selected a household in a starting cluster and sampled subsequent households across the clusters to deliberately maintain approximate distances. This is similar to a design in which every $n$th household is sampled along a street, except the repeated sampling is across geographic clusters. I marked each sampled household on the satellite image and assigned it to an enumerator. Approximately one of every twenty households in each settlement, therefore, was sampled. In the 2015 survey, twenty households were sampled per settlement through the random selection of pixels on Google Earth satellite images – a similar method that minimizes enumerator discretion.[10] These procedures yielded a sample of 2,545 households across the 111 settlements.[11]

---

[10] See Auerbach and Thachil 2018.
[11] The average number of sampled households per settlement is 22.93 with a one standard deviation of 25.18. The maximum number of sampled households is 228 and the

I accompanied the survey teams on a daily basis to ensure the integrity of the sampling procedure. The teams interviewed 80 percent of the initially sampled 2012 households and 73 percent of the initially sampled 2015 households. For locked, vacant, or unwilling households, enumerators were instructed to interview an adjacent home, alternating to the left and right. Enumerators were further instructed, when possible, to alternate the sex of the respondent from interview to interview. To ensure an occupationally diverse sample, the survey teams conducted interviews between 3 pm and 8 pm. This period straddles two key blocks of time. Between 3 pm and 5 pm, slums are mostly populated with unemployed residents and stay-at-home adults. After 5 pm, residents working outside the settlement return home. Beyond efforts to balance the number of male and female respondents, enumerators arbitrarily selected individuals in households based on availability.

### Descriptive Statistics of Surveyed Residents

The survey achieved a close balance in the sex of respondents: 46 percent are women. Seventy-four percent of respondents are Hindu and 24 percent are Muslim, with the remaining respondents identifying as Buddhists, Christians, Jains, and Sikhs. The sample includes a rich array of castes (*jati*), representing all strata of the Hindu social hierarchy and a number of Muslim castes. Over 300 *jati* are represented. While a majority of sampled households migrated to the settlement from within Rajasthan (51 percent) or Madhya Pradesh (32 percent), others migrated from states throughout India, including Bihar, Chhattisgarh, Delhi, Gujarat, Haryana, Maharashtra, Punjab, Tamil Nadu, Uttar Pradesh, and West Bengal.

The average respondent is thirty-eight years old and has five years of formal schooling. Thirty-eight percent of respondents do not have any formal education, and a similar percentage is illiterate (39 percent). The average monthly per capita income of households is Rs 2,177 with a one standard deviation of Rs 2,008 – at 2015 exchange rates, roughly a dollar per person per day.

### 6.2 OTHER SOURCES OF DATA

I complement my survey data with data from several other sources. These latter data allow me to measure and include several important variables in

---

minimum number of sampled households is 4. For a majority of settlements (88 of 111), between 10 and 35 households were sampled.

the statistical analyses below. The first of those variables is settlement population. For Bhopal, I was able to gather accurate population data from a government dataset.[12] In Jaipur, official population numbers were rough, rounded estimates. They were also uneven in their coverage across settlements. I therefore calculated population estimates for Jaipur's slums using Google Earth satellite images and area calculations. First, I selected a slum (Katarpur) with a verifiably accurate population estimate and calculated its area and population density. I then calculated the area of all slums in Jaipur using Google Earth, and estimated population numbers in relation to Katarpur's population density. While the resulting calculations face some error due to variability in population densities across settlements, they represented the best population data available on Jaipur's slums at the time of the surveys.[13]

I measured the age of settlements through interviews with veteran residents and slum leaders. Official data on slums in Jaipur and Bhopal either do not mention the age of settlements or put them in rough age bins (for instance, more or less than ten years old). While past slum lists provide a sense of whether specific settlements existed at a certain time, these lists are not exhaustive and are generated infrequently. Because India's squatter settlements are relatively new, veteran residents are knowledgeable about the formation of their settlement. In addition to providing the year when their slum was settled, they would often point to major events around its establishment, such as Jaipur's floods in the early 1980s or the 1984 Bhopal Gas Disaster.

Data on landownership categories stem from interviews and archival research. Slum residents and their informal leaders usually know the category of land on which they reside because agents of the concerned government department have likely visited to intimidate them. Second, slum leaders are often aware of landownership as a result of their claim-making efforts. Politicians and officials convey this information, often as an excuse for delays in public service provision. Official slum lists provide details on landownership too, allowing me to triangulate among several distinct sources of data.

---

[12] Bhopal 2011 RAY Dataset.
[13] I was able to access Jaipur's RAY population data in 2016, after both surveys were conducted. The two population lists are highly correlated (0.874) and results are broadly robust to the use of the government data (see Table B.18). I prefer, however, to continue to use my population calculations for Jaipur because I used these numbers for the survey sampling and in earlier publications (Auerbach 2016, 2017).

I gathered electoral data from two sources. For state assembly constituencies, electoral data are publicly available from the Election Commission of India's website. Collecting municipal election data is more challenging, requiring on-the-ground digging in dusty local government archives. I was able to photograph ward-level returns in Jaipur since its first post-decentralization elections in 1994. The same is true for Bhopal, except clerks could not find data on Bhopal's 1994 municipal elections, suggesting they are lost to time.

## 6.3 VARIABLES AND THEIR MEASUREMENT

Six development indicators serve as the outcome variables.[14] The first indicator is paved roads, which I measure as the percentage of roads in a settlement that is either paved or laid with cemented cobblestone (*farshikaran*). The second indicator is the number of streetlights per 1,000 residents.[15] The third and fourth indicators are the percentages of respondents in a settlement with household connections to piped water and sewer lines.[16] The fifth indicator is the percentage of respondents who report that municipal sweepers (*nagar nigam safai karamchari*) come to remove trash from their area of the settlement.[17] The sixth indicator is the percentage of respondents who report a government medical camp was held in their settlement in the past year.[18]

---

[14] See Table 6.1 for descriptive statistics of the variables discussed in this chapter.

[15] I measured paved roads and streetlights using Google Earth satellite images and traverse walks. A research assistant and I traversed every alleyway of the 111 settlements and marked the exact location of these goods on the satellite images.

[16] For access to water, respondents were asked, "Where does your drinking water generally come from?" A possible response was, *kood ka naal*, or personal tap. For sewers, respondents were asked, "Where do you go to the bathroom?" A possible response was, a personal toilet connected to a sewer line.

[17] For government trash removal, respondents were asked, "Do municipal workers (*nagar nigam safai karamchari*) come to remove trash from your slum?" Municipal trash collection is susceptible to the same forms of distributive politics as the other development indicators – particularistic political interventions in response to requests from slum leaders – and can be unevenly provided within a settlement (interview with sanitation inspector, Jaipur, July 13, 2018). Measuring this variable as the percentage of respondents reporting the provision of trash removal is therefore appropriate.

[18] For government medical camps, respondents were asked, "In this past year, has the government held a medical camp in your slum?" Residents within the same settlement can have variable knowledge about the provision of medical camps due to unevenness in the dissemination of information about camps – unevenness that is in part the result of politicization by politicians and their party workers. In addition to regularly scheduled government medical camps, elected representatives can spend their own funds to hold

TABLE 6.1 *Descriptive statistics of settlement-level variables*

|  | Mean | SD | Minimum | Maximum |
|---|---|---|---|---|
| Paved roads (%) | 70.05 | 37.74 | 0.00 | 100.00 |
| Streetlights per 1,000 residents | 5.73 | 5.40 | 0.00 | 25.22 |
| Water taps (%) | 42.05 | 37.50 | 0.00 | 100.00 |
| Sewer connections (%) | 27.10 | 33.53 | 0.00 | 100.00 |
| Municipal trash removal (%) | 42.41 | 26.05 | 0.00 | 100.00 |
| Government medical camps (%) | 24.43 | 16.90 | 0.00 | 95.00 |
| Development index 1 | −0.00 | 1.54 | −2.86 | 3.98 |
| Development index 2 | −0.00 | 1.16 | −3.54 | 2.48 |
| Development index 3 | −0.00 | 0.96 | −2.04 | 2.38 |
| Party worker density | 1.90 | 1.47 | 0.00 | 6.17 |
| Party representational balance | 0.42 | 0.40 | 0.00 | 1.00 |
| Population | 2,395.43 | 2,956.50 | 307.00 | 2,3811.00 |
| Log population | 7.35 | 0.90 | 5.73 | 10.08 |
| Settlement age (*years*) | 33.86 | 10.30 | 8.00 | 65.00 |
| Average education (*years*) | 5.10 | 2.13 | 0.00 | 10.20 |
| Monthly household (HH) income per capita (*in Rs*) | 2,178.80 | 562.90 | 914.88 | 4,826.51 |
| Central land | 0.23 | 0.43 | 0.00 | 1.00 |
| Private land | 0.10 | 0.30 | 0.00 | 1.00 |
| Caste diversity | 0.80 | 0.15 | 0.00 | 0.97 |
| Religious diversity | 0.17 | 0.17 | 0.00 | 0.50 |
| Region of origin diversity | 0.28 | 0.22 | 0.00 | 0.78 |
| Ethnic diversity index | −0.00 | 1.21 | −4.54 | 2.18 |
| AC electoral competition (%) | 15.30 | 4.39 | 8.90 | 25.16 |
| Ward electoral competition (%) | 13.28 | 6.29 | 3.28 | 37.91 |
| Social capital index 1 | 0.00 | 1.65 | −4.33 | 3.35 |
| Social capital index 2 | −0.00 | 1.22 | −2.58 | 2.81 |
| Land titles (%) | 12.09 | 22.19 | 0.00 | 95.00 |
| Settlement notification | 0.73 | 0.45 | 0.00 | 1.00 |

*Note:* N = 111, except for "party representational balance" (N = 91).

camps with government doctors, and their decision where to hold these camps is open to political calculation (interview with Public Health Department officer, Jaipur, July 13, 2018; interview with Public Health Department medical doctor, Jaipur, July 27, 2018). Consequently, measuring the provision of government medical camps as a percentage of residents reporting their provision is appropriate.

Using principal component analysis, I also create development indices that combine these six development indicators. The first component (eigenvalue of 2.37) explains 39.53 percent of the variation across the six development indicators and is the closest to a global measure of local development since each indicator is positively associated with it. The second component (eigenvalue of 1.35) is more difficult to interpret, as it is only positively correlated with paved roads and trash collection. It explains 22.52 percent of the variation across the indicators. The third component has an eigenvalue of 0.917 and explains 15.28 percent of the variation across the indicators. It is negatively correlated with the two most capital-intensive goods, and the only two indicators with which party worker density does not exhibit a positive, statistically significant association – sewers and piped water.

### Party Worker Density and Party Representational Balance

The explanatory variables of primary interest are party worker density and party representational balance. Party worker density is simply the number of party workers per 1,000 residents in a settlement. Party representational balance is a continuous variable, based on the Laakso and Taagepera measure of effective number of parties, which captures how balanced or lopsided the distribution of partisan affiliations is among party workers in a settlement.[19] It is bound between 0 and 1, with a score of 0 representing a situation in which all party workers in a settlement are from the same party, and a score of 1 representing a situation in which party workers are equally split between the two parties in competition in Bhopal and Jaipur (the BJP and INC).[20] Settlements without party workers are treated as missing data with respect to party representational balance.

---

[19] Laakso and Taagepera 1979. Party representational balance is measured as $\left(\frac{1}{\sum p_j^2}\right) - 1$, where $p$ is the proportion of party workers from party $j$.

[20] The INC and BJP are the two major parties in competition in Jaipur and Bhopal. In 2017, these two parties held 93.18 percent of municipal seats across the two cities (84/91 seats in Jaipur and 80/85 seats in Bhopal). All of the municipal seats not held by the INC or BJP were held by independents, with the exception of one Bahujan Samaj Party (BSP) councillor in Bhopal. In 2017, at the state level, the INC and BJP held 94.65 percent of state legislative assembly seats across Rajasthan and Madhya Pradesh (184/200 seats in Rajasthan and 223/230 seats in Madhya Pradesh).

## Alternative Explanations

Several literatures in comparative politics and related fields offer alternative explanations to examine alongside party worker density and party representational balance. First, scholars have found that ethnic diversity can undermine cooperation and public goods provision.[21] This literature would anticipate that ethnic diversity introduces divergent social norms and behavioral expectations in India's slums, undercutting the ability of residents to organize to improve local conditions. To assess this, I calculate ethnic diversity scores along three dimensions – caste (*jati*), religion, and region (state) of origin – using a standard measure based on the Herfindahl Index.[22] I then generate an ethnic diversity index using principal component analysis.[23]

Another alternative explanation is social capital.[24] My survey included seven questions tapping perceptions of interhousehold trust and cooperation.[25] Using principal component analysis, I derive underlying factors among the seven indicators and construct two indices of social capital.[26] In addition to explaining the most variation, the first index is clear in its interpretation because all seven social capital indicators are positively correlated

---

[21] On this literature, see Miguel 2004 and Habyarimana et al. 2009.

[22] I use the conventional fractionalization score, $1 - \sum e_i^2$, where $e$ is group $i$'s proportion in the settlement (Easterly and Levine 1997; Miguel 2004). To measure regional (state) diversity, survey respondents were first asked whether they were born in the settlement. Respondents born outside the settlement were asked, "in which state were you born?" Respondents born inside the settlement were asked, "from which state does your family originate?" These questions capture regional identities that often prove to be socially salient in settlements (as illustrated in several of the case studies), both for the residents who personally migrated as well as for their children born in the settlement.

[23] Only one component exhibits an eigenvalue above 1. This component is positively related to all three ethnic diversity measures and explains nearly half of the variation across them. The use of the index is preferable to including the individual measures of caste, religious, and region of origin diversity for at least three reasons. First, it reduces the number of tested hypotheses: given three ethnic diversity measures and six development indicators, I would otherwise be conducting 18 separate tests. The use of the index collapses the tests to six. Second, the three dimensions of ethnicity are not completely independent. A settlement that is more diverse in terms of religion or region of origin will have a higher number of castes (*jati*). The index addresses such overlapping identities. Third, I do not have an a priori theoretical reason for why certain dimensions of ethnic diversity should be significant and not others.

[24] Varshney 2002; Krishna 2002; Putnam 1994.

[25] For comparability with other research on social capital, the questions mirror those from the World Bank's Social Capital Assessment Tool and Krishna 2002. Table A.1 lists these survey questions.

[26] The first has an eigenvalue of 2.71 (explaining 38.73 percent of the variation among the variables) and the second has an eigenvalue of 1.49 (explaining 21.24 percent of the variation among the variables).

with it. The second index is positively correlated with three of the seven indicators. Following convention, I include both indices in the statistical models because they have eigenvalues above one. However, because the second index is less interpretable, I place less emphasis on it in the discussion below.

Studies have found that levels of electoral competition shape public spending in India.[27] We might expect slums within competitive municipal wards or state assembly constituencies to benefit from close elections because incumbents in those constituencies have greater incentives to work hard to chase after every last vote. Using electoral data from municipal elections (since 1994 in Jaipur and 1999 in Bhopal) and state assembly elections (since 1980), I calculate the vote margins between winners and runners-up in constituencies. Since the dataset is cross-sectional, I average constituency-level scores across elections and match settlements with their average ward and assembly constituency (AC) competition scores.

Without formal land titles, residents may have fewer incentives to invest time and resources in improving local conditions.[28] Having land titles might also pave the way for more programmatic access to local public goods and services. Settlements can exhibit internal variability in household possession of land titles because of local differences in the timing of resident arrival, uneven topographies and environmental sensitivities of the land, and shifting cutoff dates in state titling programs. I therefore include a variable for the percentage of respondents in a settlement who have full, formal land titles.[29]

A settlement's "notification" status – whether or not the state officially recognizes it – also relates to land tenure security. This status originates in the Slum Areas Act of 1956, which stipulates that notified slums are to be extended some protections from sudden eviction. Scholars portray the process of notification as politicized.[30] The same underlying factors that explain notification, then, likely explain the provision of local public goods and services. Moreover, there are non-notified settlements in my sample with public infrastructure and services and notified settlements

[27] Chhibber and Nooruddin 2004; Sáez and Sinha 2010.
[28] Lall et al. 2004; Field 2005; Galiani and Schargrodsky 2010.
[29] In Bhopal, some residents have temporary land titles. These were originally distributed in the mid-1980s under Arjun Singh, the chief minister of Madhya Pradesh at that time. I code these temporary titles as zeros because they are not full land titles and many have lapsed. Moreover, they are unique to Madhya Pradesh. Renters, who make up a small portion of the sample (221 of 2,545 respondents), are treated as missing data in calculations of the percentage of respondents with full land titles because the underlying status of their rented home is unobserved.
[30] Risbud 1988, p. 60; Risbud 2014, p. 180.

without them, suggesting that notification is neither necessary nor sufficient for local development.[31] Still, given its prominent place in studies of India's slums,[32] I examine a dichotomous variable for settlement notification.

Studies of distributive politics anticipate that the partisan leanings of settlements will impact public service provision.[33] First, and consistent with "swing" targeting, settlements with higher proportions of swing voters – voters who are not committed to any one party – might be privileged in the allocation of local public goods because they are likely to shift their support if neglected. In comparison, settlements mostly home to committed co-partisan voters will stick with the party even in the face of some neglect, and settlements mostly home to committed opposition voters cannot be easily swayed and are thus unattractive places to allocate scarce resources. Second, and consistent with "core" targeting, a settlement that is a party stronghold, and has been regularly exposed to elected representatives from that party over time, might be better off than a settlement that is a stronghold for a party that has rarely or never been in power. Third, and distinct from theories of top-down targeting, settlements that are internally split in their party preferences might be less capable of organizing for claim-making and protest than those settlements with more homogenous party preferences among residents.

To examine these three alternative explanations, I draw on survey responses to questions about respondents' current party preferences and whether they have voted for different parties over the last several elections.[34] It is important to note that because the dataset is cross-sectional, it is limited in its ability to fully investigate the relationship between resident party preferences/electoral behavior and public service provision because the current distribution of party preferences in a settlement may not reflect past distributions. Given a lack of historical data on neighborhood-level electoral returns in Bhopal and Jaipur, this limitation is likely unavoidable.[35]

---

[31] In the city of Sangli, Maharashtra, Joshi et al. (2002, p. 227) similarly find that while "a number of slums in Sangli have been declared, very few have been provided with basic infrastructure."

[32] Nakamura 2014.

[33] Cox and McCubbins 1986; Lindbeck and Weibull 1987; Dixit and Londregan 1996; Stokes 2005; Nichter 2008. See Golden and Min 2013 for an overview of the distributive politics literature.

[34] These questions were asked as part of the Auerbach and Thachil 2015 resident survey.

[35] Obtaining polling booth-level data, as well as information about the exact boundaries of their catchment areas, is notoriously difficult in India. After visiting the state election commissions in Bhopal and Jaipur, I determined that it would not be possible to gather

## Control Variables

I include a number of control variables in the following regressions. The first is the average household income of respondents in settlements (measured in monthly per capita terms). Residents with higher household incomes may be better able to forgo lost wages to engage in collective action.[36] The second is the average education of respondents in settlements. Better-educated residents may be in a stronger position to command state responsiveness because they are more informed about their rights and eligibility for government programs and can more effectively navigate state institutions.[37] The third is landownership categories. I aggregate landownership categories into three groups: central government land, private land, and state or municipal land. MLAs and ward councillors have considerable discretion over development on state and municipal lands yet face greater obstacles in delivering local public goods on private lands and central lands – Forest or Railway Department land, for example. The fourth is settlement age. Older settlements are likely to be more developed because residents have simply had more time to make claims on the state. The fifth is settlement population. The impact of population can cut in opposite ways. Increasing population might undermine collective action due to its impact on free riding.[38] Conversely, increasing population might encourage the provision of local public goods by increasing the scale of protest and the size of a slum's "vote bank" and, thus, its electoral appeal to politicians. The sixth and seventh are a dummy variable for city (Jaipur = 0, Bhopal = 1) and a dummy variable for whether the settlement was surveyed in 2015.

## 6.4 STATISTICAL MODELS AND RESULTS

The main regression results – Ordinary Least Squares (OLS) models with robust standard errors – are reported in Tables 6.2–6.5.[39] I first discuss the relationship between party worker density and the development measures,

---

polling booth-level data and information on catchment areas for even a single election, let alone all local, state, and national elections in the two cities since the early 1980s. Even if this data could be acquired, polling booth catchment areas do not conform to the boundaries of neighborhoods, and so there would be a nontrivial and uneven degree of slippage between electoral returns and the boundaries of slum settlements.

[36] Income data comes from the Auerbach and Thachil 2015 resident survey.
[37] On the roles of citizen education and information in generating government responsiveness, see Besley and Burgess 2002, Keefer and Khemani 2005, and Khemani 2011.
[38] Olson 1965.
[39] Figure B.2 presents a scatterplot showing the bivariate relationship between party worker density and overall community development.

TABLE 6.2 Paved roads and streetlights

|  | Paved road coverage (%) |  |  | Streetlights per 1,000 residents |  |  |
|---|---|---|---|---|---|---|
|  | M1 | M2 | M3 | M4 | M5 | M6 |
| Party worker density | 6.574** | 6.721*** | 12.33*** | 1.161*** | 1.116*** | 1.519** |
|  | (2.590) | (2.287) | (3.462) | (0.402) | (0.419) | (0.685) |
| City | 24.21*** | 35.67*** | 42.74*** | −6.931*** | −5.047*** | −5.095*** |
|  | (8.310) | (9.492) | (7.146) | (1.307) | (1.538) | (1.809) |
| Log population | 17.19*** | 14.74*** | 12.32*** | −0.150 | 0.181 | 0.314 |
|  | (4.274) | (3.741) | (2.988) | (0.623) | (0.646) | (0.803) |
| 2015 Settlement | 4.520 | −2.584 | 4.220 | −0.192 | 0.552 | 0.742 |
|  | (6.732) | (11.69) | (8.833) | (0.934) | (1.479) | (1.747) |
| Settlement age | 0.193 | 0.246 | 0.0346 | 0.00211 | 0.0189 | 0.0188 |
|  | (0.368) | (0.370) | (0.316) | (0.0358) | (0.0437) | (0.0565) |
| Average education | 1.608 | 0.0920 | 0.380 | 0.441** | 0.129 | 0.0936 |
|  | (2.107) | (2.332) | (1.680) | (0.222) | (0.250) | (0.333) |
| Monthly HH income per capita | 0.00546 | 0.00814 | 0.0139** | 0.0000383 | −0.000111 | 0.000231 |
|  | (0.00626) | (0.00636) | (0.00545) | (0.0000690) | (0.000748) | (0.000918) |
| Ethnic diversity index | −1.530 | −1.758 | −1.907 | 0.272 | 0.212 | 0.0845 |
|  | (2.940) | (2.659) | (2.143) | (0.400) | (0.433) | (0.578) |
| Central land |  | 3.485 | 14.55** |  | 0.271 | 0.563 |
|  |  | (7.795) | (6.981) |  | (1.051) | (1.247) |
| Private land |  | −26.02** | −25.53*** |  | 0.513 | 0.387 |
|  |  | (10.07) | (8.908) |  | (1.957) | (2.312) |

*(continued)*

TABLE 6.2 (continued)

| | Paved road coverage (%) | | Streetlights per 1,000 residents | |
|---|---|---|---|---|
| AC electoral competition | -0.559 | -0.532 | -0.113 | -0.116 |
| | (0.771) | (0.666) | (0.0964) | (0.118) |
| Ward electoral competition | -0.630 | -0.594 | 0.0791 | 0.0648 |
| | (0.473) | (0.461) | (0.0598) | (0.0779) |
| Social capital index 1 | 2.204 | 4.822** | 0.668** | 0.929** |
| | (2.416) | (1.936) | (0.266) | (0.405) |
| Social capital index 2 | 4.633 | 1.999 | 0.0950 | -0.147 |
| | (4.345) | (3.535) | (0.433) | (0.608) |
| Land titles | 0.310** | 0.372*** | 0.00744 | 0.00520 |
| | (0.127) | (0.122) | (0.0175) | (0.0230) |
| Party representational balance | | 31.49** | | 0.266 |
| | | (12.35) | | (2.213) |
| PW density * PR balance | | -15.96*** | | -0.673 |
| | | (4.384) | | (1.068) |
| Constant | -109.7*** | -86.60*** | 4.270 | 2.647 |
| | (37.98) | (31.45) | (5.722) | (7.407) |
| Observations | 111 | 91 | 111 | 91 |
| $R^2$ | 0.369 | 0.595 | 0.534 | 0.513 |

*Note*: OLS models; robust standard errors in parentheses
* $p < 0.10$, ** $p < 0.05$, *** $p < 0.01$

TABLE 6.3 *Piped water and sewer connections*

|  | Household access to piped water (%) |  |  | Household access to sewer connections (%) |  |  |
| --- | --- | --- | --- | --- | --- | --- |
|  | M7 | M8 | M9 | M10 | M11 | M12 |
| Party worker density | 1.292 | 1.695 | 7.265 | −0.181 | −0.154 | 2.441 |
|  | (2.387) | (2.241) | (4.727) | (2.323) | (1.843) | (3.384) |
| City | −36.11*** | −28.65*** | −27.51*** | −19.42*** | −7.327 | −11.37 |
|  | (6.854) | (8.518) | (8.190) | (6.585) | (7.327) | (8.253) |
| Log population | 5.091 | 2.832 | 7.794* | 9.385** | 7.946** | 9.203** |
|  | (3.801) | (3.803) | (3.965) | (3.978) | (3.203) | (3.624) |
| 2015 Settlement | 23.15*** | 27.78*** | 18.23* | 4.574 | 9.401 | 6.078 |
|  | (6.754) | (9.601) | (10.07) | (5.643) | (8.626) | (10.90) |
| Settlement age | −0.209 | −0.290 | 0.335 | 0.435 | 0.368 | 0.668** |
|  | (0.315) | (0.318) | (0.348) | (0.331) | (0.280) | (0.258) |
| Average education | 3.824** | 2.204 | 2.148 | 0.979 | −1.202 | −0.165 |
|  | (1.468) | (1.643) | (1.743) | (1.431) | (1.436) | (1.750) |
| Monthly HH income per capita | 0.00373 | 0.00772 | 0.0108** | 0.0128** | 0.0176*** | 0.0184*** |
|  | (0.00485) | (0.00530) | (0.00486) | (0.00573) | (0.00615) | (0.00655) |
| Ethnic diversity index | −3.797 | −3.582 | −5.467* | −3.460 | −3.139 | −3.424 |
|  | (2.671) | (2.756) | (2.912) | (2.493) | (2.495) | (2.938) |
| Central land | −7.103 | −7.103 | −12.83* |  | −13.44** | −15.73** |
|  | (7.808) | (7.808) | (7.510) |  | (6.218) | (6.922) |
| Private land | −9.697 | −9.697 | 3.428 |  | −22.91** | −13.47 |
|  | (8.581) | (8.581) | (9.593) |  | (9.679) | (10.68) |

*(continued)*

TABLE 6.3 (continued)

|  | Household access to piped water (%) |  | Household access to sewer connections (%) |  |
|---|---|---|---|---|
| AC electoral competition |  | −0.148 |  | 0.709 |
|  |  | (0.823) |  | (0.712) |
|  |  |  | 0.226 |  |
|  |  |  | (0.662) |  |
| Ward electoral competition |  | −0.240 |  | 0.283 |
|  |  | (0.405) |  | (0.425) |
|  |  |  | 0.348 |  |
|  |  |  | (0.357) |  |
| Social capital index 1 |  | 0.915 |  | 3.408 |
|  |  | (2.116) |  | (2.254) |
|  |  |  | 2.577 |  |
|  |  |  | (1.655) |  |
| Social capital index 2 |  | −3.058 |  | −2.100 |
|  |  | (3.117) |  | (3.997) |
|  |  |  | −3.017 |  |
|  |  |  | (3.046) |  |
| Land titles |  | 0.379*** |  | 0.430*** |
|  |  | (0.116) |  | (0.148) |
|  |  |  | 0.512*** |  |
|  |  |  | (0.125) |  |
| Party representational balance |  | 0.368*** |  |  |
|  |  | (0.135) |  |  |
|  |  | 7.112 |  | 6.425 |
|  |  | (15.04) |  | (13.24) |
| PW density * PR balance |  | −7.336 |  | −7.311 |
|  |  | (6.085) |  | (4.641) |
| Constant | −5.295 | −75.90** | −83.17*** | −112.8*** |
|  | (31.70) | (36.28) | (28.29) | (31.67) |
|  | 11.01 | −79.83*** |  |  |
|  | (37.31) | (29.66) |  |  |
| Observations | 111 | 91 | 111 | 91 |
|  | 111 | 91 | 111 | 91 |
| $R^2$ | 0.475 | 0.656 | 0.543 | 0.616 |
|  | 0.531 | 0.377 |  |  |

Note: OLS models; robust standard errors in parentheses
* $p < 0.10$, ** $p < 0.05$, *** $p < 0.01$

TABLE 6.4 *Municipal trash removal and government medical camps*

| | Reporting municipal trash removal (%) | | | Reporting government medical camps (%) | | |
|---|---|---|---|---|---|---|
| | M13 | M14 | M15 | M16 | M17 | M18 |
| Party worker density | 2.150 | 2.346* | 1.286 | 2.973*** | 2.936** | 4.786*** |
| | (1.432) | (1.321) | (1.988) | (1.026) | (1.210) | (1.517) |
| City | 27.55*** | 38.99*** | 42.55*** | -7.810** | -2.800 | -4.952 |
| | (4.342) | (6.374) | (6.430) | (3.585) | (4.499) | (4.649) |
| Log population | 3.418 | 3.262 | 3.429 | 3.234** | 4.380** | 5.661*** |
| | (2.408) | (2.506) | (3.160) | (1.611) | (1.701) | (2.031) |
| 2015 Settlement | 7.789* | 23.14*** | 17.86** | -13.03*** | -11.39** | -5.215 |
| | (4.336) | (6.413) | (7.009) | (2.652) | (4.588) | (5.122) |
| Settlement age | 0.748*** | 0.572*** | 0.763*** | -0.258* | -0.201 | -0.342 |
| | (0.203) | (0.216) | (0.274) | (0.133) | (0.170) | (0.235) |
| Average education | 0.910 | -1.384 | -1.607 | 0.505 | -0.112 | -1.080 |
| | (1.436) | (1.605) | (1.651) | (0.932) | (0.987) | (0.904) |
| Monthly HH income per capita | 0.00653 | 0.00889** | 0.00764** | 0.0000479 | -0.000753 | 0.00305 |
| | (0.00439) | (0.00376) | (0.00376) | (0.00243) | (0.00274) | (0.00312) |
| Ethnic diversity index | -0.189 | 0.0464 | 0.515 | 0.482 | 0.377 | 0.687 |
| | (1.681) | (1.551) | (2.102) | (1.441) | (1.491) | (1.684) |
| Central land | | 9.249* | 7.574 | | 1.205 | 3.418 |
| | | (4.697) | (5.545) | | (3.466) | (3.734) |

*(continued)*

TABLE 6.4 *(continued)*

|  | Reporting municipal trash removal (%) |  | Reporting government medical camps (%) |  |
|---|---|---|---|---|
| Private land | 1.343 | 2.368 | 0.594 | 1.831 |
|  | (6.460) | (6.196) | (3.839) | (4.893) |
| AC electoral competition | −0.236 | −0.131 | −0.522 | −0.243 |
|  | (0.477) | (0.520) | (0.328) | (0.344) |
| Ward electoral competition | 0.473 | 0.543* | 0.371 | 0.219 |
|  | (0.332) | (0.274) | (0.261) | (0.241) |
| Social capital index 1 | 3.771** | 5.279*** | 1.440 | 2.109 |
|  | (1.531) | (1.577) | (1.118) | (1.269) |
| Social capital index 2 | −5.368** | −3.113 | 0.371 | −2.555 |
|  | (2.382) | (2.955) | (2.181) | (2.608) |
| Land titles | 0.332*** | 0.356*** | −0.00481 | 0.00128 |
|  | (0.114) | (0.113) | (0.0895) | (0.104) |
| Party representational balance |  | −2.979 |  | −3.436 |
|  |  | (10.34) |  | (7.995) |
| PW density * PR balance |  | 0.729 |  | −2.631 |
|  |  | (3.155) |  | (2.940) |
| Constant | −48.04** | −54.25*** | 8.915 | 3.177 |
|  | (19.33) | (20.56) | (14.85) | (16.40) |
| Observations | 111 | 111 | 111 | 91 |
| $R^2$ | 0.442 | 0.551 | 0.306 | 0.410 |

*Note:* OLS models; robust standard errors in parentheses
* $p < 0.10$, ** $p < 0.05$, *** $p < 0.01$

TABLE 6.5 *Development indices*

|  | Development index 1 |  | Development index 2 |  | Development index 3 |  |
|---|---|---|---|---|---|---|
|  | M19 | M20 | M21 | M22 | M23 | M24 |
| Party worker density | 0.249*** | 0.479*** | 0.03111 | -0.000449 | 0.209*** | 0.226** |
|  | (0.0915) | (0.111) | (0.0552) | (0.0836) | (0.0605) | (0.0991) |
| City | -0.387 | -0.382 | 1.988*** | 2.230*** | 0.610*** | 0.586** |
|  | (0.368) | (0.373) | (0.239) | (0.247) | (0.226) | (0.225) |
| Log population | 0.417*** | 0.513*** | 0.174* | 0.0975 | 0.198** | 0.158 |
|  | (0.141) | (0.146) | (0.0972) | (0.123) | (0.0995) | (0.108) |
| 2015 Settlement | 0.505 | 0.477 | 0.717** | 0.559* | -0.808*** | -0.328 |
|  | (0.382) | (0.419) | (0.273) | (0.291) | (0.241) | (0.262) |
| Settlement age | 0.00631 | 0.0162 | 0.0226*** | 0.0257*** | -0.00430 | -0.0206* |
|  | (0.0136) | (0.0132) | (0.00801) | (0.00969) | (0.00859) | (0.0109) |
| Average education | 0.0123 | 0.00979 | -0.0465 | -0.0287 | -0.0235 | -0.0789 |
|  | (0.0645) | (0.0585) | (0.0695) | (0.0651) | (0.0512) | (0.0512) |
| Monthly HH income per capita | 0.000493** | 0.000689*** | 0.000334* | 0.000273 | -0.000183 | -0.0000403 |
|  | (0.000204) | (0.000213) | (0.000168) | (0.000147) | (0.000163) | (0.000181) |
| Central land | -0.166 | -0.118 | 0.302 | 0.363* | 0.338 | 0.591*** |
|  | (0.252) | (0.276) | (0.198) | (0.216) | (0.221) | (0.196) |
| Private land | -0.678* | -0.334 | -0.299 | -0.330 | 0.178 | -0.0204 |
|  | (0.407) | (0.427) | (0.293) | (0.279) | (0.209) | (0.282) |
| Ethnic diversity index | -0.0889 | -0.123 | -0.0278 | -0.0105 | 0.0813 | 0.125 |
|  | (0.119) | (0.122) | (0.0648) | (0.0719) | (0.0659) | (0.0802) |

(*continued*)

TABLE 6.5 (continued)

|  | Development index 1 |  | Development index 2 |  | Development index 3 |  |
|---|---|---|---|---|---|---|
| AC electoral competition | −0.0242 | 0.00323 | 0.00273 | −0.00306 | −0.0297 | −0.0356* |
|  | (0.0275) | (0.0288) | (0.0191) | (0.0193) | (0.0181) | (0.0182) |
| Ward electoral competition | 0.0123 | 0.00617 | −0.00698 | −0.000207 | 0.0146 | 0.0144 |
|  | (0.0145) | (0.0161) | (0.0143) | (0.0114) | (0.0120) | (0.0128) |
| Social capital index 1 | 0.182** | 0.263*** | 0.0629 | 0.112* | 0.0782 | 0.147** |
|  | (0.0817) | (0.0882) | (0.0647) | (0.0630) | (0.0522) | (0.0591) |
| Social capital index 2 | −0.0632 | −0.0885 | −0.0867 | 0.00265 | 0.0697 | −0.134 |
|  | (0.139) | (0.168) | (0.0940) | (0.108) | (0.105) | (0.120) |
| Land titles | 0.0189*** | 0.0181** | 0.0114** | 0.0130*** | −0.00550 | −0.00423 |
|  | (0.00551) | (0.00686) | (0.00468) | (0.00457) | (0.00372) | (0.00432) |
| Party representational balance |  | 0.451 |  | 0.370 |  | −0.0553 |
|  |  | (0.481) |  | (0.424) |  | (0.430) |
| PW density * PR balance |  | −0.467** |  | −0.0761 |  | −0.0805 |
|  |  | (0.186) |  | (0.124) |  | (0.149) |
| Constant | −4.733*** | −6.774*** | −3.995*** | −3.583*** | −1.058 | −0.189 |
|  | (1.254) | (1.443) | (0.789) | (0.989) | (1.003) | (1.099) |
| Observations | 111 | 91 | 111 | 91 | 111 | 91 |
| $R^2$ | 0.608 | 0.681 | 0.603 | 0.690 | 0.462 | 0.554 |

*Note:* OLS models; robust standard errors in parentheses
* $p < 0.10$, ** $p < 0.05$, *** $p < 0.01$

with reference to those models that exclude party representational balance. Party worker density is positive and statistically significant in its association with paved road coverage, streetlight coverage, municipal trash removal, and the provision of government medical camps. An increase of 1 party worker per 1,000 residents is associated with a 6.72 percentage-point increase in paved road coverage and an increase of 1.12 streetlights per 1,000 residents.[40] And an additional party worker per 1,000 residents is associated with a 2.35 increase in the percentage of respondents reporting municipal trash removal and a 2.94 increase in the percentage of respondents reporting that government medical camps were held in their settlement in the past year.

Party worker density does not explain inter-settlement variation in the percentage of households with access to sewer connections or piped water connections. Why? First, these are capital-intensive goods. They require substantial resources and are the most technically complex to provide among the six development indicators. As a result, politicians might be less willing or able to provide sewers and piped water, especially on central government lands or private plots where they have less scope for making major changes to the land. Second, sewers and piped water are sensitive to the presence of infrastructure in surrounding areas; it is easier to provide them when sewer lines and water pipes can be extended from adjacent neighborhoods. Even settlements with dense networks of party workers, then, might be less able to secure these goods if they are absent in that small corner of the city. These factors make piped water and sewers different from the other four development indicators. Indeed, *development index 3* is only negatively correlated with piped water and sewer connections, suggesting they have a distinct pattern in their provision.

Slum residents, moreover, rely on a wide variety of sources of water. In addition to those survey respondents with household piped water (42 percent), 37 percent of survey respondents primarily access water from shared community taps; 7 percent primarily access water from truck-fed tanks; 7 percent primarily access water from bore wells; and the remainder primarily use sources such as hand pumps and open wells. Party workers, as shown in Chapter 5, are involved in solving problems related to all of these sources of water, from ensuring water trucks show up on time to having hand pumps fixed and bore wells dug. The findings on household piped water do not capture the influence of party workers on the accessibility of water more broadly.

---

[40] Given the observational nature of the data, statements on the direction, magnitude, and significance of coefficients should be read as conditional on the other covariates. For ease of exposition, I do not continue to note this below and in the following chapter.

I now turn to the development indices. Because *development index 1* exhibits the highest eigenvalue and is positively related to all six development indicators, I place greatest emphasis on it. Party worker density is positive and significant in its association with *development index 1* ($p < 0.05$). A one standard deviation increase in party worker density explains 24 percent of a standard deviation in *development index 1*. Party worker density is positive and significant in its association with *development index 3* but not *development index 2*. The latter index is only positively correlated with paved roads and trash collection. *Development index 3* is positively correlated with paved roads, streetlights, trash collection, and government medical camps.

In sum, party worker density is positive and statistically significant in its association with four of the six development indicators. Party worker density also has a positive and statistically significant association with the primary development index. These statistical results are consistent with those estimated when only examining the 80 settlements surveyed in 2012 (see Auerbach 2016). Read alongside my qualitative findings, the statistical results provide further evidence of party worker density's positive relationship with public service delivery.

### The Interaction of Party Worker Density and Party Representational Balance

How does the partisan distribution of party workers in a settlement – the extent to which party workers are split in their party affiliations – impact public service provision? To investigate this relationship, I turn to the interaction of party worker density and party representational balance. I focus on the marginal effects of party worker density conditional on the range of values for party representational balance because the coefficient on the latter cannot be substantively interpreted by itself since it cannot exist, by definition, without party workers. Marginal effects are plotted in Figures B.1.a through B.1.i.[41]

The plots exhibit limited, suggestive evidence that – assuming a linear functional form – party representational balance has an attenuating conditional influence with respect to the primary development index and a few of the development indicators.[42] However, the interactions across all

---

[41] The marginal effects plots are created using the Stata code produced by Berry et al. 2012.
[42] The marginal effect of party worker density on the primary development index, conditional on party representational balance, decreases as the values of party representational balance rises. This association retains statistical significance up to a party representational balance score of approximately 0.65. Note that this value is based on interpolation.

of the development measures are statistically insignificant for either part or all of the moderating variable's range. Moreover, there is a significant clustering of observations at zero[43] and a lack of common support across much of party representational balance's range.[44] Broadly, then, the results on the conditional influence of party representational balance should be seen as tentative, provoking questions for future research on the relationship between the partisan distribution of local party workers and outcomes in community development.

As I argue in Chapter 3, the blurred conditional impact of party representational balance may also, in part, be a consequence of the cross-cutting nature of its component mechanisms. The presence of party workers affiliated to different parties provides residents with diverse points of partisan connectivity, ensuring that there are party workers with linkages to the incumbent regardless of which party is in power. Moreover, given the stakes of having one's party in power for success in local problem-solving, partisan divisions among party workers might intensify competition for an electoral following, compelling them to be more active claim-makers. Conversely, a politician's efforts to take credit for development projects are muddled in the presence of non-co-partisan workers, who are less likely to help spread word of the politician's work. Politicians therefore have reasons to target slums where all or most party workers are co-partisans. Competing party worker networks also have incentives to undercut the other's claim-making efforts to dampen their electoral support. These countervailing mechanisms plausibly obfuscate the relationship between party representational balance and public service provision.

## Alternative Explanations

The variables capturing alternative explanations exhibit uneven explanatory power. First, the ethnic diversity index is strikingly silent across most of the models. Much of the literature on ethnic diversity and public goods provision suggests that ethnic diversity should be caustic in India's slums, where part of the impetus for development falls on the capacity of

---

The stated value should not be understood as a strict, specific point at which statistical significance is lost (Hainmueller et al. 2019).

[43] I also examine a dichotomous measure of party representational balance – whether or not a settlement has party workers affiliated to more than one party (see Tables B.16 and B.17). Results are mixed and mostly statistically insignificant.

[44] These same data limitations diminish the insights that can be gained from examining non-linear interactions. See Hainmueller et al. 2019 on nonlinearities in interaction terms.

residents to organize and make group-based claims. Importantly, against this expectation, I do not find systematic evidence of a negative relationship between ethnic diversity and public service provision. This is also true in models where I drop party worker density (Table B.1) and drop party worker density and include only basic control variables (Table B.2).[45] Recall that the second part of the theoretical framework argues that ethnic diversity is positively related to the density of party workers. Provocatively, this represents a pathway through which ethnic diversity could *positively* influence local public goods provision, potentially offsetting the negative mechanisms highlighted by other work. That there is no strong evidence here of either a positive or negative relationship between ethnic diversity and public service provision likely reflects the fact that there are numerous complex mechanisms linking the two variables,[46] which differ in the direction and magnitude of their effects. The reduced form or overall impact of ethnic diversity on public goods provision may therefore not be clear.

The principal social capital index is positive and significant in its association with the provision of streetlights and trash collection. It is also positively associated with the primary development index. Settlements home to more cooperative and trusting residents thus tend to have higher levels of local public goods provision than those in which residents are uncooperative and mistrusting. These findings are in line with prior studies of social capital.[47]

Coefficients on average margins of victory at the assembly constituency (AC) level fail to attain statistical significance in relation to the development indicators. The significance of average margins of victory at the municipal ward level is limited to its association with government medical camps. Given that I examine twelve tests of electoral competition across the six models, this finding is likely an artifact of statistical chance. The silence of average margins of victory is inconsistent with studies that posit a positive impact of electoral competition on public service provision.[48]

---

[45] Results are similar when using ethnic diversity data from the Auerbach and Thachil 2015 resident survey (Table B.19). The components of the ethnic diversity index – caste diversity, religious diversity, and regional (state) diversity – are also broadly statistically insignificant in their relationship with the development indicators (Table B.3).
[46] Habyarimana et al. 2009; Singh and vom Hau 2016.
[47] Krishna 2002; Varshney 2002.
[48] This finding, however, is consistent with Cleary's 2007 study on urban Mexico, where he finds that it is bottom-up citizen pressure, not electoral competition, that drives state responsiveness.

The coefficient on settlement population (logged) is positive and significant in its relationship with paved road coverage, household sewer connections, government medical camps, and all three of the development indices. These results lend support to the assertion that more populous settlements receive more attention in the allocation of public resources than their smaller counterparts.

Settlement notification is positively related to paved road coverage and all three of the development indices.[49] Notification, however, should not be seen as an independent cause of development but rather a consequence of state responsiveness. When controlling for settlement notification, party worker density remains positive and significant in its association with the same development indicators and indices.

I next examine whether settlements that are fragmented in the party preferences of their residents tend to have lower levels of community development. In the average settlement, 47 percent of respondents support the BJP (with a one standard deviation of 21 percentage points) and 41 percent of respondents support the INC (with a one standard deviation of 21 percentage points). An impressive fifty-eight settlements have at least 30 percent of respondents supporting the BJP and at least 30 percent of respondents supporting the INC. Twenty-five settlements have at least 40 percent of residents supporting the BJP and at least 40 percent of residents supporting the INC. Using the latter threshold, I generate a dichotomous variable for politically fragmented settlements.

Settlements that are politically fragmented do not tend to have lower levels of infrastructural development and access to public services.[50] The dichotomous variable is uniformly statistically insignificant at conventional levels across all six of the development indicators. Results are similar using cutoffs of 35 or 30 percent. As noted above, these findings should be interpreted in the context of cross sectional data that cannot take into account changes in the distribution of intra-settlement partisan preferences over time. Still, the findings provide suggestive evidence that politically fragmented settlements are not systematically less developed than those with more homogenous partisan preferences.

I next look at the relationship between the percentage of swing voters in a settlement and outcomes in local public goods provision. In the average settlement, 34 percent of respondents report having switched their votes

---

[49] See Table B.4. Notification was measured using data from the Jaipur and Bhopal RAY datasets. Eighty-one of the 111 sampled settlements are notified.
[50] Results presented in Table B.5.

between parties over the last several elections (with a one standard deviation of 13 percentage points). The results show that the percentage of swing voters lacks statistical significance across all of the development indicators except for piped water, where it is negative and statistically significant (p = 0.08).[51] I do not, therefore, find consistent evidence of a relationship between the percentage of swing voters in settlements and outcomes in local development.

Finally, I examine the interaction between the number of years that the BJP or INC has been in power in a constituency (since 1980 for state assembly constituencies and 1999 for municipal wards) and whether or not a settlement is a BJP or INC stronghold. I code settlements as BJP or INC strongholds if more than 60 percent of respondents support the BJP or INC, respectively.[52] Tables B.7 through B.10 present regression results and Table B.11 presents the marginal effects of years of party rule (BJP or INC) in constituencies (state assembly constituencies or municipal wards) when settlements are or are not party strongholds (for the BJP or INC). The marginal effects of party years in power, conditional on the settlement being a stronghold for that party, are positive and statistically significant with respect to household sewer connections and government medical camps (BJP years in the state assembly constituency and BJP strongholds) and paved roads (BJP years in the ward and BJP strongholds; INC years in the state assembly constituency and INC strongholds). The results are similar when I change what constitutes a stronghold to 65 or 70 percent support. These findings offer modest evidence of core targeting with respect to some of the local public goods under study.

### Alternative Model Specifications and P-Value Adjustments

I now discuss results from several alternative model specifications and p-value adjustments that account for multiple hypothesis testing. First, I

---

[51] See Table B.6.
[52] Sixty percent is an appropriate cutoff given that it is roughly one standard deviation above the average level of support for either of the parties. Moreover, in the average settlement, just over 12 percent of respondents support a party besides the BJP or INC (or do not participate in elections), and so 60 percent of local voters supporting a party is substantial. A dichotomous variable for party stronghold is also conceptually appropriate because politicians are unlikely to know the level of local party support with exact precision. Instead, as some of the interviews quoted in Chapter 3 suggest, politicians see settlements in more binary terms – whether or not "most" voters there support the party.

consider Tobit and fractional logit models because five of the six development indicators are bound between 0 and 100, and there is some clustering of observations at those extremes.[53] This is also true for streetlights, though only with the lower bound of zero. Results from these two specifications are consistent with the OLS results. Next, to ensure outliers are not driving the results, I examine robust regression models with Huber weights. Results are consistent with those from the OLS models, with the exception of the association between party worker density and municipal trash removal, where the p-value rises above 0.10.[54]

I address multiple hypothesis testing – that the probability of falsely rejecting at least one null hypothesis grows with the number of statistical tests conducted – in two ways. The first has already been presented: the construction of a summary index, which reduces the number of tests and provides a broad assessment of party worker density's relationship with local development. Second, I calculate adjusted p-values to control for the false discovery rate.[55] This approach controls for the expected proportion of false rejections. Party worker density continues to exhibit significance at conventional levels in relation to paved roads, streetlights, and government medical camps. The adjusted p-value for trash collection floats just above 0.10.[56] The significance of party worker density vis-à-vis the development indices, and the broad robustness of the findings after controlling for the false discovery rate, reduce concerns of multiple hypothesis testing.

To summarize, the findings on party worker density are robust to the inclusion of a wide range of theoretically important potential confounders. They are also robust to several alternative model specifications and p-value adjustments.[57] Party worker density is positively related to paved roads, streetlights, government medical camps, and with less consistency, municipal trash collection. Party worker density is also positively

---

[53] Fractional logit models take into account the boundedness of the five dependent variables that are proportions. See Papke and Wooldridge 1996 on fractional response models.
[54] See Tables B.13 through B.15 for results from the alternative model specifications.
[55] See Benjamini et al. 2006 and Anderson 2008 on the false discovery rate. I calculate adjusted p-values using the Stata code from Anderson 2008.
[56] The adjusted p-values (q-values) for party worker density are 0.024 in relation to paved roads, 0.027 in relation to streetlights, 0.034 in relation to medical camps, and 0.119 in relation to trash removal. The adjusted p-values for party worker density are 0.542 and 0.933 for piped water and sewers, respectively. For reference, the unadjusted p-values on party worker density are 0.004 (paved roads), 0.009 (streetlights), 0.017 (medical camps), 0.079 (trash removal), 0.451 (piped water), and 0.933 (sewers).
[57] Results are broadly consistent when only controlling for variables that are plausibly antecedent to the formation of party worker networks (see Table B.12).

## 6.5 CAUSALITY AND HISTORICAL SEQUENCING

The *causal* nature of the statistical relationships presented above remain murky. Concerns over endogeneity and unobserved heterogeneity cannot be fully dismissed, and a paucity of historical data on urban slums prevents an assessment of the statistical relationships over time. While causal identification is a looming challenge with such observational data, qualitative fieldwork can provide important insights into context and historical processes that improve our understanding of causality. Specifically, confidence in the statistical results can be strengthened along two fronts. First, in this section, I address issues of historical sequencing in the political organization and development of squatter settlements to reduce concerns of selection bias and reverse causality. In the following chapter, I delve into the deeper determinants of local party organization. I will argue that variation in party worker networks across settlements, in part, stems from geographical and migratory factors that are largely antecedent or unrelated to outcomes in public service delivery.

### Shared Initial Conditions of Underdevelopment and Political Disorganization

Squatter settlements emerge on greenfield sites that initially lack public infrastructure and services.[58] My interviews with veteran residents on the early conditions of their settlements, as well as historical photographs I collected in Bhopal and Jaipur, all reflect this defining feature of squatter settlements. One squatter in Bhopal, for instance, described the state of his settlement when he arrived in the late 1970s: "The roads were mud, there were no drains; there was nothing."[59] Similarly, a slum leader in another area of Bhopal, reflecting on the early conditions of his settlement, recalled, "There was nothing ... the area was entirely a field (*maedan*)."[60] Other studies of Indian squatter settlements make the same observations. Rao, for example, notes in his study of a Pune squatter settlement: "Old residents who have lived here for fifty to sixty years recollect that when

---

[58] See Figures 6.5 through 6.7 for photographs of just-established squatter settlements.
[59] Interview, Bhopal, September 2, 2011.  [60] Interview, Bhopal, September 23, 2012.

FIGURE 6.5 A squatter settlement emerging in Jaipur, early 1980s
*Note*: Photograph courtesy of Alice Garg. This photograph was previously included in my article "Informal Archives: Historical Narratives and the Preservation of Paper in India's Urban Slums." *Studies in Comparative International Development* 53, no. 3 (2018): 343–64. The photograph is reprinted here with permission from Springer Nature.

they first came here to live, the place was completely deserted except for trees, shrubs, and boulders."[61]

The origins of squatter settlements in such conditions are the result of the deliberate actions of the initial squatters. Squatters frequently set up their shanties in vacant areas that are otherwise undesirable for human habitation – for reasons of either illegality or environmental sensitivity – reducing the immediate threat of eviction. These settlements are often located in precarious areas such as riverbeds and mountainsides; along drains, highways, and railroad tracks; and next to factories and garbage dumps. Gooptu summarizes this point in her historical study of India's urban poor: "Hutments and temporary shanties ... sprouted on low lying marshy tracts, un-drained ditches and swampy river fronts, which could not be built over."[62]

Squatters in Latin America employ similar strategies. In his study of Caracas's *barrios*, Ray writes, "new migrants usually had to seek out

[61] Rao 1990, p. 41.   [62] Gooptu 2001, p. 97.

202  Demanding Development

FIGURE 6.6 A squatter settlement emerging in Jaipur, early 1980s
*Note*: Photograph courtesy of Alice Garg

FIGURE 6.7 A squatter settlement emerging in Bhopal, early 1980s
*Note*: Photograph courtesy of Jhabbu Lal Sahu

worthless bits of land – in the *quebradas* (dry creek beds), under bridges, on abandoned railroad lines, and in marshy areas – and pack themselves in as best they could."[63] Holzner describes the location of a Mexican squatter settlement in related terms: "Before 1990, the hills were ... barren and unused, too steep and too dry for agriculture and too far from the center of town to be attractive as a residential site."[64] During Burgwal's fieldwork in Quito, a squatter described the origins of his settlement on a barren plot of land: "We went up through the woods. We crossed the whole *hacienda*. It was just woodland."[65]

Another important characteristic of squatting in India and other countries in South Asia and Africa is that it commonly occurs through gradual accretion – disjointed arrivals by families and small groups of migrants that trickle in over time – not large, preplanned land invasions in which entire settlements are erected in a matter of days.[66] Squatting through gradual accretion unfolds over months and years, expanding the boundaries of settlements in the process.[67] Strong, settlement-wide forms of slum leadership – among squatters who come from different villages and states and belong to different castes and religions – do not come prefabricated, ready to spring into action upon arrival. Slum leadership and political linkages are constructed afterward, as described in Chapter 5. This is not to suggest that politicians in India's cities do not lend their assistance in thwarting eviction to allow for the rise of new "vote banks"; they do. However, slum leadership, and linkages between slum leaders and political elites, do not take shape until squatters settle the land and begin to organize for public services and security from eviction.

The unsanctioned origins of squatter settlements on barren lands, and their disjointed formation through gradual accretion, are analytically important points. They suggest that the initial waves of squatters did not self-select into areas with certain levels of local development or forms of political organization. Divergences in infrastructural development and access to public services are the result of factors that unfold after the dust of squatting settles and residents begin to organize and make demands on the state.

Moreover, as we saw in Chapters 4 and 5, party workers are recruited from slum settlements, live within those settlements, and engage in

---

[63] Ray 1969, p. 32.  [64] Holzner 2004, p. 228.  [65] Burgwal 1996, p. 52.
[66] See UN-Habitat 1982 on squatting through gradual accretion.
[67] In their study of Karachi, Schoorl et al. (1983, p. 50) refer to these as "unorganized invasions."

leadership activities for local residents. They are not dispatched to settlements by party organizations, nor do they independently rove among settlements to either enjoy higher levels of public services in more developed settlements or take advantage of greater demands for their problem-solving services in more marginalized, underdeveloped settlements. Instead, workers emerge from – and are deeply embedded in – the social networks of their settlement; to leave the settlement is to leave behind the social ties from which they derive authority. These figures move to slums with other squatters and build a following afterward by demonstrating an ability to get things done. These defining features of slum leader emergence and local party organization reduce concerns that party workers self-select into more developed settlements, introducing reverse causality.

### Formal Institutional Change in Urban India

Two formal institutional changes took place in India in the early 1990s that represent critical junctures in the political economy of slum development. First, the Seventy-Fourth Constitutional Amendment created a third tier of urban local government. Municipalities were thereafter mandated to hold local elections every five years and were given greater responsibilities over public service provision, making ward councillors and municipal officials targets of slum residents' claims. Second, and also starting in the early 1990s, are the discretionary "area development funds" that are allocated to elected representatives. These discretionary funds are frequently used to provide local public goods in slums.

All but 2 of the 111 settlements under examination in this book emerged well *before* India's decentralization reforms and the start of area development funds in the early 1990s, when local public goods and services started to be extended to slums in a more robust fashion. As illustrated in the case studies, settlement demographics largely took root beforehand, as did the rise of slum leadership and linkages with parties. Settlement demographics and leadership are, of course, not static. Nor were local public goods and services completely absent across all slums in Bhopal and Jaipur prior to the early 1990s.[68] Rather, this is to argue that

---

[68] Mitra 1988 and Risbud 1988 document forms of public service delivery in the mid-1980s – in particular, the provision of water and electricity – in some of Bhopal's slum settlements. Yet, as the case studies demonstrate, the provision of local public goods and services predominantly took off after decentralization in the early 1990s.

the foundations of settlement demographics and political organization were largely laid prior to decentralization in the early 1990s, reducing concerns of reverse causality – that levels of local development shaped the nature of local party organization.

## 6.6 CONCLUSION

Drawing on quantitative data from 111 squatter settlements in Bhopal and Jaipur, this chapter presented evidence that denser networks of party workers are associated with higher levels of infrastructural development and public service provision. Party worker density is positively related to paved road coverage, streetlight coverage, municipal trash collection, and the provision of government medical camps, as well as the primary development index. Definitively ruling out the possibility of unobserved variables confounding the results is, of course, challenging in an observational study. Yet the fact that I obtain consistent results for party worker density after accounting for theoretically important potential confounders lends confidence to the findings.

The statistical results presented in this chapter provide evidence of a positive relationship between party worker density and public service provision, not estimates of causal effects. Given the complex, time-intensive processes of political organization and development in slums, this is likely an unavoidable limitation. Still, the quantitative results, taken together with the qualitative findings presented in the preceding chapters, underscore the positive relationship between party worker density and local public goods provision. Furthermore, the origins of squatter settlements in undeveloped conditions, as well as the timing and nature of their political organization and development, provide considerable reason to conclude that the statistical relationships can be explained through the theoretical framework. I now turn to examining the formation of party worker networks and why they vary so strikingly in their density and partisan distribution across settlements.

# 7

# Why Party Worker Networks Spread Unevenly Across Settlements

Urban slums are often portrayed as places rife with clientelistic politics, where we would expect party workers to be widespread in their presence, solving resident problems and engaging in acts of voter mobilization for politicians.[1] Yet, this book demonstrates that party workers vary remarkably in their density and partisan distribution across the slum settlements of two major north Indian cities. Such variation represents a significant and unexplored puzzle for studies of distributive politics. Why are party workers so uneven in their presence and concentration across slum settlements – neighborhoods that politicians in India's cities often refer to as electorally crucial "vote banks"?

The answer to this question has immediate analytical consequence for the findings presented in the preceding chapter. Chapter 6 showed that the density of party workers – the per capita number of party workers in a settlement – is positively related to the provision of several local public goods and services – paved roads, streetlights, municipal trash collection, and government medical camps. These findings beg the question of why some settlements are full of party workers while others are thin or absent of them. This chapter takes up this antecedent question.

I argue that two variables largely drive the uneven spread of party worker networks across settlements. The first is settlement population. A settlement's population shapes electoral incentives for parties to expend limited organizational positions and party patronage. It is more advantageous for party elites to allocate a unit of these resources to larger slums

---

[1] For examples, see Gay 1994, Auyero 2001, Hansen 2001, Edelman and Mitra 2007, and Murillo et al. 2019.

because informal leaders in those settlements have bigger potential crowds of voters to deliver during elections and rallies. Moreover, and from the bottom-up, residents of more populous settlements have greater incentives to enter the fray of slum leadership given the larger pools of residents from which they can aspire to draw fees for problem-solving activities, demand party patronage during elections, and generate the public support that fuels party promotions. Such incentives in larger settlements generate dense concentrations of slum leaders and, in turn, more slum leaders for parties to bring into their organizations.

The second variable is ethnic diversity. Higher levels of ethnic diversity tend to increase the density of informal leaders because residents often prefer to support co-ethnic slum leaders.[2] Over time, parties seek to bring slum leaders into their organizations to establish local nodes of party influence, and so settlements with denser concentrations of slum leaders tend to produce denser networks of party workers. There is not, however, a one-to-one match between ethnic groups and informal leaders in India's slums. Because of the importance of non-ethnic criteria in slum leader selection – charisma, occupational connectivity to municipal officials, and sufficient education to engage in written claim-making, to name just a few[3] – many residents are without co-ethnic slum leaders. Residents of smaller ethnic groups within a settlement also have reasons to look outside their narrow group for effective leadership and numbers in claim-making. Thus, while higher levels of ethnic heterogeneity tend to increase the density of party workers, ethnicity does not rigidly define linkages between residents and party workers. The market for a following extends beyond a party worker's own ethnic group, widening the arena of competition among party workers for resident support.

I begin this chapter by investigating the correlates of party worker density and party representational balance. I then take a step backward in the historical sequencing of events to probe why squatter settlements exhibit differences in their population sizes and levels of ethnic diversity. I will argue that these two demographic variables are largely the result of geographic and migratory factors that are unrelated to party organization and public service delivery, providing analytical leverage in assessing their impact on the rise of party worker networks and, in turn, local development.

---

[2] Auerbach and Thachil 2018.
[3] See Auerbach and Thachil 2018 on the attributes that slum residents look for in their slum leaders.

## 7.1 THE CORRELATES OF PARTY WORKER DENSITY AND PARTY REPRESENTATIONAL BALANCE

The two explanatory variables of theoretical interest are settlement population and ethnic diversity. I combine three key dimensions of ethnicity in urban India – caste (*jati*), religion, and region (state) of origin – into a single measure of ethnic diversity using principal component analysis. I do so for two reasons. First, they are, in part, overlapping. A settlement with residents who migrated from more than one state in India will, by extension, likely have more than one caste group because of the localized nature of *jati*. Further, a settlement home to residents of more than one religion will likely have more than one caste group given the religion-specific nature of *jati*. Combining the three categories of ethnicity into a single measure accounts for this. Second, a single measure cuts the number of hypotheses tested about ethnic diversity by two-thirds, reducing concerns of multiple hypothesis testing. This is important in the absence of a priori hypotheses on which dimension of ethnic diversity will prove most salient. Only one component has an eigenvalue greater than one (and is positively related to all three dimensions of ethnicity), suggesting it is a good overall measure of ethnic diversity.

I examine several other potential explanations of variation in party worker density and party representational balance. The first is the average level of electoral competition that settlements have been exposed to since their establishment. Settlements situated in constituencies that have historically been competitive might have denser concentrations of party workers since parties have greater incentives to extend their networks into neighborhoods to chase after every vote. I examine this at the municipal ward (since 1994 in Jaipur and 1999 in Bhopal) and state assembly constituency (since 1980) levels. Since the dataset is cross-sectional, I average competition scores – margins of victory between winners and runner-ups – over time in the wards and assembly constituencies (AC) within which settlements are located.

A second potential explanation is the broad ethnic makeup of settlements, which may attract or discourage parties from making investments in local network building.[4] The BJP's exclusionary Hindu nationalism

---

[4] For seminal studies on ethnicity and distributive politics in India and sub-Saharan Africa, see Chandra 2004 and Posner 2005, respectively.

# Explaining the Uneven Spread of Party Worker Networks

would suggest that Muslim-majority settlements are likely to have few or no BJP workers. The BJP's conventionally understood electoral base among "Bania-Brahmin," upper-caste Hindus[5] would also suggest that settlements mostly home to residents belonging to the Scheduled Castes (SCs) and Scheduled Tribes (STs) are more likely to be thin or absent of BJP workers. I therefore examine the association between the percentages of Muslims and SC/STs in settlements and party worker density, disaggregated by party.

I control for several other variables. The first is settlement age, accounting for the fact that older settlements have simply had a longer period of time to develop networks of party workers. I also control for the average income and education of residents, the percentage of residents who have formal land titles, landownership categories, whether the settlement was surveyed in 2015, and the city in which the settlement is located (Jaipur = 0, Bhopal = 1).

## Party Worker Density

When party worker density is the outcome variable under examination, Tobit is an appropriate model specification because party worker density can be understood as bottom censored, with a latent stock of aspiring party workers who have not yet been extended party positions. There is also a clustering of observations at zero, further making Tobit an appropriate model specification.

Settlement population (logged) is positive and statistically significant in its association with party worker density (Table 7.1). The ethnic diversity index is also positive and statistically significant in its association with party worker density. Larger and more ethnically diverse settlements thus tend to have higher levels of party worker density than smaller and less ethnically diverse settlements.

With respect to the other explanatory variables, the coefficient on average electoral competition at the state assembly constituency level is statistically significant. The direction of that coefficient, however, is counterintuitive: a positive coefficient means that *larger* vote margins are associated with higher levels of party worker density. In other words,

---

[5] See Thachil 2014 on this conventional understanding of the BJP's core base of support.

TABLE 7.1 *Correlates of party worker density*

|  | Party worker density (OLS) | | Party worker density (Tobit) | |
| --- | --- | --- | --- | --- |
|  | M1 | M2 | M3 | M4 |
| City | 0.399 | 0.195 | 0.527 | 0.296 |
|  | (0.333) | (0.393) | (0.375) | (0.421) |
| Log population | 0.438** | 0.474** | 0.603*** | 0.638*** |
|  | (0.200) | (0.206) | (0.204) | (0.208) |
| 2015 Settlement | 0.203 | 0.135 | 0.312 | 0.230 |
|  | (0.287) | (0.293) | (0.350) | (0.351) |
| Settlement age | 0.0101 | 0.00762 | 0.00983 | 0.00582 |
|  | (0.0121) | (0.0141) | (0.0157) | (0.0162) |
| Average education | 0.0678 | 0.0835 | 0.0826 | 0.0960 |
|  | (0.0722) | (0.0749) | (0.0893) | (0.0932) |
| Monthly HH income per capita | 0.000120 | 0.0000922 | 0.000218 | 0.000191 |
|  | (0.000272) | (0.000288) | (0.000313) | (0.000314) |
| Ethnic diversity index | 0.240** | 0.244** | 0.353** | 0.367** |
|  | (0.105) | (0.110) | (0.144) | (0.144) |
| Central land |  | −0.207 |  | −0.142 |
|  |  | (0.338) |  | (0.379) |
| Private land |  | 0.225 |  | 0.333 |
|  |  | (0.537) |  | (0.508) |
| AC electoral competition |  | 0.0560* |  | 0.0712* |
|  |  | (0.0333) |  | (0.0388) |
| Ward electoral competition |  | 0.0128 |  | 0.0145 |
|  |  | (0.0202) |  | (0.0247) |
| Land titles |  | −0.000833 |  | 0.00144 |
|  |  | (0.00755) |  | (0.00802) |
| Constant | −2.533* | −3.594** | −4.315** | −5.599*** |
|  | (1.521) | (1.481) | (1.709) | (1.884) |
| Sigma |  |  | 1.512*** | 1.485*** |
|  |  |  | (0.116) | (0.114) |
| Observations | 111 | 111 | 111 | 111 |
| $R^2$/pseudo $R^2$ | 0.209 | 0.234 | 0.083 | 0.093 |

*Note*: Standard errors in parentheses (robust standard errors for OLS models)
* $p < 0.10$, ** $p < 0.05$, *** $p < 0.01$

settlements in *less* competitive assembly constituencies exhibit higher party worker densities. The coefficient on electoral competition at the municipal ward level is positive in sign but statistically insignificant. The remaining explanatory variables fail to attain statistical significance. Older settlements are not more likely to have higher levels of party worker density than more recently established ones. Settlements with higher average household incomes and education levels are not more or less likely to have dense networks of party workers than those with lower average household incomes and education levels. The coefficients on landownership categories and the percentage of residents with land titles similarly lack statistical significance.

After disaggregating party worker density into its INC and BJP components (see Table 7.2), I find that the percentage of SCs/STs in settlements is not related to either BJP or INC worker density. The percentage of Muslim residents, however, is negative and statistically significant in its association with BJP worker density and positive and statistically significant in its association with INC worker density. These findings are consistent with conventional wisdom regarding the BJP's exclusionary Hindu nationalism[6] and the popularly understood political status of Muslims in Bhopal and Jaipur as a base of support for the INC. That said, I enumerated a surprisingly high number of Muslim BJP workers across the sampled settlements: 28 percent of enumerated Muslim party workers (47 of 168) are affiliated with the BJP. While the regressions show a negative association between the percentage of Muslim residents and BJP worker density, the nontrivial degree of BJP support among Muslim party workers is noteworthy and suggestive of some organizational efforts by the BJP in settlements with Muslim residents. Such efforts are illustrated in the case of Jaipur's Pahari settlement (see Chapter 5).

## Party Representational Balance

Why do settlements with party workers vary in the degree to which those party workers are split in their partisan affiliations? To examine the correlates of party representational balance, I estimate Tobit and fractional logit models. These model specifications are appropriate given the number of settlements with one-party representation (40) and the boundedness of the variable between 0 and 1.

---

[6] See Jaffrelot 1998 and Hansen 1999 on Hindu nationalism and the BJP.

TABLE 7.2 *Disaggregating INC and BJP party worker densities*

|  | INC worker density |  | BJP worker density |  |
|---|---|---|---|---|
|  | M5 (OLS) | M6 (Tobit) | M7 (OLS) | M8 (Tobit) |
| City | −0.0171 | −0.0415 | 0.0506** | 0.0785** |
|  | (0.0290) | (0.0410) | (0.0228) | (0.0341) |
| Log population | 0.0241** | 0.0680*** | 0.0354** | 0.0592*** |
|  | (0.0106) | (0.0202) | (0.0161) | (0.0161) |
| 2015 Settlement | −0.0221 | −0.0395 | 0.0342 | 0.0505* |
|  | (0.0216) | (0.0360) | (0.0221) | (0.0286) |
| Settlement age | 0.000324 | −0.000123 | 0.000636 | 0.000827 |
|  | (0.000906) | (0.00155) | (0.00105) | (0.00132) |
| Average education | 0.00425 | 0.00900 | 0.00633 | 0.00679 |
|  | (0.00534) | (0.0103) | (0.00549) | (0.00805) |
| Monthly HH income per capita | 0.0000217 | 0.0000451 | −0.00000714 | −0.00000309 |
|  | (0.0000192) | (0.0000301) | (0.0000182) | (0.0000254) |
| Central land | −0.00583 | −0.0125 | −0.0179 | −0.0176 |
|  | (0.0232) | (0.0378) | (0.0239) | (0.0312) |
| Private land | 0.0125 | 0.0152 | −0.00136 | 0.00907 |
|  | (0.0385) | (0.0501) | (0.0345) | (0.0417) |
| Percent Muslim | 0.00101** | 0.00144** | −0.000660* | −0.000973* |
|  | (0.000433) | (0.000648) | (0.000381) | (0.000553) |
| Percent SC/ST | 0.000110 | −0.0000471 | −0.000186 | −0.000172 |
|  | (0.000407) | (0.000740) | (0.000435) | (0.000601) |
| AC electoral competition | 0.000826 | 0.00330 | 0.00484* | 0.00597* |
|  | (0.00222) | (0.00409) | (0.00289) | (0.00325) |
| Ward electoral competition | 0.00125 | 0.00237 | −0.0000692 | −0.000743 |
|  | (0.00139) | (0.00258) | (0.00161) | (0.00204) |
| Land titles | −0.0000841 | −0.0000393 | −0.000286 | −0.000160 |
|  | (0.000612) | (0.000751) | (0.000516) | (0.000666) |
| Constant | −0.226** | −0.708*** | −0.258* | −0.498*** |
|  | (0.0871) | (0.197) | (0.131) | (0.147) |
| Sigma |  | 0.133*** |  | 0.118*** |
|  |  | (0.0132) |  | (0.00967) |
| Observations | 111 | 111 | 111 | 111 |
| $R^2$/pseudo $R^2$ | 0.223 | 1.645 | 0.252 | −1.075 |

*Note*: Standard errors in parentheses (robust standard errors for OLS models)
\* $p < 0.10$, ** $p < 0.05$, *** $p < 0.01$

The coefficient on settlement population (logged) is positive and statistically significant – larger settlements tend to have party worker networks that are more balanced between the BJP and INC. This relationship holds across the models in Table 7.3. If I use a dichotomous measure of party representational balance (whether settlements have at least one INC and one BJP worker), the results are similar. The coefficient on the ethnic diversity index is positive but insignificant at conventional levels in the fractional logit model. It also lacks statistical significance in the OLS specification, though it is significant and positive ($p < 0.10$) in the Tobit model. Hence, evidence of a relationship between ethnic diversity and party representational balance is modest.

Coefficients on the control variables mostly fail to attain statistical significance. There is some evidence of a positive relationship between average household income per capita and party representational balance, but otherwise the coefficients on settlement age, average education, land titles, and landownership categories are statistically insignificant.

## 7.2 WHY ARE SOME SETTLEMENTS MORE POPULOUS AND ETHNICALLY DIVERSE THAN OTHERS?

The analyses above provoke the question of why some settlements are larger and more ethnically diverse than others. Unearthing these "critical antecedents" is important,[7] as they set in motion the formation of party worker networks and, consequently, shape the capacity of residents to demand and secure development from the state. I argue below that settlement population and ethnic diversity are largely generated by factors unrelated to local party organization and development, strengthening the basis on which I assert population and ethnic diversity have a causal impact on party worker density and, in turn, local public goods provision.

### Settlement Size

The formation of squatter settlements in India, as in much of Asia and Africa, commonly occurs through a process of gradual accretion, wherein squatters trickle onto the land over time without large-scale, preplanned coordination.[8] It is rare for whole settlements to organize land invasions, as they sometimes do in Latin America, with strong forms of resident

---

[7] Slater and Simmons 2010.    [8] UN-Habitat 1982, p. 15.

TABLE 7.3 *Correlates of party representational balance*

|  | Party representational balance (OLS) |  | Party representational balance (fractional logit) |  | Party representational balance (Tobit) |  |
|---|---|---|---|---|---|---|
|  | M9 | M10 | M11 | M12 | M13 | M14 |
| City | −0.0631 | −0.0908 | −0.318 | −0.635 | −0.168 | −0.288 |
|  | (0.104) | (0.135) | (0.497) | (0.696) | (0.166) | (0.203) |
| Log population | 0.213*** | 0.215*** | 1.120*** | 1.203*** | 0.370*** | 0.387*** |
|  | (0.0500) | (0.0494) | (0.309) | (0.308) | (0.0942) | (0.0978) |
| 2015 Settlement | −0.0500 | −0.0601 | −0.326 | −0.426 | −0.0823 | −0.112 |
|  | (0.0777) | (0.0829) | (0.414) | (0.424) | (0.159) | (0.160) |
| Settlement age | −0.00239 | −0.00135 | −0.0159 | −0.0121 | −0.00542 | −0.00332 |
|  | (0.00386) | (0.00424) | (0.0197) | (0.0213) | (0.00762) | (0.00797) |
| Average education | 0.0201 | 0.0161 | 0.111 | 0.102 | 0.0353 | 0.0357 |
|  | (0.0189) | (0.0227) | (0.0991) | (0.121) | (0.0437) | (0.0457) |
| Monthly HH income per capita | 0.000114* | 0.000112 | 0.000677* | 0.000783* | 0.000140 | 0.000120 |
|  | (0.0000652) | (0.0000766) | (0.000394) | (0.000453) | (0.000133) | (0.000137) |
| Ethnic diversity index | 0.0643* | 0.0623 | 0.332 | 0.362 | 0.121* | 0.129* |
|  | (0.0384) | (0.0402) | (0.220) | (0.225) | (0.0670) | (0.0696) |
| Central land |  | −0.0689 |  | −0.372 |  | −0.165 |
|  |  | (0.0992) |  | (0.502) |  | (0.172) |
| Private land |  | 0.0993 |  | 1.001 |  | 0.237 |
|  |  | (0.148) |  | (0.795) |  | (0.239) |

|  |  |  |  |  |
|---|---|---|---|---|
| AC electoral competition | −1.432*** | 0.00659 |  | 0.0236 |
|  | (0.456) | (0.00994) |  | (0.0185) |
| Ward electoral competition |  | −0.00294 | 0.0647 | −0.00515 |
|  |  | (0.00608) | (0.0561) | (0.0123) |
| Land titles |  | 0.00001000 | −0.0207 | −0.000505 |
|  |  | (0.00171) | (0.0363) | (0.00348) |
| Constant |  | −1.494*** | −0.000530 | −3.160*** |
|  |  | (0.465) | (0.00881) | (0.945) |
|  |  |  | −11.72*** | −2.799*** |
|  |  |  | (2.963) | (0.810) |
|  |  | −10.20*** |  |  |
|  |  | (2.817) |  |  |
| Sigma |  |  | 0.562*** | 0.553*** |
|  |  |  | (0.0667) | (0.0655) |
| Observations | 91 | 91 | 91 | 91 |
| $R^2$/pseudo $R^2$ | 0.356 | 0.369 | 0.195 | 0.212 |

*Note:* Standard errors in parentheses (robust standard errors for OLS models)
* $p < 0.10$, ** $p < 0.05$, *** $p < 0.01$

leadership and thick relationships with politicians.[9] This is not to say that politicians are uninvolved in the formation of squatter settlements in India; on the contrary, they often encourage squatting to create bases of new supporters. Instead, it suggests that squatters typically construct their settlements in a fragmented, ad hoc fashion – processes that, in the eight case study settlements, unfolded over years, until the settlements approached their geographic limits. These limits can be physical – rivers, sand dunes, mountains, preexisting neighborhoods – or they can be institutional, based on landownership boundaries that, once crossed, provoke the ire of a government agency or private party.

Settlement eviction, while a looming threat for slum residents, has been infrequent in Bhopal and Jaipur. The vast majority of settlements listed in government reports and academic texts from the 1980s and 1990s still exist today.[10] While estimating the number of evictions is difficult without reliable government data, it appears that most slums in Bhopal and Jaipur have evaded eviction – so far – allowing them to expand toward the limits of the available land around them. While some settlements were never able to form because the initial squatters were promptly pushed off the land, having survived such incipient threats of eviction is a constant across the hundreds of squatter settlements that are now scattered across Bhopal and Jaipur.

Several factors facilitate the survival of squatter settlements once they are established. The first stems from conditions that dissuade other residential and commercial interests from competing for the land. Squatters often face reduced threats of eviction because of their location on environmentally sensitive lands.[11] Squatting on such lands is a deliberate tactic to avoid stirring the interests of competing groups in the city. Middle-class citizens have the means to avoid living on floodprone riverbeds, alongside railroad tracks, and on the slopes of

---

[9] On preplanned land invasions, see Perlman 1976, Gilbert 1998, and Lanjouw and Levy 2002. Also see UN-Habitat 1982 for a detailed discussion on the differences between land invasions and squatting through gradual accretion.

[10] Examples include Mitra 1988, Agnihotri 1994, Singhi 1997, and the Jaipur Municipal Corporation's 2004 slum survey.

[11] Scholars have long noted the draw of squatters to hazardous and otherwise undesirable lands. Singh and de Souza write, "Favored locations of squatters seem to be abandoned graveyards, embankments of drains, pits filled with refuse, dumping grounds, railway lands, and open undeveloped plots reserved for public buildings. These sites are favored for the very pragmatic reason that they offer the most secure tenure. There are usually no immediate alternative development plans for such land, and political pressure may be more easily exerted to prevent or delay eviction" (Singh and de Souza 1980, p. 42).

mountains.[12] Squatters on central government lands benefit from being in areas where formal housing construction is illegal, diminishing competing demands. As for those settlements on private lands under legal dispute, cases can become stuck in the slow grind of India's court system for years, allowing settlements to expand and making eviction more difficult with each additional shanty.

The second factor is rooted in simple electoral politics. Politicians often lend their support in thwarting eviction to cultivate loyal bases of supporters.[13] These political interventions undermine the ability of nonelected officials to dispatch bulldozers to clear the land. Moreover, such hurdles to eviction are raised once settlements find their way into official lists as "notified" slums, providing them a degree of protection from unannounced eviction.

Despite the real and continued threat of eviction, most slum settlements in Bhopal and Jaipur have remained in place, allowing them to expand over time to their surroundings. Given this scope for expansion, what determines the size of settlements?

One key determinant is idiosyncratic features of the local geography. These include rivers, lakes, sand dunes, mountainsides, and ravines, which form hard limits to where squatters can build their homes. Other constraints are part of the built space – factories, railroad tracks, storm drains, highways, markets, and preexisting neighborhoods. Landownership boundaries can also stop the expansion of settlements. For instance, many squatter settlements grow tightly parallel to railroad tracks, careful not to cross into nonrailroad land, which might encourage local actors to see them swiftly evicted. These physical and institutional features of the land define the extent to which slums can grow, generating much of their variation in size.

For an example, take Ganeshpuri, a squatter settlement in Jaipur. Migrants settled Ganeshpuri in 2003, after an eviction of squatters in the same location a few years prior. To the northeast of the settlement are the jagged mountains that flank Jaipur's eastern edge. The mountainside is

---

[12] Schoorl et al. make a similar point in their study of Karachi's slums: "Almost everywhere in the world squatter settlements tend to be located in areas of second choice, e.g. in riverbeds, and at the periphery of the cities. In the case of Karachi, indeed, one of the concentration areas is alongside watercourses" (Schoorl et al. 1983, p. 43).
[13] See Holland 2016 on such politicized acts of "forbearance" – the "intentional and revocable non-enforcement of law" (p. 232) – toward urban street venders and squatters in Latin America.

too steep and unstable for housing. Equally restrictive are the sand dunes beneath the mountains, located to the north and east of the settlement. It is difficult to get a stick to stand upright in the sand, let alone a *jhuggi* (shanty). To the south is a middle-class neighborhood that predated the settlement. And to the west is a drainage basin and temple grounds. Ganeshpuri has expanded to its maximum limits and now stands at 1,500 residents. Relative to its counterparts elsewhere in Jaipur, which have an average population of roughly 2,500 residents, Ganeshpuri will never be a large cluster of voters because of the physical boundaries that surround it.

To provide a second example, consider Rawan Mandi, a squatter settlement in central Jaipur that is constrained in its growth on all four sides by prior human development. Squatters began to settle Rawan Mandi in the early 2000s. To the north and east of Rawan Mandi are busy roads, as well as Jaipur's above-ground metro rail (started in 2010). To the west is a middle-class neighborhood that, like the roads, emerged before the arrival of the squatters. To the south is a privately owned plot of land, guarded by a tall and sturdy brick wall. Rawan Mandi has spread out to its maximum limits and is now home to about 400 residents. Because of their small numbers, residents of Rawan Mandi cannot position themselves as a large group of voters in the distributive politics of the city.

Constraints stemming from local geography thus drive much of the variation in the size of squatter settlements. As noted in Chapter 6, the average settlement in my sample was established thirteen years prior to decentralization and the establishment of area development funds in the early 1990s. Only two sampled settlements were established after this period. Most settlements had therefore expanded toward their maximum area by the time local public goods and services were more robustly provided to settlements in the mid-1990s and onward, reducing concerns of reverse causality – that party worker density generates slum size.

## Settlement Diversity

Why are India's urban slums so ethnically diverse in terms of caste, religion, and region of origin? Why don't poor migrants sort themselves into ethnic enclaves, generating settlements that are mostly homogenous? Prior studies on rural-urban migration in India have established that kinship and village networks do facilitate the migration process for individuals and small

Explaining the Uneven Spread of Party Worker Networks 219

groups. Migrants frequently self-select into settlements where they know a family member or someone from their *janam bhoomi* (place of birth) who can set them up with a place to stay and maybe even a job.[14] However, prior to their arrival, migrants do not anticipate the full nature and extent of ethnic diversity in the host settlement. The importance of having someone who can help with housing and employment narrows the degree to which squatters can shop around for socially desirable neighborhoods in the city. Additionally, a scarcity of land for squatting and the need to be in close proximity to local labor markets prevent squatters from sorting themselves into homogenous enclaves, even if they want to do so. These preferences and constraints generate the impressive ethnic diversity found in India's urban slums. Indeed, even the smallest clusters of adjacent households in India's slums are often socially diverse: a majority of survey respondents in 2012 (62 percent) said that at least one of their *immediate* neighbors belongs to a caste (*jati*) other than their own, and an even higher percentage (85 percent) stated that at least one of their immediate neighbors is from a village other than their own village of origin.[15]

I asked the 1,925 residents surveyed in 2012 to explain why they chose their specific settlement out of the hundreds of other settlements in Bhopal or Jaipur.[16] Respondents mostly stated preferences to be in close proximity to kin, opportunities for work, and available plots of land on which to squat. They rarely noted self-selecting into settlements based on ethnic considerations.[17] The movement of poor squatters, guided by preferences to be close to a known person and employment, creates diverse conditions like the one described by Rao: "During the course of the last twenty years or so, hundreds of families of different castes came and settled here [in

---

[14] See Mitra 2003.
[15] These micro-geographies of social diversity also reflect squatting through gradual accretion.
[16] Respondents were asked, "Jaipur/ Bhopal is a big city with many slum settlements. Why did you move to this *particular* settlement?"
[17] The breakdown of responses are as follows: to join family members (619 respondents); to work inside or nearby the slum (413 respondents); land available for squatting (493 respondents); rooms available for rent (77 respondents); proximity to public transportation (17 respondents); to live near fellow villagers (59 respondents); to live near caste fellows (54 respondents); was attracted to the development of the settlement (36 respondents). A total of 181 respondents said they "didn't know," and 37 observations are missing. Respondents were allowed to provide multiple responses, though few (46 respondents) provided more than one response.

a Pune slum] and this has affected the caste composition of [the slum] to a great extent."[18]

One axis along which a considerable degree of sorting does take place is religion. That the average fractionalization score for religion (0.17) is lower than the fractionalization scores for caste (0.80) and region of origin (0.28) is not surprising given several post-Independence episodes of Hindu-Muslim riots in Bhopal and Jaipur.[19] Gayer and Jaffrelot find Muslims to be marginalized and segregated in other large Indian cities.[20] Yet even segregation along religious lines in Bhopal and Jaipur's slums is dampened by the constraints over ethnic sorting described above. Indeed, the majority of the sampled settlements (70 of 111) *do* have both Hindu and Muslim residents (with many housing Buddhists and Sikhs as well). To a nontrivial degree, then, the compulsions and constraints of migration bring people of different castes, regions of origin, and religions into the same settlements, producing forms of ethnic diversity not found in the countryside.

## 7.3 CONCLUSION

This chapter investigated why party worker networks are uneven in their density and partisan balance across slum settlements. I argued that two variables largely drive this unevenness. The first is settlement population. From a party's perspective, a unit of limited party resources – party positions and patronage – has increasing returns in relation to settlement size. Leaders of larger slums have bigger potential crowds of voters to deliver during elections and so they command greater attention in the allocation of party positions than their counterparts in smaller slums. Residents of larger slums, moreover, have greater incentives to engage in slum leadership because they have a wider resident base from which to extract rents and party patronage. These top-down and bottom-up factors converge to produce dense networks of party workers in larger slums.

The second variable is ethnic diversity. Ethnic diversity tends to increase the density of slum leaders because residents often prefer to

---

[18] Rao 1990, p. 113. [19] See Mayaram 1993 on Hindu-Muslim riots in Jaipur.
[20] Gayer and Jaffrelot 2012.

support coethnic slum leaders.[21] Parties seek to build ties with slum leaders to absorb their local followings, and so more diverse settlements tend to produce denser networks of party workers. Most ethnic groups within slums, however, lack the size to pursue group claim-making alone, pushing them to look outward for numbers and informal leadership. And while residents may hold preferences for coethnic leaders, the importance of nonethnic criteria in slum leader selection leaves most without one. Ethnic diversity, then, tends to increase party worker density, though it does not fully define resident-party worker linkages.

The statistical analyses demonstrated that population and ethnic diversity have positive, statistically significant associations with party worker density. Both are also positively associated with party representational balance, though only the former exhibits a robust association at conventional levels of statistical significance.

I ended the chapter by asserting that settlement size and ethnic diversity flow from several factors that are independent of outcomes in political organization and public service provision. I argued that most settlements have avoided eviction because of political interventions as well as their location on otherwise undesirable lands, allowing them to balloon out toward the spatial limits around them. I then argued that due to a dearth of available land upon which to squat, and a desire to live near a family member or a contact who can help them get set up in the city, poor migrants move to slum settlements with people from different villages and states, belonging to different castes and religions. Because settlement population and ethnic diversity are largely shaped by geographic constraints and migratory decisions that are unrelated to local political organization and development, they anchor the theoretical framework to a largely exogenous foundation.

---

[21] Auerbach and Thachil 2018.

# 8

# Conclusion

In September 2010, during my first week of fieldwork in Jaipur's Ganpati settlement, a resident sat me down in front of his home and, hoping to spare me the trouble of having to conduct further interviews in Rajasthan's oppressive summer heat, gave me his all-purpose explanation of "slum politics" in India: "Look, slums are only vote banks in India. Politicians make promises that are not fulfilled."[1] This sentiment was echoed time and again during my interviews in Jaipur and Bhopal's slum settlements. Politicians, too, were frank in confirming that such cynicism is justified. A former INC MLA in Bhopal, for example, unapologetically told me, "After winning an election, parties are afraid to give slum dwellers all the facilities, like education, healthcare, roads, and other things, because they will become independent and not go around seeking help. That is a loss for the parties."[2]

Slums exhibit several characteristics arising from their general position in urban India that, taken together, suggest they should be widely marginalized in the distributive politics of India's cities, as the quotes above imply. These are low-income neighborhoods, where residents lack the resources to provide themselves many essential public goods and services. Slums are pervaded with informality in employment and housing and are commonly seen as bastions of clientelistic politics. Yet, despite sharing these broader vulnerabilities as a class of neighborhoods in India's cities, this book exposed striking variation across slum settlements in their access to local public goods and services. In some settlements, residents have

---

[1] Interview with Ganpati resident, Jaipur, September 24, 2010.
[2] Interview with former INC MLA, Bhopal, September 13, 2011.

managed to demand and secure paved roads, streetlights, piped water, sewers, municipal trash removal, and government medical camps. In other settlements, claims for these same public goods and services have been ignored. As a result, streets are dark, muddy, and full of garbage. Water is scarce and residents have no choice but to go to the bathroom in the open. Most settlements exist somewhere in between, suspended between complete squalor and full access to public services.

Uneven development across India's slums motivated the central question of this book: Why are some vulnerable communities able to demand and secure development from the state while others fail? This concluding chapter reviews the book's arguments and findings. It then outlines the contributions of the book to several literatures in comparative politics and discusses its implications for community-driven development efforts in cities of the Global South.

## 8.1 REVISITING THE THEORY AND FINDINGS

In the face of India's sprawling population of people living in slums, public resources for infrastructure and services in slums are limited – a situation exacerbated by the slow grind of government and leakage in funding as it trickles down to neighborhoods. These resources are also, as I argued in Chapter 2, largely politicized in their provision, and access is frequently mediated through hierarchical networks of political brokers. In this context, slum residents cannot passively wait for public goods and services to flow from citizen entitlements. Instead, they must be actively demanded from the state, with as much political heft as residents can muster.

Central to the political economy of development in India's slums are slum leaders. These actors operate in an informal space between residents and the larger political currents of the city. They emerge from the ranks of ordinary residents and become focal points of efforts to demand development because they possess attributes that allow them to get things done. Literacy and some formal education are two such attributes, as slum leaders must be able to write petitions and navigate state institutions. Some also possess humble forms of bureaucratic connectivity through their jobs – city clerks, security guards, or public sweepers – offering residents a valuable link to officials.[3]

---

[3] See Auerbach and Thachil 2018 on the qualities that residents look for in their slum leaders.

Chapters 4 and 5 showed that the emergence of slum leaders takes place through several pathways of resident selection. In some settlements, groups of residents sit to discuss who is best fit to lead. Other settlements hold informal elections, with campaigns and makeshift ballots. Other slum leaders rise to power more gradually, attracting resident support with their reputations for efficacy in problem-solving. Importantly, parties do not impose these figures on settlements. Instead, slum leaders migrate to the city like their neighbors and build personal followings afterward. It is this embedded status that makes them so attractive to parties.

Slum leaders play a prominent role in resident efforts to improve local conditions. The preceding pages documented slum leaders organizing residents for modest projects – digging drains, replacing hand pumps, fixing potholes, and sweeping trash. They write petitions, collect signatures, and lead residents to government offices to make demands. They also galvanize residents for settlement-wide protest. The many slum leaders profiled in this book engage in a wide assortment of other activities too, such as dispute resolution, overseeing the construction of temples and mosques, and assisting residents in securing ration cards and voter IDs.

Participating in the rough-and-tumble world of slum leadership invites material rewards and social prestige. Residents look to slum leaders to solve problems, ensuring a stream of fees for those slum leaders who are capable and responsive. A large following also attracts patronage and promotion in party organizations. Further, slum leaders live in settlements with their families and want public services for their own sake. This motivation should not be overlooked, as the social rootedness of slum leaders distinguishes them from the outside party activists that parachute into settlements during elections.

Of specific focus in this book are those slum leaders who have been absorbed into parties and given positions within their organizational hierarchies. I argued that slums with dense networks of these party workers – those with high per capita numbers of party workers – can more effectively claim public goods and services than those that are thin or absent of party workers.

Three mechanisms link party worker density with outcomes in local development. First, dense networks of party workers intensify competition among them for a personal following, pushing party workers to be responsive to resident demands or risk losing their base of public support. Informal accountability is further encouraged from above, as parties sanction workers if they undermine the party brand through inattentiveness to resident problems or thuggish behavior. Second, dense networks of party workers provide residents with numerous points of political connectivity. When slum leaders are members of party organizations, they have lines of communication with party elites. These vertical linkages are fostered through routine, face-to-face meetings between party workers and political elites. Connectivity also reveals and exerts itself through the use of party stationery when petitioning officials for public services. Third, dense networks of party workers offer an organizational structure for rallying residents, strengthening a slum's mobilizational capacity. Party workers can also activate larger party organizations in the city to draw attention to local problems. These three mechanisms were illustrated in Chapters 3, 4, and 5 with a rich assortment of qualitative data.

The theorized relationship between party worker density and local public goods provision was inductively derived from comparative ethnographic fieldwork in eight case study settlements. To test that theory with a larger, representative sample of slums in Bhopal and Jaipur, I conducted a survey across 111 squatter settlements in the two cities. Drawing on this quantitative data, I found party worker density to be positive and statistically significant in its association with the provision of most of the public goods and services under study: paved roads, streetlights, municipal trash collection, and government medical camps. These results, as demonstrated in Chapter 6, are robust to the inclusion of a wide range of potential confounders as well as several model specifications and post-estimation tests. The statistical findings thus provide compelling evidence that party worker density is positively related to local public goods provision.

The 111 settlements revealed wide variation in the party representational balance of their party workers – the extent to which party workers are split in their partisan affiliations. In some settlements, party workers all belong to the same party – either the BJP or INC. Others contain both BJP and INC workers, introducing a partisan element to competition among local party workers for resident support. I argued that the presence of party workers from competing parties has crosscutting effects on public service provision. On the one hand, because of the stakes of having one's party in power for claim-making, it can intensify competition for resident support, increasing incentives for party workers to be active problem solvers. It also provides residents with diverse partisan nodes of political connectivity – an asset in India's fluid electoral environment. On the other hand, rival party networks have incentives to undercut the other's mobilization efforts to diminish their electoral prospects, even to the detriment of local development. Further, elected representatives may believe that opposition party workers will undermine their credit-claiming efforts and therefore be less likely to extend public resources to settlements with opposition party workers.

Interviews with politicians and slum leaders, as well as ethnographic fieldwork in the eight case study settlements, provided qualitative evidence for these crosscutting mechanisms. Quantitatively, I found limited, suggestive evidence that higher levels of party representational balance conditionally attenuate the positive influence of party worker density with respect to some of the development indicators. However, considering the interactions across all of the development indicators, as well as taking into account a lack of observations for much of the variable's range, the quantitative results on party representational balance should be viewed as tentative. I argued this blurred statistical relationship between party representational balance and community development partially reflects the countervailing nature of its component mechanisms. The relationship between the partisan distribution of party workers in a settlement and outcomes in local development represents an important path for future research.

The central role of party workers in the drama of slum development raised an ancillary question: What explains variation in the density of party workers across settlements? I argued that two demographic factors – a settlement's population and level of ethnic diversity – powerfully influence the emergence of party worker networks. In the allocation of limited party positions and patronage, slum leaders in larger settlements tend to take priority over those in smaller settlements. This is because a party position invested in a larger settlement has higher electoral returns than in a smaller settlement. Slum leaders in larger settlements can potentially deliver larger blocs of votes, and are thus more crucial to cultivate as party workers. There are also bottom-up reasons why party workers proliferate in larger settlements. In larger settlements, there are bigger numbers of voters to mobilize and offer problem-solving assistance, generating rich opportunities to engage in rent seeking and political career building.

In addition to settlement size, I argued that ethnic diversity is positively related to the density of party worker networks. Increasing levels of ethnic diversity tend to increase the density of slum leaders within settlements because residents often prefer to support and turn to coethnic slum leaders. More diverse settlements consequently tend to develop more slum leaders per capita and, in turn, denser networks of party workers. Yet, because of the importance of nonethnic criteria in slum leader selection, many residents are without coethnic slum leaders, pushing them to look outside their narrow group for effective problem-solvers and greater numbers in claim-making. Slum leaders, moreover, are not limited to attracting the support of coethnics. Rather, they have incentives to work to attract non-coethnics to maximize their following in the settlement, extending the arena of competition for followers. Drawing on quantitative data from the 111 sampled settlements, I found that both population and levels of ethnic diversity are positively associated with party worker density.

Several aspects of the formation of squatter settlements lend confidence that the statistical results can be explained through the book's theoretical framework. The shared origins of squatter settlements in conditions of underdevelopment and political disorganization suggest that the first waves of squatters did not self-select into settlements with certain levels of party organization and access to public services. Further, all but two of the sampled settlements emerged before decentralization reforms and the start of area development funds in the early 1990s, when public service provision in Bhopal and Jaipur's slums sharply expanded. Hence, settlement demographics were largely defined before public goods and services were extended more robustly after decentralization, reducing concerns of reverse causality – that levels of public service provision shape settlement demographics and, in turn, the rise of slum leaders and party workers. Slum leaders also emerge from within settlements and do not rove among them to either enjoy public services in developed areas or exploit demands for informal leadership in neglected ones. The rooted nature of slum leadership reduces concerns of reverse causality as well – that party workers sort themselves in response to the outcome variables under study.

I also argued that local geographical features of the land, both natural and human-made, define the area in which a slum can physically expand – for instance, the space between a riverbed and factory, the base of a mountainside, or the area between the train tracks and a middle-class neighborhood. Invisible boundaries exist as well, fixed by landownership categories that carve cities into private and government-administered lands. To foster "vote banks", politicians keep the bulldozers at bay, allowing settlements to balloon outward toward their spatial limits. The size of slums, then, is largely generated by factors unrelated to party organization, providing analytical leverage in assessing the impact of population on party worker density and, in turn, local development.

## 8.2 IMPLICATIONS OF THE BOOK'S FINDINGS

In explaining the variable success of India's slum residents in demanding and securing development from the state, this book advances several literatures in the field of comparative politics. This final section outlines those contributions. It then concludes by discussing the implications of the book for the design and implementation of community-driven development programs in the expanding cities of the Global South.

### Democracy and Distributive Politics in the Indian City

Studies of distributive politics often cast poor voters as passive targets of material inducements, provided by parties to encourage electoral support and turnout.[4] Yet this book documents substantial political agency among India's slum residents – low-income voters, residing in neighborhoods with weak or absent formal property rights, who should typify constrained clients. Slum residents define and articulate their claims from the bottom-up, between the votes; they do not wait for public resources to be dangled in front of them during elections. They engage in "active" forms of citizenship that extend beyond voting, from forming neighborhood associations to routinely making claims on the state.[5] Furthermore, slum residents frequently select their slum leaders through community meetings, informal elections, and the daily choices of individual residents over whom to seek help from and follow. Slum residents are therefore pivotal in the construction of the political networks that link them to the state. In tracing the roots of local development, these active forms of citizenship require that we look past the election-time dispersal of cheap handouts to the daily efforts of poor voters to demand public infrastructure and services. They require us to rethink accounts of distributive politics that view party-voter linkages as top-down in formation and function.

Studies of distributive politics commonly assume that political brokers are uniformly present across the space under study, and that during elections these actors are poised to persuade and mobilize voters in their local domains of influence. In contrast, this book establishes that the presence, density, and partisan balance of party workers vary remarkably

---

[4] Stokes 2005; Nichter 2008; Gonzalez-Ocantos et al. 2012.
[5] Kruks-Wisner (2018, p. 9) defines active citizenship as "the quotidian practices through which citizens negotiate their social rights vis-à-vis the state. Citizenship in this sense is both a status (a set of rights) and an exercise (a set of practices)."

across neighborhoods. This book is, to my knowledge, the first to enumerate political intermediaries across a large and representative sample of urban neighborhoods and to examine the impact of uneven party worker networks on local development. A key contribution of this book, then, is to demonstrate that the geography of political brokerage – and by extension the claim-making capacity of localities – shapes distributive outcomes.

This book also demonstrates that in explaining variation in public service provision, slum residents are not usefully approached as atomistic voters who operate independently of space. Resident collective action and claim-making erupt in response to settlement-specific problems. Residents identify with their settlements, and the informal status of slum leaders flows from resident support. Politicians see slums as named pockets of the city with distinct social groups and patterns of informal leadership. The emphasis in the literature on individual voters – or large administrative or electoral units – misses this intermediary and informal level of political organization. Socially defined *neighborhoods* should thus enjoy far more prominence as units of analysis than they currently do in studies of distributive politics.

Chapters 4 and 5 provided descriptive accounts of the emergence and activities of slum leaders, shedding light on the nature of informal authority in settlements that are proliferating across many cities in the Global South. I argued that the activities and political compulsions of slum leaders must be assessed beyond their election-time party work. Slum leaders emerge from the pool of residents, face the same vulnerabilities as their neighbors, and most often become position-holding party workers after amassing a following through acts of problem-solving. Their party connections are important for growing and maintaining a following, but they are not the core source of a slum leader's informal authority. A narrow focus on election-time activities misses the quotidian ways that slum leaders emerge and work to improve their neighborhoods.

We saw in the previous chapters that India's slums are highly competitive brokerage environments, housing multiple slum leaders who jostle with one another to build a following, pushing them to demonstrate efficacy or else lose support to those who do. These are high-information environments, where the distribution of public support for slum leaders can rapidly transform in response to rumors of incompetence or thuggish behavior. Studies of political brokers often overlook such dynamics, sidestepping the possibility of locally competitive, multifocal brokerage.[6] As such, they fail to consider the consequences of inter-broker competition for broker responsiveness and local public goods provision. It is precisely the multifocal nature of slum leadership and competitive market for followers that compel these actors to engage in the many problem-solving activities documented in this book. In explaining distributive outcomes in "mediated states,"[7] scholars should investigate the nature of local competition among political brokers, which can produce a degree of responsiveness and accountability in political networks that are otherwise assumed to be mostly devoid of them.

### The Limits of Political Organization in India's Slums

Taking the political agency of slum residents seriously is not to suggest that such agency is unconstrained. This book identified serious manifestations of social marginalization and economic deprivation in India's slums that curtail the ability of residents to expand what Amartya Sen would refer to as their capabilities and freedoms.[8] These constraints stem from weak or absent formal property rights, material poverty, low rates of formal education, and a complex blend of economic and social forces that threaten to push them off the land. While the political struggles described in this book at times yield access to public services, it is important to place such victories within the context of larger structures that generate deep spatial inequalities in India's cities, which, as Heller and his coauthors assert, fragment the quality of citizenship across neighborhoods.[9]

It is similarly crucial to recognize the hard limits of the types of local organization documented in this book. The forms of resident claim-making encountered in previous chapters were mostly animated by and exerted to address settlement-specific problems. While slum federations were present in Bhopal and Jaipur (like the INC's *Jhuggi Jhopri Maha Sangh* in Bhopal), slum leaders mostly used these federations as vehicles to petition the state for *their* settlements. Political organization is thus splintered along settlement lines. I encountered little intersettlement organization to push for larger changes in city governance. The only meaningful examples that go against this trend are dated, stretching back to the work of the Communist Party in Bhopal and Jaipur in the

---

[6] Important exceptions include Auyero 2001 and Camp 2015.   [7] Berenschot 2010.
[8] Sen 1999.   [9] Heller et al. 2015.

1960s and 1970s. Hence, there is substantial need for organizational efforts across settlements to demand larger, systemic changes in land tenure security and access to public services.

## Political Parties and Local Problem-Solving

India's political parties are commonly described as organizationally weak, especially below the level of the district.[10] In this light, we would expect party workers to play little or no role in neighborhood mobilization. Such descriptions of weak parties, however, mostly flow from studies of rural India. This book documents structured and active party organizations in India's cities. Party organizational networks fan out across neighborhoods and stretch upward, through ranked committees at the booth, ward, block, and district levels to the highest strata of party leadership in cities. In India's slums, where migrants hail from a diversity of villages and states and belong to different castes and religions, parties cannot turn to long-held forms of social authority to mobilize voters. Instead, they must actively bring slum leaders into their fold to broadcast influence downward into these urban "vote banks." The networks that result from such organizational efforts play an instrumental role in local development.

Scholarly assessments of weak party organizations are often made from the perspective of political elites – that the leading or even sole function of party workers is to be in a constant, frenzied state of persuading and monitoring voters. This book broadens the view of the activities and motivations of party workers. Party workers in India's slums emerge from within settlements to resist eviction and demand development. It is these acts of problem-solving that generate public support, which parties lean on during elections. In assessing the strength of party organizations, studies should widen their focus to the everyday activities of party workers. Sleepy party offices between elections, or observations that party workers are not frantically struggling to sway voters, should not be interpreted as weak or inactive party organizations.

A unique form of political competition revealed itself in this book: day-to-day competition among local party workers for a base of public support. Such competition is distinct from electoral competition among parties and candidates, which animates most studies on the politics of public goods provision.[11] Competition among local party workers is

---

[10] Kohli 1991; de Souza and Sridharan 2006; Krishna 2007; Manor 2010.
[11] Chhibber and Nooruddin 2004; Sáez and Sinha 2010; Boulding and Brown 2014.

distinct because it is informal, locally rooted, and waged between the votes. This book advances our understanding of political competition by emphasizing a quotidian form of competition among local party workers.

### Ethnic Diversity and Community Development

This book documents impressive levels of ethnic diversity in India's urban slums, manifested along the lines of caste (*jati*), religion, and region of origin. I argued that a scarcity of land for squatting (negligible space on which to squat in any corner of the city, forcing migrants from various castes, religions, villages, and states into the same densely packed settlements), gradual accretion in settlement formation (single ethnic groups do not dominate specific settlements through large-scale, preplanned land invasions), and constrained choices over location (settlement choice is mostly driven by preferences to live near a family member or village contact who can help find housing and work in the city) generate the rich patterns of ethnic diversity in India's slums.

A large literature in political economy finds that ethnic diversity can undermine cooperation and public goods provision.[12] Given the larger thrust of this literature, we would expect ethnic heterogeneity to have deleterious effects in informal urban settlements, where the mobilizational capacity of residents, in part, drives local public goods provision. This book, however, finds no systematic evidence of a negative relationship between ethnic diversity and public goods provision. It further points to a pathway through which ethnic diversity can positively influence public service provision – through its influence on the formation of dense, competitive party worker networks. The mechanisms operating between ethnic diversity and public goods provision are of course complex, numerous, and likely uneven in the direction and magnitude of their effects. The arguments and findings presented in the preceding chapters nevertheless suggest that scholars should, in addition to looking at more conventional mechanisms such as ethnic diversity's impact on horizontal cooperation, investigate how ethnic heterogeneity shapes the contours of political brokerage in communities and, by extension, the ability of residents to command state responsiveness through vertical political networks.

---

[12] Alesina et al. 1999; Banerjee et al. 2005; Habyarimana et al. 2009.

Moreover, in fighting to improve their settlements and push back against eviction, this book shows that India's slum residents routinely organize across ethnic lines. Such interethnic organization takes on a variety of forms, from acts of group claim-making to constructing multiethnic neighborhood associations. In unearthing these surprising patterns of political life in India's slums, this book provides insights into how urbanization in India is reshaping local ethnic politics.

## Community-Driven Development in Cities of the Global South

For the last several decades, international development organizations have emphasized citizen participation in the design and implementation of local development projects. Scholars and practitioners argue that participation bends development projects toward the preferences of communities, harnesses local knowledge, and, alongside decentralization, increases political accountability, as citizens are more proximate to officials, elected representatives, and service providers. Much of the language on participation has been folded into models of community-driven development. In a sweeping account of this approach, Mansuri and Rao estimated that the World Bank alone had spent $85 billion on community-driven development projects between 2003 and 2013.[13] Specific to cities, local participation was a guiding theme at Habitat III in Quito. It is woven into several Habitat III issue papers, including those on urban governance, economic development, and informal settlements.[14]

Rajiv Awas Yojana (RAY) was at the height of its implementation during the bulk of my fieldwork. RAY aimed to improve public infrastructure and services as well as land tenure security in India's urban slums. I saw municipal offices in Jaipur and Bhopal abuzz with RAY planning and survey work. Construction crews were breaking ground on new multistory flats for slum residents, either in situ or on the outskirts of the city. Echoing the discourse of participatory development, the Ministry of Housing and Urban Poverty Alleviation created a handbook

---

[13] This estimate is provided in Mansuri and Rao 2013, p. ix.
[14] See Habitat III, Papers 6, 12, and 24. A relevant example of the language of participation: "[Participatory slum upgrading] engages and puts all key urban stakeholders ... at the heart of the process to improve slums' living standards ... Slum dwellers, in particular, have important knowledge, skills and capacity to contribute, direct and own the upgrading process" (Habitat III, Issue Paper 24, p. 2).

for municipal governments in how to involve slum residents in RAY projects.[15] Community-based organizations (CBOs), at least on paper, were tasked with assisting in survey work, organizing residents, and listing local needs. Provocatively, RAY guidelines mandated that residents *without* ties to political parties should staff the CBOs. These guidelines sought to circumvent party workers – the actors at the very center of this book.

This book has several lessons for community-driven development in cities of the Global South. First, the description of slum leaders in the preceding pages deviates from popular accounts of these figures as inevitably thuggish and criminal. Slum leaders, in fact, are frequently selected by residents and exert considerable effort to solve resident problems. Practitioners should be aware of how informal authority emerges and operates before making interventions in these spaces. It cannot be assumed that slum leaders are too soaked in criminality and void of public support to be involved in local development projects.

Second, and related, informal authority in India's slums is not likely to be swept aside or circumvented by outside agencies. These figures have emerged in a larger field of politics to claim public services from the state – activities that will persist long after a single project is completed. In those neighborhoods with active and popular slum leaders, the potential for state-society synergy presents itself.[16] Prior to building partnerships with these actors, though, practitioners should probe the nature of informal community governance and both identify and address groups of residents who are marginalized by extant slum leadership.

Third, ethnic diversity is often assumed to be an impediment to community mobilization, particularly in places like urban slums that are thought to represent governance "brown spots."[17] For example, a prominent NGO working in Delhi's slums asserts in a publication: "In conditions of overcrowding and insufficiency, people are likely to perceive their neighbors as little more than competitors for space, water and other scarce facilities. This perception is exacerbated by the artificiality of many slum 'communities,' which draw migrants from several states that may not share common languages, religions or caste."[18] A Government of India report similarly notes, "Given the degree of heterogeneity in urban set-ups, social fragmentation becomes yet another distinct inconvenience

---

[15] Government of India 2011.
[16] See Evans 1996 and Ostrom 1996 on state-society synergy in development.
[17] O'Donnell 1993.   [18] Asha Report 2011, p. 55.

for the urban poor."[19] This book shows that ethnic diversity does not undermine local public goods provision in these spaces.

Fourth, given India's expansive population of slum settlements, development programs in any city must prioritize some settlements over others. In my trips to government and consultant offices, I often observed program staff making rubrics of socioeconomic vulnerabilities to rank a city's slums in terms of their levels of material deprivation and land tenure insecurity. This book suggests that the political characteristics of settlements should be taken into account as well. Many settlements struggle to demand and secure development from the state because of weak organizational capacity and a lack of political connectivity, sidelining them in the distributive politics of cities. Alongside other sources of marginalization, practitioners should identify settlements that would otherwise struggle to obtain public goods and services through local forms of claim-making.

[19] Chatterjee 2016, p. 3.

# APPENDIX A

# Measuring Social Capital

TABLE A.1 *Measuring social capital*

| Survey question | Coding |
|---|---|
| If a family here is short of money, or has a member who is sick or dies, will people here in the settlement help that family in need? | No = 0; Yes = 1 |
| If you were short of money and needed Rs 1,000, would your neighbors in the settlement lend you the money? | No = 0; Maybe = 1; Yes = 2 |
| In your opinion, would your neighbors in the settlement give time or money to improve the development of the settlement? | No = 0; Maybe = 1; Yes = 2 |
| If there were a big problem in the settlement, like no water or electricity for several days, would people in this settlement unite to solve the problem? | No = 0; Yes = 1 |
| When people here are free, do they mostly socialize and spend time with their own social group (*samaj*) or do they mix with other social groups? | Mostly with own group = 0; Mix with other groups = 1 |
| Is the following true or false: people in this settlement only really care about their own household and don't care about the welfare of the settlement as a whole? | True = 0; False = 1 |
| Generally speaking, how much do you trust people in this settlement? | Don't trust at all = 0; Trust a little = 1; Trust a lot = 2 |

# APPENDIX B

# Additional Tables and Figures

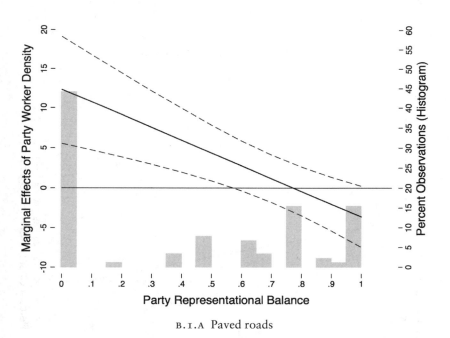

B.1.A Paved roads

FIGURES B.1.A THROUGH B.1.I: Marginal effects of party worker density on the outcome variables, conditional on party representational balance (dashed curves depict 95% confidence intervals)

238    Appendix B: Additional Tables and Figures

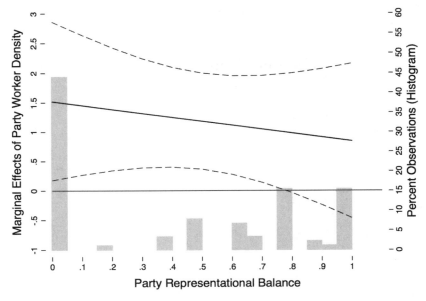

B.1.B Streetlights

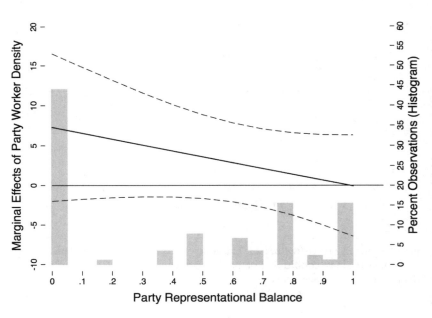

B.1.C Piped water

## Appendix B: Additional Tables and Figures

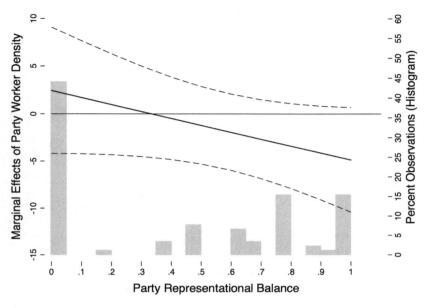

B.1.D Sewers

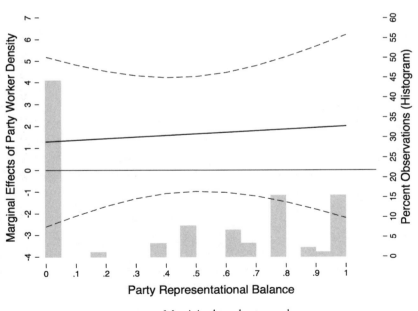

B.1.E Municipal trash removal

## Appendix B: Additional Tables and Figures

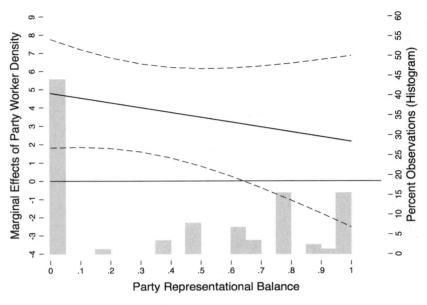

B.1.F Government medical camps

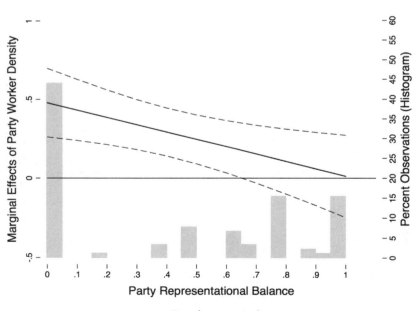

B.1.G Development index 1

*Appendix B: Additional Tables and Figures* 241

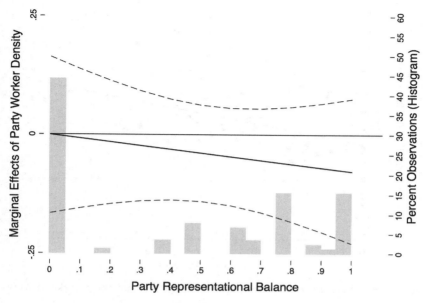

B.1.H Development index 2

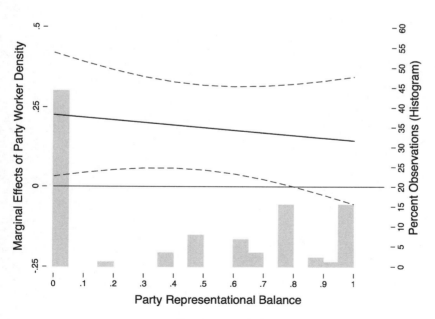

B.1.I Development index 3

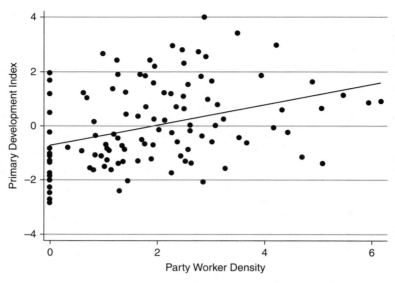

FIGURE B.2 Scatterplot of primary development index and party worker density

TABLE B.1 *Dropping party worker density*

| | Paved roads | Streetlights | Piped water | Sewers | Trash removal | Medical camps | Dev. index 1 |
|---|---|---|---|---|---|---|---|
| City | 38.28*** | -4.613*** | -27.99*** | -7.387 | 39.90*** | -1.660 | -0.290 |
| | (10.16) | (1.503) | (8.307) | (7.324) | (6.378) | (4.543) | (0.362) |
| Log population | 18.30*** | 0.771 | 3.729 | 7.865** | 4.502* | 5.932*** | 0.548*** |
| | (3.894) | (0.636) | (3.636) | (3.101) | (2.387) | (1.603) | (0.132) |
| 2015 Settlement | -4.706 | 0.199 | 27.24*** | 9.450 | 22.40*** | -12.31*** | 0.426 |
| | (12.06) | (1.602) | (9.759) | (8.485) | (6.740) | (4.661) | (0.410) |
| Settlement age | 0.340 | 0.0345 | -0.266 | 0.366 | 0.605*** | -0.160 | 0.00980 |
| | (0.383) | (0.0435) | (0.316) | (0.277) | (0.218) | (0.164) | (0.0137) |
| Average education | 0.498 | 0.196 | 2.306 | -1.212 | -1.242 | 0.0655 | 0.0273 |
| | (2.501) | (0.292) | (1.668) | (1.410) | (1.617) | (1.031) | (0.0746) |
| Monthly household (HH) income per capita | 0.00813 | -0.000113 | 0.00771 | 0.0176*** | 0.00889** | -0.000757 | 0.000493** |
| | (0.00645) | (0.000856) | (0.00532) | (0.00611) | (0.00387) | (0.00283) | (0.000218) |
| Central land | 1.545 | -0.0510 | -7.593 | -13.39** | 8.572* | 0.357 | -0.238 |
| | (8.157) | (1.170) | (7.817) | (6.104) | (4.745) | (3.544) | (0.263) |
| Private land | -24.25** | 0.806 | -9.253 | -22.95** | 1.958 | 1.364 | -0.612 |
| | (10.48) | (1.844) | (8.518) | (9.574) | (6.807) | (4.147) | (0.406) |
| Ethnic diversity index | -0.196 | 0.471 | -3.188 | -3.175 | 0.591 | 1.059 | -0.0310 |
| | (2.863) | (0.451) | (2.619) | (2.460) | (1.487) | (1.403) | (0.119) |

*(continued)*

TABLE B.1 (*continued*)

| | Paved roads | Streetlights | Piped water | Sewers | Trash removal | Medical camps | Dev. index 1 |
|---|---|---|---|---|---|---|---|
| AC electoral competition | -0.198 | -0.0535 | -0.0573 | 0.218 | -0.111 | -0.365 | -0.0109 |
| | (0.804) | (0.0991) | (0.813) | (0.638) | (0.471) | (0.330) | (0.0277) |
| Ward electoral competition | -0.519 | 0.0975 | -0.212 | 0.346 | 0.512 | 0.419* | 0.0164 |
| | (0.514) | (0.0622) | (0.404) | (0.357) | (0.328) | (0.249) | (0.0154) |
| Social capital index 1 | 2.623 | 0.738*** | 1.020 | 2.568 | 3.917** | 1.623 | 0.197** |
| | (2.509) | (0.269) | (2.066) | (1.638) | (1.568) | (1.073) | (0.0823) |
| Social capital index 2 | 6.414 | 0.391 | -2.608 | -3.058 | -4.746* | 1.149 | 0.00289 |
| | (4.344) | (0.451) | (3.132) | (2.949) | (2.400) | (2.150) | (0.140) |
| Land titles | 0.294** | 0.00480 | 0.375*** | 0.512*** | 0.327*** | -0.0118 | 0.0183*** |
| | (0.142) | (0.0201) | (0.117) | (0.124) | (0.117) | (0.0911) | (0.00586) |
| Constant | -107.1*** | -0.0270 | 4.483 | -82.58*** | -63.28*** | -8.126 | -5.693*** |
| | (37.00) | (5.563) | (36.33) | (27.54) | (20.29) | (16.12) | (1.214) |
| Observations | 111 | 111 | 111 | 111 | 111 | 111 | 111 |
| $R^2$ | 0.422 | 0.465 | 0.528 | 0.543 | 0.538 | 0.294 | 0.566 |

*Note:* OLS models; robust standard errors in parentheses
* $p < 0.10$, ** $p < 0.05$, *** $p < 0.01$

TABLE B.2 *Ethnic diversity reduced models*

| | Paved roads | Streetlights | Piped water | Sewers | Trash removal | Medical camps | Dev. index 1 |
|---|---|---|---|---|---|---|---|
| City | 28.73*** | -5.777*** | -30.57*** | -19.74*** | 28.75*** | -5.710 | -0.855*** |
| | (7.365) | (1.203) | (6.845) | (6.117) | (4.313) | (3.541) | (0.303) |
| Log population | 21.48*** | 0.698 | 8.313** | 11.05*** | 5.707** | 5.033*** | 0.677*** |
| | (3.949) | (0.591) | (3.673) | (3.899) | (2.395) | (1.729) | (0.148) |
| 2015 Settlement | 10.38 | 0.687 | 27.42*** | 5.454 | 11.19** | -11.58*** | 0.496* |
| | (6.864) | (0.988) | (6.593) | (5.775) | (4.546) | (2.709) | (0.279) |
| Settlement age | 0.448 | 0.0353 | 0.0954 | 0.742*** | 0.832*** | -0.199 | 0.0225 |
| | (0.354) | (0.0405) | (0.299) | (0.268) | (0.209) | (0.128) | (0.0134) |
| Central land | -0.312 | -0.264 | -13.03* | -18.89*** | 3.619 | -0.465 | -0.479* |
| | (7.264) | (1.117) | (6.756) | (5.409) | (4.815) | (3.456) | (0.243) |
| Private land | -20.95 | 1.736 | -3.978 | -17.77 | 7.183 | 3.404 | -0.278 |
| | (12.79) | (1.868) | (9.695) | (11.09) | (8.245) | (3.413) | (0.517) |
| Ethnic diversity index | 0.0796 | 0.565 | -3.571 | -3.487 | 0.644 | 1.226 | -0.0268 |
| | (3.027) | (0.459) | (2.897) | (2.755) | (1.747) | (1.469) | (0.141) |
| Constant | -119.2*** | 2.228 | -9.933 | -63.91** | -47.93** | 0.275 | -5.274*** |
| | (35.14) | (5.423) | (30.31) | (30.87) | (19.76) | (15.17) | (1.314) |
| Observations | 111 | 111 | 111 | 111 | 111 | 111 | 111 |
| $R^2$ | 0.319 | 0.395 | 0.443 | 0.392 | 0.406 | 0.251 | 0.415 |

*Note:* OLS models; robust standard errors in parentheses
* $p < 0.10$, ** $p < 0.05$, *** $p < 0.01$

TABLE B.3 *Ethnic diversity components*

| | Paved roads | Streetlights | Piped water | Sewers | Trash removal | Medical camps | Dev. index 1 |
|---|---|---|---|---|---|---|---|
| City | 29.42*** | −5.606*** | −30.49*** | −19.36*** | 29.09*** | −5.346 | −0.818*** |
| | (7.318) | (1.114) | (6.874) | (6.045) | (4.308) | (3.431) | (0.290) |
| Log population | 22.62*** | 0.545 | 6.307* | 12.33*** | 6.237** | 5.083** | 0.672*** |
| | (4.103) | (0.614) | (3.765) | (3.788) | (2.517) | (2.042) | (0.158) |
| 2015 Settlement | 11.99* | 0.450 | 24.47*** | 7.286 | 11.94** | −11.54*** | 0.486* |
| | (7.037) | (1.011) | (6.448) | (5.872) | (4.774) | (2.787) | (0.278) |
| Settlement age | 0.360 | 0.0279 | 0.156 | 0.673** | 0.790*** | −0.227 | 0.0200 |
| | (0.352) | (0.0415) | (0.312) | (0.271) | (0.218) | (0.143) | (0.0143) |
| Central land | −0.625 | 0.274 | −10.02 | −20.00*** | 3.498 | 0.148 | −0.402 |
| | (7.855) | (1.262) | (6.410) | (5.960) | (4.664) | (3.633) | (0.260) |
| Private land | −19.15 | 1.989 | −4.702 | −16.51 | 8.044 | 4.106 | −0.211 |
| | (12.99) | (1.832) | (9.742) | (10.52) | (8.166) | (3.563) | (0.509) |
| Caste diversity | −28.65 | 2.606 | 18.43 | −41.35 | −11.00 | −0.752 | −0.531 |
| | (26.22) | (3.442) | (24.72) | (30.10) | (16.59) | (19.69) | (1.469) |
| Religious diversity | 20.33 | 5.925* | −14.55 | 0.291 | 11.87 | 13.51 | 0.836 |
| | (20.98) | (3.482) | (18.10) | (15.62) | (13.36) | (10.83) | (0.908) |
| State diversity | 5.768 | −2.060 | −31.08** | 2.180 | 3.961 | −0.225 | −0.487 |
| | (16.59) | (2.261) | (13.45) | (13.07) | (9.415) | (6.714) | (0.523) |
| Constant | −107.6*** | 0.914 | −0.682 | −39.06 | −45.15** | −1.168 | −4.771*** |
| | (33.48) | (4.404) | (28.73) | (31.20) | (19.40) | (16.46) | (1.355) |
| Observations | 111 | 111 | 111 | 111 | 111 | 111 | 111 |
| $R^2$ | 0.334 | 0.421 | 0.465 | 0.406 | 0.413 | 0.260 | 0.427 |

*Note:* OLS models; robust standard errors in parentheses
* $p < 0.10$, ** $p < 0.05$, *** $p < 0.01$

TABLE B.4 *Settlement notification*

| | Paved roads | Streetlights | Piped water | Sewers | Trash removal | Medical camps | Dev. index 1 |
|---|---|---|---|---|---|---|---|
| Party worker density | 5.709** | 1.108*** | 1.579 | −0.680 | 2.153* | 2.743** | 0.224** |
| | (2.209) | (0.415) | (2.283) | (1.875) | (1.294) | (1.247) | (0.0921) |
| City | 40.10*** | −5.010*** | −28.14*** | −5.024 | 39.83*** | −1.955 | −0.278 |
| | (9.048) | (1.495) | (8.279) | (7.262) | (6.546) | (4.661) | (0.352) |
| Log population | 13.64*** | 0.172 | 2.706 | 7.374** | 3.052 | 4.169** | 0.390*** |
| | (3.844) | (0.674) | (3.948) | (3.240) | (2.484) | (1.711) | (0.146) |
| 2015 Settlement | −0.278 | 0.571 | 28.04*** | 10.60 | 23.58*** | −10.95** | 0.562 |
| | (11.15) | (1.489) | (9.643) | (8.747) | (6.559) | (4.670) | (0.376) |
| Settlement age | 0.340 | 0.0196 | −0.279 | 0.416 | 0.590*** | −0.184 | 0.00862 |
| | (0.360) | (0.0435) | (0.321) | (0.272) | (0.223) | (0.172) | (0.0132) |
| Average education | 0.172 | 0.130 | 2.213 | −1.161 | −1.368 | −0.0965 | 0.0142 |
| | (2.108) | (0.251) | (1.643) | (1.393) | (1.589) | (0.984) | (0.0601) |
| Monthly HH income per capita | 0.00893 | −0.000105 | 0.00781 | 0.0180*** | 0.00904** | −0.000604 | 0.000512*** |
| | (0.00584) | (0.000751) | (0.00531) | (0.00608) | (0.00380) | (0.00278) | (0.000194) |
| Central land | 7.889* | 0.308 | −6.597 | −11.15* | 10.09** | 2.045 | −0.0575 |
| | (7.660) | (1.127) | (7.920) | (6.309) | (4.999) | (3.692) | (0.257) |
| Private land | −19.43* | 0.568 | −8.940 | −19.49* | 2.596 | 1.851 | −0.516 |
| | (10.90) | (2.007) | (9.014) | (10.03) | (7.018) | (4.273) | (0.429) |
| Ethnic diversity index | −1.158 | 0.216 | −3.513 | −2.828 | 0.160 | 0.491 | −0.0742 |
| | (2.556) | (0.442) | (2.811) | (2.503) | (1.558) | (1.508) | (0.120) |

(*continued*)

TABLE B.4 (continued)

|  | Paved roads | Streetlights | Piped water | Sewers | Trash removal | Medical camps | Dev. index 1 |
|---|---|---|---|---|---|---|---|
| AC electoral competition | -0.235 | -0.111 | -0.111 | 0.395 | -0.175 | -0.461 | -0.0163 |
|  | (0.766) | (0.0988) | (0.845) | (0.681) | (0.482) | (0.329) | (0.0272) |
| Ward electoral competition | -0.664 | 0.0788 | -0.244 | 0.331 | 0.467 | 0.364 | 0.0115 |
|  | (0.460) | (0.0601) | (0.408) | (0.364) | (0.330) | (0.262) | (0.0142) |
| Social capital index 1 | 2.108 | 0.668** | 0.904 | 2.528 | 3.752** | 1.422 | 0.180** |
|  | (2.323) | (0.268) | (2.122) | (1.643) | (1.527) | (1.104) | (0.0800) |
| Social capital index 2 | 3.830 | 0.0884 | -3.150 | -3.434 | -5.521** | 0.218 | -0.0829 |
|  | (4.294) | (0.443) | (3.126) | (3.092) | (2.433) | (2.168) | (0.138) |
| Land titles | 0.312*** | 0.00746 | 0.380*** | 0.513*** | 0.333*** | -0.00435 | 0.0189*** |
|  | (0.118) | (0.0177) | (0.117) | (0.127) | (0.113) | (0.0915) | (0.00562) |
| Notification | 17.58** | 0.146 | 2.020 | 9.132 | 3.343 | 3.354 | 0.432* |
|  | (7.606) | (1.040) | (7.578) | (5.599) | (5.824) | (3.349) | (0.248) |
| Constant | -98.59** | 4.126 | 9.014 | -92.19*** | -57.55** | -0.134 | -5.160*** |
|  | (37.63) | (5.532) | (36.24) | (29.12) | (22.00) | (17.08) | (1.218) |
| Observations | 111 | 111 | 111 | 111 | 111 | 111 | 111 |
| $R^2$ | 0.500 | 0.534 | 0.532 | 0.553 | 0.553 | 0.347 | 0.618 |

*Note*: OLS models; robust standard errors in parentheses
* $p < 0.10$, ** $p < 0.05$, *** $p < 0.01$

TABLE B.5 *Politically fragmented settlements*

| | Paved roads | Streetlights | Piped water | Sewers | Trash removal | Medical camps | Dev. index 1 |
|---|---|---|---|---|---|---|---|
| Party worker density | 6.753*** | 1.122** | 1.663 | −0.102 | 2.329* | 2.971** | 0.251*** |
| | (2.331) | (0.430) | (2.185) | (1.899) | (1.329) | (1.209) | (0.0928) |
| City | 35.45*** | −5.085*** | −28.53*** | −7.674 | 39.08*** | −3.035 | −0.400 |
| | (9.646) | (1.573) | (8.431) | (7.448) | (6.389) | (4.530) | (0.375) |
| Log population | 14.75*** | 0.191 | 3.592 | 7.894** | 3.431 | 4.332** | 0.427*** |
| | (3.834) | (0.683) | (3.673) | (3.218) | (2.534) | (1.695) | (0.145) |
| 2015 Settlement | −3.252 | 0.438 | 28.35*** | 8.336 | 23.46*** | −12.11** | 0.469 |
| | (11.70) | (1.500) | (9.838) | (8.811) | (6.497) | (4.660) | (0.387) |
| Settlement age | 0.276 | 0.0248 | −0.236 | 0.409 | 0.576** | −0.175 | 0.00896 |
| | (0.374) | (0.0436) | (0.315) | (0.277) | (0.221) | (0.165) | (0.0133) |
| Average education | −0.0439 | 0.0999 | 1.786 | −1.375 | −1.438 | −0.220 | −0.00210 |
| | (2.402) | (0.253) | (1.636) | (1.455) | (1.643) | (0.999) | (0.0665) |
| Monthly HH income per capita | 0.00724 | −0.000290 | 0.00634 | 0.0163** | 0.00885** | −0.00158 | 0.000416** |
| | (0.00655) | (0.000758) | (0.00557) | (0.00623) | (0.00383) | (0.00273) | (0.000208) |
| Central land | 2.702 | 0.124 | −7.700 | −14.58** | 9.344* | 0.449 | −0.224 |
| | (8.055) | (1.053) | (7.983) | (6.206) | (4.839) | (3.545) | (0.251) |
| Private land | −26.14** | 0.489 | −9.952 | −23.07** | 1.321 | 0.492 | −0.689 |
| | (10.21) | (1.991) | (8.838) | (10.01) | (6.508) | (3.877) | (0.422) |
| Ethnic diversity index | −2.541 | 0.0529 | −5.171* | −4.202 | −0.0821 | −0.308 | −0.161 |
| | (2.894) | (0.441) | (2.664) | (2.567) | (1.759) | (1.535) | (0.112) |

*(continued)*

TABLE B.5 (continued)

|  | Paved roads | Streetlights | Piped water | Sewers | Trash removal | Medical camps | Dev. index 1 |
|---|---|---|---|---|---|---|---|
| AC electoral competition | -0.526 | -0.108 | -0.164 | 0.277 | -0.249 | -0.488 | -0.0224 |
|  | (0.765) | (0.0977) | (0.814) | (0.658) | (0.472) | (0.337) | (0.0272) |
| Ward electoral competition | -0.625 | 0.0794 | -0.295 | 0.361 | 0.459 | 0.380 | 0.0119 |
|  | (0.478) | (0.0601) | (0.410) | (0.358) | (0.327) | (0.260) | (0.0145) |
| Social capital index 1 | 2.370 | 0.696*** | 0.729 | 2.845 | 3.680** | 1.623 | 0.190** |
|  | (2.364) | (0.253) | (2.158) | (1.727) | (1.558) | (1.167) | (0.0827) |
| Social capital index 2 | 4.865 | 0.137 | -3.042 | -2.665 | -5.433** | 0.607 | -0.0480 |
|  | (4.336) | (0.435) | (3.160) | (3.089) | (2.373) | (2.178) | (0.138) |
| Land titles | 0.310** | 0.00756 | 0.385*** | 0.512*** | 0.333*** | -0.00495 | 0.0190*** |
|  | (0.125) | (0.0178) | (0.120) | (0.126) | (0.116) | (0.0904) | (0.00562) |
| Politically fragmented settlement | 1.360 | 0.150 | -8.313 | 2.754 | -2.271 | 1.990 | -0.0239 |
|  | (6.119) | (0.986) | (5.683) | (5.050) | (3.685) | (2.997) | (0.235) |
| Constant | -79.82** | 4.537 | 12.05 | -81.09*** | -54.43*** | 4.554 | -4.627*** |
|  | (36.12) | (5.845) | (36.71) | (28.57) | (20.58) | (16.36) | (1.275) |
| Observations | 110 | 110 | 110 | 110 | 110 | 110 | 110 |
| $R^2$ | 0.460 | 0.537 | 0.553 | 0.551 | 0.541 | 0.347 | 0.617 |

*Note:* OLS models; robust standard errors in parentheses. Settlements are defined as politically fragmented if at least 40 percent of survey respondents support the BJP and at least 40 percent of survey respondents support the INC. Twenty-six of the 111 settlements are above this threshold. Results are similar with thresholds of 30 or 35 percent.

* $p < 0.10$, ** $p < 0.05$, *** $p < 0.01$

TABLE B.6 *Swing voters*

| | Paved roads | Streetlights | Piped water | Sewers | Trash removal | Medical camps | Dev. index 1 |
|---|---|---|---|---|---|---|---|
| Party worker density | 6.781*** | 1.110*** | 1.812 | −0.102 | 2.381* | 2.977** | 0.253*** |
| | (2.322) | (0.405) | (2.264) | (1.867) | (1.320) | (1.206) | (0.0940) |
| City | 35.41*** | −5.048*** | −29.17*** | −7.598 | 38.88*** | −2.995 | −0.405 |
| | (9.713) | (1.517) | (8.591) | (7.452) | (6.455) | (4.534) | (0.377) |
| Log population | 14.65*** | 0.251 | 2.696 | 7.962** | 3.135 | 4.355** | 0.419*** |
| | (3.846) | (0.654) | (3.740) | (3.263) | (2.523) | (1.685) | (0.145) |
| 2015 Settlement | −2.257 | 0.265 | 28.26*** | 9.290 | 23.64*** | −11.31** | 0.492 |
| | (11.66) | (1.482) | (9.684) | (8.779) | (6.601) | (4.625) | (0.385) |
| Settlement age | 0.252 | 0.0307 | −0.270 | 0.393 | 0.560** | −0.190 | 0.00818 |
| | (0.375) | (0.0434) | (0.318) | (0.281) | (0.226) | (0.167) | (0.0134) |
| Average education | 0.0985 | 0.0562 | 2.171 | −1.309 | −1.290 | −0.151 | 0.00377 |
| | (2.420) | (0.252) | (1.635) | (1.490) | (1.650) | (0.992) | (0.0667) |
| Monthly HH income per capita | 0.00657 | −0.0000864 | 0.00457 | 0.0160** | 0.00816** | −0.00191 | 0.000389* |
| | (0.00664) | (0.000744) | (0.00519) | (0.00649) | (0.00395) | (0.00272) | (0.000206) |
| Central land | 2.244 | 0.295 | −9.584 | −14.68** | 8.668* | 0.296 | −0.247 |
| | (7.980) | (1.037) | (7.793) | (6.051) | (4.848) | (3.516) | (0.247) |
| Private land | −26.69** | 0.637 | −10.98 | −23.41** | 0.889 | 0.167 | −0.709* |
| | (10.29) | (1.916) | (8.798) | (9.945) | (6.906) | (3.771) | (0.423) |
| Ethnic diversity index | −2.205 | −0.0324 | −4.634* | −3.981 | 0.154 | −0.102 | −0.149 |
| | (2.861) | (0.462) | (2.673) | (2.583) | (1.790) | (1.448) | (0.110) |

*(continued)*

TABLE B.6 (continued)

|  | Paved roads | Streetlights | Piped water | Sewers | Trash removal | Medical camps | Dev. index 1 |
|---|---|---|---|---|---|---|---|
| AC electoral competition | −0.408 | −0.143 | 0.137 | 0.335 | −0.132 | −0.428 | −0.0176 |
|  | (0.770) | (0.0998) | (0.863) | (0.672) | (0.501) | (0.332) | (0.0277) |
| Ward electoral competition | −0.659 | 0.0855 | −0.294 | 0.329 | 0.452 | 0.353 | 0.0111 |
|  | (0.478) | (0.0602) | (0.397) | (0.363) | (0.328) | (0.268) | (0.0148) |
| Social capital index 1 | 2.274 | 0.697** | 1.073 | 2.694 | 3.766** | 1.509 | 0.190** |
|  | (2.432) | (0.266) | (2.119) | (1.670) | (1.543) | (1.107) | (0.0817) |
| Social capital index 2 | 4.743 | 0.147 | −2.804 | −2.822 | −5.385** | 0.485 | −0.0493 |
|  | (4.334) | (0.426) | (3.056) | (3.058) | (2.403) | (2.136) | (0.136) |
| Land titles | 0.313** | 0.00703 | 0.386*** | 0.514*** | 0.334*** | −0.00268 | 0.0190*** |
|  | (0.126) | (0.0200) | (0.107) | (0.124) | (0.117) | (0.0878) | (0.00538) |
| Percent swing voters | −0.186 | 0.0494 | −0.343* | −0.114 | −0.145 | −0.109 | −0.00660 |
|  | (0.187) | (0.0303) | (0.194) | (0.208) | (0.155) | (0.108) | (0.00745) |
| Constant | −72.56* | 2.520 | 27.36 | −76.97** | −48.20** | 8.578 | −4.357*** |
|  | (38.32) | (6.055) | (37.42) | (30.25) | (20.92) | (17.66) | (1.378) |
| Observations | 110 | 110 | 110 | 110 | 110 | 110 | 110 |
| $R^2$ | 0.464 | 0.549 | 0.557 | 0.552 | 0.545 | 0.351 | 0.619 |

*Note:* OLS models; robust standard errors in parentheses

* $p < 0.10$, ** $p < 0.05$, *** $p < 0.01$

TABLE B.7 *BJP strongholds and years of BJP rule in assembly constituency*

|  | Paved roads | Streetlights | Piped water | Sewers | Trash removal | Medical camps | Dev. index 1 |
|---|---|---|---|---|---|---|---|
| Party worker density | 6.566*** | 1.179*** | 1.556 | 0.317 | 2.314* | 3.360*** | 0.266*** |
|  | (2.339) | (0.443) | (2.248) | (1.931) | (1.295) | (1.141) | (0.0948) |
| City | 33.49*** | -4.822*** | -26.87*** | -5.552 | 40.42*** | -1.826 | -0.312 |
|  | (9.957) | (1.549) | (8.763) | (7.359) | (6.368) | (4.485) | (0.362) |
| Log population | 14.92*** | 0.113 | 3.340 | 6.402* | 3.121 | 3.368* | 0.377** |
|  | (4.020) | (0.679) | (3.947) | (3.364) | (2.598) | (1.890) | (0.149) |
| 2015 Settlement | -6.954 | 0.793 | 29.17*** | 7.805 | 23.36*** | -11.59** | 0.475 |
|  | (11.25) | (1.537) | (10.16) | (8.395) | (6.475) | (4.793) | (0.369) |
| Settlement age | 0.333 | 0.0283 | -0.330 | 0.415 | 0.519** | -0.193 | 0.00797 |
|  | (0.415) | (0.0441) | (0.332) | (0.292) | (0.223) | (0.177) | (0.0140) |
| Average education | 0.256 | 0.171 | 2.036 | -1.164 | -0.801 | -0.148 | 0.0192 |
|  | (2.384) | (0.270) | (1.817) | (1.516) | (1.653) | (1.038) | (0.0680) |
| Monthly HH income per capita | 0.00700 | -0.000171 | 0.00620 | 0.0181*** | 0.00926** | -0.000581 | 0.000470** |
|  | (0.00670) | (0.000770) | (0.00552) | (0.00615) | (0.00381) | (0.00260) | (0.000203) |
| Central land | 1.173 | 0.659 | -6.326 | -15.19** | 11.28** | 0.189 | -0.175 |
|  | (8.440) | (1.118) | (8.189) | (5.993) | (4.627) | (3.678) | (0.247) |
| Private land | -27.59** | 0.101 | -9.401 | -23.22** | -0.101 | 0.800 | -0.737* |
|  | (10.82) | (2.005) | (9.252) | (10.03) | (6.218) | (3.990) | (0.433) |
| Ethnic diversity index | -1.140 | -0.0524 | -5.501** | -4.708 | 0.0539 | -1.258 | -0.184 |
|  | (3.322) | (0.438) | (2.680) | (2.921) | (1.939) | (1.549) | (0.117) |

*(continued)*

TABLE B.7 (continued)

| | Paved roads | Streetlights | Piped water | Sewers | Trash removal | Medical camps | Dev. index 1 |
|---|---|---|---|---|---|---|---|
| AC electoral competition | 0.792 | −0.0587 | −0.580 | −0.662 | 0.0882 | −1.525** | −0.0403 |
| | (1.262) | (0.164) | (1.160) | (1.140) | (0.809) | (0.721) | (0.0432) |
| Ward electoral competition | −0.737 | 0.0779 | −0.155 | 0.245 | 0.494 | 0.366 | 0.0107 |
| | (0.501) | (0.0637) | (0.406) | (0.358) | (0.315) | (0.261) | (0.0150) |
| Social capital index 1 | 1.994 | 0.714*** | 1.498 | 2.387 | 3.928** | 1.315 | 0.188** |
| | (2.368) | (0.271) | (2.216) | (1.573) | (1.528) | (1.128) | (0.0787) |
| Social capital index 2 | 5.995 | 0.0896 | −2.934 | −3.531 | −5.105** | −0.410 | −0.0679 |
| | (4.231) | (0.443) | (3.211) | (3.005) | (2.492) | (2.154) | (0.137) |
| Land titles | 0.292** | 0.0111 | 0.400*** | 0.539*** | 0.351*** | 0.0157 | 0.0202*** |
| | (0.133) | (0.0174) | (0.126) | (0.128) | (0.110) | (0.0936) | (0.00555) |
| BJP AC years in power | −0.786 | −0.0925 | 0.394 | 0.164 | −0.238 | 0.495 | −0.00137 |
| | (0.717) | (0.0897) | (0.564) | (0.522) | (0.468) | (0.366) | (0.0242) |
| BJP stronghold | 6.873 | −5.081** | −4.355 | −24.37* | −13.75 | −10.34 | −1.083 |
| | (20.13) | (2.291) | (19.77) | (12.41) | (10.03) | (8.512) | (0.688) |
| BJP AC years in power*BJP stronghold | −0.289 | 0.173** | 0.104 | 0.965** | 0.359 | 0.353 | 0.0371 |
| | (0.752) | (0.0858) | (0.729) | (0.464) | (0.387) | (0.296) | (0.0255) |
| Constant | −81.26** | 5.704 | 9.071 | −64.56** | −54.38** | 13.32 | −4.174*** |
| | (39.30) | (5.755) | (37.39) | (29.80) | (21.05) | (17.95) | (1.291) |
| Observations | 108 | 108 | 108 | 108 | 108 | 108 | 108 |
| $R^2$ | 0.477 | 0.558 | 0.552 | 0.573 | 0.580 | 0.388 | 0.633 |

*Note*: OLS models; robust standard errors in parentheses
* $p < 0.10$, ** $p < 0.05$, *** $p < 0.01$

TABLE B.8 *BJP strongholds and years of BJP rule in municipal ward*

| | Paved roads | Streetlights | Piped water | Sewers | Trash removal | Medical camps | Dev. index 1 |
|---|---|---|---|---|---|---|---|
| Party worker density | 6.623*** | 1.127** | 1.368 | −0.0119 | 2.199 | 3.235*** | 0.251*** |
| | (2.437) | (0.448) | (2.319) | (1.959) | (1.338) | (1.146) | (0.0930) |
| City | 32.44*** | −4.750*** | −29.24*** | −7.545 | 38.99*** | −4.051 | −0.425 |
| | (9.582) | (1.581) | (8.940) | (7.606) | (6.574) | (4.438) | (0.374) |
| Log population | 14.13*** | 0.369 | 2.778 | 8.534** | 2.674 | 3.838** | 0.423** |
| | (4.254) | (0.712) | (4.343) | (3.660) | (2.779) | (1.778) | (0.162) |
| 2015 Settlement | −7.831 | 0.522 | 27.04*** | 7.466 | 23.50*** | −13.43*** | 0.379 |
| | (12.03) | (1.600) | (9.986) | (9.036) | (6.512) | (4.688) | (0.387) |
| Settlement age | 0.284 | 0.0188 | −0.326 | 0.440 | 0.472** | −0.139 | 0.00770 |
| | (0.398) | (0.0446) | (0.330) | (0.305) | (0.220) | (0.162) | (0.0142) |
| Average education | 0.0453 | 0.152 | 2.281 | −1.445 | −0.713 | −0.130 | 0.0153 |
| | (2.558) | (0.274) | (1.790) | (1.452) | (1.749) | (1.095) | (0.0684) |
| Monthly HH income per capita | 0.00674 | −0.000479 | 0.00656 | 0.0155** | 0.00979** | −0.00133 | 0.000395* |
| | (0.00698) | (0.000805) | (0.00561) | (0.00663) | (0.00403) | (0.00285) | (0.000213) |
| Central land | 3.711 | 0.442 | −6.544 | −12.69** | 11.82** | 1.169 | −0.113 |
| | (8.500) | (1.115) | (8.324) | (6.429) | (4.740) | (3.701) | (0.245) |
| Private land | −25.05** | 0.770 | −11.54 | −21.11* | −1.460 | 0.128 | −0.668 |
| | (10.92) | (1.918) | (8.715) | (10.78) | (6.554) | (4.017) | (0.428) |
| Ethnic diversity index | −0.385 | 0.0621 | −4.550 | −3.434 | 0.0601 | −0.109 | −0.114 |
| | (3.265) | (0.465) | (2.767) | (2.884) | (1.993) | (1.613) | (0.117) |
| AC electoral competition | −0.0986 | −0.0800 | 0.189 | 0.422 | 0.0328 | −0.466 | −0.00649 |
| | (0.806) | (0.0981) | (0.864) | (0.720) | (0.505) | (0.362) | (0.0285) |

*(continued)*

TABLE B.8 (continued)

| | Paved roads | Streetlights | Piped water | Sewers | Trash removal | Medical camps | Dev. index 1 |
|---|---|---|---|---|---|---|---|
| Ward electoral competition | −0.579 | 0.104* | −0.208 | 0.387 | 0.493 | 0.324 | 0.0154 |
| | (0.482) | (0.0625) | (0.433) | (0.377) | (0.328) | (0.290) | (0.0153) |
| Social capital index 1 | 1.531 | 0.748** | 1.110 | 2.671 | 3.751** | 1.175 | 0.182** |
| | (2.524) | (0.285) | (2.252) | (1.788) | (1.671) | (1.193) | (0.0841) |
| Social capital index 2 | 5.070 | 0.107 | −2.166 | −3.030 | −5.024** | 0.242 | −0.0460 |
| | (4.374) | (0.447) | (3.208) | (3.130) | (2.382) | (2.172) | (0.139) |
| Land titles | 0.356*** | 0.0122 | 0.392*** | 0.547*** | 0.348*** | 0.0148 | 0.0209*** |
| | (0.130) | (0.0190) | (0.122) | (0.127) | (0.107) | (0.0863) | (0.00541) |
| BJP ward years in power | 0.235 | 0.127 | −0.428 | 0.645 | −0.495 | 0.0733 | 0.0159 |
| | (0.762) | (0.118) | (0.650) | (0.613) | (0.573) | (0.345) | (0.0269) |
| BJP stronghold | −18.00 | 0.346 | −9.437 | −6.579 | −13.46 | −9.715 | −0.625 |
| | (11.46) | (1.661) | (15.40) | (10.86) | (8.916) | (8.860) | (0.533) |
| BJP ward years in power*BJP stronghold | 2.386** | −0.135 | 0.932 | 0.710 | 0.934 | 0.959 | 0.0571 |
| | (1.133) | (0.177) | (1.684) | (1.217) | (0.912) | (0.894) | (0.0563) |
| Constant | −81.54** | 1.721 | 15.30 | −92.62*** | −50.35** | 6.687 | −4.967*** |
| | (40.22) | (6.215) | (41.66) | (32.84) | (23.60) | (16.88) | (1.447) |
| Observations | 108 | 108 | 108 | 108 | 108 | 108 | 108 |
| $R^2$ | 0.471 | 0.545 | 0.548 | 0.556 | 0.580 | 0.363 | 0.626 |

*Note:* OLS models; robust standard errors in parentheses
* $p < 0.10$, ** $p < 0.05$, *** $p < 0.01$

TABLE B.9 *INC strongholds and years of INC rule in assembly constituency*

| | Paved roads | Streetlights | Piped water | Sewers | Trash removal | Medical camps | Dev. index 1 |
|---|---|---|---|---|---|---|---|
| Party worker density | 7.008*** | 1.110*** | 1.610 | -0.345 | 2.037 | 3.194*** | 0.250*** |
| | (2.093) | (0.407) | (2.282) | (1.852) | (1.266) | (1.152) | (0.0856) |
| City | 38.55*** | -4.657*** | -26.57*** | -8.293 | 41.38*** | -2.861 | -0.297 |
| | (7.910) | (1.444) | (8.072) | (7.830) | (6.232) | (4.649) | (0.341) |
| Log population | 13.43*** | 0.199 | 2.938 | 7.250** | 3.407 | 3.540* | 0.383*** |
| | (3.577) | (0.605) | (3.876) | (3.342) | (2.480) | (1.952) | (0.138) |
| 2015 Settlement | -7.093 | 0.753 | 32.06*** | 8.079 | 24.01*** | -9.651 | 0.550 |
| | (12.16) | (1.656) | (10.57) | (8.283) | (6.073) | (5.567) | (0.420) |
| Settlement age | 0.353 | 0.0183 | -0.360 | 0.385 | 0.510** | -0.219 | 0.00593 |
| | (0.350) | (0.0451) | (0.335) | (0.290) | (0.214) | (0.181) | (0.0134) |
| Average education | 1.837 | 0.260 | 2.549 | -2.037 | -0.711 | -0.0441 | 0.0381 |
| | (2.083) | (0.285) | (1.887) | (1.616) | (1.704) | (1.076) | (0.0723) |
| Monthly HH income per capita | 0.00812 | -0.000274 | 0.00631 | 0.0180*** | 0.00912** | -0.000849 | 0.000466** |
| | (0.00692) | (0.000795) | (0.00550) | (0.00581) | (0.00375) | (0.00265) | (0.000213) |
| Central land | 4.051 | 0.600 | -6.220 | -17.38*** | 11.16** | -0.409 | -0.195 |
| | (7.637) | (1.122) | (7.973) | (6.047) | (4.570) | (3.737) | (0.247) |
| Private land | -32.48*** | 0.0450 | -10.35 | -20.64** | -0.0832 | 0.880 | -0.761* |
| | (10.32) | (1.892) | (8.912) | (9.944) | (6.120) | (3.780) | (0.395) |
| Ethnic diversity index | -1.211 | 0.134 | -5.298** | -4.257 | 0.685 | -0.817 | -0.146 |
| | (2.900) | (0.459) | (2.638) | (2.769) | (1.835) | (1.584) | (0.114) |
| AC electoral competition | 0.646 | -0.0482 | -0.903 | -0.913 | -0.00711 | -1.559* | -0.0503 |
| | (1.248) | (0.169) | (1.174) | (1.248) | (0.837) | (0.808) | (0.0476) |

*(continued)*

TABLE B.9 *(continued)*

|  | Paved roads | Streetlights | Piped water | Sewers | Trash removal | Medical camps | Dev. index 1 |
|---|---|---|---|---|---|---|---|
| Ward electoral competition | −0.817* | 0.0785 | −0.180 | 0.305 | 0.472 | 0.363 | 0.0104 |
|  | (0.471) | (0.0610) | (0.415) | (0.336) | (0.342) | (0.244) | (0.0141) |
| Social capital index 1 | 0.992 | 0.658** | 1.334 | 2.702 | 3.786** | 1.355 | 0.175** |
|  | (2.090) | (0.269) | (2.200) | (1.676) | (1.504) | (1.173) | (0.0801) |
| Social capital index 2 | 5.282 | 0.139 | −3.279 | −2.911 | −4.993** | −0.309 | −0.0631 |
|  | (4.435) | (0.456) | (3.383) | (2.908) | (2.360) | (2.325) | (0.150) |
| Land titles | 0.347** | 0.0127 | 0.424*** | 0.500*** | 0.355*** | 0.0179 | 0.0206*** |
|  | (0.143) | (0.0177) | (0.127) | (0.126) | (0.115) | (0.0953) | (0.00569) |
| INC AC years in power | 0.740 | 0.0122 | −0.828 | −0.777 | −0.0208 | −0.799 | −0.0283 |
|  | (0.750) | (0.0948) | (0.682) | (0.664) | (0.519) | (0.493) | (0.0299) |
| INC stronghold | −22.57 | −1.200 | −1.350 | −15.20 | −8.301 | 0.0945 | −0.635 |
|  | (22.32) | (3.293) | (21.14) | (21.54) | (13.17) | (11.19) | (0.879) |
| INC AC years in power*INC stronghold | 3.140* | 0.225 | 0.658 | 0.485 | 1.084 | 0.176 | 0.0771 |
|  | (1.737) | (0.211) | (1.567) | (1.718) | (0.923) | (0.752) | (0.0668) |
| Constant | −113.7*** | 2.038 | 30.09 | −44.62 | −63.13** | 33.13 | −3.952** |
|  | (43.07) | (5.749) | (43.97) | (39.88) | (31.57) | (27.62) | (1.718) |
| Observations | 108 | 108 | 108 | 108 | 108 | 108 | 108 |
| $R^2$ | 0.533 | 0.557 | 0.560 | 0.570 | 0.583 | 0.383 | 0.637 |

*Note:* OLS models; robust standard errors in parentheses
* $p < 0.10$, ** $p < 0.05$, *** $p < 0.01$

TABLE B.10 *INC strongholds and years of INC rule in municipal ward*

| | Paved roads | Streetlights | Piped water | Sewers | Trash removal | Medical camps | Dev. index 1 |
|---|---|---|---|---|---|---|---|
| Party worker density | 7.159*** | 1.101*** | 1.295 | −0.317 | 2.197 | 3.070** | 0.246*** |
| | (2.162) | (0.404) | (2.350) | (1.865) | (1.340) | (1.185) | (0.0846) |
| City | 36.39*** | −5.100*** | −29.06*** | −7.524 | 42.05*** | −3.386 | −0.383 |
| | (8.994) | (1.403) | (8.860) | (7.851) | (6.395) | (5.103) | (0.358) |
| Log population | 13.62*** | 0.146 | 2.884 | 8.828** | 3.984 | 4.013** | 0.416*** |
| | (3.685) | (0.618) | (3.892) | (3.490) | (2.431) | (1.813) | (0.140) |
| 2015 Settlement | −3.155 | 0.619 | 26.54** | 9.997 | 25.53*** | −12.51** | 0.495 |
| | (12.92) | (1.522) | (10.42) | (9.345) | (6.300) | (4.889) | (0.397) |
| Settlement age | 0.185 | 0.00776 | −0.382 | 0.440 | 0.496** | −0.181 | 0.00447 |
| | (0.385) | (0.0468) | (0.332) | (0.299) | (0.239) | (0.171) | (0.0143) |
| Average education | 1.910 | 0.257 | 2.817 | −2.179 | −0.697 | 0.0211 | 0.0412 |
| | (2.408) | (0.291) | (1.961) | (1.513) | (1.723) | (1.098) | (0.0714) |
| Monthly HH income per capita | 0.00603 | −0.000422 | 0.00596 | 0.0161** | 0.00840** | −0.00129 | 0.000386* |
| | (0.00698) | (0.000808) | (0.00567) | (0.00633) | (0.00385) | (0.00275) | (0.000227) |
| Central land | 4.535 | 0.598 | −6.664 | −13.86** | 11.59** | 0.243 | −0.128 |
| | (7.955) | (1.090) | (8.173) | (6.485) | (4.520) | (3.684) | (0.242) |
| Private land | −30.44*** | −0.166 | −13.45 | −20.79* | 1.518 | −0.784 | −0.821* |
| | (11.23) | (1.827) | (8.943) | (10.51) | (6.591) | (3.898) | (0.420) |
| Ethnic diversity index | −1.298 | 0.205 | −4.382 | −4.194 | 0.442 | −0.370 | −0.122 |
| | (2.997) | (0.442) | (2.804) | (2.668) | (1.797) | (1.645) | (0.114) |
| AC electoral competition | −0.0331 | −0.0399 | 0.299 | 0.202 | 0.00506 | −0.508 | −0.00512 |
| | (0.787) | (0.101) | (0.883) | (0.710) | (0.476) | (0.370) | (0.0276) |

*(continued)*

TABLE B.10 (continued)

| | Paved roads | Streetlights | Piped water | Sewers | Trash removal | Medical camps | Dev. index 1 |
|---|---|---|---|---|---|---|---|
| Ward electoral competition | −0.480 | 0.105* | −0.187 | 0.436 | 0.496 | 0.326 | 0.0175 |
| | (0.450) | (0.0628) | (0.433) | (0.368) | (0.347) | (0.280) | (0.0149) |
| Social capital index 1 | 1.733 | 0.712** | 1.015 | 3.267* | 4.003*** | 1.271 | 0.192** |
| | (2.320) | (0.279) | (2.226) | (1.804) | (1.519) | (1.176) | (0.0824) |
| Social capital index 2 | 4.124 | 0.0926 | −2.051 | −2.833 | −5.215** | 0.484 | −0.0491 |
| | (4.739) | (0.449) | (3.346) | (3.111) | (2.248) | (2.232) | (0.143) |
| Land titles | 0.408*** | 0.0164 | 0.389*** | 0.512*** | 0.364*** | −0.00600 | 0.0209*** |
| | (0.136) | (0.0180) | (0.126) | (0.124) | (0.109) | (0.0905) | (0.00552) |
| INC ward years in power | −0.983 | −0.124 | 0.507 | −0.605 | −0.0158 | 0.230 | −0.0195 |
| | (0.889) | (0.130) | (0.814) | (0.693) | (0.692) | (0.435) | (0.0302) |
| INC stronghold | 11.63 | −0.0846 | 4.095 | −8.672 | 9.312 | 2.311 | 0.126 |
| | (11.26) | (1.687) | (10.25) | (11.93) | (7.697) | (6.941) | (0.453) |
| INC ward years in power*INC stronghold | 1.783 | 0.369 | 0.443 | 0.489 | −0.527 | −0.00564 | 0.0602 |
| | (1.641) | (0.302) | (1.576) | (1.636) | (1.190) | (0.861) | (0.0708) |
| Constant | −87.87** | 3.622 | 5.783 | −79.92** | −67.58*** | 5.366 | −4.926*** |
| | (35.34) | (5.419) | (37.83) | (30.90) | (20.62) | (17.94) | (1.321) |
| Observations | 108 | 108 | 108 | 108 | 108 | 108 | 108 |
| $R^2$ | 0.497 | 0.558 | 0.553 | 0.554 | 0.578 | 0.352 | 0.628 |

*Note:* OLS models; robust standard errors in parentheses
* $p < 0.10$, ** $p < 0.05$, *** $p < 0.01$

TABLE B.11 *Marginal effects of party years in power, conditional on party stronghold*

|  | Paved roads | Streetlights | Piped water | Sewers | Trash removal | Medical camps | Dev. index 1 |
|---|---|---|---|---|---|---|---|
| *Marginal effects of BJP years in power in the state assembly constituency* |
| BJP party stronghold = 0 | −0.79 | −0.09 | 0.39 | 0.16 | −0.24 | 0.50 | −0.00 |
|  | (0.72) | (0.09) | (0.56) | (0.52) | (0.47) | (0.37) | (0.02) |
| BJP party stronghold = 1 | −1.08 | 0.08 | 0.50 | 1.13* | 0.12 | 0.85** | 0.04 |
|  | (0.76) | (0.10) | (0.78) | (0.56) | (0.43) | (0.41) | (0.03) |
| *Marginal effects of BJP years in power in the municipal ward* |
| BJP party stronghold = 0 | 0.23 | 0.13 | −0.43 | 0.65 | −0.49 | 0.07 | 0.02 |
|  | (0.76) | (0.19) | (0.65) | (0.61) | (0.57) | (0.34) | (0.03) |
| BJP party stronghold = 1 | 2.62** | −0.01 | 0.50 | 1.36 | 0.44 | 1.03 | 0.07 |
|  | (1.05) | (0.18) | (1.56) | (1.11) | (0.76) | (0.82) | (0.05) |
| *Marginal effects of INC years in power in the state assembly constituency* |
| INC party stronghold = 0 | 0.74 | 0.01 | −0.83 | −0.78 | −0.02 | −0.80 | −0.03 |
|  | (0.75) | (0.09) | (0.68) | (0.66) | (0.52) | (0.49) | (0.03) |
| INC party stronghold = 1 | 3.88** | 0.24 | −0.17 | −0.29 | 1.06 | −0.62 | 0.05 |
|  | (1.68) | (0.22) | (1.51) | (1.65) | (0.93) | (0.75) | (0.07) |
| *Marginal effects of INC years in power in the municipal ward* |
| INC party stronghold = 0 | −0.98 | −0.12 | 0.51 | −0.61 | −0.02 | 0.23 | −0.02 |
|  | (0.89) | (0.13) | (0.81) | (0.69) | (0.69) | (0.44) | (0.03) |
| INC party stronghold = 1 | 0.80 | 0.25 | 0.95 | −0.12 | −0.54 | 0.22 | 0.04 |
|  | (1.43) | (0.27) | (1.50) | (1.52) | (1.06) | (0.78) | (0.06) |

*Note:* Standard errors in parentheses

TABLE B.12 *Party worker density reduced models*

| | Paved roads | Streetlights | Piped water | Sewers | Trash removal | Medical camps | Dev. index |
|---|---|---|---|---|---|---|---|
| Party worker density | 7.377*** | 1.212*** | 1.973 | 0.477 | 2.478 | 3.017*** | 0.280*** |
| | (2.308) | (0.421) | (2.463) | (2.331) | (1.525) | (1.037) | (0.105) |
| City | 25.22*** | −6.353*** | −31.51*** | −19.97*** | 27.57*** | −7.142** | −0.988*** |
| | (7.361) | (1.215) | (6.978) | (6.321) | (4.357) | (3.465) | (0.308) |
| Log population | 17.84*** | 0.0999 | 7.340* | 10.82*** | 4.486* | 3.546** | 0.539*** |
| | (4.124) | (0.635) | (3.937) | (4.017) | (2.506) | (1.639) | (0.168) |
| 2015 Settlement | 8.213 | 0.331 | 26.84*** | 5.314 | 10.46** | −12.46*** | 0.414 |
| | (6.421) | (0.894) | (6.625) | (5.910) | (4.539) | (2.563) | (0.261) |
| Settlement age | 0.345 | 0.0184 | 0.0679 | 0.736*** | 0.798*** | −0.241* | 0.0186 |
| | (0.332) | (0.0400) | (0.300) | (0.275) | (0.207) | (0.129) | (0.0129) |
| Central land | 0.283 | −0.167 | −12.87* | −18.85*** | 3.819 | −0.222 | −0.457* |
| | (6.873) | (1.000) | (6.801) | (5.478) | (4.857) | (3.366) | (0.234) |
| Private land | −22.93* | 1.411 | −4.507 | −17.89 | 6.518 | 2.594 | −0.353 |
| | (11.92) | (1.962) | (9.753) | (11.20) | (7.813) | (3.020) | (0.496) |
| Ethnic diversity index | −1.723 | 0.268 | −4.053 | −3.604 | 0.0383 | 0.489 | −0.0953 |
| | (2.840) | (0.419) | (2.997) | (2.846) | (1.773) | (1.494) | (0.137) |
| Constant | −100.5*** | 5.303 | −4.929 | −62.70* | −41.65** | 7.927 | −4.564*** |
| | (36.13) | (5.433) | (31.99) | (31.70) | (20.35) | (14.43) | (1.425) |
| Observations | 111 | 111 | 111 | 111 | 111 | 111 | 111 |
| $R^2$ | 0.385 | 0.482 | 0.448 | 0.392 | 0.421 | 0.305 | 0.472 |

*Note:* OLS models; robust standard errors in parentheses
* $p < 0.10$, ** $p < 0.05$, *** $p < 0.01$

TABLE B.13 *Tobit models*

| | Paved roads | Streetlights | Piped water | Sewers | Trash removal | Medical camps |
|---|---|---|---|---|---|---|
| Party worker density | 10.71*** | 1.354*** | 3.238 | 0.251 | 2.482* | 2.982*** |
| | (3.794) | (0.356) | (2.616) | (2.674) | (1.422) | (1.126) |
| City | 57.39*** | −5.998*** | −36.36*** | −2.303 | 40.93*** | −3.405 |
| | (16.19) | (1.487) | (11.05) | (11.07) | (5.947) | (4.701) |
| Log population | 16.21** | 0.872 | 8.185 | 18.66*** | 3.749 | 5.491** |
| | (7.184) | (0.701) | (5.153) | (5.312) | (2.717) | (2.193) |
| 2015 Settlement | −3.321 | 0.419 | 43.63*** | 15.73 | 25.06*** | −12.32** |
| | (18.84) | (1.832) | (13.38) | (13.05) | (7.013) | (5.528) |
| Settlement age | 0.273 | 0.0363 | −0.476 | 0.449 | 0.531** | −0.233 |
| | (0.548) | (0.0516) | (0.382) | (0.391) | (0.204) | (0.161) |
| Average education | 0.161 | 0.139 | 3.811 | −2.518 | −1.239 | 0.145 |
| | (3.465) | (0.331) | (2.500) | (2.426) | (1.274) | (1.011) |
| Monthly HH income per capita | 0.0168 | −0.0000397 | 0.00805 | 0.0237*** | 0.00930** | −0.00142 |
| | (0.0111) | (0.000991) | (0.00760) | (0.00739) | (0.00400) | (0.00315) |
| Central land | 14.56 | −0.489 | −11.40 | −20.06** | 10.68** | −0.000506 |
| | (12.92) | (1.220) | (9.075) | (8.982) | (4.791) | (3.807) |
| Private land | −42.17** | 0.813 | −16.87 | −35.66*** | 3.300 | 1.306 |
| | (18.49) | (1.577) | (12.29) | (12.70) | (6.473) | (5.084) |
| Ethnic diversity index | −1.615 | 0.346 | −5.285 | −3.550 | 0.417 | 0.851 |
| | (4.769) | (0.458) | (3.361) | (3.442) | (1.789) | (1.425) |
| AC electoral competition | −1.149 | −0.111 | −0.790 | 0.391 | −0.168 | −0.549 |
| | (1.298) | (0.127) | (0.939) | (0.942) | (0.494) | (0.395) |

*(continued)*

TABLE B.13 (continued)

| | Paved roads | Streetlights | Piped water | Sewers | Trash removal | Medical camps |
|---|---|---|---|---|---|---|
| Ward electoral competition | −1.077 | 0.140* | 0.0336 | 1.062* | 0.423 | 0.467* |
| | (0.814) | (0.0817) | (0.591) | (0.614) | (0.309) | (0.245) |
| Social capital index 1 | 4.709 | 1.028** | 1.300 | 6.598** | 3.827*** | 1.546 |
| | (3.845) | (0.402) | (2.812) | (3.001) | (1.455) | (1.170) |
| Social capital index 2 | 9.701 | 0.375 | −4.804 | −1.315 | −6.187** | 0.820 |
| | (6.649) | (0.649) | (4.667) | (4.740) | (2.489) | (1.956) |
| Land titles | 0.493* | 0.000651 | 0.443** | 0.561*** | 0.377*** | −0.0237 |
| | (0.282) | (0.0244) | (0.191) | (0.180) | (0.103) | (0.0806) |
| Constant | −111.6* | −3.238 | −31.98 | −197.0*** | −62.15*** | −4.601 |
| | (63.31) | (6.211) | (44.51) | (48.05) | (23.65) | (18.88) |
| Sigma | 45.89*** | 4.479*** | 33.23*** | 32.04*** | 18.71*** | 14.82*** |
| | (4.833) | (0.365) | (2.845) | (3.002) | (1.342) | (1.071) |
| Observations | 111 | 111 | 111 | 111 | 111 | 111 |
| Pseudo $R^2$ | 0.076 | 0.148 | 0.100 | 0.100 | 0.089 | 0.053 |

*Note:* Standard errors in parentheses
* $p < 0.10$, ** $p < 0.05$, *** $p < 0.01$

TABLE B.14 *Fractional logit models*

| | Paved roads | Piped water | Sewers | Trash removal | Medical camps |
|---|---|---|---|---|---|
| Party worker density | 0.501*** | 0.0836 | -0.0144 | 0.124** | 0.151** |
| | (0.150) | (0.114) | (0.113) | (0.0588) | (0.0622) |
| City | 2.370*** | -1.481*** | -0.361 | 1.842*** | -0.102 |
| | (0.630) | (0.449) | (0.396) | (0.296) | (0.229) |
| Log population | 1.105*** | 0.149 | 0.714*** | 0.141 | 0.267*** |
| | (0.259) | (0.214) | (0.213) | (0.106) | (0.0960) |
| 2015 Settlement | -0.0813 | 1.825*** | 0.623 | 1.088*** | -0.647** |
| | (0.708) | (0.598) | (0.563) | (0.287) | (0.273) |
| Settlement age | 0.0328 | -0.0202 | 0.0266 | 0.0282*** | -0.00988 |
| | (0.0267) | (0.0169) | (0.0162) | (0.00994) | (0.00910) |
| Average education | -0.0251 | 0.132 | -0.0932 | -0.0600 | -0.0103 |
| | (0.130) | (0.0950) | (0.0935) | (0.0680) | (0.0533) |
| Monthly HH income per capita | 0.000437 | 0.000559* | 0.00109*** | 0.000423*** | -0.0000308 |
| | (0.000437) | (0.000299) | (0.000345) | (0.000164) | (0.000139) |
| Central land | 0.142 | -0.433 | -0.985** | 0.447** | 0.0294 |
| | (0.507) | (0.430) | (0.411) | (0.219) | (0.188) |
| Private land | -1.779*** | -0.793* | -1.712** | 0.0699 | -0.0167 |
| | (0.510) | (0.444) | (0.668) | (0.270) | (0.208) |
| Ethnic diversity index | -0.140 | -0.204 | -0.289* | 0.0105 | 0.0182 |
| | (0.146) | (0.147) | (0.154) | (0.0742) | (0.0826) |

*(continued)*

TABLE B.14 (continued)

|  | Paved roads | Piped water | Sewers | Trash removal | Medical camps |
|---|---|---|---|---|---|
| AC electoral competition | −0.0557 | −0.0152 | 0.0220 | −0.0141 | −0.0288 |
|  | (0.0493) | (0.0428) | (0.0407) | (0.0213) | (0.0184) |
| Ward electoral competition | −0.0287 | −0.0187 | 0.0398 | 0.0220 | 0.0254* |
|  | (0.0232) | (0.0241) | (0.0270) | (0.0142) | (0.0142) |
| Social capital index 1 | 0.174 | 0.0721 | 0.281** | 0.172** | 0.102 |
|  | (0.136) | (0.122) | (0.129) | (0.0676) | (0.0649) |
| Social capital index 2 | 0.224 | −0.282 | −0.153 | −0.269** | 0.0102 |
|  | (0.259) | (0.199) | (0.214) | (0.109) | (0.128) |
| Land titles | 0.0188* | 0.0251*** | 0.0235*** | 0.0158*** | −0.000176 |
|  | (0.0105) | (0.00603) | (0.00768) | (0.00508) | (0.00448) |
| Constant | −9.790*** | −2.172 | −10.09*** | −4.896*** | −2.668*** |
|  | (2.464) | (1.993) | (2.084) | (0.918) | (0.911) |
| Observations | 111 | 111 | 111 | 111 | 111 |

*Note:* Robust standard errors in parentheses
* $p < 0.10$, ** $p < 0.05$, *** $p < 0.01$

TABLE B.15 *Robust regression with Huber weights*

| | Paved roads | Streetlights | Piped water | Sewers | Trash removal | Medical camps | Dev. index 1 |
|---|---|---|---|---|---|---|---|
| Party worker density | 6.873*** | 1.281*** | 1.415 | 0.000867 | 1.701 | 2.592** | 0.270*** |
| | (2.312) | (0.289) | (2.234) | (1.748) | (1.513) | (1.061) | (0.0829) |
| City | 39.90*** | −5.356*** | −30.72*** | 0.0716 | 41.66*** | −2.543 | −0.474 |
| | (9.604) | (1.199) | (9.278) | (7.260) | (6.284) | (4.405) | (0.344) |
| Log population | 14.76*** | 0.115 | 3.857 | 7.425** | 3.578 | 5.115** | 0.396** |
| | (4.438) | (0.554) | (4.288) | (3.355) | (2.904) | (2.036) | (0.159) |
| 2015 Settlement | −8.022 | 1.208 | 25.28** | 9.794 | 23.13*** | −12.27** | 0.395 |
| | (11.29) | (1.409) | (10.90) | (8.532) | (7.386) | (5.177) | (0.405) |
| Settlement age | 0.149 | 0.0102 | −0.194 | 0.342 | 0.628*** | −0.160 | 0.00333 |
| | (0.331) | (0.0413) | (0.320) | (0.250) | (0.217) | (0.152) | (0.0119) |
| Average education | 0.810 | 0.00628 | 1.816 | −0.295 | −0.331 | −0.187 | 0.0310 |
| | (2.060) | (0.257) | (1.990) | (1.557) | (1.348) | (0.945) | (0.0738) |
| Monthly HH income per capita | 0.0105 | 0.000309 | 0.00791 | 0.0148*** | 0.00530 | −0.000568 | 0.000500** |
| | (0.00646) | (0.000806) | (0.00624) | (0.00488) | (0.00422) | (0.00296) | (0.000231) |
| Central land | 6.399 | −0.0863 | −8.725 | −10.68* | 8.972* | 1.310 | −0.156 |
| | (7.770) | (0.970) | (7.506) | (5.873) | (5.084) | (3.564) | (0.279) |
| Private land | −23.87** | 2.047 | −8.882 | −22.10*** | −0.0675 | 2.105 | −0.565 |
| | (10.49) | (1.309) | (10.13) | (7.929) | (6.864) | (4.811) | (0.376) |

*(continued)*

TABLE B.15 *(continued)*

|  | Paved roads | Streetlights | Piped water | Sewers | Trash removal | Medical camps | Dev. index 1 |
|---|---|---|---|---|---|---|---|
| Ethnic diversity index | -1.736 | -0.0919 | -3.262 | 0.142 | 0.0639 | 1.189 | -0.0712 |
|  | (2.868) | (0.358) | (2.771) | (2.168) | (1.877) | (1.316) | (0.103) |
| AC electoral competition | -0.307 | -0.0790 | 0.0160 | -0.0802 | -0.127 | -0.368 | -0.0156 |
|  | (0.805) | (0.100) | (0.778) | (0.609) | (0.527) | (0.369) | (0.0289) |
| Ward electoral competition | -0.708 | 0.0228 | -0.0363 | 0.259 | 0.606* | 0.403* | 0.0120 |
|  | (0.501) | (0.0625) | (0.484) | (0.379) | (0.328) | (0.230) | (0.0180) |
| Social capital index 1 | 1.170 | 0.436 | 0.568 | 1.020 | 4.712*** | 1.352 | 0.148* |
|  | (2.350) | (0.293) | (2.271) | (1.777) | (1.538) | (1.078) | (0.0843) |
| Social capital index 2 | 6.958* | -0.0568 | -2.092 | -2.562 | -4.951* | 1.562 | -0.0300 |
|  | (3.977) | (0.496) | (3.842) | (3.006) | (2.602) | (1.824) | (0.143) |
| Land titles | 0.393** | 0.00864 | 0.398** | 0.643*** | 0.377*** | -0.0657 | 0.0187*** |
|  | (0.165) | (0.0206) | (0.159) | (0.124) | (0.108) | (0.0755) | (0.00590) |
| Constant | -92.81** | 4.425 | -2.448 | -82.47*** | -60.06** | -5.787 | -4.695*** |
|  | (38.45) | (4.800) | (37.15) | (29.07) | (25.16) | (17.64) | (1.378) |
| Observations | 111 | 111 | 111 | 111 | 111 | 111 | 111 |

*Note:* Standard errors in parentheses

* $p < 0.10$, ** $p < 0.05$, *** $p < 0.01$

TABLE B.16 *Using party representational balance (dichotomous measure)*

|  | Paved roads | Streetlights | Piped water | Sewers | Trash removal | Medical camps | Dev. index 1 |
|---|---|---|---|---|---|---|---|
| Party worker density | 8.186** | 0.188 | 8.763 | 3.355 | 1.357 | 2.679 | 0.320** |
|  | (4.013) | (0.700) | (5.927) | (3.323) | (2.510) | (1.833) | (0.123) |
| PRB (dichotomous) | 17.28 | -2.543 | 9.131 | 8.252 | -4.460 | -4.677 | 0.0883 |
|  | (11.64) | (1.741) | (12.94) | (11.23) | (9.047) | (6.208) | (0.407) |
| PWD * PRB (dichotomous) | -6.567 | 1.252 | -7.324 | -6.629 | 0.719 | 0.677 | -0.139 |
|  | (4.688) | (0.892) | (6.091) | (4.163) | (3.036) | (2.404) | (0.163) |
| City | 43.09*** | -4.701** | -29.31*** | -12.97 | 42.39*** | -4.953 | -0.394 |
|  | (7.936) | (1.819) | (8.407) | (8.140) | (6.676) | (4.909) | (0.399) |
| Log population | 11.24*** | 0.173 | 7.489* | 8.666** | 3.911 | 4.809** | 0.467*** |
|  | (3.387) | (0.825) | (3.962) | (3.952) | (3.119) | (2.290) | (0.173) |
| 2015 Settlement | 1.975 | 0.233 | 19.27* | 6.763 | 18.41*** | -5.912 | 0.426 |
|  | (10.39) | (1.915) | (10.22) | (11.41) | (6.875) | (5.002) | (0.458) |
| Settlement age | -0.000704 | 0.0110 | 0.304 | 0.639** | 0.748*** | -0.365 | 0.0138 |
|  | (0.326) | (0.0544) | (0.358) | (0.266) | (0.277) | (0.242) | (0.0139) |
| Average education | 0.604 | 0.167 | 2.130 | -0.142 | -1.622 | -0.894 | 0.0216 |
|  | (1.720) | (0.344) | (1.678) | (1.736) | (1.666) | (0.938) | (0.0612) |
| Monthly HH income per capita | 0.0108* | -0.000250 | 0.00971** | 0.0170*** | 0.00778** | 0.00150 | 0.000555*** |
|  | (0.00559) | (0.000902) | (0.00468) | (0.00630) | (0.00370) | (0.00289) | (0.000201) |
| Central land | 12.82* | 0.142 | -12.55 | -15.57** | 7.502 | 2.876 | -0.176 |
|  | (7.324) | (1.166) | (7.552) | (6.710) | (5.551) | (3.790) | (0.273) |
| Private land | -27.63*** | 0.210 | 2.240 | -14.67 | 2.313 | 1.124 | -0.417 |
|  | (9.796) | (2.504) | (10.00) | (10.91) | (6.083) | (4.734) | (0.469) |

*(continued)*

TABLE B.16 (continued)

| | Paved roads | Streetlights | Piped water | Sewers | Trash removal | Medical camps | Dev. index 1 |
|---|---|---|---|---|---|---|---|
| Ethnic diversity index | -2.868 | -0.160 | -5.512* | -3.589 | 0.549 | 0.0933 | -0.167 |
| | (2.127) | (0.532) | (2.888) | (2.902) | (2.149) | (1.934) | (0.128) |
| AC electoral competition | -0.567 | -0.109 | 0.883 | 0.659 | -0.134 | -0.244 | 0.00200 |
| | (0.682) | (0.116) | (0.863) | (0.705) | (0.519) | (0.347) | (0.0293) |
| Ward electoral competition | -0.590 | 0.0699 | -0.403 | 0.282 | 0.545** | 0.232 | 0.00682 |
| | (0.466) | (0.0754) | (0.461) | (0.423) | (0.273) | (0.239) | (0.0165) |
| Social capital index 1 | 4.133* | 0.780* | 0.721 | 3.189 | 5.391*** | 1.621 | 0.231** |
| | (2.275) | (0.399) | (2.260) | (2.337) | (1.560) | (1.279) | (0.0967) |
| Social capital index 2 | 2.876 | 0.0703 | -0.357 | -2.355 | -3.316 | -2.222 | -0.0658 |
| | (3.969) | (0.655) | (3.961) | (4.143) | (2.923) | (2.540) | (0.184) |
| Land titles | 0.385*** | 0.0122 | 0.354*** | 0.419*** | 0.358*** | 0.00872 | 0.0186*** |
| | (0.119) | (0.0207) | (0.133) | (0.150) | (0.112) | (0.106) | (0.00667) |
| Constant | -64.59* | 6.472 | -70.94** | -105.4*** | -60.88** | 3.844 | -5.853*** |
| | (33.75) | (7.560) | (34.96) | (34.38) | (26.67) | (22.65) | (1.615) |
| Observations | 91 | 91 | 91 | 91 | 91 | 91 | 91 |
| $R^2$ | 0.550 | 0.518 | 0.654 | 0.611 | 0.583 | 0.381 | 0.649 |

*Note*: OLS models; robust standard errors in parentheses
* $p < 0.10$, ** $p < 0.05$, *** $p < 0.01$

TABLE.B.17 *Marginal effects of party worker density, conditional on PRB (dichotomous measure)*

| | MFX party worker density ||||||| 
|---|---|---|---|---|---|---|---|
| | Paved roads | Streetlights | Piped water | Sewers | Trash removal | Medical camps | Dev. index 1 |
| PRB (dichotomous) = 0 | 8.19** | 0.19 | 8.76 | 3.36 | 1.36 | 2.68 | 0.32** |
| | (4.01) | (0.70) | (5.93) | (3.32) | (2.51) | (1.83) | (0.12) |
| PRB (dichotomous) = 1 | 1.62 | 1.44** | 1.44 | −3.27 | 2.08 | 3.36* | 0.18 |
| | (2.59) | (0.54) | (2.45) | (2.38) | (1.72) | (1.75) | (0.17) |

*Note:* Standard errors in parentheses

TABLE B.18 *Using Jaipur RAY population data*

| | Paved roads | Streetlights | Piped water | Sewers | Trash removal | Medical camps | Dev. index 1 |
|---|---|---|---|---|---|---|---|
| Party worker density | 3.175* | 2.332*** | 1.195 | 1.624** | 1.596** | 0.103 | 0.109** |
| | (1.772) | (0.290) | (0.978) | (0.800) | (0.637) | (0.683) | (0.0545) |
| City | 32.73*** | -9.525*** | -28.35*** | -10.03 | 38.08*** | -2.152 | -0.414 |
| | (9.599) | (2.180) | (8.155) | (7.437) | (6.122) | (4.330) | (0.345) |
| Log population | 14.49*** | -1.821** | 3.678 | 5.515* | 1.941 | 7.866*** | 0.491*** |
| | (4.103) | (0.887) | (3.846) | (2.963) | (2.588) | (1.610) | (0.129) |
| 2015 Settlement | -4.972 | 0.347 | 27.21*** | 9.136 | 21.83*** | -11.56** | 0.426 |
| | (11.75) | (2.148) | (9.724) | (8.520) | (6.611) | (4.545) | (0.396) |
| Settlement age | 0.140 | -0.0127 | -0.341 | 0.253 | 0.478** | -0.123 | 0.00332 |
| | (0.417) | (0.0809) | (0.352) | (0.303) | (0.231) | (0.184) | (0.0150) |
| Average education | 0.786 | 0.706* | 2.222 | -1.1119 | -1.293 | 0.253 | 0.0310 |
| | (2.469) | (0.407) | (1.603) | (1.408) | (1.612) | (0.999) | (0.0702) |
| Monthly HH income per capita | 0.00894 | 0.000200 | 0.00773 | 0.0180*** | 0.00929** | -0.000940 | 0.000507** |
| | (0.00645) | (0.00122) | (0.00517) | (0.00603) | (0.00388) | (0.00277) | (0.000203) |
| Central land | 3.148 | 2.156 | -7.221 | -12.62** | 9.202* | 0.526 | -0.191 |
| | (8.083) | (1.540) | (7.839) | (6.191) | (4.715) | (3.441) | (0.255) |
| Private land | -23.78** | -0.254 | -8.580 | -22.43** | 3.038 | 0.373 | -0.585 |
| | (10.70) | (2.972) | (8.443) | (9.817) | (6.716) | (3.744) | (0.406) |

*(continued)*

| | | | | | | |
|---|---|---|---|---|---|---|
| Ethnic diversity index | −0.991 (2.867) | 0.205 (0.602) | −3.842 (2.677) | −3.468 (2.486) | 0.382 (1.563) | 0.467 (1.432) | −0.0775 (0.117) |
| AC electoral competition | −0.0692 (0.808) | −0.0769 (0.161) | −0.0277 (0.815) | 0.271 (0.639) | −0.0839 (0.456) | −0.312 (0.318) | −0.00676 (0.0271) |
| Ward electoral competition | −0.781 (0.518) | 0.105 (0.0795) | −0.283 (0.447) | 0.190 (0.366) | 0.332 (0.361) | 0.509* (0.267) | 0.00941 (0.0159) |
| Social capital index 1 | 1.804 (2.496) | 0.341 (0.401) | 0.855 (2.114) | 2.144 (1.672) | 3.532** (1.560) | 1.656 (1.023) | 0.176** (0.0813) |
| Social capital index 2 | 5.551 (4.310) | 0.114 (0.694) | −2.875 (3.211) | −3.624 (2.866) | −5.481** (2.461) | 1.653 (2.205) | −0.0198 (0.135) |
| Land titles | 0.334** (0.129) | 0.0473 (0.0345) | 0.375*** (0.115) | 0.527*** (0.124) | 0.328*** (0.110) | 0.00867 (0.0908) | 0.0192*** (0.00544) |
| Constant | −77.60* (41.14) | 16.08** (7.398) | 5.947 (40.31) | −63.75** (26.71) | −41.57* (22.97) | −25.33 (16.81) | −5.225*** (1.258) |
| Observations | 111 | 111 | 111 | 111 | 111 | 111 | 111 |
| $R^2$ | 0.435 | 0.756 | 0.535 | 0.547 | 0.549 | 0.339 | 0.592 |

*Note:* OLS models; robust standard errors in parentheses
* $p < 0.10$, ** $p < 0.05$, *** $p < 0.01$

TABLE B.19 *2015 Ethnic diversity index*

| | Paved roads | Streetlights | Piped water | Sewers | Trash removal | Medical camps | Dev. index 1 |
|---|---|---|---|---|---|---|---|
| Party worker density | 6.764*** | 1.146*** | 1.393 | -0.291 | 2.466* | 2.853** | 0.246*** |
| | (2.309) | (0.419) | (2.236) | (1.828) | (1.341) | (1.148) | (0.0905) |
| City | 35.19*** | -4.881*** | -30.83*** | -8.846 | 39.38*** | -2.927 | -0.430 |
| | (9.083) | (1.488) | (8.075) | (7.373) | (6.169) | (4.431) | (0.357) |
| Log population | 14.81*** | 0.279 | 1.780 | 7.413** | 3.631 | 4.140** | 0.402*** |
| | (3.730) | (0.627) | (3.809) | (3.071) | (2.447) | (1.871) | (0.139) |
| 2015 Settlement | -3.346 | 0.627 | 26.41*** | 8.143 | 23.10*** | -11.19** | 0.469 |
| | (11.51) | (1.451) | (9.486) | (8.659) | (6.453) | (4.473) | (0.376) |
| Settlement age | 0.241 | 0.0223 | -0.332 | 0.341 | 0.582*** | -0.206 | 0.00557 |
| | (0.358) | (0.0436) | (0.314) | (0.278) | (0.211) | (0.175) | (0.0133) |
| Average education | 0.352 | 0.115 | 2.537 | -0.846 | -1.329 | -0.205 | 0.0224 |
| | (2.206) | (0.246) | (1.574) | (1.384) | (1.577) | (0.990) | (0.0604) |
| Monthly HH income per capita | 0.00778 | -0.0000802 | 0.00712 | 0.0170*** | 0.00886** | -0.000649 | 0.000477** |
| | (0.00633) | (0.000745) | (0.00540) | (0.00611) | (0.00381) | (0.00267) | (0.000207) |
| Central land | 3.141 | 0.249 | -7.090 | -13.66** | 9.036* | 1.413 | -0.172 |
| | (7.801) | (1.053) | (7.890) | (6.233) | (4.720) | (3.496) | (0.254) |
| Private land | -26.96*** | 0.463 | -9.777 | -23.58** | 0.797 | 1.142 | -0.697* |
| | (9.845) | (1.949) | (8.713) | (9.542) | (6.353) | (3.745) | (0.405) |

*(continued)*

|  |  |  |  |  |  |  |
|---|---|---|---|---|---|---|
| 2015 Ethnic diversity index | −2.887 | 0.0222 | −2.237 | −3.152 | −1.058 | 1.308 | −0.0906 |
|  | (2.864) | (0.381) | (2.665) | (2.358) | (1.565) | (1.195) | (0.119) |
| AC electoral competition | −0.484 | −0.118 | −0.0464 | 0.332 | −0.223 | −0.548* | −0.0212 |
|  | (0.751) | (0.0969) | (0.819) | (0.679) | (0.474) | (0.318) | (0.0274) |
| Ward electoral competition | −0.661 | 0.0771 | −0.238 | 0.329 | 0.454 | 0.389 | 0.0117 |
|  | (0.484) | (0.0606) | (0.404) | (0.362) | (0.326) | (0.256) | (0.0145) |
| Social capital index 1 | 2.117 | 0.692** | 0.590 | 2.341 | 3.819** | 1.430 | 0.175** |
|  | (2.301) | (0.270) | (2.070) | (1.615) | (1.501) | (1.140) | (0.0793) |
| Social capital index 2 | 4.535 | 0.0834 | −2.995 | −3.048 | −5.447** | 0.442 | −0.0642 |
|  | (4.282) | (0.430) | (3.167) | (3.079) | (2.385) | (2.152) | (0.138) |
| Land titles | 0.300** | 0.00601 | 0.389*** | 0.510*** | 0.323*** | 0.00289 | 0.0188*** |
|  | (0.127) | (0.0177) | (0.116) | (0.128) | (0.115) | (0.0914) | (0.00571) |
| Constant | −82.15** | 3.392 | 20.23 | −78.72*** | −57.67*** | 5.467 | −4.611*** |
|  | (35.78) | (5.526) | (38.69) | (26.28) | (20.09) | (17.97) | (1.237) |
| Observations | 111 | 111 | 111 | 111 | 111 | 111 | 111 |
| $R^2$ | 0.478 | 0.532 | 0.526 | 0.545 | 0.553 | 0.349 | 0.609 |

*Note*: OLS models; robust standard errors in parentheses
* $p < 0.10$, ** $p < 0.05$, *** $p < 0.01$

# Bibliography

Acemoglu, Daron, Tristan Reed, and James Robinson. 2014. "Chiefs: Economic Development and Elite Control of Civil Society in Sierra Leone." *Journal of Political Economy* 122, no. 2: 319–68.

Agarwala, Rina. 2013. *Informal Labor, Formal Politics, and Dignified Discontent in India*. New York: Cambridge University Press.

Agnihotri, Pushpa. 1994. *Poverty Amidst Prosperity: Survey of Slums*. New Delhi: M.D. Publications.

Ahuja, Amit and Pradeep Chhibber. 2012. "Why the Poor Vote in India: 'If I Don't Vote, I Am Dead to the State.'" *Studies in Comparative International Development* 47, no. 4: 389–410.

Alesina, Alberto, Reza Baqir, and William Easterly. 1999. "Public Goods and Ethnic Divisions." *The Quarterly Journal of Economics* 114, no. 4: 1243–84.

Anand, Nikhil. 2017. *Hydraulic City: Water and the Infrastructures of Citizenship in Mumbai*. Durham, NC: Duke University Press.

Anderson, Michael. 2008. "Multiple Inference and Gender Differences in the Effects of Early Intervention: A Reevaluation of the Abecedarian, Perry Preschool, and Early Training Projects." *Journal of the American Statistical Association* 103, no. 484: 1481–95.

Anjaria, Jonathan Shapiro. 2016. *The Slow Boil: Street Food, Rights, and Public Space in Mumbai*. Stanford, CA: Stanford University Press.

Asian Development Bank. 2016. "India: Urban Water Supply and Environmental Improvement in Madhya Pradesh Project." Project Completion Report.

Auerbach, Adam Michael. 2016. "Clients and Communities: The Political Economy of Party Network Organization and Development in India's Urban Slums." *World Politics* 68, no. 1: 111–48.

Auerbach, Adam Michael. 2017. "Neighborhood Associations and the Urban Poor: India's Slum Development Committees." *World Development* 96: 119–35.

Auerbach, Adam Michael. 2018. "Informal Archives: Historical Narratives and the Preservation of Paper in India's Urban Slums." *Studies in Comparative International Development* 53, no.3: 343–64.

Auerbach, Adam Michael and Tariq Thachil. 2018. "How Clients Select Brokers: Competition and Choice in India's Slums." *American Political Science Review* 112, no. 4: 775–91.

Auerbach, Adam Michael, Adrienne LeBas, Alison Post, and Rebecca Weitz-Shapiro. 2018. "State, Society, and Informality in Cities of the Global South." *Studies in Comparative International Development* 53, no. 3: 261–80.

Auyero, Javier. 2001. *Poor People's Politics: Peronist Survival Networks and the Legacy of Evita*. Durham, NC: Duke University Press.

Bag, Sugata, Suman Seth, and Anish Gupta. 2016. "A Comparative Study of Living Conditions in Slums of Three Metro Cities in India." Leeds University Business School Research Paper Series (no. 16–07).

Bagchi, Soumen and Soumyadeep Chattopadhyay. 2004. "Decentralised Urban Governance in India: Implications for Financing of Urban Infrastructure." *Economic and Political Weekly* 39, no. 49: 5253–60.

Bailey, F. G. 1963. *Politics and Social Change: Orissa in 1959*. Berkeley, CA: University of California Press.

Baldwin, Kate. 2015. *The Paradox of Traditional Chiefs in Democratic Africa*. New York: Cambridge University Press.

Banda, Subhadra, Varsha Bhaik, Bijendra Jha, Ben Mandelkern, and Shahana Sheikh. 2014. "Negotiating Citizenship in F Block: A Jhuggi Jhopri Cluster in Delhi." A Report of the Cities of Delhi Project, Centre for Policy Research, New Delhi.

Banerjee, Abhijit, Lakshmi Iyer, and Rohini Somanathan. 2005. "History, Social Divisions, and Public Goods in Rural India." *Journal of the European Economic Association* 3, no. 2–3: 639–47.

Banerjee, Abhijit, Rohini Pande, and Michael Walton. 2012. "Delhi's Slum-Dwellers: Deprivation, Preferences, and Political Engagement among the Urban Poor." International Growth Centre Working Paper.

Banerjee, Banashree. 2002. "Security of Tenure in Indian Cities." In *Holding their Ground: Secure Land Tenure for the Urban Poor in Developing Countries* (edited by Alain Durand-Lasserve and Lauren Royston). London: Earthscan.

Banks, Nicola. 2008. "A Tale of Two Wards: Political Participation and the Urban Poor in Dhaka City." *Environment and Urbanization* 20, no. 2: 361–76.

Bapat, Meera and Indu Agarwal. 2003. "Our Needs, Our Priorities: Women and Men from the Slums in Mumbai and Pune Talk about their Needs for Water and Sanitation." *Environment and Urbanization* 15, no. 2: 71–86.

Bardhan, Pranab and Dilip Mookherjee. 2006. *Decentralization and Local Governance in Developing Countries*. Cambridge, MA: MIT Press.

Barnes, Sandra. 1986. *Patrons and Power: Creating a Political Community in Metropolitan Lagos*. Bloomington, IN: Indiana University Press.

Batra, Lalit. 2009. "A Review of Urbanisation and Urban Policy in Post-Independent India." Centre for the Study of Law and Governance Working Paper Series, Jawaharlal Nehru University, New Delhi.

Basu, Amrita. 1994. "Bhopal Revisited: The View from Below." *Bulletin of Concerned Asian Scholars* 26, no. 1–2: 3–14.

Baud, I. S. A. and Joop de Wit. 2008. *New Forms of Urban Governance in India*. New Delhi: Sage.

Bayat, Asef. 1997. *Street Politics: Poor People's Movements in Iran*. New York: Columbia University Press.

Benjamin, Solomon. 2008. "Occupancy Urbanism: Radicalizing Politics and Economy beyond Policy and Programs." *International Journal of Urban and Regional Research* 32, no. 3: 719–29.

Benjamin, Solomon and R. Bhuvaneswari. 2001. "Democracy, Inclusive Governance and Poverty in Bangalore." University of Birmingham: Urban Governance, Partnership and Poverty Working Paper 26.

Benjamini, Yoav, Abba Krieger, and Daniel Yekutieli. 2006. "Adaptive Linear Step-Up Procedures that Control for the False Discovery Rate." *Biometrika* 93, no.3: 491–507.

Berenschot, Ward. 2010. "Everyday Mediation: The Politics of Public Service Delivery in Gujarat, India." *Development and Change* 41, no.5: 883–905.

Berenschot, Ward. 2011. "Political Fixers and the Rise of Hindu Nationalism in Gujarat, India: Lubricating a Patronage Democracy." *South Asia: Journal of South Asian Studies* XXXIV, no. 3: 382–401.

Berry, William, Matt Golder, and Daniel Milton. 2012. "Improving Tests of Theories Positing Interaction." *Journal of Politics* 74, no. 3: 653–71.

Bertorelli, Ebony, Patrick Heller, Siddharth Swaminathan, and Ashutosh Varshney. 2014. "Citizenship in Urban India: Evidence from Bangalore." *Janaagraha-Brown India Initiative Citizenship Index Report*.

Besley, Timothy and Robin Burgess. 2002. "The Political Economy of Government Responsiveness: Theory and Evidence from India." *Quarterly Journal of Economics* 117, no. 4: 1415–51.

Besley, Timothy, Rohini Pande, Lupin Rahman, and Vijayendra Rao. 2004. "The Politics of Public Goods Provision: Evidence from Indian Local Governments." *Journal of the European Economic Association* 2, no. 2–3: 416–26.

Bhagat, R. B. 2011. "Emerging Pattern of Urbanisation in India." *Economic and Political Weekly* 46, no. 34: 10–12.

Bhan, Gautam. 2016. *In the Public's Interest: Evictions, Citizenship and Inequality in Contemporary Delhi*. Athens, GA: University of Georgia Press.

Bhan, Gautam, Amlanjyoti Goswami, and Aromar Revi. 2014. "The Intent to Reside: Spatial Illegality, Inclusive Planning, and Urban Social Security." In *Inclusive Urban Planning: State of the Urban Poor Report 2013* (edited by Om Prakash Mathur). New Delhi: Oxford University Press.

Bhan, Gautam and Arindam Jana. 2013. "Of Slums or Poverty: Notes of Caution from Census 2011." *Economic and Political Weekly* 48, no. 18: 13–16.

Bhan, Gautam and Arindam Jana. 2015. "Reading Spatial Inequality in Urban India." *Economic and Political Weekly* 50, no. 22: 49–54.

Bhatnagar, Mridula. 2010. *Urban Slums and Poverty*. Jaipur: Ritu Publications.

Bhatt, Mahesh and V. K. Chavda. 1979. *The Anatomy of Urban Poverty: A Study of Slums in Ahmedabad City*. Ahmedabad: Gujarat University Press.

Bhavnani, Rikhil. 2009. "Do Electoral Quotas Work after They Are Withdrawn? Evidence from a Natural Experiment in India." *American Political Science Review* 103, no. 1: 23–35.

Björkman, Lisa. 2014. "'Vote Banking' as Politics in Mumbai." In *Patronage as Politics in South Asia* (edited by Anastasia Piliavsky). New York: Cambridge University Press.

Björkman, Lisa. 2015. *Pipe Politics, Contested Waters: Embedded Infrastructures of Millennial Mumbai.* Durham, NC: Duke University Press.

Bohlken, Anjali. 2018. "Targeting Ordinary Voters or Political Elites? Why Pork Is Distributed Along Partisan Lines in India." *American Journal of Political Science* 62, no. 4: 796–812.

Boulding, Carew and David Brown. 2014. "Political Competition and Local Social Spending: Evidence from Brazil." *Studies in Comparative International Development* 49, no. 2: 197–216.

Bowles, Samuel and Herbert Gintis. 2002. "Social Capital and Community Governance." *The Economic Journal* 112, no. 483: 419–36.

Bowles, Samuel and Herbert Gintis. 2004. "Persistent Parochialism: Trust and Exclusion in Ethnic Networks." *Journal of Economic Behavior & Organization* 55, no. 1: 1–23.

Brass, Paul. 1965. *Factional Politics in an Indian State: The Congress Party in Uttar Pradesh.* Berkeley, CA: University of California Press.

Breeding, Mary. 2011. "The Micro-Politics of Vote Banks in Karnataka." *Economic and Political Weekly* 46, no. 14: 71–77.

Breman, Jan. 1996. *Footloose Labour: Working in India's Informal Economy.* New York: Cambridge University Press.

Breman, Jan. 2013. *At Work in the Informal Economy of India.* New York: Oxford University Press.

Burgwal, Gerrit. 1996. *Struggle of the Poor: Neighborhood Organization and Clientelist Practice in a Quito Squatter Settlement.* Amsterdam: CEDLA.

Bussell, Jennifer. 2019. *Clients and Constituents: Political Responsiveness in Patronage Democracies.* New York: Oxford University Press.

Calvo, Ernesto and Maria Victoria Murillo. 2013. "When Parties Meet Voters: Assessing Political Linkages through Partisan Networks and Distributive Expectations in Argentina and Chile." *Comparative Political Studies* 46, no. 7: 851–82.

Camp, Edwin. 2015. "Cultivating Effective Brokers: A Party Leader's Dilemma." *British Journal of Political Science*: 1–23.

Carpenter, Jeffrey, Amrita Daniere, and Lois Takahashi. 2004. "Cooperation, Trust, and Social Capital in Southeast Asian Urban Slums." *Journal of Economic Behavior and Organization* 55, no. 4: 533–51.

Census of India. 2013. *Primary Census Abstract for Slum, 2011.* New Delhi: Office of the Registrar General and Census Commissioner.

Chandra, Kanchan. 2004. *Why Ethnic Parties Succeed: Patronage and Ethnic Head Counts in India.* New York: Cambridge University Press.

Chandra, Kanchan. 2006. "What Is Ethnic Identity and Does It Matter?" *Annual Review of Political Science* 9: 397–24.

Chatterjee, Partha. 2004. *Politics of the Governed: Reflections on Popular Politics in Most of the World.* New York: Columbia University Press.

Chatterjee, Partha. 2008. "Democracy and Economic Transformation in India." *Economic and Political Weekly* 43, no. 16: 53–62.

Chatterjee, Nandita. 2016. "Gender Perspectives in Addressing Urban Poverty: India's Efforts." In *State of the Urban Poor Report 2015: Gender and Urban Poverty* (edited by Om Prakash Mathur). New Delhi: Oxford University Press.

Chauchard, Simon. 2018. "Electoral Handouts in Mumbai Elections: The Cost of Political Competition." *Asian Survey* 58, no. 2: 341–64.

Chhibber, Pradeep and Irfan Nooruddin. 2004. "Do Party Systems Count? The Number of Parties and Government Performance in the Indian States." *Comparative Political Studies* 37, no. 2: 152–87.

Chhibber, Pradeep, Francesca Jensenius, and Pavithra Suryanarayan. 2014. "Party Organization and Party Proliferation in India." *Party Politics* 20, no. 4: 489–505.

Chidambaram, Soundarya. 2012. "The 'Right' Kind of Welfare in South India's Urban Slums: *Seva* vs. Patronage and the Success of Hindu Nationalist Organizations." *Asian Survey* 52, no. 2: 298–320.

Chubb, Judith. 1982. *Patronage, Power, and Poverty in Southern Italy: A Tale of Two Cities*. New York: Cambridge University Press.

Cleary, Matthew. 2007. "Electoral Competition, Participation, and Government Responsiveness in Mexico." *American Journal of Political Science* 51, no. 2: 283–99.

Collier, David. 1976. *Squatters and Oligarchs: Authoritarian Rule and Policy Change in Peru*. Baltimore, MD: The Johns Hopkins University Press.

Corbridge, Stuart, Glyn Williams, Manoj Srivastava, and René Véron. 2005. *Seeing the State: Governance and Governmentality in India*. New York: Cambridge University Press.

Cornelius, Wayne. 1975. *Politics and the Migrant Poor in Mexico City*. Stanford, CA: Stanford University Press.

Corstange, Daniel. 2016. *The Price of a Vote in the Middle East: Clientelism and Communal Politics in Lebanon and Yemen*. New York: Cambridge University Press.

Cox, Gary and Matthew McCubbins. 1986. "Electoral Politics as a Redistributive Game." *Journal of Politics* 48, no. 2: 370–89.

Crook, Richard and James Manor. 1998. *Democracy and Decentralisation in South Asia and West Africa*. New York: Cambridge University Press.

Cross, John. 1998. *Informal Politics: Street Vendors and the State in Mexico City*. Stanford, CA: Stanford University Press.

Das, Veena. 2011. "State, Citizenship, and the Urban Poor." *Citizenship Studies* 15, no. 3–4: 319–33.

Das, Veena and Michael Walton. 2015. "Political Leadership and the Urban Poor." *Current Anthropology* 56, Supplement 11: S44–S54.

Datta, Ayona. 2012. "'Mongrel City': Cosmopolitan Neighbourliness in a Delhi Squatter Settlement." *Antipode* 44, no. 3: 745–63.

Davis, Mike. 2007. *Planet of Slums*. New York: Verso Books.

Denis, Eric, Partha Mukhopadhyay, and Marie-Helene Zerah. 2012. "Subaltern Urbanisation in India." *Economic and Political Weekly* 47, no. 30: 52–62.

de Soto, Hernando. 2003. *The Mystery of Capital*. New York: Basic Books.

de Souza, Peter Ronald and E. Sridharan (eds.). 2006. *India's Political Parties*. New Delhi: Sage.

de Wit, Joop. 1997. *Poverty, Policy and Politics in Madras Slums: Dynamics of Survival, Gender and Leadership*. New Delhi: Sage.

de Wit, Joop. 2017. *Urban Poverty, Local Governance and Everyday Politics in Mumbai*. New York: Routledge.

de Wit, Joop, and Erhard Berner. 2009. "Progressive Patronage? Municipalities, NGOs, CBOs and the Limits to Slum Dwellers' Empowerment." *Development and Change* 40, no. 5: 927–47.

Diaz-Cayeros, Alberto, Federico Estévez, and Beatriz Magaloni. 2016. *The Political Logic of Poverty Relief: Electoral Strategies and Social Policy in Mexico*. New York: Cambridge University Press.

Dixit, Avinash and John Londregan. 1996. "The Determinants of Success of Special Interests in Redistributive Politics." *Journal of Politics* 58, no. 4: 1132–55.

Dosh, Paul. 2010. *Demanding the Land: Urban Popular Movements in Peru and Ecuador, 1990–2005*. University Park, PA: Pennsylvania State University Press.

Dunning, Thad and Janhavi Nilekani. 2013. "Ethnic Quotas and Political Mobilization: Caste, Parties, and Distribution in Indian Village Councils." *American Political Science Review* 107, no. 1: 35–56.

Dupont, Véronique and Usha Ramanathan. 2008. "The Courts and the Squatter Settlements in Delhi." In *New Forms of Urban Governance in India* (edited by I. S. A. Baud and Joop de Wit). New Delhi: Sage.

Durand-Lasserve, Alain and Lauren Royston. 2002. *Holding Their Ground: Secure Land Tenure for the Urban Poor in Developing Countries*. London: Earthscan.

Easterly, William and Ross Levine. 1997. "Africa's Growth Tragedy: Policies and Ethnic Divisions." *Quarterly Journal of Economics* 112, no. 4: 1203–50.

Edelman, Brent and Arup Mitra. 2007. "Slums as Vote Banks and Residents' Access to Basic Amenities: The Role of Political Contact and its Determinants." *Indian Journal of Human Development* 1, no. 1: 129–50.

Erie, Steven. 1988. *Rainbow's End: Irish-Americans and the Dilemmas of Urban Machine Politics, 1840–1985*. Berkeley, CA: University of California Press.

Evans, Peter. 1996. "Government Action, Social Capital and Development: Reviewing the Evidence on Synergy." *World Development* 24, no. 6: 1119–32.

Fernandes, Leela. 2006. *India's New Middle Class: Democratic Politics in an Era of Economic Reform*. Minneapolis, MN: University of Minnesota Press.

Field, Erica. 2005. "Property Rights and Investment in Urban Slums." *Journal of the European Economic Association* 3, no. 2–3: 279–90.

Fischer, Brodwyn. 2010. *A Poverty of Rights: Citizenship and Inequality in Twentieth-Century Rio de Janeiro*. Palo Alto, CA: Stanford University Press.

Fox, Jonathan. 1994. "The Difficult Transition from Clientelism to Citizenship: Lessons from Mexico." *World Politics* 46, no. 2: 151–84.

Fox, Jonathan. 2012. "State Power and Clientelism: Eight Propositions for Discussion." In *Clientelism in Everyday Latin American Politics* (edited by Tina Hilgers). New York: Palgrave Macmillan.

Galiani, Sebastian and Ernesto Schargrodsky. 2010. "Property Rights for the Poor: Effects of Land Titling." *Journal of Public Economics* 94, no. 9–10: 700–29.

Gay, Robert. 1990. "Community Organization and Clientelist Politics in Contemporary Brazil: A Case Study from Suburban Rio de Janeiro." *International Journal of Urban and Regional Research* 14, no. 4: 648–66.

Gay, Robert. 1994. *Popular Organization and Democracy in Rio de Janeiro: A Tale of Two Favelas.* Philadelphia, PA: Temple University Press.

Gayer, Laurent and Christophe Jaffrelot (eds.). 2012. *Muslims in Indian Cities: Trajectories of Marginalisation.* New Delhi: HarperCollins.

Ghertner, D. Asher. 2015. *Rule by Aesthetics: World-Class City Making in Delhi.* New York: Oxford University Press.

Gilbert, Alan. 1998. *The Latin American City.* New York: Monthly Review Press.

Gill, Kaveri. 2009. *Of Poverty and Plastic: Scavenging and Scrap Trading Entrepreneurs in India's Urban Informal Economy.* New Delhi: Oxford University Press.

Golden, Miriam and Brian Min. 2013. "Distributive Politics Around the World." *Annual Review of Political Science* 16: 73–99.

Gonzalez-Ocantos, Ezequiel, Chad Kiewiet de Jonge, Carlos Melendez, Javier Osorio, and David Nickerson. 2012. "Vote Buying and Social Desirability Bias: Experimental Evidence from Nicaragua." *American Journal of Political Science* 56, no. 1: 202–17.

Gooptu, Nandini. 2001. *The Politics of the Urban Poor in Early Twentieth-Century India.* New York: Cambridge University Press.

Gosnell, Harold. 1937. *Machine Politics: Chicago Model.* Chicago: Chicago University Press.

Government of India. 2009. *India Urban Poverty Report 2009.* New Delhi: Oxford University Press.

Government of India. 2010. *Report of the Committee on Slum Statistics/Census.* New Delhi: Ministry of Housing and Urban Poverty Alleviation.

Government of India. 2011. *Rajiv Awas Yojana, Guidelines for Community Participation.* New Delhi: Ministry of Housing and Urban Poverty Alleviation.

Government of India. 2014. *Report of the Expert Group to Review the Methodology for Measurement of Poverty.* New Delhi: Planning Commission.

Government of India. 2015. *Slums in India: A Statistical Compendium.* New Delhi: Ministry of Housing and Urban Poverty Alleviation.

Greene, Kenneth. 2007. *Why Dominant Parties Lose: Mexico's Democratization in Comparative Perspective.* New York: Cambridge University Press.

Gupta, Akhil. 1995. "Blurred Boundaries: The Discourse of Corruption, the Culture of Politics, and the Imagined State." *American Ethnologist* 22, no. 2: 375–402.

Gupta, Akhil. 2012. *Red Tape: Bureaucracy, Structural Violence, and Poverty in India.* Durham, NC: Duke University Press.

Gupta, Kamla, Fred Arnold, and H. Lhungdim. 2009. *Health and Living Conditions in Eight Indian Cities.* National Family Health Survey, India, 2005–06. Mumbai: International Institute for Population Sciences.

Habyarimana, James, Macartan Humphreys, Daniel Posner, and Jeremy Weinstein. 2009. *Coethnicity: Diversity and the Dilemmas of Collective Action.* New York: Russell Sage Foundation.

Hainmueller, Jens, Jonathan Mummolo, and Yiqing Xu. 2019. "How Much Should We Trust Estimates from Multiplicative Interaction Models? Simple Tools to Improve Empirical Practice." *Political Analysis* 27, no. 2: 163–92.

Hanna, Bridget, Ward Morehouse, and Satinath Sarangi. 2005. *The Bhopal Reader: Remembering Twenty Years of the World's Worst Industrial Disaster*. New York: The Apex Press.
Hansen, Thomas Blom. 1999. *The Saffron Wave: Democracy and Hindu Nationalism in Modern India*. Princeton, NJ: Princeton University Press.
Hansen, Thomas Blom. 2001. *Wages of Violence: Naming and Identity in Postcolonial Bombay*. Princeton, NJ: Princeton University Press.
Harding, Robin. 2015. "Attribution and Accountability: Voting for Roads in Ghana." *World Politics* 67, no. 4: 656–89.
Harriss, John. 2005. "Political Participation, Representation, and the Urban Poor: Findings from Research in Delhi." *Economic and Political Weekly* 40, no. 11: 1041–54.
Harriss, John. 2007. "Antinomies of Empowerment: Observations on Civil Society, Politics, and Urban Governance in India." *Economic and Political Weekly* 42, no. 26: 2716–24.
Heller, Patrick and Peter Evans. 2010. "Taking Tilly South: Durable Inequalities, Democratic Contestation, and Citizenship in the Southern Metropolis." *Theory and Society* 39: 433–50.
Heller, Patrick, Partha Mukhopadhyay, Subhadra Banda, and Shahana Sheikh. 2015. "Exclusion, Informality, and Predation in the Cities of Delhi." New Delhi: Centre for Policy Research.
Helmke, Gretchen and Steven Levitsky. 2004. "Informal Institutions and Comparative Politics: A Research Agenda." *Perspectives on Politics* 2, no. 4: 725–40.
Herrera, Veronica. 2017. *Water and Politics: Clientelism and Reform in Urban Mexico*. Ann Arbor, MI: University of Michigan Press.
Herrera, Veronica and Alison Post. 2014. "Can Developing Countries Both Decentralize and Depoliticize Urban Water Services? Evaluating the Legacy of the 1990s Reform Wave." *World Development* 64: 621–41.
Herring, Ronald. 1999. "Embedded Particularism: India's Failed Developmental State." In *The Developmental State* (edited by Meredith Woo-Cumings). Ithaca, NY: Cornell University Press.
Hicken, Allen. 2011. "Clientelism." *Annual Review of Political Science* 14: 289–310.
Holland, Alisha. 2016. "Forbearance." *American Political Science Review* 110, no. 2: 232–46.
Holland, Alisha and Brian Palmer-Rubin. 2015. "Beyond the Machine: Clientelistic Brokers and Interest Organizations in Latin America." *Comparative Political Studies* 48, no. 9: 1186–223.
Holston, James. 2009. *Insurgent Citizenship: Disjunctions of Democracy and Modernity in Brazil*. Princeton, NJ: Princeton University Press.
Holzner, Claudio. 2004. "The End of Clientelism? Strong and Weak Networks in a Mexican Squatter Movement." *Mobilization* 9, no. 3: 223–40.
Holzner, Claudio. 2010. *Poverty of Democracy: The Institutional Roots of Political Participation in Mexico*. Pittsburgh, PA: Pittsburgh University Press.
Houtzager, Peter and Arnab Acharya. 2011. "Associations, Active Citizenship, and the Quality of Democracy in Brazil and Mexico." *Theory and Society* 40: 1–36.

International Labour Organization. 2013. *Women and Men in the Informal Economy: A Statistical Picture*. Geneva: International Labour Office.

Jaffrelot, Christophe. 1998. *The Hindu Nationalist Movement in India*. New York: Columbia University Press.

Jayal, Niraja Gopal, Amit Prakash, and Pradeep Sharma. 2007. *Local Governance in India: Decentralization and Beyond*. New Delhi: Oxford University Press.

Jeffrey, Craig. 2010. *Timepass: Youth, Class, and the Politics of Waiting in India*. Palo Alto, CA: Stanford University Press.

Jenkins, Rob. 2000. *Democratic Politics and Economic Reform in India*. New York: Cambridge University Press.

Jensenius, Francesca. 2017. *Social Justice through Inclusion: The Consequences of Electoral Quotas in India*. New York: Oxford University Press.

Jha, Saumitra, Vijayendra Rao, and Michael Woolcock. 2007. "Governance in the Gullies: Democratic Responsiveness and Leadership in Delhi's Slums." *World Development* 35, no. 2: 230–46.

Joshi, Pratima, Srinanda Sen, and Jane Hobson. 2002. "Experiences with Surveying and Mapping Pune and Sangli Slums on a Geographical Information System (GIS)." *Environment and Urbanization* 14, no. 2: 225–40.

Kamath, Lalitha and M. Vijayabaskar. 2014. "Middle-Class and Slum-Based Collective Action in Bangalore: Contestations and Convergences in a Time of Market Reforms." *Journal of South Asian Development* 9, no. 2: 147–71.

Kapur, Devesh. 2017. "How Will India's Urban Future Affect Social Identities?" *Urbanisation* 2, no. 1: 1–8.

Keefer, Philip and Stuti Khemani. 2005. "Democracy, Public Expenditures, and the Poor: Understanding Political Incentives for Providing Public Services." *World Bank Research Observer* 20, no. 1: 1–27.

Keefer, Philip and Stuti Khemani. 2009. "When do Legislators Pass on Pork? The Role of Political Parties in Determining Legislator Effort." *American Political Science Review* 103, no. 1: 99–112.

Khwaja, Asim. 2009. "Can Good Projects Succeed in Bad Communities?" *Journal of Public Economics* 93, no. 7–8: 899–916.

Kitschelt, Herbert and Steven Wilkinson (eds.). 2007. *Patrons, Clients, and Policies: Patterns of Democratic Accountability and Political Competition*. New York: Cambridge University Press.

Kohli, Atul. 1991. *Democracy and Discontent: India's Growing Crisis of Governability*. New York: Cambridge University Press.

Kohli, Atul. 2006. "Politics of Economic Growth in India, 1980–2005: Part I: The 1980s." *Economic and Political Weekly* 41, no. 13: 1251–59.

Kohli, Atul. 2012. *Poverty Amid Plenty in the New India*. New York: Cambridge University Press.

Koster, Martijn and Pieter A. de Vries. 2012. "Slum Politics: Community Leaders, Everyday Needs, and Utopian Aspirations in Recife, Brazil." *Focaal* 62: 83–98.

Kramon, Eric. 2016. "Electoral Handouts as Information: Explaining Unmonitored Vote Buying." *World Politics* 68, no. 3: 454–98.

Krishna, Anirudh. 2002. *Active Social Capital: Tracing the Roots of Development and Democracy*. New York: Columbia University Press.

Krishna, Anirudh. 2007. "Politics in the Middle: Mediating Relationships between the Citizens and the State in Rural North India." In *Patrons, Clients, and Policies: Patterns of Democratic Accountability and Political Competition* (edited by Herbert Kitschelt and Steven Wilkinson). New York: Cambridge University Press.

Krishna, Anirudh. 2011. "Gaining Access to Public Services and the Democratic State in India: Institutions in the Middle." *Studies in Comparative International Development* 46, no. 1: 98–117.

Krishna, Anirudh. 2013. "Stuck in Place: Investigating Social Mobility in 14 Bangalore Slums." *Journal of Development Studies* 49, no. 7: 1010–28.

Krishna, Anirudh, M. S. Sriram, and Purnima Prakash. 2014. "Slum Types and Adaptation Strategies: Identifying Policy-Relevant Differences in Bangalore." *Environment and Urbanization* 26, no. 2: 568–85.

Krishna, Anirudh, Emily Rains, Jeremy Spater, and Erik Wibbels. 2018. "Informal Housing Markets in Bangalore." Working Paper, Duke University.

Kruks-Wisner, Gabrielle. 2018. *Claiming the State: Active Citizenship and Social Welfare in Rural India.* New York: Cambridge University Press.

Kumar, Tanu, Alison Post, and Isha Ray. 2018. "Flows, Leaks, and Blockages in Informational Interventions: A Field Experimental Study of Bangalore's Water Sector." *World Development* 106: 149–60.

Kundu, Amitabh. 2011. "Method in Madness: Urban Data from 2011 Census." *Economic and Political Weekly* 46, no. 40: 13–16.

Kundu, Debolina. 2014. "Urban Development Programmes in India: A Critique of JNNURM." *Social Change* 44, no. 4: 615–32.

Laakso, Markku and Rein Taagepera 1979. "Effective Number of Parties: A Measure with Application to West Europe." *Comparative Political Studies* 12, no. 1: 3–27.

Lall, Somik, Ajay Suri, and Uwe Deichmann. 2006. "Household Savings and Residential Mobility in Informal Settlements in Bhopal, India." *Urban Studies* 43, no. 7: 1025–39.

Lall, Somik, Uwe Deichmann, Mattias Lundberg, and Nazmul Chaudhury. 2004. "Tenure, Diversity and Commitment: Community Participation for Urban Service Provision." *Journal of Development Studies* 40, no. 3: 1–26.

Lanjouw, Jean and Philip Levy. 2002. "Untitled: A Study of Formal and Informal Property Rights in Urban Ecuador." *The Economic Journal* 112, no. 482: 986–1019.

Lapierre, Dominique and Javier Moro. 2002. *Five Past Midnight in Bhopal.* New York: Grand Central Publishing.

Larreguy, Horacio, John Marshall, and Pablo Querubin. 2016. "Parties, Brokers, and Voter Mobilization: How Turnout Buying Depends upon the Party's Capacity to Monitor Brokers." *American Political Science Review* 110, no. 1: 160–79.

Lee, Yok-Shiu. 1998. "Intermediary Institutions, Community Organizations, and Urban Environmental Management: The Case of Three Bangkok Slums." *World Development* 26, no. 6: 993–1011.

Lee, Alexander. 2018. "Ethnic Diversity and Ethnic Discrimination: Explaining Local Public Goods." *Comparative Political Studies* 51, no. 10: 1351–83.
Levitsky, Steven. 2003. *Transforming Labor-Based Parties in Latin America: Argentine Peronism in Comparative Perspective*. New York: Cambridge University Press.
Lindbeck, Assar and Jörgen Weibull. 1987. "Balanced-Budget Redistribution as the Outcome of Political Competition." *Public Choice* 52, no. 3: 273–97.
Lynch, Owen. 1974. "Political Mobilization and Ethnicity among Adi-Dravidas in a Bombay Slum." *Economic and Political Weekly* 9, no. 39: 1657–68.
Magaloni, Beatriz. 2008. *Voting for Autocracy: Hegemonic Party Survival and Its Demise in Mexico*. New York: Cambridge University Press.
Mahoney, James and Kathleen Thelen. 2015. *Advances in Comparative-Historical Analysis*. New York: Cambridge University Press.
Manor, James. 2000. "Small-Time Political Fixers in India's States." *Asian Survey* 40, no. 5: 816–35.
Manor, James. 2005. "In Part, a Myth: The BJP's Organisational Strength." In *Coalition Politics and Hindu Nationalism* (edited by Katharine Adeney and Lawrence Sáez). London: Routledge.
Manor, James. 2010. "What Do They Know of India Who Only India Know? The Uses of Comparative Politics." *Commonwealth and Comparative Politics* 48, no. 4: 505–16.
Mansuri, Ghazala and Vijayendra Rao. 2013. "Localizing Development: Does Participation Work?" World Bank Policy Research Report. Washington, D.C.
Marx, Benjamin, Thomas Stoker, and Tavneet Suri. 2013. "The Economics of Slums in the Developing World." *Journal of Economic Perspectives* 27, no. 4: 187–210.
Marx, Benjamin, Thomas Stoker, and Tavneet Suri. 2017. "There Is No Free House: Ethnic Patronage in a Kenyan Slum." Working Paper, Massachusetts Institute of Technology.
Mathur, Om Prakash (ed.). 2014. *Inclusive Urban Planning: State of the Urban Poor Report 2013*. New Delhi: Oxford University Press.
Mathur, Shiv. 1996. *Political Attitudes of Slum Dwellers*. Jaipur: Aalekh Publishers.
Mayaram, Shail. 1993. "Communal Violence in Jaipur." *Economic and Political Weekly* 28, no. 46/47: 2524–41.
McFarlane, Colin. 2004. "Geographical Imaginations and Spaces of Political Engagement: Examples from the Indian Alliance." *Antipode* 36, no. 5: 890–916.
Miguel, Edward. 2004. "Tribe or Nation? Nation Building and Public Goods in Kenya versus Tanzania." *World Politics* 56, no. 3: 327–62.
Min, Brian. 2015. *Power and the Vote: Elections and Electricity in the Developing World*. New York: Cambridge University Press.
Mishra, Arun Kumar and Shubhagato Dasgupta. 2014. "Evolution of National Policies for Basic Services, Affordable Housing, and Livelihoods for the Urban Poor." In *Inclusive Urban Planning: State of the Urban Poor Report 2013* (edited by Om Prakash Mathur). New Delhi: Oxford University Press.

Mitra, Arup. 2003. *Occupational Choices, Networks, and Transfers: An Exegesis Based on Micro Data from Delhi Slums.* New Delhi: Manohar Publishers.
Mitra, Arup. 2010. "Migration, Livelihood and Well-Being: Evidence from Indian City Slums." *Urban Studies* 47, no. 7: 1371–90.
Mitra, Banashree. 1988. *Impact of Tenure Regularisation and Environmental Upgrading Programmes on Shelter Consolidation in Squatter Settlements in Bhopal.* New Delhi: Indian Human Settlements Programme.
Montgomery, Mark. 2008. "The Urban Transformation of the Developing World." *Science* 319, no. 5864: 761–64.
Morrison, Nicky. 2017. "Playing by the Rules? New Institutionalism, Path Dependency and Informal Settlements in Sub-Saharan Africa." *Environment and Planning A* 49, no. 11: 2558–77.
Motiram, Sripad and Vamsi Vakulabharanam. 2012. "Understanding Poverty and Inequality in Urban India since Reforms." *Economic and Political Weekly* 47, no. 47/48: 44–52.
Murillo, Maria Victoria, Virginia Oliveros, and Rodrigo Zarazaga. 2019. "The Most Vulnerable Poor: Clientelism among Slum Dwellers." Working Paper.
Mushkat, Jerome. 1971. *Tammany: The Evolution of a Political Machine, 1789–1865.* Syracuse, NY: Syracuse University Press.
Nakamura, Shohei. 2014. "Impact of Slum Formalization on Self-Help Housing Construction: A Case of Slum Notification in India." *Urban Studies* 51, no. 16: 3420–44.
Nakamura, Shohei. 2017. "Does Slum Formalisation without Title Provision Stimulate Housing Improvement? A Case of Slum Declaration in Pune, India." *Urban Studies* 54, no. 7: 1715–35.
Naidu, Ratna. 2009. "Dilapidation and Slum Formation." In *Urban Studies* (edited by Sujata Patel and Kushal Deb). New Delhi: Oxford University Press.
Nair, Shalini. 2015. "35 Percent Urban India Is BPL, Says Unreleased Data." *The Indian Express* (July 17).
Narayan, Deepa and Lant Pritchett. 1999. "Cents and Sociability: Household Income and Social Capital in Rural Tanzania."*Economic Development and Cultural Change* 47, no. 4: 871–97.
Nathan, Noah. 2016. "Local Ethnic Geography, Expectations of Favoritism, and Voting in Urban Ghana." *Comparative Political Studies* 49, no. 14: 1896–29.
Nathan, Noah. 2019. "Does Participation Reinforce Patronage? Policy Preferences, Turnout, and Class in Urban Ghana." *British Journal of Political Science* 49, no. 1: 229–55.
National Sample Survey Office. 2014. "Urban Slums in India, 2012." Report 561. New Delhi: Ministry of Statistics and Programme Implementation.
National Sample Survey Office. 2014. "Drinking Water, Sanitation, Hygiene, and Housing Condition in India." Report 556. New Delhi: Ministry of Statistics and Programme Implementation.
Nichter, Simeon. 2008. "Vote Buying or Turnout Buying? Machine Politics and the Secret Ballot." *American Political Science Review* 102, no. 1: 19–31.
O'Donnell, Guillermo. 1993. "On the State, Democratization, and Some Conceptual Problems: A Latin American View with Glances at Some Post-Communist Countries." Kellogg Working Paper Series, University of Notre Dame.

Oldenburg, Philip. 1976. *Big City Government in India: Councilor, Administrator, and Citizen in Delhi*. Tucson, AZ: University of Arizona Press.

Oldenburg, Philip. 1987. "Middlemen in Third-World Corruption: Implications of an Indian Case." *World Politics* 39, no. 4: 508–35.

Olken, Benjamin. 2010. "Direct Democracy and Local Public Goods: Evidence from a Field Experiment in Indonesia." *American Political Science Review* 104, no. 2: 243–67.

Olson, Mancur. 1965. *The Logic of Collective Action: Public Goods and the Theory of Groups*. Cambridge, MA: Harvard University Press.

Ostrom, Elinor. 1990. *Governing the Commons: The Evolution of Institutions for Collective Action*. New York: Cambridge University Press.

Ostrom, Elinor. 1996. "Crossing the Great Divide: Coproduction, Synergy, and Development." *World Development* 24, no. 6: 1073–87.

Padhi, Bijaya, Kelly Baker, Ambarish Dutta, Oliver Cumming, Matthew Freeman, Radhanatha Satpathy, Bhabani Das, and Pinaki Panigrahi. 2015. "Risk of Adverse Pregnancy Outcomes among Women Practicing Poor Sanitation in Rural India: A Population-Based Prospective Cohort Study." *PLoS Medicine* 12, no. 7: 1–18.

Paller, Jeffrey. 2014. "Informal Institutions and Personal Rule in Urban Ghana." *African Studies Review* 57, no. 3: 123–42.

Pande, Rohini. 2011. "Can Informed Voters Enforce Better Governance? Experiments in Low-Income Democracies." *Annual Review of Economics* 3: 215–37.

Paniagua, Victoria. 2018. "When Clients Elect Brokers: Elections, Participation, and Public Goods Provision in Urban Slums" Working Paper, Duke University.

Papke, Leslie and Jeffrey Wooldridge. 1996. "Econometric Methods for Fractional Response Variables with an Application to 401(K) Plan Participation Rates." *Journal of Applied Econometrics* 11, no. 6: 619–32.

Perlman, Janice. 1976. *The Myth of Marginality: Urban Poverty and Politics in Rio de Janeiro*. Berkeley, CA: University of California Press.

Posner, Daniel. 2005. *Institutions and Ethnic Politics in Africa*. New York: Cambridge University Press.

Post, Alison. 2018. "Cities and Politics in the Developing World." *Annual Review of Political Science* 21: 115–33.

Post, Alison, Vivian Bronsoler, and Lana Salman. 2017. "Hybrid Regimes for Local Public Goods Provision: A Framework for Analysis." *Perspectives on Politics* 15, no. 4: 952–66.

Pradhan, Kanhu Charan. 2013. "Unacknowledged Urbanisation: New Census Towns of India." *Economic and Political Weekly* 48, no. 36: 43–51.

Putnam, Robert. 1994. *Making Democracy Work: Civic Traditions in Modern Italy*. Princeton, NJ: Princeton University Press.

Raghunandan, T. R. 2017. "Re-Energizing Democratic Decentralization in India." In *Rethinking Public Institutions in India* (edited by Devesh Kapur, Pratap Bhanu Mehta, and Milan Vaishnav). New York: Oxford University Press.

Rains, Emily, Anirudh Krishna, and Erik Wibbels. 2019. "Combining Satellite and Survey Data to Study Indian Slums." *Environment and Urbanization* 31, no. 1: 267–92.

Ramanathan, Ramesh. 2007. "Federalism, Urban Decentralization, and Citizen Participation." *Economic and Political Weekly* 42, no. 8: 674–81.

Rao, K. Ranga and M.S.A. Rao. 1984. *Cities and Slums: A Study of a Squatters' Settlement in the City of Vijayawada*. New Delhi: Concept Publishing.

Rao, Ratna. 1990. *Social Organisation in an Indian Slum*. New Delhi: Mittal.

Rao, Vijayendra, Kripa Ananthpur, and Kabir Malik. 2017. "The Anatomy of Failure: An Ethnography of a Randomized Trial to Deepen Democracy in Rural India." *World Development* 99: 481–97.

Ray, Talton. 1969. *The Politics of the Barrios of Venezuela*. Berkeley, CA: University of California Press.

Reddy, G. R. and G. Haragopal. 1985. "The Pyraveekar: The 'Fixer' in Rural India." *Asian Survey* 25, no. 11: 1148–62.

Resnick, Danielle. 2014. *Urban Poverty and Party Populism in African Democracies*. New York: Cambridge University Press.

Risbud, Neelima. 1988. *Socio-Physical Evolution of Popular Settlements and Government Supports: Case Study of Bhopal*. New Delhi: Indian Human Settlements Programme.

Risbud, Neelima. 2002. "Policies for Tenure Security in Delhi." In *Holding Their Ground: Secure Land Tenure for the Urban Poor in Developing Countries* (edited by Alain Durand-Lasserve and Lauren Royston). London: Earthscan.

Risbud, Neelima. 2009. "The Poor and Morphology of Cities." In *India Urban Poverty Report 2009*. New Delhi: Oxford University Press.

Risbud, Neelima. 2014. "Experience of Security of Tenure toward Inclusion: Indore and Jaipur." In *Inclusive Urban Planning: State of the Urban Poor Report 2013* (edited by Om Prakash Mathur). New Delhi: Oxford University Press.

Roy, Ananya. 2002. *City Requiem, Calcutta: Gender and the Politics of Poverty*. Minneapolis, MN: University of Minnesota Press.

Roy, Ananya. 2009. "Why India Cannot Plan Its Cities: Informality, Insurgence and the Idiom of Urbanization." *Planning Theory* 80, no. 1: 76–87.

Roy, Ananya. 2014. "The Inclusive City: A New Paradigm of Urban Planning in India?" In *Inclusive Urban Planning: State of the Urban Poor Report 2013* (edited by Om Prakash Mathur). New Delhi: Oxford University Press.

Rudolph, Lloyd and Susanne Rudolph. 1984. *The Modernity of Tradition: Political Development in India*. Chicago: University of Chicago Press.

Ruet, Joel and Stéphanie Tawa Lama-Rewal. 2009. *Governing India's Metropolises: Case Studies of Four Cities*. New Delhi: Routledge.

Sáez, Lawrence and Aseema Sinha. 2010. "Political Cycles, Political Institutions and Public Expenditure in India, 1980–2000." *British Journal of Political Science* 40, no. 1: 91–113.

Samuelson, Paul. 1954. "The Pure Theory of Public Expenditure." *The Review of Economics and Statistics* 36, no. 4: 387–89.

Sankhe, Shirish, Ireena Vittal, Richard Dobbs, Ajit Mohan, Ankur Gulati, Jonathan Ablett, Shishir Gupta, Alex Kim, Sudipto Paul, Aditya Sanghvi, and Gurpreet Sethy. 2010. "India's Urban Awakening: Building Inclusive Cities, Sustaining Economic Growth." *McKinsey Global Institute Report*.

Schaffer, Frederic (ed.). 2007. *Elections for Sale: The Causes and Consequences of Vote Buying*. New York: Lynne Rienner.

Schaffer, Joby and Andy Baker. 2015. "Clientelism as Persuasion-Buying: Evidence from Latin America." *Comparative Political Studies* 48, no. 9: 1093–126.
Schenk, Hans (ed.). 2001. *Living in India's Slums: A Case Study of Bangalore.* New Delhi: Manohar Publishers.
Schneider, Mark. forthcoming. "Do Local Leaders Know Their Voters? A Test of Guessability in India." *Electoral Studies.*
Schoorl, J. W., J. J. van der Linden, and K. S. Yap (eds.). 1983. *Between Basti Dwellers and Bureaucrats: Lessons in Squatter Settlement Upgrading in Karachi.* Oxford: Pergamon.
Scott, James. 1977. "Patron-Client Politics and Political Change in Southeast Asia." In *Friends, Followers, Factions: A Reader in Political Clientelism* (edited by Steffen Schmidt, James Scott, Carl Lande, and Laura Guasti). Berkeley, CA: University of California Press.
Sen, Amartya. 1999. *Development as Freedom.* New York: Knopf.
Shami, Mahvish. 2012. "Collective Action, Clientelism, and Connectivity." *American Political Science Review* 106, no. 3: 588–606.
Shami, Mahvish and Hadia Majid. 2014. "The Political Economy of Public Goods Provision in Slums." London: International Growth Centre, Working Paper.
Sharalaya, Nandan. 2017. "Financing Indian Cities." *Ideas for India* (July 12).
Singh, Andrea and Alfred de Souza. 1980. *The Urban Poor: Slum and Pavement Dwellers in the Major Cities of India.* New Delhi: Manohar Publications.
Singh, Prerna and Matthias vom Hau. 2016. "Ethnicity in Time: Politics, History, and the Relationship between Ethnic Diversity and Public Goods Provision." *Comparative Political Studies* 49, no. 10: 1303–40.
Singhi, N. K. 1997. *Pro-Poor City Planning: Social Mapping of Jaipur City.* Jaipur: Institute of Development Studies, Jaipur Report.
Sivaramakrishnan, K. C., Amitabh Kundu, and B. N. Singh. 2006. *Oxford Handbook of Urbanization in India.* New Delhi: Oxford University Press.
Slater, Dan and Erica Simmons. 2010. "Informative Regress: Critical Antecedents in Comparative Politics." *Comparative Political Studies* 43, no. 7: 886–917.
Snell-Rood, Claire. 2015. *No One Will Let Her Live: Women's Struggle for Well-Being in a Delhi Slum.* Berkeley, CA: University of California.
Srivastava, Sanjay. 2012. "Duplicity, Intimacy, Community: An Ethnography of ID Cards, Permits and Other Fake Documents in Delhi." *Thesis Eleven* 113, no. 1: 78–93.
Stokes, Susan. 1995. *Cultures in Conflict: Social Movements and the State in Peru.* Berkeley, CA: University of California Press.
Stokes, Susan. 2005. "Perverse Accountability: A Formal Model of Machine Politics with Evidence from Argentina." *American Political Science Review* 99, no. 3: 315–25.
Stokes, Susan, Thad Dunning, Marcelo Nazareno, and Valeria Brusco. 2013. *Brokers, Voters, and Clientelism: The Puzzle of Distributive Politics.* New York: Cambridge University Press.
Sukhtankar, Sandip. 2016. "India's National Rural Employment Guarantee Scheme: What Do We Really Know about the World's Largest Workfare Program?" New Delhi: India Policy Forum.

Suttles, Gerald. 1968. *The Social Order of the Slum: Ethnicity and Territory in the Inner City*. Chicago: University of Chicago Press.

Szwarcberg, Mariela. 2015. *Mobilizing Poor Voters: Machine Politics, Clientelism, and Social Networks in Argentina*. New York: Cambridge University Press.

Tarlo, Emily. 2001. "Paper Truths: The Emergency and Slum Clearance through Forgotten Files." In *The Everyday State in Modern India* (edited by C. J. Fuller and Veronique Benei). London: Hurst and Company.

Tarlo, Emily. 2003. *Unsettling Memories: Narratives of the Emergency in Delhi*. Berkeley, CA: University of California Press.

Tewari, V. 2002. *An Assessment of SJSRY in Rajasthan*. New Delhi: National Institute of Urban Affairs Report.

Thachil, Tariq. 2014. *Elite Parties, Poor Voters: How Social Services Win Votes in India*. New York: Cambridge University Press.

Thachil, Tariq. 2017. "Do Rural Migrants Divide Ethnically in the City? Evidence from an Ethnographic Experiment in India." *American Journal of Political Science* 61, no. 4: 908–26.

Thomas, Rosamma. 2017. "Jaipur Slum Dwellers March Seeking Better Facilities." *Times of India, Jaipur City News* (March 29, 2017).

Tiebout, Charles. 1967. "A Pure Theory of Local Expenditures." *Journal of Political Economy* 64, no. 5: 416–24.

Tsai, Lily. 2007. *Accountability without Democracy: Solidary Groups and Public Goods Provision in Rural China*. New York: Cambridge University Press.

UN-Habitat. 1982. *Survey of Slum and Squatter Settlements*. Dublin: Tycooly International.

UN-Habitat. 2003. *The Challenge of Slums: Global Report on Human Settlements 2003*. London: Earthscan.

UN-Habitat. 2006a. *Financial Resource Mapping for Pro-Poor Governance*. New Delhi: Water for Asian Cities, India Programme.

UN-Habitat. 2006b. *State of the World's Cities, 2006/2007*. London: Earthscan.

UN-Habitat. 2007a. *Poverty Mapping: Prioritising Interventions, Intra-Slum Inequalities Analysis, Bhopal*. Bhopal: UN-Habitat and Water-Aid Office.

UN-Habitat. 2007b. *Poverty Mapping: Prioritising Interventions, Intra-Slum Inequalities Analysis, Jabalpur*. Bhopal: UN-Habitat and Water-Aid Office.

UN-Habitat. 2013. *State of the World's Cities, 2012/2013*. New York: Earthscan from Routledge.

United Nations. 2015. *World Urbanization Prospects: The 2014 Revision*. New York: United Nations Publications (ST/ESA/SER.A/366).

Vaishnav, Milan. 2017. *When Crime Pays: Money and Muscle in Indian Politics*. New Haven, CT: Yale University Press.

Vaishnav, Milan and Neelanjan Sircar. 2013. "Core or Swing? The Role of Electoral Context in Shaping Pork Barrel." Working Paper.

Vaishnav, Milan and Jamie Hintson. 2019. "India's Emerging Crisis of Representation." Washington, DC: Carnegie Endowment for International Peace.

Varshney, Ashutosh. 1998. *Democracy, Development, and the Countryside: Urban-Rural Struggles in India*. New York: Cambridge University Press.

Varshney, Ashutosh. 2002. *Ethnic Conflict and Civic Life: Hindus and Muslims in India*. New Haven, CT: Yale University Press.

Véron, René, Stuart Corbridge, Glyn Williams, and Manoj Srivastava. 2003. "The Everyday State and Political Society in Eastern India: Structuring Access to the Employment Assurance Scheme." *Journal of Development Studies* 39, no. 5: 1–28.

Wade, Robert. 1988. *Village Republics: Economic Conditions for Collective Action in South India*. New York: Cambridge University Press.

Weiner, Myron. 1967. *Party Building in a New Nation: The Indian National Congress*. Chicago: University of Chicago Press.

Weinstein, Liza. 2014. *The Durable Slum: Dharavi and the Right to Stay Put in Globalizing Mumbai*. Minneapolis, MN: University of Minnesota Press.

Weitz-Shapiro, Rebecca. 2014. *Curbing Clientelism in Argentina: Politics, Poverty, and Social Policy*. New York: Cambridge University Press.

Wiebe, Paul. 1975. *Social Life in an Indian Slum*. New Delhi: Vikas Publishing House.

Williams, Glyn, J. Devika, and Guro Aandahl. 2015. "Making Space for Women in Urban Governance? Leadership and Claims-Making in a Kerala Slum." *Environment and Planning A* 47, no. 5: 1113–31.

Witsoe, Jeffrey. 2012. "Everyday Corruption and the Political Mediation of the Indian State: An Ethnographic Exploration of Brokers in Bihar." *Economic and Political Weekly* 47, no. 6: 47–54.

Ziegfeld, Adam. 2016. *Why Regional Parties? Clientelism, Elites, and the Indian Party System*. New York: Cambridge University Press.

# Index

accountability
　informal, 39–40
　opposition party workers in, 166
　of party workers, 4, 21, 22–23, 71–73, 224–225
accretion, gradual, 203, 213–216, 232
age
　of settlements, 177, 184, 209, 213
　of surveyed residents, 176
agency
　in clientelism, 69n6
　of parties in party worker selection, 84
　of residents, 5, 28, 100–101, 228
Ahmed, Taqiuddin, 116
Andhra Pradesh, 48
archives, informal, of slum leaders, 115n2, 115–116, 156, 159–160, 161
area development funds, 54–55, 204–205
Atal Mission for Rejuvenation and Urban Transformation (AMRUT), 46, 52
authority
　in community-driven development, 234
　construction of, 99, 133
　informal, 24, 33, 40, 109, 114, 234
　and party worker networks, 68–73, 83, 86–87, 89
Ayodhya Basti Yojana (Madhya Pradesh), 54

Basic Services for the Urban Poor (BSUP), 52–53
Bhopal, Madhya Pradesh. *see also* Madhya Pradesh
　BJP in, 143
　case studies in, 143–164, *see also under* settlement name
　delays of improvement projects in, 53n54
　federal development funding in, 52–53
　income in, 10
　party organization in, 59–63
　party worker density in, 144–145, 225
　population of, 45
　population of squatter settlements in, 48–49, 143n143, 149, 158,
　short-term land titles in, 182n29
　survey design and data collection in, 35–36, 170–176
　uneven development in, 12–13
　urbanization in, 46
BJP (Bharatiya Janata Party)
　in Bhopal, 143
　Ganpati network of, 137–140
　in Jaipur, 116
　in Pahari, 133–134
　party worker density of, 208–209, 211–212
　in Rudra, 162–164
　in Saraswati, 127–128
　slum leaders and party workers of, 17
　structure of, 59–63
booth-level presidents, 109n57, 109, 127–128
BPL cards, 10, 102, 104, 137, 140
brokers, political. *see* party workers
Buddhists, in Tulsi Nagar, 149, 152
built space, 27, 46, 217
bureaucrats. *see* officials

capacity, organizational, 4, 90, 114, 165, 235
capital-intensive goods, 180, 193
capital projects, urban, 52
case studies
  comparative observations in, 164–168
  role of, 114–115
  selection of, 36–38
castes. *see also* diversity, caste
  casteism, 126n55, 152
  in construction of informal leadership, 99
  in measuring ethnic diversity, 208
  Scheduled Castes (SCs), 17, 32, 49, 60, 208–209, 211
causality and historical sequencing, 37, 114, 168, 200–205, 227
Census of India, slums defined in, 30n96
centralization/decentralization, political, 26, 27, 49–56
Chhattisgarh, 48
*Chhattisgarh Mazdoor Sangh* (Chhattisgarh Laborer Association), Durga Nagar, 154–155
Chouhan, Ishwar Singh, 146–147, 151, 156
citizenship, active, 228n6, 228, 230, 233–235
citizen-state relationships, 27, 56–57, 234
claim-making
  competition in, 68–73, 90
  connectivity in, 39–40, 73–76
  direct, 55–56
  in distributive politics, 25, 229
  in Durga Nagar, 156–157
  limits of political organization in, 230
  partisanship in undercutting of, 195
  party worker density in, 21–22, 167–168, 169, 224–225
  politicization of, 42
  post-decentralization, 50
  in provision of public goods and services, 2, 5, 21–22, 33, 63, 164–165
  in Saraswati, 127–129
  slum leaders in, 63, 94–96, 101, 103, 113, 114, 120, 122, 165
class, socioeconomic, 36–37
clientelism, 4, 68, 69n6, 69, 107, 206, 222–223
co-ethnicity. *see also* diversity, ethnic
  in cooperation and political organization, 88–89
  and party worker density, 5, 24, 220, 226–227
  in slum leader selection, 207, 233
collective action. *see also* protests, petitions, written, claim-making
  constraints on, 29, 184
  development committees in, 167
  in distributive politics, 229
  internal self-provision, 93–94, 94n5, 164–165
  and partisan competition, 81
  settlements as units of, 33
  slum leaders in, 40, 97
colonies, resettlement, 30, 170
colonies, unauthorized, 30, 170–171
community asset maps, 39
Community Based Organizations (CBOs), 233–234, *see also* neighborhood associations, development committees
community centers, 103, 157, 158, 164
community events, 101, 103
community meetings, 100–101, 106, 125, 147, 151–152, 224, 228
competition
  among party workers, 68–73, 114, 133–134, 151, 166, 169, 195, 224–225, 229–230
  electoral, 29, 49–50, 172, 182, 196, 208, 209–211
  and credit-claiming, 22–23, 82n43, 82–83, 90, 195, 225
  in distributive politics, 25
  in Ganpati, 137, 141–142
  inter-development committee, in Rudra, 161
  negative effects of, 22–23, 81–83, 133–134, 141–142, 166, 169, 225
  in Pahari, 133–134
  and party worker density, 65–80, 90, 167–168, 208, 224–225
  in problem-solving, 231–232
  in slum leadership, 100, 101, 113, 162, 166
connectivity
  in claim-making, 39–40, 73–76
  in distributive politics, 58
  in Durga Nagar, 155
  face-to-face interactions in, 73, 83–84, 224
  lack of in Ram Nagar, 122
  of Pahari's slum leaders, 135
  and party representational balance, 225

and party worker density, 21–22, 80–81, 90, 166, 167–168, 195, 224
of party workers, 73–78, 169
to political elites, 4, 21–22, 73–76, 224
in Rudra, 159
of Saraswati's president, 127–128
of slum leaders, 58, 135, 203, 223
of women party workers in Tulsi Nagar, 153
Constitutional Amendment, 74th, 49–50, 204
core targeting, 82, 183, 198
corruption, 70, 108, 136, 144, 161
credit-claiming
  and partisan competition, 22–23, 82n43, 82–83, 90, 195, 225
  by politicians, 42

*Dalit Sudharan Samiti* (Dalit Improvement Committee), 151–152
decentralization reforms, 49–56, 204–205
democracy and distributive politics in Indian cities, 228–230
development committees. *see also* neighborhood associations, Community Based Organizations (CBOs)
  collective action by, 167
  in Gandhi Nagar, 146–147, 148
  in Ganpati, 137
  in Pahari, 130–133
  in Ram Nagar, 122
  in Rudra, 159–162
  in Saraswati, 126
  in Tulsi Nagar, 151–152
development, local
  alternative explanations of, 29, 181–183, 195–198
  indicators of, 12–13, 39, 178–179n18, 178–180
  indices of, 180, 205
  and party worker density, 21–24, 184–200, 205
  public financing of, 51–56
  unevenness of, 11–16
dignity, 15–16, 157
disease, 15–16
disorganization, political. *see* organization/disorganization, political
disparities in provision of public goods and services

and government medical camps, 178–179n18
informality in, 8–9, 27–29
in municipal trash collection, 178n17
party workers and local development in, 16–26
puzzle of, in slum settlements, 7–16
dispute resolution, 121, 130, 165
distributive politics
  claim-making in, 25, 229
  competition in, 25
  co-partisan linkages in, 183
  and democracy in Indian cities, 228–230
  development funding sources in, 56–59
  and disparities in public goods provision, 4, 10–11, 21
  in municipal trash collection, 178n17
  neighborhood focus in, 24–25, 229
  party worker density in, 21, 228
  slum leaders in, 35, 40, 58, 92–93
diversity, caste
  in Durga Nagar, 154
  factors in, 218–220
  in Gandhi Nagar, 146
  in Ganpati, 135–136
  in index of ethnic diversity, 181
  in party network formation, 5, 88–89, 221
  in Ram Nagar, 117, 122
  of residents surveyed, 87n58, 176
  in Rudra, 160
  in Saraswati, 123, 126
  in Tulsi Nagar, 149
diversity, ethnic. *see also* co-ethnicity
  as an explanatory variable, 5, 27, 181, 195–196, 218–219, 232–233
  in community development, 232–233, 234–235
  in Durga Nagar, 154
  factors in, 218–220, 221
  in Gandhi Nagar, 146
  in Ganpati, 135–136
  index of, 181n23, 181
  in India's slums, 32–33
  measuring, 181n23, 208
  in Pahari, 129
  in party network formation, 87–90
  and party organization, 59
  and party representational balance, 213
  and party worker density, 24, 207, 209, 220, 226–227

diversity, ethnic (cont.)
  in party worker networks, 5, 87–90, 207
  in Ram Nagar, 117, 122
  in Rudra, 160
  in Saraswati, 123, 126
  and settlement population, 32
  of slum settlements, 32–33
  in Tulsi Nagar, 149
  urban geography in, 40, 232
diversity, religious, 149, 154, 160
documents, government-issued
  in low-income neighborhoods, 10
  party workers in procuring, 137, 148
  slum leaders in procuring, 92, 102, 104, 113, 127
dominating behavior (*dadagiri*), 126, 166
drainage systems, 15, 42, 146, 148–149, *see also* public goods and services, provision of
Durga Nagar settlement, Bhopal, 93, 96n10, 144, 154–158

economies, urban, 45–47
education
  as an explanation of service provision, 184
  and party representational balance, 213
  and party worker density, 24, 209–211
  of slum leaders, 119, 162–163, 223
  of surveyed residents, 176
efficacy/effectiveness in problem-solving
  and party worker density, 4, 21
  of party workers, 69, 114, 169
  of Rudra's committees, 161
  of slum leaders, 40, 99–100, 101, 224, 229–230
elections
  informal, 100–101, 125–126, 130, 147, 160, 165, 224
  municipal, 49, 151, 204
  participation in, 10–11, 18
  and party worker networks, 83–85
  slum leaders' activities in, 105–108
  sources of data for, 178
Electricity Department (*Vidyut Bhavan*), 51
elites, political
  in claim-making effectiveness, 55–56
  connectivity to, 4, 21–22, 73–76, 224
  credit-claiming by, 42
  election season visits by, 105–106

  factionalism by, 62
  interviews of, 37
  in monitoring party workers, 70–71
  and opposition party workers, 76–77
  in preventing eviction, 227
  in squatter settlement formation and size, 213–216, 221
  value of slum leaders to, 84–85, 92–93
  and vote bank politics, 222
employment, 8, 53–54, *see also* occupations
entrepreneurship by slum leaders, 99, 166
Environmental Improvement of Urban Slums Scheme of 1972, 51–52
environment, physical
  and granting temporary land titles, 54, 182
  dangers from, 130
  degradation of, 46–47
  in defining squatter settlements, 31
  sensitivity and hazards from, in settlement survival, 201, 216n11, 216–217, 221,
ethnography
  in data collection, 37, 115–116
  on social diversity, 33
eviction, threat of
  as constraint on political organization, 230
  in Durga Nagar, 157
  in Gandhi Nagar, 149
  mitigating factors in, 216–217
  in mobilization of protests, 79
  in Pahari, 130
  in Ram Nagar, 117–119
  in Saraswati, 125, 126
  in Tulsi Nagar, 149

face-to-face network interactions, 73, 83–84, 224
fees for service, 108, 155
finance, public. *see* resources for slum development
Forest Department, 116, 117–119, 125, 136
frequency of requests to slum leaders, 103–105

Gandhi Nagar settlement, Bhopal, 144–145, 146–149
Ganeshpuri settlement, Jaipur, 217–218
Ganpati settlement, Jaipur, 2, 117, 135–142
gender of surveyed residents, 176
gentrification, 171

geography/geographic location
  of Bhopal settlements, 143, 146, 149
  in defining slum settlements, 35
  in ethnic diversity, 40, 232
  of Jaipur settlements, 116, 123, 129
  of political brokerage, 228
  in settlement size, 40, 213–216, 217–218, 221, 227
Global South, 3, 26, 233–235
group-based strategies, 94–96, 164–165, 195–196, *see also* protests, petitions, written, claim-making

Habitat III, Quito, 233
Hindu-Buddhist conflict, 152, 220
Hindu-Muslim riots, 133, 147
historical sequencing, 168, 200–205
households, sampling of, 174–176
housing
  in defining slums, 29–30
  informalities in, 8–9
  in urban development programs, 52

INC (Indian National Congress)
  in Bhopal, 143
  in Durga Nagar, 156
  factors in party worker density of, 211–212
  in Ganpati, 140
  in Pahari, 131, 133–135
  in Rudra, 161–164
  slum leaders and party workers of, 17
  structure of, 59–63
  in Tulsi Nagar, 150–151
incentives/disincentives
  bottom-up, 23, 39, 86–87, 220
  competition-generated, 72, 90
  counterproductive, partisanship in, 225
  electoral, 4
  material, 39, 108, 113, 224
  multiparty competition as, 90
  in party organizations, 62
  and party worker density, 80–81, 169
  patronage as, 92, 108, 113, 224
  for slum leaders, 87, 90, 108–109, 113, 224
  top-down, 5, 23, 29, 39, 84, 87, 220
  for voter mobilization, 120–121
income
  in distributive politics, 222
  household, 184
  in party representational balance, 213
  in party worker density, 209–211
  of surveyed households, 176
  and uneven provision of public goods and services, 7, 9–10
Indian Ministry of Housing and Urban Poverty Alleviation, 233–234
indicators of development, 178–180
Indore, Madhya Pradesh, 12
inequality, socioeconomic, 6, 46–47
informality
  in accountability, 39–40
  of authority, 24, 33, 114, 234
  and disparities in provision of public goods and services, 7, 8–9
  in employment and housing, 8–9, 222
  in property rights, 130, 165
  of slum leadership, 97–98, 113, 124, 167
  and the state, 27–29
information, provision of, by slum leaders, 16, 104, 120, *see also* rumors
infrastructure
  and capital-intensive projects, 193
  in Durga Nagar, 158
  in Gandhi Nagar, 148–149
  in Ganpati, 142
  lack of, in settlement emergence, 200–201
  lack of resources for, 223
  in Pahari, 135
  for piped water and sewer systems, 193
  in Ram Nagar, 119, 123
  in Rudra, 164
  tagging of, in credit-claiming, 83, 109
  urbanization and failures of, 46–47
institutional change, formal, 204–205
inter-household trust and cooperation, 181
intermediaries, political, 11, *see also* slum leaders (*basti neta*), party workers
intervention, political, 55–56, 78, 217

Jabalpur, Madhya Pradesh, 12
Jaipur Development Authority (JDA), 116
Jaipur Municipal Corporation, 116
Jaipur, Rajasthan
  case studies in, 116–142, *see also under name of settlement*
  Congress *Kachi Basti Prakosht* (slum cell), 86
  federal development funding in, 52–53
  income in, 10

Jaipur, Rajasthan (cont.)
    non-programmatic distributive politics in, 58
    party organization in, 59–63
    party worker density and provision of public goods and services in, 225
    population of, 45
    population of squatter settlements in, 116, 122, 123, 135–136
    proliferation of squatter settlements in, 48–49
    protests in, 96–97
    survey design and data collection in, 35–36, 170–176
    uneven development in, 12–13
    urbanization in, 46
*jati* (sub-caste). *see* castes
*jati panchayat*, 121
Jawaharlal Nehru National Urban Renewal Mission (JNNURM), 46, 52–53
*Jhuggi Jhopri Ekta Samiti*, Rudra, 161
*Jhuggi Jhopri Maha Sangh* (Grand Slum Organization), 146–147, 148, 156
*Jhuggi Jhopri Prakosht* (Madhya Pradesh), 60
job training, 53–54, 101
justice, slum leaders in, 102, 121, 155

Kamal Nagar, 19–21
*Kachi Basti Prakosht* (Rajasthan), 60
Kerala, 48
kinship ties, 218–220

labor, collective, 164–165
labor markets, 116, 143, 218–220
land
    distribution of, 130
    government, 143, 149, 216–217
    ownership of, 177, 184, 209, 213, 227
    scarcity of, 218–220, 232
    titles to (*pattas*), 8–9, 120, 143–144, 154, 182, 209, 213
    urban, 33, 200–201, 203
Latin American cities, 28, 67–68, 72, 201

machine politics, 65–68, *see also* parties, political
Madhya Pradesh, 48, 51–52, 53n55, 54, 143–144, *see also* Bhopal, Madhya Pradesh
Mazdoor Nagar, 18

mediation
    in discretionary resource distribution, 223
    monetary rewards of, 108
    political, 16, 58–59
    by slum leaders, 102
medical camps, government, 178–179n18, 178, 184, 194, 205, *see also* public goods and services, provision of
migrant labor in settlement of Saraswati, 123
MLAs (members of legislative assembly), 50, 54–55, 63, 73–77, 184
mobilization. *see also* rallies, political
    capacity for, 39–40, 129
    ethnic diversity in, 234–235
    and party worker density, 224
    party workers in, 16, 22
    people power in, 79
    political parties in, 231
    for protest, 78–80, 183
    by slum leaders, 105–106, 120–121
    of women, 139
money collection, 95–96, 96n10, 130, 152, 157, 164–165
motivations. *see* incentives/disincentives
MPs (members of parliament), 50
multifocal brokerage
    competitive, 69, 229
    in distributive outcomes, 25
    in distributive politics, 229–230
    in slum leadership, 98, 100, 101, 113
municipal governments, post-decentralization, 49–51
Muslim-majority settlements, 208–209, 220

narratives, historical, 114–116, *see also under settlement name*
Nehru Rozgar Yojana, 53–54
neighborhood associations, 154–155, 167, 228, *see also* development committees, Community Based Organizations (CBOs)
neighborhoods
    in distributive politics, 24–25, 229
    old city, 29, 30, 170–171

occupations. *see also* employment
    in Gandhi Nagar, 146
    in Ganpati, 135–136
    in Jaipur, 116
    in Pahari, 129, 133

in Ram Nagar, 117
in Saraswati, 123
in Tulsi Nagar, 149
officials
  hostility of, to Ram Nagar, 117–119
  incentives for, in claim-making success, 55–56
  interviews of, 37
  and opposition party workers, 76–77
  and party worker connectivity, 74–75
  in post-decentralization governance, 51
  predation by, in Ganpati, 136
  as targets of claim-making, 63
organization/disorganization, political
  construction of, 203–204
  development committees in, 167
  ethnic diversity in, 88–89, 195–196, 233
  limits of, 230–231
  in origins of squatter settlements, 200–204, 205, 227
  party worker density in, 224
  of Rudra, 159
  and underdevelopment, 168, 200–204, 205, 227
  and uneven provision of public goods and services, 4
organization, inter-settlement, 230
origins of squatter settlements, 168, 171, 200–204, 205, 227, *see also* under *settlement narratives*

*Pahari Kachi Basti Vikas Samiti*, 130–133
Pahari settlement, Jaipur, 117, 129–135
Parnami, Ashok, 122
parties, political. *see also* INC (Indian National Congress), BJP (Bharatiya Janata Party)
  in Bhopal and Jaipur, 59–63
  in constructing slum leadership, 99
  in Durga Nagar, 156
  in Ganpati protests, 141–142
  linkages of, with slum leaders, 83–85
  in local problem-solving, 18–21, 231–232
  in Pahari, 133–135
  party-voter linkages in uneven service provision, 4
  in Rudra, 161–164
  in settlement protests, 96
  structure of, 59–63
  turnover of, 76, 78, 81, 116
  visibility of, 17

years in power, 198
party positions/position holders (*padadhikari*)
  in Gandhi Nagar, 147–148
  lack of in Ram Nagar, 122
  in Pahari, 134–135
  in party hierarchies, 61–62
  population in allocation of, 85, 90, 220
  slum leaders as, 109, 224
  in Tulsi Nagar, 151
party representational balance/partisanship
  and core targeting, 82
  negative effects of, 39, 225
  as outcome variable, 180, 183
  in Pahari, 133–134
  and party worker density, 80–83, 90, 167, 194–195, 208–213
  and political competition, 26, 80–83, 90, 166
  in provision of public goods and services, 4, 22–23, 197, 225–226
party worker density
  and accountability, 224–225
  in Bhopal, 144–145, 225
  and claim-making, 21–22, 167–168, 169, 224–225
  and competition, 65–80, 90, 167–168, 208, 209–211, 224–225
  and connectivity, 65–76, 90
  and development, 21–24, 184–200, 205
  in distributive politics, 21, 228
  in Durga Nagar, 144
  and ethnicity, 5, 24, 208–209, 220, 226–227
  factors in, 23–24, 39, 90, 207–211, 226
  in Gandhi Nagar, 144–145
  in Ganpati, 117
  in Jaipur, 117
  and mobilization capacity, 78–80
  as an outcome variable, 180
  in Pahari, 117, 133–134
  and party representational balance, 80–83, 90, 167, 194–195, 208–213
  and people power, 165
  population in, 23, 206, 209–211, 220, 226
  in provision of public goods and services, 4, 40, 167–168, 199, 205
  in Ram Nagar, 117
  in Rudra, 144, 162
  in Saraswati, 117, 129

party worker density (cont.)
    in Tulsi Nagar, 144
    variation in, 68, 167
party worker networks
    competition, connections, and
        mobilization capacity in, 63, 65–80
    and density of slum leadership, 206–207
    in Durga Nagar, 156, 157
    and ethnic diversity, 5, 87–90, 207
    in Gandhi Nagar, 148
    in Ganpati, 136–142
    network, defined, 21n58
    in Pahari, 133–135
    in problem-solving, 231
    in Rudra, 162–164
    in Tulsi Nagar, 144, 150–153
    unevenness in across settlements, 206–221
    variations in, 83–90, 206–207
party workers
    accountability of, 4, 21, 22–23, 71–73, 224–225
    census of, 38
    competition among, 68–73, 114, 133–134, 151, 166, 169, 195, 224–225, 229–230
    connectivity of, 63, 73–78
    in mobilizing protests, 78–80
    opposition party workers, 76–78, 166
    and party representational balance, 80–83, 111–113, 167
    in problem-solving, 231
    in provision of public goods and services, 2, 4, 16–26
    slum leaders as, 63, 109–113
    as slum residents, 203–204
patronage
    agency in, 69n6
    distribution of, 86–87, 224
    as motivation for slum leaders, 92, 108, 113, 224
    in party worker networks, 65, 84
    population and allocation of, 4, 23, 85–87, 90, 206, 220, 226
Patta Act of 1984 (Madhya Pradesh), 54, 143–144
pavement dwellers, 9n27
people power (*lokshakti*), 79, 89, 94–95, 122, 165
petitions, written
    in claim-making, 22, 94–96, 103, 113, 224
    in demanding public goods and services, 164–165
    in Durga Nagar, 156–157
    by Gandhi Nagar's development committees, 146
    by Ganpati's slum leaders, 136–138
    in informal archives, 115n3, 115–116
    by Pahari's slum leaders, 132–133, 135
    by Ram Nagar slum leaders, 120
    residents in financing of, 95–96, 96n10
    by Saraswati's slum leaders, 128
    by slum federations, 230
    by Tulsi Nagar's development committees, 151–152
political economy, 5–6, 18, 28–29, 56, 204–205, 223, 232
politicians. *see* elites, political
politicization
    of government medical camps, 178–179n18
    of the notification process, 182
    of provision of public goods and services, 42–43
    of public resource distribution, 55–58, 223
politics, urban popular, 7, 10–11, 57
popularity of slum leaders, 23, 86n56, 100, 166
population of squatter settlements
    of Bhopal settlements, 48, 143n143, 146, 149, 154
    data sources for, 176
    factors in, 213–220
    of Jaipur settlements, 116, 122, 123, 135–136
    and party representational balance, 213
    and party worker density, 23, 206, 209–211, 220, 226
    and party worker networks, 4, 85–87
    in prioritization of development, 235
    and provision of public goods and services, 4, 168, 184, 197
    of settlements surveyed, 170
    and social diversity, 32
    urban, in the Global South, 3
population, urban, 44–45, 48, 59, 63
poverty
    as constraint on political organization, 230

urban, 9–10, 27, 46–47
Pradhan Matri Awas Yojana, 52
Pradhan, Shelender, 155, 164
*prakoshts* (party cells), 60
problem-solving
    competition in, 69, 231–232
    and constructing slum leadership, 99–100, 101, 166
    in distributive politics, 229
    in Durga Nagar, 154–155, 156–157
    in historical narratives, 115
    household-level, 102–103, 165
    individual-level, 102–104, 133
    and party politics, 18
    and party worker density, 21, 22
    by Ram Nagar slum leaders, 120
    in Saraswati, 127–128
    slum leaders in, 16, 18–21, 92–93, 101–105, 113, 165
Project UDAY, 54
property rights, 29, 31n103, 31, 52, 130, 165, 230
protests
    capacity for, 4, 165
    in demanding public goods and services, 164–165
    in Ganpati, 141–142
    opposition party workers in, 76, 166
    and party representational balance, 183
    and party-slum leader linkages, 84
    and party worker density, 78–80, 167–168, 169
    and slum leaders, 96–97, 224
    in state responsiveness, 22
public goods and services, provision of
    alternative explanations for, 181–183
    in Bhopal settlements, 143–145
    claim-making in, 63, 95, 127–129, 164–165
    as development indicators, 39
    in Durga Nagar, 157, 158
    and ethnic diversity, 5, 27, 218–219, 232
    in Gandhi Nagar, 148–149
    in Ganpati, 138, 142
    internal self-provision of, 93–94, 164–165
    in Jaipur settlements, 117
    non-programmatic, 56–58
    in Pahari, 132–133, 135

    and party worker density, 117, 199, 205, 224
    politicization of, 42–43
    in Ram Nagar, 122–123
    in Rudra, 164
    in Saraswati, 128–129
    and slum leaders, 103, 224
    in Tulsi Nagar, 152, 153
    unevenness in, 7–16
Public Health and Engineering Department (PHED), 51
public support in constructing slum leadership, 99–101
Public Works Department, 51

Rajasthan, 48, 53–54, *see also* Jaipur, Rajasthan
Rajiv Awas Yojana (RAY), 52–53, 233–234
Rajiv settlement, Jaipur, 93
rallies, political. *see also* mobilization
    and party worker density, 22, 224
    and party workers, 71
    in revealing leaders' followings, 86n56
    slum leaders' roles in, 105–106
    in urban politics, 10–11
Ram Nagar settlement, Jaipur, 1–2, 117–123
*Ram Nagar Vikas Samiti*, 122
Rangarajan Expert Group, 47
Rawan Mandi settlement, Jaipur, 218
regions of origin. *see also* diversity, ethnic
    diversity in, 33
    in Durga Nagar, 154
    and ethnic diversity, 5, 87, 181, 208, 218–219, 232
    in Ganpati, 135
    in Ram Nagar, 117
    in Saraswati, 123
regularization of listed slums, 171
religion
    diversity of, 149, 154, 160
    in measurement of ethnic diversity, 208
    and partisan composition of party networks, 211
    in Rudra, 160
    of surveyed residents, 176
rent seeking, 108, 226, *see also* incentives/disincentives
representatives, elected, 50, 54–55, *see also* ward councillors, MPs (members of parliament), MLAs (members of legislative assembly)

reputation
  of party workers, 70–71, 72, 139
  of slum leaders, 108, 109, 165
residents
  agency of, 5, 28, 100–101, 228
  caste diversity of, 87n58, 176
  in constructing slum leadership, 98–101, 113, 166, 224
  cooperation and trust among, 89, 196
  descriptive statistics of those interviewed, 176
  direct claim-making by, 55–56
  in estimating settlement age, 177
  in group claim-making, 94–96
  in internal self-provision, 93–94
  interviews conducted with, 176
  in settlement protests, 96–97
  slum leaders as, 16, 33, 99, 110, 168, 224, 227
resources for slum development
  constraints on, 85, 143–144, 193, 223
  discretionary, 54–56
  distributive politics of access to, 56–59
  electoral competition in spending, 182
  public, 52–53, 55–58, 223
  sources of finance for, 51–56, 63
responsiveness
  of party workers, 72, 90
  of the state, 21–23, 55–57, 71–72, 73–76, 81
revenue (*nazul*) department lands, 143, 149
roads, paved, 15, 178, 184, 194, 197, 205, *see also* public goods and services, provision of
Royla, Raj Kumar, 135
Rudra settlement, Bhopal, 144, 158–164
*Rudra Shetriya Jhuggi Jhopri Samiti* (Rudra Area Slum Committee), 160–162
rumors
  in party worker network competition, 69, 70, 76
  in slum leadership competition, 100, 229–230

sampling, context-driven, of squatter settlements, 172–173
sanitation services, 11, 123, 128, 132, 138, 142, 148–149, 157
Sanjay Bhatta, Jaipur, 54–55
Saraf, Kali Charan, 116, 119, 122, 135, 137

Saraswati settlement, Jaipur, 93, 95, 117, 123–129
Satnami, Bhopal, 112–113
Scheduled Castes (SCs), 17, 32, 49, 60, 208–209, 211
Scheduled Tribes (STs), 60, 208–209, 211
scope conditions, 26–27
self-organization
  by residents from Uttar Pradesh in Pahari, 133
  in Saraswati, 124, 128–129, 133
self-provision, internal, 94n5, 164–165
sewer systems, 178, 180, 193, *see also* public goods and services, provision of
Sharma, P.C., 146–147, 155–157
Shiv Nagar, Bhopal, 112–113
Singh, Arjun, 143–144
Slum Areas Act of 1956, 182
Slum Development Policy of 2012, 52–53
Slum Improvement and Clearance Act of 1956, 51
slum improvement schemes, 11
slum leaders (*basti neta*)
  in claim-making, 63, 94–96, 101, 103, 113, 114, 120, 122, 165
  in distributive politics, 35, 40, 58, 92–93
  in Durga Nagar, 155–158
  electoral activities of, 92, 105–108
  and ethnic diversity, 226–227
  followings of, 86–87
  in Gandhi Nagar, 146–148
  in Ganpati, 136–140
  incentives/disincentives for, 87, 90, 92, 108–109, 113, 224
  informal archives of, 37, 115n2, 115–116
  as informal leaders, 97–98
  in internal self-provision, 93–94
  in party worker networks, 83–85, 206–207
  as party workers, 63, 109–113
  as political actors, 92–93
  in the political economy of development, 223
  problem-solving by, 16, 18–21, 92–93, 101–105, 113, 165
  in protests, 96–97, 224
  in provision of public goods and services, 1–2, 16–21
  qualities of, 83, 89, 99, 119, 137, 162–164, 207, 223
  in Ram Nagar, 119–123

as residents, 16, 33, 99, 110, 168, 224, 227
in Rudra, 159–162
selection of, 165, 207, 228, 233
strategies of, in demanding development, 78, 93–97
in Tulsi Nagar, 150–152
slum leadership
activities of (*netagiri*), 2, 83–84, 87
construction of, 40, 98–101, 203–204, 224
ethnic diversity in development and formation of, 87–90
in historical sequence of slum development, 205
informal elections in, 100–101, 165, 224
informality of, 97–98
multiparty representation in fragmentation of, 81
population in incentives of, 206, 220
slum organizations/federations, 230
slums
defined, 29–35, 30n96, 31n103, 48–49, 51
listed, 170–176
proliferation of, 47–49
social capital, 29, 181, 196
social work (*samajik seva*), 75, 97, 102, 126, 137, 139
Socio-Economic and Caste Census, 2011, 9
squatter settlements. *see also under settlement name*
defined, 29–31, 48–49, 63
origins of, 168, 171, 200–204, 205, 227
sampling of, 38
as social/spatial units, 33–35
in survey design and data collection, 170–176
in urban distributive politics, 24
urban geography in size of, 40
and urbanization, 46–47
state assembly constituencies, 36–37, 116, 178, 182, 198
state-level programs in slum development, 54
state-society relations, 234
stationery, letterhead, 22, 73, 95–96, 96n10, 97, 135, 159, 224
statutory towns, 44n4, 48
streetlights, 15, 184, 205, *see also* public goods and services, provision of

survey design and data, 170–176
Swarna Jayanti Shehari Rozgar Yojana (SJSRY), 53–54
swing voter targeting, 183, 197–198

tenure security/insecurity, 8–9, 51, 182, 216–217, *see also* eviction, threat of
thuggish behavior, 70, 124, 126, 166, 224, 229–230
trash collection, municipal, 178n17, 178, 184, 194, 205, *see also* public goods and services, provision of
Tulsi Nagar settlement, Bhopal, 144, 149–153

underdevelopment
in Gandhi Nagar, 144–145
informal leadership emerging in, 136–137
in mobilization of protests, 79
in origins of squatter settlements, 168, 200–204, 205
and political disorganization, 168, 200–204, 205, 227
UN-Habitat, 30n96, 31n103
Union Carbide factory explosion, 144
United States, machine politics in, 65–67
Urban Basic Services for the Poor and National Slum Development Program (NSDP), 51–52
urbanization
effects of, on cities and towns, 44–47
in the Global South, 3
and local ethnic politics, 232–233
Urban Services for the Poor (UK Department for International Development), 54

Valmiki Ambedkar Awas Yojana of 2001 (VAMBAY), 51–52
*Van Vibhag* (Forest Department) lands, Jaipur, 58
Vijay Nagar, Jaipur, 54–55
villages, urban, 170–171
violence
and party worker competition, 70, 81
in slum leader competition, 166
Visakhapatnam, 48
vote banks. *see also* population of squatter settlements
as eviction protection, 227
Ganpati as, 136

vote banks (cont.)
    in non-programmatic distributive
        politics, 58
    Pahari as, 131
    and party worker density, 23, 206, 220, 226
    politics of, in survival of settlements, 23, 217
    and provision of public goods and
        services, 4, 7, 10–11
    in resisting eviction, 117–119
    Rudra as, 163
    slums as, for politicians, 222
    and variation in party networks, 85–86, 90
voter turnout
    party networks in mobilization of, 4, 11,
        16, 59, 84–85, 86n56, 157
    slum leaders in, 92, 107

ward councillors
    in citizen-state relations, 27
    in claim-making, 63, 74–75,
        95, 157
    election-time handouts by,
        107
    in Ganpati, 137–139, 140–142
    in post-decentralization governance,
        50
    in provision of public goods and services,
        204
    in public resource distribution,
        42
water, piped, 15, 42, 95, 128–129, 178, 180,
    193, *see also* public goods and services,
    provision of

Other Books in the Series (*continued from page iii*)

David Austen-Smith, Jeffry A. Frieden, Miriam A. Golden, Karl Ove Moene, and Adam Przeworski, eds., *Selected Works of Michael Wallerstein: The Political Economy of Inequality, Unions, and Social Democracy*
S. Erdem Aytaç and Susan C. Stokes, *Why Bother? Rethinking Participation in Elections and Protests*
Andy Baker, *The Market and the Masses in Latin America: Policy Reform and Consumption in Liberalizing Economies*
Laia Balcells, *Rivalry and Revenge: The Politics of Violence during Civil War*
Lisa Baldez, *Why Women Protest? Women's Movements in Chile*
Kate Baldwin, *The Paradox of Traditional Chiefs in Democratic Africa*
Stefano Bartolini, *The Political Mobilization of the European Left, 1860–1980: The Class Cleavage*
Robert Bates, *When Things Fell Apart: State Failure in Late-Century Africa*
Mark Beissinger, *Nationalist Mobilization and the Collapse of the Soviet State*
Pablo Beramendi, *The Political Geography of Inequality: Regions and Redistribution*
Nancy Bermeo, ed., *Unemployment in the New Europe*
Carles Boix, *Democracy and Redistribution*
Carles Boix, *Political Order and Inequality: Their Foundations and their Consequences for Human Welfare*
Carles Boix, *Political Parties, Growth, and Equality: Conservative and Social Democratic Economic Strategies in the World Economy*
Catherine Boone, *Merchant Capital and the Roots of State Power in Senegal, 1930–1985*
Catherine Boone, *Political Topographies of the African State: Territorial Authority and Institutional Change*
Catherine Boone, *Property and Political Order in Africa: Land Rights and the Structure of Politics*
Michael Bratton and Nicolas van de Walle, *Democratic Experiments in Africa: Regime Transitions in Comparative Perspective*
Michael Bratton, Robert Mattes, and E. Gyimah-Boadi, *Public Opinion, Democracy, and Market Reform in Africa*
Valerie Bunce, *Leaving Socialism and Leaving the State: The End of Yugoslavia, the Soviet Union, and Czechoslovakia*
Daniele Caramani, *The Nationalization of Politics: The Formation of National Electorates and Party Systems in Europe*
John M. Carey, *Legislative Voting and Accountability*
Kanchan Chandra, *Why Ethnic Parties Succeed: Patronage and Ethnic Headcounts in India*
Eric C. C. Chang, Mark Andreas Kayser, Drew A. Linzer, and Ronald Rogowski, *Electoral Systems and the Balance of Consumer-Producer Power*

José Antonio Cheibub, *Presidentialism, Parliamentarism, and Democracy*
Ruth Berins Collier, *Paths toward Democracy: The Working Class and Elites in Western Europe and South America*
Daniel Corstange, *The Price of a Vote in the Middle East: Clientelism and Communal Politics in Lebanon and Yemen*
Pepper D. Culpepper, *Quiet Politics and Business Power: Corporate Control in Europe and Japan*
Sarah Zukerman Daly, *Organized Violence after Civil War: The Geography of Recruitment in Latin America*
Christian Davenport, *State Repression and the Domestic Democratic Peace*
Donatella della Porta, *Social Movements, Political Violence, and the State*
Alberto Diaz-Cayeros, *Federalism, Fiscal Authority, and Centralization in Latin America*
Alberto Diaz-Cayeros, Federico Estévez, Beatriz Magaloni, *The Political Logic of Poverty Relief: Electoral Strategies and Social Policy in Mexico*
Jesse Driscoll, *Warlords and Coalition Politics in Post-Soviet States*
Thad Dunning, *Crude Democracy: Natural Resource Wealth and Political Regimes*
Thad Dunning et al., *Information, Accountability, and Cumulative Learning: Lessons from Metaketa I*
Gerald Easter, *Reconstructing the State: Personal Networks and Elite Identity*
Margarita Estevez-Abe, *Welfare and Capitalism in Postwar Japan: Party, Bureaucracy, and Business*
Henry Farrell, *The Political Economy of Trust: Institutions, Interests, and Inter-Firm Cooperation in Italy and Germany*
Karen E. Ferree, *Framing the Race in South Africa: The Political Origins of Racial Census Elections*
M. Steven Fish, *Democracy Derailed in Russia: The Failure of Open Politics*
Robert F. Franzese, *Macroeconomic Policies of Developed Democracies*
Roberto Franzosi, *The Puzzle of Strikes: Class and State Strategies in Postwar Italy*
Timothy Frye, *Building States and Markets After Communism: The Perils of Polarized Democracy*
Mary E. Gallagher, *Authoritarian Legality in China: Law, Workers, and the State*
Geoffrey Garrett, *Partisan Politics in the Global Economy*
Scott Gehlbach, *Representation through Taxation: Revenue, Politics, and Development in Postcommunist States*
Edward L. Gibson, *Boundary Control: Subnational Authoritarianism in Federal Democracies*
Jane R. Gingrich, *Making Markets in the Welfare State: The Politics of Varying Market Reforms*
Miriam Golden, *Heroic Defeats: The Politics of Job Loss*
Jeff Goodwin, *No Other Way Out: States and Revolutionary Movements*
Merilee Serrill Grindle, *Changing the State*
Anna Grzymala-Busse, *Rebuilding Leviathan: Party Competition and State Exploitation in Post-Communist Democracies*
Anna Grzymala-Busse, *Redeeming the Communist Past: The Regeneration of Communist Parties in East Central Europe*

Frances Hagopian, *Traditional Politics and Regime Change in Brazil*
Mark Hallerberg, Rolf Ranier Strauch, Jürgen von Hagen, *Fiscal Governance in Europe*
Henry E. Hale, *The Foundations of Ethnic Politics: Separatism of States and Nations in Eurasia and the World*
Stephen E. Hanson, *Post-Imperial Democracies: Ideology and Party Formation in Third Republic France, Weimar Germany, and Post-Soviet Russia*
Michael Hechter, *Alien Rule*
Timothy Hellwig, *Globalization and Mass Politics: Retaining the Room to Maneuver*
Gretchen Helmke, *Institutions on the Edge: The Origins and Consequences of Inter-Branch Crises in Latin America*
Gretchen Helmke, *Courts Under Constraints: Judges, Generals, and Presidents in Argentina*
Yoshiko Herrera, *Imagined Economies: The Sources of Russian Regionalism*
Alisha C. Holland, *Forbearance as Redistribution: The Politics of Informal Welfare in Latin America*
J. Rogers Hollingsworth and Robert Boyer, eds., *Contemporary Capitalism: The Embeddedness of Institutions*
Yue Hou, *The Private Sector in Public Office: Selective Property Rights in China*
John D. Huber, *Exclusion by Elections: Inequality, Ethnic Identity, and Democracy*
John D. Huber and Charles R. Shipan, *Deliberate Discretion? The Institutional Foundations of Bureaucratic Autonomy*
Ellen Immergut, *Health Politics: Interests and Institutions in Western Europe*
Torben Iversen, *Capitalism, Democracy, and Welfare*
Torben Iversen, *Contested Economic Institutions*
Torben Iversen, Jonas Pontussen, and David Soskice, eds., *Unions, Employers, and Central Banks: Macroeconomic Coordination and Institutional Change in Social Market Economics*
Thomas Janoski and Alexander M. Hicks, eds., *The Comparative Political Economy of the Welfare State*
Joseph Jupille, *Procedural Politics: Issues, Influence, and Institutional Choice in the European Union*
Karen Jusko, *Who Speaks for the Poor? Electoral Geography, Party Entry, and Representation*
Stathis Kalyvas, *The Logic of Violence in Civil War*
Stephen B. Kaplan, *Globalization and Austerity Politics in Latin America*
David C. Kang, *Crony Capitalism: Corruption and Capitalism in South Korea and the Philippines*
Junko Kato, *Regressive Taxation and the Welfare State*
Orit Kedar, *Voting for Policy, Not Parties: How Voters Compensate for Power Sharing*
Robert O. Keohane and Helen B. Milner, eds., *Internationalization and Domestic Politics*
Herbert Kitschelt, *The Transformation of European Social Democracy*

Herbert Kitschelt, Kirk A. Hawkins, Juan Pablo Luna, Guillermo Rosas, and Elizabeth J. Zechmeister, *Latin American Party Systems*

Herbert Kitschelt, Peter Lange, Gary Marks, and John D. Stephens, eds., *Continuity and Change in Contemporary Capitalism*

Herbert Kitschelt, Zdenka Mansfeldova, Radek Markowski, and Gabor Toka, *Post-Communist Party Systems*

David Knoke, Franz Urban Pappi, Jeffrey Broadbent, and Yutaka Tsujinaka, eds., *Comparing Policy Networks*

Ken Kollman, *Perils of Centralization: Lessons from Church, State, and Corporation*

Allan Kornberg and Harold D. Clarke, *Citizens and Community: Political Support in a Representative Democracy*

Amie Kreppel, *The European Parliament and the Supranational Party System*

David D. Laitin, *Language Repertoires and State Construction in Africa*

Fabrice E. Lehoucq and Ivan Molina, *Stuffing the Ballot Box: Fraud, Electoral Reform, and Democratization in Costa Rica*

Benjamin Lessing, *Making Peace in Drug Wars: Crackdowns and Cartels in Latin America*

Mark Irving Lichbach and Alan S. Zuckerman, eds., *Comparative Politics: Rationality, Culture, and Structure, 2nd edition*

Evan Lieberman, *Race and Regionalism in the Politics of Taxation in Brazil and South Africa*

Richard M. Locke, *The Promise and Limits of Private Power: Promoting Labor Standards in a Global Economy*

Julia Lynch, *Age in the Welfare State: The Origins of Social Spending on Pensioners, Workers, and Children*

Pauline Jones Luong, *Institutional Change and Political Continuity in Post-Soviet Central Asia*

Pauline Jones Luong and Erika Weinthal, *Oil is Not a Curse: Ownership Structure and Institutions in Soviet Successor States*

Doug McAdam, John McCarthy, and Mayer Zald, eds., *Comparative Perspectives on Social Movements*

Gwyneth H. McClendon and Rachel Beatty Riedl, *From Pews to Politics in Africa: Religious Sermons and Political Behavior*

Lauren M. MacLean, *Informal Institutions and Citizenship in Rural Africa: Risk and Reciprocity in Ghana and Côte d'Ivoire*

Beatriz Magaloni, *Voting for Autocracy: Hegemonic Party Survival and its Demise in Mexico*

James Mahoney, *Colonialism and Postcolonial Development: Spanish America in Comparative Perspective*

James Mahoney and Dietrich Rueschemeyer, eds., *Historical Analysis and the Social Sciences*

Scott Mainwaring and Matthew Soberg Shugart, eds., *Presidentialism and Democracy in Latin America*

Melanie Manion, *Information for Autocrats: Representation in Chinese Local Congresses*

Isabela Mares, *From Open Secrets to Secret Voting: Democratic Electoral Reforms and Voter Autonomy*
Isabela Mares, *The Politics of Social Risk: Business and Welfare State Development*
Isabela Mares, *Taxation, Wage Bargaining, and Unemployment*
Cathie Jo Martin and Duane Swank, *The Political Construction of Business Interests: Coordination, Growth, and Equality*
Anthony W. Marx, *Making Race, Making Nations: A Comparison of South Africa, the United States, and Brazil*
Bonnie M. Meguid, *Party Competition between Unequals: Strategies and Electoral Fortunes in Western Europe*
Joel S. Migdal, *State in Society: Studying How States and Societies Constitute One Another*
Joel S. Migdal, Atul Kohli, and Vivienne Shue, eds., *State Power and Social Forces: Domination and Transformation in the Third World*
Scott Morgenstern and Benito Nacif, eds., *Legislative Politics in Latin America*
Kevin M. Morrison, *Nontaxation and Representation: The Fiscal Foundations of Political Stability*
Layna Mosley, *Global Capital and National Governments*
Layna Mosley, *Labor Rights and Multinational Production*
Wolfgang C. Müller and Kaare Strøm, *Policy, Office, or Votes?*
Maria Victoria Murillo, *Political Competition, Partisanship, and Policy Making in Latin American Public Utilities*
Maria Victoria Murillo, *Labor Unions, Partisan Coalitions, and Market Reforms in Latin America*
Monika Nalepa, *Skeletons in the Closet: Transitional Justice in Post-Communist Europe*
Noah L. Nathan, *Electoral Politics and Africa's Urban Transition: Class and Ethnicity in Ghana*
Ton Notermans, *Money, Markets, and the State: Social Democratic Economic Policies since 1918*
Simeon Nichter, *Votes for Survival: Relational Clientelism in Latin America*
Richard A. Nielsen, *Deadly Clerics: Blocked Ambition and the Paths to Jihad*
Aníbal Pérez-Liñán, *Presidential Impeachment and the New Political Instability in Latin America*
Roger D. Petersen, *Understanding Ethnic Violence: Fear, Hatred, and Resentment in 20th Century Eastern Europe*
Roger D. Petersen, *Western Intervention in the Balkans: The Strategic Use of Emotion in Conflict*
Simona Piattoni, ed., *Clientelism, Interests, and Democratic Representation*
Paul Pierson, *Dismantling the Welfare State? Reagan, Thatcher, and the Politics of Retrenchment*
Marino Regini, *Uncertain Boundaries: The Social and Political Construction of European Economies*
Kenneth M. Roberts, *Changing Course in Latin America: Party Systems in the Neoliberal Era*
Marc Howard Ross, *Cultural Contestation in Ethnic Conflict*

David Rueda and Daniel Stegmueller, *Who Wants What? Redistribution Preferences in Comparative Perspective*
Ignacio Sánchez-Cuenca, *The Historical Roots of Political Violence: Revolutionary Terrorism in Affluent Countries*
Ben Ross Schneider, *Hierarchical Capitalism in Latin America: Business, Labor, and the Challenges of Equitable Development*
Roger Schoenman, *Networks and Institutions in Europe's Emerging Markets*
Lyle Scruggs, *Sustaining Abundance: Environmental Performance in Industrial Democracies*
Jefferey M. Sellers, *Governing from Below: Urban Regions and the Global Economy*
Yossi Shain and Juan Linz, eds., *Interim Governments and Democratic Transitions*
Beverly Silver, *Forces of Labor: Workers' Movements and Globalization since 1870*
Prerna Singh, *How Solidarity Works for Welfare: Subnationalism and Social Development in India*
Theda Skocpol, *Social Revolutions in the Modern World*
Austin Smith et al., *Selected Works of Michael Wallerstein*
Regina Smyth, *Candidate Strategies and Electoral Competition in the Russian Federation: Democracy Without Foundation*
Richard Snyder, *Politics after Neoliberalism: Reregulation in Mexico*
David Stark and László Bruszt, *Postsocialist Pathways: Transforming Politics and Property in East Central Europe*
Sven Steinmo, *The Evolution of Modern States: Sweden, Japan, and the United States*
Sven Steinmo, Kathleen Thelen, and Frank Longstreth, eds., *Structuring Politics: Historical Institutionalism in Comparative Analysis*
Susan C. Stokes, *Mandates and Democracy: Neoliberalism by Surprise in Latin America*
Susan C. Stokes, ed., *Public Support for Market Reforms in New Democracies*
Susan C. Stokes, Thad Dunning, Marcelo Nazareno, and Valeria Brusco, *Brokers, Voters, and Clientelism: The Puzzle of Distributive Politics*
Milan W. Svolik, *The Politics of Authoritarian Rule*
Duane Swank, *Global Capital, Political Institutions, and Policy Change in Developed Welfare States*
Sidney Tarrow, *Power in Movement: Social Movements and Contentious Politics*
Sidney Tarrow, *Power in Movement: Social Movements and Contentious Politics, Revised and Updated Third Edition*
Tariq Thachil, *Elite Parties, Poor Voters: How Social Services Win Votes in India*
Kathleen Thelen, *How Institutions Evolve: The Political Economy of Skills in Germany, Britain, the United States, and Japan*
Kathleen Thelen, *Varieties of Liberalization and the New Politics of Social Solidarity*
Charles Tilly, *Trust and Rule*
Daniel Treisman, *The Architecture of Government: Rethinking Political Decentralization*

Guillermo Trejo, *Popular Movements in Autocracies: Religion, Repression, and Indigenous Collective Action in Mexico*
Rory Truex, *Making Autocracy Work: Representation and Responsiveness in Modern China*
Lily Lee Tsai, *Accountability without Democracy: How Solidary Groups Provide Public Goods in Rural China*
Joshua Tucker, *Regional Economic Voting: Russia, Poland, Hungary, Slovakia and the Czech Republic, 1990–1999*
Ashutosh Varshney, *Democracy, Development, and the Countryside*
Yuhua Wang, *Tying the Autocrat's Hand: The Rise of The Rule of Law in China*
Jeremy M. Weinstein, *Inside Rebellion: The Politics of Insurgent Violence*
Stephen I. Wilkinson, *Votes and Violence: Electoral Competition and Ethnic Riots in India*
Andreas Wimmer, *Waves of War: Nationalism, State Formation, and Ethnic Exclusion in the Modern World*
Jason Wittenberg, *Crucibles of Political Loyalty: Church Institutions and Electoral Continuity in Hungary*
Elisabeth J. Wood, *Forging Democracy from Below: Insurgent Transitions in South Africa and El Salvador*
Elisabeth J. Wood, *Insurgent Collective Action and Civil War in El Salvador*
Deborah J. Yashar, *Homicidal Ecologies: Illicit Economies and Complicit States in Latin America*
Daniel Ziblatt, *Conservative Parties and the Birth of Democracy*